Foundations

CRITICAL THINKING, READING, AND WRITING

Foundations

CRITICAL THINKING, READING, AND WRITING

SECOND EDITION

Victor Shea
York University

William Whitla
York University

PEARSON
Prentice
Hall

Toronto

National Library of Canada Cataloguing in Publication

Shea, Victor Norman, 1960–
    Foundations : critical thinking, reading and writing/Victor Shea,
William Whitla.—2nd ed.

Includes bibliographic references and index.
ISBN 0-13-123631-8

   1. Study skills. 2. Report writing. 3. Critical thinking. I. Whitla, William, 1934– II. Title.

LB2369.S45 2004   378.1′70281   C2003-906097-7

ISBN 0-13-123631-8

Vice President, Editorial Director: Michael J. Young
Executive Editor: Dave Ward
Marketing Manager: Toivo Pajo
Developmental Editor: Jon Maxfield
Production Editor: Lara Caplan
Copy Editor: Rohini Herbert
Proofreader: David Handelsman
Production Coordinator: Anita Heyna
Page Layout: Heidi Palfrey
Art Director: Julia Hall
Cover Design: Monica Kompter
Cover Image: Getty Images

 25 26 27 CP 16 15 14

Printed and bound in Canada.

Contents

Chapter 8   Researching Print Sources   186

Chapter 9   References and Documentation: Acknowledging Your Sources   202

PART FOUR: THE ESSAY FROM FIRST DRAFT TO FINAL COPY TO GETTING IT BACK   226

Chapter 10   The Planning and Pre-Writing Stage   226

Chapter 11   The Writing Stage   239

Preface

We have written *Foundations: Critical Thinking, Reading, and Writing* over a number of years: first as a series of handouts, then as a handbook for students taking our second-year interdisciplinary course in Humanities at York University, and afterwards, with substantial revision, as part of our university's mandate to foreground critical skills as part of a new foundations program. This second edition has continued this process of revision with advice from students, colleagues at York University using the book, professors across Canada, and a group of selected assessors unknown to us. We were pleased when Pearson Education Canada/Prentice-Hall asked us to prepare a second edition, and we undertook major revisions. We emphasized students' concerns by providing reasons for strategic choices in critical reading and writing, by amplifying our examples and suggestions, and by setting out the practical advantages for improvement in academic skills.

Current students are faced with numerous new challenges when they come to university from high school or return after a period away. Their old skills might be rusty, some essential skills for successful university work might be seriously underdeveloped, and some new skills which they need might have been unexplored in their previous education. New developments in computer technology, classroom configurations and facilities, research resources on the Internet and in libraries, and continuing pressure for students to perform to a better academic standard have made urgent the need for such a textbook to help students cope with this changed academic environment. As well as addressing these innovations, we have retained some of the more traditional methods of organizing arguments and pursuing research systematically, as well as the now-widely-accepted notion that teaching critical skills will continue to be crucial in a variety of courses across the curriculum. Accordingly, we have drawn our examples from a range of disciplines, including English, history, sociology, media studies, and interdisciplinary studies in the humanities and social sciences.

In light of the pressures described above, *Foundations* addresses three major areas of concern. First, our discussion of survival skills addresses professors' expectations of how students are to perform. The problem with these expectations, for example, in listening in lectures and seminars and taking notes, is that they are rarely spoken about but are assumed. Where the expectations are spelled out in such areas as documentation and formatting, avoiding plagiarism, and grammar for standard written English, we give a reference guide to these areas in an accessible and easy-to-use format.

A second major area of emphasis is the development of a critical frame of mind. *Foundations* is guided by the fundamental need to move students from stating an opinion to formulating a reasoned and grounded position. Furthermore, students need to be able to think strategically when approaching readings and assignments, that is, to read and write with specific goals in mind and to adapt different methods to different requirements.

A third major area of concern involves more advanced skills that we introduce and extend but that can be continued into a lifetime of learning. In particular, these skills involve logic in argument and writing, different levels of reading, different strategic paths for undertaking research, as well as the most fundamental critical skill of all, learning to question and revise received positions to formulate new ones.

ORGANIZATION

From the first day at university, students are expected to attend lectures and take notes, begin reading textbooks, and prepare first assignments. The opening part of *Foundations* is devoted to lecture and classroom strategies for success in meeting university-level requirements and to improvements in all areas that will ensure that students get the most from their studies. Part I introduces what we call "survival skills," techniques to empower students to negotiate the first few weeks of classes successfully.

The four chapters in Part II are devoted to critical thinking and reading. We begin with an introduction to critical thinking, stressing the development of a critical attitude of mind. Chapter 4 extends that critical attitude to reading practices, showing how reading skills can be improved and applied. Chapter 5 discusses the essential building blocks of critical thinking, reading, and writing: language components and the extension of word power and vocabulary. Finally, Chapter 6 is devoted to methods and examples of critical argument. It shows how to use a critical attitude and reading strategies to assess the logic and persuasiveness of different types of texts. It also equips students to perceive and question logical weaknesses, to correct them, and so to formulate their own strong and defensible positions in presentations, essays, and examinations.

Part III of *Foundations* applies critical thinking skills to systematic research. Students learn how to gather essential materials for courses and assignments and how to annotate them, keep files, document them, and avoid charges of plagiarism. Above all, students learn how to approach research logically, systematically, and critically, using both electronic and printed sources.

Part IV of *Foundations* concentrates on planning an essay, writing it, and getting it back. All three parts are essential stages in a critical approach to academic work. This part of the book takes an assignment from the research stage, perhaps not quite completed yet, through to the submission of it—where many people think the exercise concludes—and to the day when it is returned, building on an instructor's comments to improve for the next round.

In the book's concluding part, Part V, we draw together the skills learned throughout the book and the course, stressing that a test or an examination should not be considered a negative experience fraught with anxiety but, rather, an opportunity to demonstrate what has been learned. In this final chapter, we examine various resources for preparing for exams. Studying is not merely memorizing facts or remembering isolated bits of data but requires critical thinking; that is, writing exams is a skill that requires practice and thinking with a purpose. Studying involves mapping out a course before getting down to acquiring the details, and the writing of an exam requires planning and organization before putting pen to paper.

This last chapter foregrounds the two principles of organization used throughout the book, discussing the final examination as both the end of the academic term and the culmination of the materials taught in the course. As this outline indicates, *Foundations* is organized to follow the sequence of the academic year, from the first lecture to the final examination, or to follow a student from entering university to graduation. The book is also cumulative in that it builds from basic survival skills to more advanced critical thinking, reading, and writing. For instance, in the first chapter, we address the need for different reading approaches, such as skimming for an overview, to address the possible culture shock a new student faces in an apparently impossible reading load. Later, in Chapter 4, we discuss in detail five more complex reading practices—literal, formal, expository, comparative, and analytical—as well as terminology and concepts from new theories to read narrative and multi-media. Similar principles of sequential and cumulative organization are used for developing arguments, preparing assignments and formal essays, and documenting sources, moving from basic requirements to more developed levels as a course progresses through the academic year or a student undertakes a series of more demanding courses or years of study.

This arrangement allows the instructor considerable flexibility in using *Foundations*. For instance, our experience has been that for students entering university, most of the material in the first two chapters needs to be worked through in lectures and tutorials, while for many second-year students, the first two chapters could be most usefully assigned as important refreshers. Similarly, while the chapters on grammar and studying for exams are addressed to a beginning student, more advanced students can also use them to advantage. All students can benefit from classroom study of more advanced critical skills, such as developing arguments, new reading practices, essay research, and working through the requirements for an essay in terms of thesis statements and opening and concluding paragraphs. The level of intervention and direct instruction will depend upon the students' previous preparation.

The materials in *Foundations* can be re-arranged easily. For instance, if a research-based assignment is scheduled early in the term, then Chapters 7 and 8 can be moved before Chapters 4 and 5. If students demonstrate little familiarity with standard written English or the conventions of grammar, then an instructor might wish to spend classroom time on Chapter 12 early in the year. In any case, the academic year upon which the book is principally organized is not uniform and consistent across all courses of study in Canadian universities, and therefore, instructors can easily adapt the order of the chapters according to their needs.

NEW TO THIS EDITION

About two-thirds of *Foundations* has been re-written, and the whole book has been re-organized to clarify the application of critical skills to all aspects of academic work. While most students now entering university and many continuing students can use computers in quite sophisticated ways and are adept in using them for entertainment or games, many are not familiar with using computers and the Internet for more challenging academic purposes, such as undertaking systematic research or writing, editing, and formatting more complicated essays or assignments. We have addressed these issues throughout, including ways of using the new electronic resources of university libraries and the Net, methods of assessing the reliability of Web sites for their academic reliability, and ways of avoiding plagiarism when using materials from the Web.

While every chapter has been extensively revised, the most important changes involve the following:

- Thorough re-organization of the chapters to foreground the sequence of cumulative skills acquired during the school year.

- Inclusion of new learning objectives and learning outcomes to indicate what every chapter covers, the kinds of questions answered and what a student should be expected to have achieved at the end of each chapter.
- Supplementing each chapter with new figures, tables, charts, and Tips boxes to present information and concepts graphically.
- Crucial integration of computer skills and applications throughout.
- Addition of many more key terms and concepts with explanations.
- Extensive revision and clarification of the essential chapter on survival skills, with additional practical advice on time management, control of your study environment, and taking notes in lectures and seminars.
- Addition of a new separate chapter on changing expectations in university life and academic work, with additional sections on learning styles and new classroom formats.
- Comprehensive treatment of advanced reading strategies to cover literal, formal, expository, comparative, and analytical levels of reading, with examples of each.
- Improved organization of chapters on critical thinking and writing, especially on implementing a critical attitude and arguing a position, with simplified sections on formal logic.
- Revision of chapters on research using the Internet and print resources to take into account the increasingly computerized collections of e-resources in university libraries.
- Extended treatment of planning and writing an essay, with enlarged sections on a thesis statement, opening and concluding paragraphs, major problems to watch out for, and how to write with clarity. Samples of student writing, and corrected essays have been included.
- Expanded and revised treatment of the chapter on documenting sources, including conformity with the most recent MLA (6th edition, 2003) and APA (5th edition, 2001) revisions. The presentation and explanation of examples has been thoroughly revised and clarified, and fuller treatment is given to citations from and references to multi-media and electronic (Web) resources.
- Extended section on what to do after getting the mid-term exam back.
- Simplified sections on the etymology of words.
- New sections on the following:
  - The changing electronic classroom
  - Different classroom formats, including e-wired and wi-fi learning environments
  - Learning skills and how to adapt them to university work
  - Paraphrase and summary
  - How to evaluate Web sites for research
  - How to avoid charges of plagiarism when using the Web
  - Sample student essays with corrections marked in them
  - Critical attitudes in electronic learning environments
- Thorough revision of Web sites adding many new references for further reading.
- Supplementary materials that have been added on the *Foundations* Web site.

FEATURES

Foundations has a large number of educational features that make the book useful to students and helpful to teachers whether assigned for individual study or for classroom discussion. In particular, *Foundations*

- outlines clear learning objectives and outcomes at the beginning and end of each chapter in questions and answers that enable students to know just what is covered;
- integrates practical advice with theoretical and expository background and information;
- sets out difficult concepts and relationships in graphs and charts;
- provides a comprehensive index to direct readers to detailed treatment of topics;
- includes useful Tips boxes throughout to summarize procedures for making study efficient;
- highlights and defines difficult or technical terms and uses them in an appropriate academic context;
- follows the rhythm of the school year, beginning with survival skills needed for the first lectures and seminars, through classroom presentations, assignments, and essays, to the mid-term test and final exam;
- builds cumulative learning with increasing complexity, while providing both introductory and more advanced skills, for instance, in critical reading practices, and in research methods and documentation;
- provides an interdisciplinary approach to teaching foundational skills and critical thinking across the curriculum;
- explains thoroughly why certain study strategies are appropriate, shows how they work, and gives practical advice about how to use them;
- draws examples from a variety of disciplines in the humanities and social sciences, including literature, history, sociology, and media studies, and the procedures are transferable to any discipline;
- illustrates concepts with Canadian examples;
- adapts to instructors' particular needs, so the sequence of chapters makes sense for a particular course;
- accommodates both in-class and at-home study. The whole book may be taken up in sections, or parts of the text for in-class work, say, the sections on taking lecture notes, formulating critical arguments, planning and writing essays (with the sections on a thesis statement, or opening and closing paragraphs), or undertaking special kinds of research;
- gives flexibility to students who can use parts of *Foundations* to review on their own, perhaps the sections on grammar and punctuation or the chapter on changing university expectations. If difficulties arise in reviewing the readings in class, further work can be undertaken; and
- concludes each chapter with a "Further Readings" list of relevant Web sites and print resources.

SUPPLEMENTS

- *Foundations* is supported by a Web site that outlines the book in detail, gives a complete specimen chapter, provides hot links to all the Web sites mentioned in the book, as well as numerous other sites to supplement them, and provides the learning objectives for each chapter and a series of short answers to major questions that each chapter addresses. In addition, the Web site contains additional materials that expand specific sections in the printed text, such as a list of commonly misused words, expanded discussions of dictionaries, and a fuller treatment of formal logic.

Acknowledgments

We are grateful to York University students in Humanities 1970 (Worlds of Childhood), 2320 (Cultures of North America), and 2640 (Modes of Fantasy), who, over many years, have helped us hone these skills and direct them as clearly as possible to students' needs and classroom practice. We are particularly grateful to those students who took our courses from 1996 to 2003, for and with whom much of this material was written and revised. Various people have helped us by making suggestions and by reading parts of the manuscript, among whom we would like to thank the following:

- Our colleagues in the Division of Humanities at York University.
- At Pearson Education Canada, we have been greatly helped by Matthew Christian, Joel Gladstone, Jon Maxfield, Jennifer Murray, Madhu Ranadive, David Stover, and Dave Ward. Marcia Miron and Rohini Herbert have been highly proficient copy editors.
- The following reviewers provided thoughtful comments and suggestions: Diane Luu, University College of the Fraser Valley; Trudy MacCormack, St. Francis Xavier University; Colleen Mahy, George Brown College; Patrick Malcolmson, St. Thomas University; David Rubeli, Algonquin College; Mathew Zachariah, University of Calgary.
- Particular individuals, including Oriana Barbato, Kym Bird, Sue Collins, Rob Finlayson, Doug Freake, Lisa Haberman, Robert Hanke, Jennifer Hosein, Peggy Keall, Rob Lawrence, Steve Mason, Kirsten McKnight, Peter Mitchell, Gwen Norman, Pat Rockman, Dylani Shea, Tashiana Shea, Ron Sheese, Marlene Shore, Patricia Stamp, Peter Turner, Susan Warwick, Nancy Whitla, and Lisa Wood.
- Various institutions have also helped us, including Founders College, the Centre for Academic Writing and the Centre for Computer Assisted Writing at York University, and the Teaching with Technology Lab at Calumet College, York University.

Victor Shea and William Whitla
Division of Humanities, York University

part one

改变方式. &gear:齿轮. 排档.

Shifting Gears: Ways of Adapting to University

chapter one

Survival Skills

This chapter introduces the fundamental academic skills and critical methods you need and also can serve as a refresher for students already experienced in university work, as well as for those who are returning to it after a time away.

LEARNING OBJECTIVES

This section will answer the following questions:

- How can you develop good study habits and concentration skills?
- How do you schedule your time in the face of many demands on you from school, family, friends, and work? 面对.
- How can you read and understand so many assigned texts?
- How can you get the information you need from large lectures and small classes?
- How can you best take notes in lectures and seminars?

CHANGING SCHOOLS: FUNDAMENTAL ACADEMIC SKILLS

Students come to university now with different skills from those of 10 or 20 years ago. You probably have a much greater ability than previous university students to work with computers, but you still may need help to write well at a university level. You may be an expert in all kinds of current music and movies but may have not yet developed many resources for describing, evaluating, or analyzing what you read and are expected to learn. You are suddenly faced with many new challenges, not the least of which is being on your own in a new environment, where you have to take responsibility for your own education in important ways. And just when you enter this changing environment with its new expectations, you are faced with apprehensions about your ability to succeed. This book directly addresses these concerns by providing skills and strategies for academic success.

Your university professors expect you to work independently and to have ability in thinking, reading, writing, taking lecture notes, and making class presentations. Some of these expectations undoubtedly will cause some anxiety—and not only for beginning students. In what follows, we first set out some of the fundamental skills that will help you survive and flourish. Better than that, they will enable you to cope, from the start, with your lectures and seminars and with your assignments and readings. Even better, they will train you in study methods and instill study habits that will continue to benefit you in the rest of your years at university and even in life-long learning.

To shift into successful university work (whether you are in the first year or are seeking to improve your skills in later years), you have to commit yourself to three things:

1. Attend your lectures, classes, and seminars, even when attendance is not taken.
2. Take good notes at classes and lectures.
3. Keep up with your weekly readings.

These are the keys to completing university courses successfully. Because of work or personal commitments, however, no student can always entirely keep up the pace demanded by a course schedule. It is good to realize at the outset that always keeping up is impossible. Nevertheless, your goal should be trying to keep up and finding ways to make a recovery when you slip behind a little. Having your reading completed *before* the lecture or class where it is discussed will allow you to understand the ways in which the material is being taught and also provide you with a foundation for successful completion of the course.

Because, for the most part, nobody monitors your reading or note taking on a weekly basis, you are expected to monitor yourself. But it is easy at this point to lose your motivation. Without learning habits of good concentration, you will very likely face a crisis mid-way through the first term when the first essay or mid-term examination is due. A major difficulty many students encounter is finding the mind-set that will allow them to concentrate. Dr. Samuel Johnson, a famous 18th-century British literary figure, made a remark about the increased powers of concentration available when faced with death in two weeks: "Depend upon it, Sir, when a man knows he is to be hanged in a fortnight, it concentrates his mind wonderfully." For a student, that moment might seem to be an essay deadline, but improved study habits that you can learn will help you keep up with your reading and write your essays as a normal part of academic life, not as a moment of life-threatening crisis.

The following sections set out the fundamental academic skills that will enable you to shift gears into your university's academic term. You will learn how to analyze your own study habits and improve your concentration, how to manage your time in accordance with your workload and personal commitments, and how to listen and take notes during lectures and seminars.

Learning good study habits is a matter of training. It is possible for you to move into a new frame of mind where your study habits really work well for you. To do so, you have to examine your present habits critically, break them down into their parts, and then modify some of them, one or two at a time. In this self-examination of the ways that your study habits facilitate your concentration on readings and classes, you are embarking on your first exercise in critical thinking.

STUDY HABITS

Whether your most common place of study is the library, your residence room, your home, or any number of places in between classes (the bus, the pub, the lunch room, the park), you should be in control of your study space and what you bring to it to help you concentrate and use your best time to your advantage. Dartmouth College notes that large numbers of students—from 8 percent to as high as 50 percent—have difficulty concentrating on their studies on a regular basis, and virtually all students have this difficulty from time to time ("Concentration"; see the Works Cited list at the end of the book. We explain this convention in Chapter 9).

Studies show that a combination of three factors influences your ability to concentrate:

1. External reasons (environment, distractions, noise and light levels)
2. Methods of concentration adapted to the purpose and goals of a particular study task (using your best time for the hardest task)
3. Internal reasons (motivational problems, worries, and anxieties) (see Figure 1.1).

No one can expect that after a great summer partying, or one combining work and courses to complete your degree faster, you can show up for the first week of lectures and plug in immediately to the old study routines that you had learned, or perhaps only partly learned, in your high school days or earlier in your university career. Study skills, including concentration, are learned habits, and they have to be acquired and nurtured carefully to bring improved results. Such improvement is a life-long project for everybody at university, including your teachers. This section will show you how to develop these fundamental academic skills. You should not be discouraged if you revert to old habits (we all do at times) but, rather, should try to isolate the causes of losing your concentration and should follow the goals that you set for yourself until you can successfully focus on reading or studying for increasingly longer periods. When you are successful, you can give yourself a reward.

It is a good idea to assess the reasons for being distracted. If you can learn what it is that causes poor attention generally and then determine if that cause applies to you, then you are well on your way to bringing more focus to your studying. The key is to make it habitual to control over your environment and yourself to realize your best academic potential.

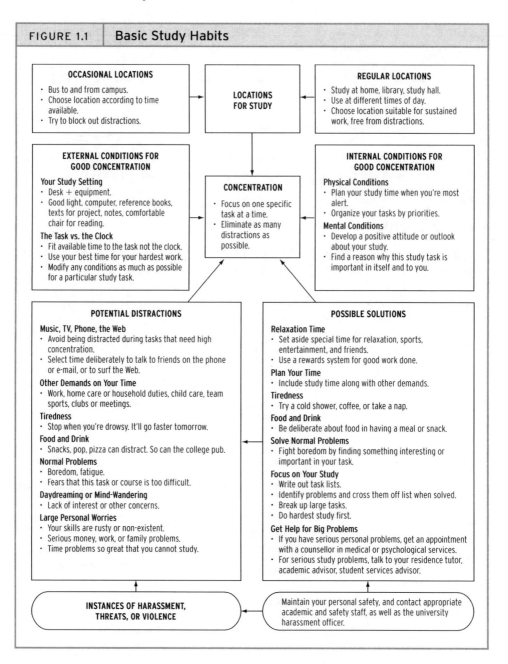

FIGURE 1.1 | Basic Study Habits

OCCASIONAL LOCATIONS
- Bus to and from campus.
- Choose location according to time available.
- Try to block out distractions.

LOCATIONS FOR STUDY

REGULAR LOCATIONS
- Study at home, library, study hall.
- Use at different times of day.
- Choose location suitable for sustained work, free from distractions.

EXTERNAL CONDITIONS FOR GOOD CONCENTRATION

Your Study Setting
- Desk + equipment.
- Good light, computer, reference books, texts for project, notes, comfortable chair for reading.

The Task vs. the Clock
- Fit available time to the task not the clock.
- Use your best time for your hardest work.
- Modify any conditions as much as possible for a particular study task.

CONCENTRATION
- Focus on one specific task at a time.
- Eliminate as many distractions as possible.

INTERNAL CONDITIONS FOR GOOD CONCENTRATION

Physical Conditions
- Plan your study time when you're most alert.
- Organize your tasks by priorities.

Mental Conditions
- Develop a positive attitude or outlook about your study.
- Find a reason why this study task is important in itself and to you.

POTENTIAL DISTRACTIONS

Music, TV, Phone, the Web
- Avoid being distracted during tasks that need high concentration.
- Select time deliberately to talk to friends on the phone or e-mail, or to surf the Web.

Other Demands on Your Time
- Work, home care or household duties, child care, team sports, clubs or meetings.

Tiredness
- Stop when you're drowsy. It'll go faster tomorrow.

Food and Drink
- Snacks, pop, pizza can distract. So can the college pub.

Normal Problems
- Boredom, fatigue.
- Fears that this task or course is too difficult.

Daydreaming or Mind-Wandering
- Lack of interest or other concerns.

Large Personal Worries
- Your skills are rusty or non-existent.
- Serious money, work, or family problems.
- Time problems so great that you cannot study.

POSSIBLE SOLUTIONS

Relaxation Time
- Set aside special time for relaxation, sports, entertainment, and friends.
- Use a rewards system for good work done.

Plan Your Time
- Include study time along with other demands.

Tiredness
- Try a cold shower, coffee, or take a nap.

Food and Drink
- Be deliberate about food in having a meal or snack.

Solve Normal Problems
- Fight boredom by finding something interesting or important in your task.

Focus on Your Study
- Write out task lists.
- Identify problems and cross them off list when solved.
- Break up large tasks.
- Do hardest study first.

Get Help for Big Problems
- If you have serious personal problems, get an appointment with a counsellor in medical or psychological services.
- For serious study problems, talk to your residence tutor, academic advisor, student services advisor.

INSTANCES OF HARASSMENT, THREATS, OR VIOLENCE

Maintain your personal safety, and contact appropriate academic and safety staff, as well as the university harassment officer.

External Conditions for Good Concentration

Your Environment

Whether you live at home or in residence or share an apartment, you will want to spend time with your friends and in various forms of sports and recreation. While it is enjoyable to spend time relaxing, it is also useful to catch whatever time you can for study—say, in that hour or two you may have between classes when you have a chapter to read. That study time can best be spent where you can devote your attention to your reading. Spending the time in the pub, where there is constant coming and going and the big TV screen dominates all conversation, might not be the best choice. The library is better, but avoid the study space taken over by groups working loudly on joint projects. One of the study halls or a carrel in the library stacks might be appropriate, or find any other location that works for you so that you can concentrate without distraction.

Your Equipment

Besides the occasional time you have for reading, such as on the bus or between classes, you need a place for study on a regular basis that is equipped with what you need for your particular study task, such as a good reading light, a comfortable chair, a desk, your computer, writing materials, your notes, a bookstand to keep your book propped open so your hands are free to use the computer or to write in your notebook, and a dictionary. That is, you have to create the conditions you need to focus on your work so that you are not constantly running around searching for a pencil, a highlighter, and so on.

Music and TV

What about noise, especially music? If you find yourself reading the same paragraph several times because your friends are laughing their way through *The Simpsons,* you might be better off either joining them or going to the library. Probably most students already have developed the habit of listening to music when studying in high school. In the case of certain tasks that require undivided attention, music, even if you think it is only background noise, will distract you. What applies to music applies to TV even more stringently. You need to set aside your time for watching TV and listening to music and to try to follow that timetable carefully. You will get more enjoyment out of your relaxation and also out of your studying.

Concentration for Particular Study Tasks

You often will have only a little time at your disposal, in which case you have to take advantage of that time to do what you can. But when you set aside more time for study, take all the time you need. Be controlled by the demands of the task you set for yourself, rather than by the clock. The clock can be a major distraction. Do your most demanding studying when you are at your best, whether morning or evening, but you should also plan to set aside that premium time when there are fewest competing activities demanding your attention—work, sports, partying, or your favourite TV shows. Besides following your timetable, you need to be aware that some of the most demanding tasks should determine their own length of time (see the section on time scheduling on page 8). It is best to stop studying when you get tired, your concentration begins to fade seriously, and none of the tricks to keep focus seems to be working.

Internal Conditions for Good Concentration

Your Physical State

It is important to plan to study your most difficult material when you are most alert. Some people work best in the early morning and others late at night. You need to choose your time carefully for demanding work and try to prevent other things from encroaching upon this special time. Physical hunger is a sure source of distraction; soft drinks, beer, or snacks will tempt you to turn away from the books to indulge yourself (or, in the case of beer, fall asleep). It is best to have a deliberate snack before you start studying and to do a little physical exercise as a tune-up. Studying when you are drowsy will not produce good results.

Your Mental State

Good study habits depend upon a positive mental outlook. But for most of us, there are any number of inhibitors of good study habits, including boredom, anxiety, personal worries, and poor study methods. The greatest deterrent is the notion that studying is a chore that *must* be performed, when you have to summon every ounce of will power to open the book and get through that first paragraph. Here, the problem is primarily one of attitude. Success in studying depends on getting the work done efficiently, block by building block.

It helps to shift your attitude to find a reason that satisfies you for taking a class, such as that you are interested in the materials covered or that success in this course will make achieving other goals possible. Talking to your professor or to other students will sometimes help. Getting the readings done for the next lecture so that you see for yourself how much more you get out of it when properly prepared will also result in a lot of satisfaction. If you are anxious about the difficulty of the course, you can try to solve the particular problem that you are stuck on, or you can talk to your instructor to sort out the problem. Or, if this course is more demanding than others, you can find ways of putting its demands in perspective, such as the following:

- Using a notebook to write out your tasks and striking them out when they are accomplished
- Identifying your problems in a particular project or reading and addressing each of them systematically
- Breaking up large tasks into their component parts
- Doing the most difficult task first, when you are most alert

Daydreaming or Mind-Wandering

When you find your attention slipping, you need to note what is distracting you. If it is part of your environment, you can take steps to correct it. If it is daydreaming that is pulling you away, you might write down the interrupting thought and turn back to the books. The point is that if you objectify the thought, you will be able to set it aside and regain your direction more easily. Another trick is simply to make a check mark on a piece of paper whenever you catch yourself daydreaming and to try to reduce the number of checks in an hour. On the other hand, you can turn deliberately away from your books, daydream freely for as long as you wish, and then return to your study. The idea is to try to avoid studying and daydreaming at the same time.

Personal Worries

You might be troubled by other problems that interfere with your academic study. You may have withdrawn from study for several months or years to work and now wonder if your old skills are rusty. You might be worried about how to finance the costs of spiralling tuition and so have taken a part-time job that cuts into your study time; you might be anxious about

---

TIPS Increasing Your Concentration

1. Analyze your own study habits realistically and identify how and when you lose concentration. Work on eliminating your bad habits one or two at a time.

2. Set aside a regular amount of time for study and then gradually increase your attention span.

3. Set out your tasks or goals for a particular session in order (the number of pages to be read, the problems to be solved), and check them off when you complete them.

4. Vary your activities among reading, writing, reviewing, memorizing, solving problems, planning for the next day, and so on.

5. Plan your breaks and do something different so that you enjoy them.

---

your job prospects upon graduation; you might be forced to live at home for financial reasons but would rather live in residence; you might have moved into a new and ethnically diverse academic community where you are exposed to challenging new experiences; or your family might be going through a major crisis, such as a divorce. Almost all students are faced with some of these challenges, though you may not know it. There are also new challenges in the classroom, not only in the first year but every year, when you have new teachers to get used to, new classmates to relate to, and new course materials to master.

Every university has facilities to help students cope with problems in their life situations. There are financial aid officers, organizations for mature students, clubs and associations for particular language and cultural groups, and a number of people with specialized training and resources to help you with accommodation and family or personal difficulties. The helpful and discreet resources of the student association and the counselling offices are available. The same professionals, as well as your school's job placement or employment office, can help you cope with worries about your future job prospects or about your present balance of academics and work. All of these student resources have particular roles in smoothing out your university life, and you should use them as you need them. Clearing away as many worries and personal difficulties as you can will help you concentrate on your academic work and will make the kinds of academic skills that are addressed in this book far more useful to you.

Instances of Harassment, Threats, or Violence

In cases of serious disruptions or harassment, by either faculty or other students, there are important avenues to be followed. First, you need to maintain your own personal safety in the situation, and second, if someone in authority is harassing you, you need to preserve your academic integrity against reprisals by reporting it to the appropriate authority. Having done that, you should follow the procedures that your university sets out for dealing with each problem. Appropriate people to contact are the course director, the head of a department, the student or faculty ombudsperson, the academic dean or dean of students, the sexual harassment office (anonymity can be preserved), the women's support office, the campus police, medical staff, chaplains, and so on. If you live in residence, your residence don or dean can be of help. We have discussed four different levels of internal distractions that might affect your concentration and study. We are by no means suggesting, however, that daydreaming can be equated with harassment or violence. Improving your mental state by simple modes of better concentration and avoiding daydreaming require time and effort, but serious personal worries can be much harder to solve, and you might well need some help with them. That is almost certainly true for the most serious problems, those of harassment, threats, or violence.

Getting any of these difficulties out of the way leaves you ready to tackle your academic work afresh. The key is to break down and isolate the distractions, worries, or threats, and to take steps to eliminate the parts that hinder your building up better concentration skills.

TIME SCHEDULING

"We'd draw up a timetable," say over-stretched students, "but we haven't had a moment." Little do they know that by not planning, they are wasting valuable study time.

Some people think that scheduling their time limits their freedom unnecessarily and destroys their spontaneity. In fact, we all have obligations and duties of various kinds, whether we ignore them or not, and are not as free as we think. When it comes to planning time for study or recreation, we are really setting our priorities.

Within your complex life, you need to set out priorities so that a realistic plan is in place for you to do well in your university courses. Other aspects of your life might be just as important to you, such as earning money for school, avoiding an enormous student loan, caring for parents or children, and so on. When you schedule time for studying, you are choosing to set your academic goals in relationship to the rest of your life, and only you can determine what the best balance should be. However, it may be that in appraising the demands on your time realistically, you will find that a normal five-course load is too heavy, or at least that your grades will suffer, if you must maintain the other demands on your time outside university work (see Box 1.1).

Setting out a Plan

The workload for a particular course is set at the beginning of the year, and you must estimate the demands of that workload in relation to other demands on your time. A normal minimal expectation for university work is that you spend two hours outside class for every hour in class. Following this minimal demand, your time spent in a full-time five-course load will require at least 45 hours per week: 15 hours spent in class and 30 hours spent outside reading and writing. The time commitment to a full-time course load, therefore, is more than a full-time job, which is now usually 37 to 40 hours a week.

These time frames are not meant to discourage you but to provide a reality check. Without the commitment of time to your studies, your grades will suffer considerably. If work or other commitments mean that you cannot devote this much time to your study, assess that early on and cut back on the number of courses that you are taking. In our experience, more and more students are taking fewer courses per year, better balancing their academic commitments and the employment necessary to pay for their schooling. Many students find it practical and very helpful to map out the year, the term, the month, and the week.

BOX 1.1	**Mapping Time**

How much time does a student have for a full-year course? In this model, adapted from one by Professor Susan Warwick, we assume that a full-year course involves 30 weeks, with three hours of classes a week. In our sample there are 3500 pages of readings to complete in the year, including all texts and a course kit, but not counting any extra reading for assignments. We also assume that our sample student is taking a full course load of five courses and is also working for 25 hours a week.

Time Available

168 hours in a week   = 5040 hours in a 30-week year

Commitments

5 courses @ 15 hours a week	= 450 hours
Sleeping @ 8 hours a night	= 1680 hours
Work @ 25 hours a week	= 750 hours
Travel @ 2 hours a day, 10 hours a week	= 300 hours
Entertaining @ 2 hours a day, 10 hours a week	= 300 hours
Misc. (eating, shopping, etc.) @ 2 hours a day, 10 hours a week	= 300 hours
Total	= 3780 hours
Hence 1260 hours are left	= 1260 hours
To be fair, take only 2/3 of that amount	= 840 hours
Divided by the five courses	= 168 hours per course per year
Realistic estimate of course time available	= 5.6 hours a week per course

That amount of time comes close to the recommended minimum of two hours of studying or reading outside class for every hour spent in class. You will have to schedule more than your allotted time for assignments in some weeks, but for many weeks you can spend the full time on course readings. Two models calculate the reading load. Column A divides the course readings into weekly and daily numbers of pages to read all of the course materials. Column B assumes an average reader and calculates the time needed on the basis of the number of words to be read and average reading speed.

Column A

Actual page count of sample course
  = 3500 pages
  = 116 pages each week
  = 20 pages a day, excluding
    Saturdays and Sundays
With about five and a half hours available, that also comes out to about 20 pages a day for a five-day week.

Column B

3500 pages = 1 225 000 words
          @ 350 per page
Most Canadian college students read 250–300 words a minute. A good reader will read about 500, a slow reader 150–250. Take the lowest of the average readers, 250 words a minute. Therefore, an average student will take 4900 minutes to read all of the readings.
  = 81.6 hours for the year, or
  = 2.7 hours a week to do all of the readings, about half of the allotted time, with time left over for research and assignments.

The Year

If your courses are on a yearly schedule, you need to note the important dates of assignments, essays, reports or class presentations, projects, quizzes, and examinations (mid-terms and finals) as well as any other highlights. You need to be sure to mark down the key dates by which you must drop the course in order to receive a partial fee refund or to avoid receiving a failing grade and the last day to hand in term work. These dates are published in your university calendar and are on the university's Web page. Of course, your yearly schedule will also include special events, such as religious holidays, parties, concerts, and so on.

TIPS   Getting Organized

1. Many student organizations make academic timetable forms available in the first week of classes. Get a couple and hang them prominently near your desk.

2. Buy a watch.

3. Keep and use a date book.

4. Most student centres recommend that you spend at least twice the number of hours a week reading or studying for a course as you spend in the classroom. For more difficult work and when assignments are due, you will have to schedule more time for study.

5. Use odd periods of time—such as time spent on the bus—for reviewing or reading that is not too demanding.

6. Always carry some notes or a book with you that you can work on for that 15-minute period. Such use of time adds up profitably.

7. If you have a free day with no classes, do not plan to use it for weekly study marathons, as it will be hard to maintain your concentration. Instead, break it up into two-hour sessions (at most), do different work within those sessions, and relax between sessions.

8. Before you go to bed, put some of your material in order for the next day and make a brief list of upcoming tasks (a "things-to-do" list).

The Term, Semester, or Quarter

Like the yearly schedule, the term schedule will also record the key dates for university and course deadlines, as well as other events, such as concerts and long weekends. But here, your time is more compressed. You might also wish to extend the term schedules into a yearly pattern, especially if some of your courses are year-long courses and some are semester courses or, in some universities, full and half courses.

The Month

Most students who draw up this schedule position the month with a week added into the next month. To organize a month of good work and then find that the next week contains two assignments will come as a shock. The week added at the end is insurance that when you schedule the next month, you will have no surprises, since the due dates for your essays, other assignments, and examinations have already been entered into your fuller timetable.

The Week

For the first weeks in the term, it helps to make detailed timetables of your week, first listing all classes, seminars, labs, and other fixed activities, such as work or other responsibilities. Then, you should total all of the time that you customarily spend eating, sleeping, shopping, attending meetings, and commuting, as well as any other time requirements, such as those for family, work, or regular recreation. You should allow yourself an hour for lunch on most days, if your classes allow, and more time than that for dinner so that you can use some of that time for relaxation. After calculating the time that you have left, you can deduct from that a reasonable amount of recreational time for the week. You can include the time that you intend to take off on the weekends and the time that you will spend partying, reading for pleasure, or watching TV. The amount of time that you have left is what you have for your academic study and reading.

Next, you should estimate the time that you need for studying for each course and plan it in blocks so that you can split your time working on a number of courses in a block to give variety and minimize loss of concentration. Some students find that thinking of blocks of time as morning, afternoon, and evening is a help. It is a good idea to put your most difficult work into the peak study period when you have the fewest distractions and your concentration is at its best. If this map allows you sufficient time for the two hours of study to one hour of classes, your management is under control; if not, you need to decide where you can make adjustments and check the schedule again to see whether it is practical and realistic.

You can then post your schedule over your desk and be prepared to amend it as the week goes by. You will likely need to revise the schedule for the second week to fit your needs and goals. It is your strategy map, and all that you do academically can be charted on it.

The Day

You might set out a daily timetable based on your weekly timetable with the specifics added about where you are supposed to be. You can put in the locations and precise tasks that you have to complete and sketch in the details the night before. Such a schedule will have to be modified depending on when your classes begin. It might look like this:

9:00 a.m.	wake up and leave by 9:45
10:30	return library books; look over Geography notes
11:30–1:00	Geography lecture
1:00–2:00	library; look up 2 different encyc. articles to photocopy on Adam Smith and Ricardo for Economic History

Note: assignment due next Wednesday

2:00–3:30	free time
3:30–4:00	review vocabulary for Spanish class
4:00–5:00	Spanish class
5:00–5:15	appointment with Prof. Lewis re economics paper

| 5:15–8:00 | free time |
| 8:00–11:00 | study—desk |

8:00–9:00	1. read textbook on Smith and Ricardo
	2. read and compare the two encyclopedia articles
	3. make notes on text and on articles
9:00–10:00	1. Spanish vocab. 1/2 hour
	2. Spanish grammar from text 1/2 hour
	Note: Quiz next Thursday
10:00–11:00	1. read chapters 4–8 of Dickens's *Hard Times* for English
	Note: Try to complete novel by weekend

| 11:00 | free time |

You can see that the details are set out carefully, especially in the evening study time but also in the library so that the time does not drift by. A good habit is to make short lists of things to do on a daily basis and to tick items off when completed. Of course, it will not all work out easily, and there will be problems, but the scheme sets out a pattern that you can then vary or modify. As well, the daily plan fits into the weekly and monthly schedules. Even if you fall behind, and we all do, you have a map of your own expectations based on your course demands and can make adjustments the next day to catch up, perhaps by taking less free time.

When You Fall Behind: A Schedule to Catch Up

Everybody falls behind. Sometimes, your schedule does not work and your unfinished school work piles up. Now is the time to invoke the "catch-up schedule." It has three simple principles: first, keep from falling further behind; second, prioritize the incomplete work; and third, implement a method to catch up on some of it every day.

Keep from Falling Further Behind

Be rigorous in what you have to do to keep up. That may mean skimming a bit or taking some shortcuts—anything to cut free a bit of time that you can use for getting some of the unfinished work done. But in planning for that, you cannot afford to let other things slip. Do not try to economize by skipping classes. Make careful lists of your readings, decide what you can do, and complete it at least in the overview method (see the advice on reading for an overview on page 15); go to lectures and labs, concentrating as well as you can; identify what is most important; and keep up with any new deadlines.

Prioritize Your Unfinished Work

Sort unfinished work into four categories: *urgent* (*U:* this work has to be done as soon as possible; grade loss is threatened by this item); *essential* (*E:* this item has to be done soon and is related to understanding a major component or part of the course; direct grade loss is not imminent, but this item is vital to the final examination); *important* (*I:* it would be good and useful to get this item completed within a specific time for general comprehension, but it is neither urgent nor essential); and *postpone* (*P:* this item can safely be postponed until your schedule allows it to be taken up; realistically, you put items in this category only when you are aware that they may not be completed and accepting that fact does not put you at risk).

Next, list all of the work that you have not done, fitting it into one of the categories. Colour code them, with the *U* items marked in red. Then, estimate the amount of time that you will need for each task. Be as complete and as specific as you can be, listing all readings unfinished, lectures missed, notes incomplete, work not handed in, and deadlines missed. The chances are that your estimated times will greatly exceed your available time. So, go back over the list and cut back once more, eliminating what you can safely, reducing the time for lesser tasks, and giving the most time to the high-priority items. The aim here is not to get you more and more discouraged or to render you immobile from the shock of what is incomplete but to set out what you should do to get out of the swamp. Everyone gets into these swamps at different times as the work piles up; the important thing is to devise a strategy to get out.

Deal first with the deadlines you have missed or the work you have not handed in. Check with your professors about whether you can still submit it, even if there is a late penalty. Then, make a plan to get the work done, concentrating on what is most difficult first, or what is latest, or what carries the greatest weight or greatest penalty. Mark on your schedule specific times for beginning this work and for each part of it until it is finished, and stick to the time you allot for it. Do not feel you have to go only for perfection—hand in something—a low grade is better than a zero. Try to have the first item completed within three days, according to a realistic schedule.

When you are drawing up your priorities, you will see some materials that have long passed in the course, so, unless they are essential for understanding the present concepts of the course or you are missing a gap that cannot be filled later, skip them for now and return to them later when (or if) there is a lull in your workload.

When you are more modestly behind in your readings, again concentrate on moving through the older material to get caught up. Reading for comprehension, rather than for detail, would be a good idea here.

Catch Up Bit by Bit

In the time that you have saved from your other work, take some time every day to get your overdue work back into shape. Each week you should be chipping away at the unfinished tasks and removing them from your list, and meanwhile, you will not be falling further behind.

When you are struggling to catch up, ask for help from your friends or your teachers. Delegate some of the work to others. Perhaps a friend can take notes once for you (do not make this practice a habit) while you complete your library work. Many students, when falling behind, make a habit of skipping classes to make up for lost time; this practice, when habitual, is ultimately counter-productive because the classes missed result in falling further behind. Class time is usually an efficient way of keeping in touch with course materials and requirements. Even if you do not have time to complete the readings, attendance at lectures and seminars will at least keep you up to date. Professors are not sympathetic to repeating material covered in class that you have missed because of your scheduling problems.

When you have fallen behind, give up some tasks as impossible and just accept that fact. Reorganize some part of your life to get a fresh angle and to stimulate your motivation;

sometimes just cleaning up your desk or room or reorganizing your workplace a little can help. Do not give in, however, to making this the important task in order to avoid doing what you are behind in. Get something done, and you will move ahead with the rest of your list to get caught up.

Problems with Time Management

"I'm supposed to be doing this survey in Psychology on procrastination," says the worried student, "but I just can't seem to get around to doing it."

Things get put off and put off until the last possible moment, and then, in a frantic flurry of activity, you struggle to get papers handed in, to study for exams, or to complete whatever task has you in a panic at the moment. Typically, procrastinators fail to learn from this pattern of disaster, but when the chance to defer comes up again, even in the face of horrible results, the same behavioural pattern kicks in. Or, they fall back on the excuse that many of us have invoked, "I'll do that when I feel like it"—except that we almost never feel like it. The key problem is that procrastinators really do believe that they do their best work under the extreme pressure of an absolute deadline, and so they cannot move until that moment is imminent. It is as though all of their inertia has accumulated to render them immobile until the final moment—or beyond the final moment—when in a frenzy they struggle to complete an almost impossible task.

Impairing the life of a procrastinator is the loss of self-confidence, as all of the promises you have made to yourself are broken. But despite your doubts or your ingrained habits, many recent studies have assured sufferers (and most students and professors have been sufferers at one time or another—you are not alone) that their problem can be reduced and cured. In an article in the *New York Times,* Jane Brody writes that "there are a host of techniques, many of which have been tested on some of the nation's most egregious procrastinators, to help you overcome the tendency to postpone or ignore tasks you find forbidding, offensive or just plain disagreeable" (C12). For a more detailed discussion of these kinds of procrastinators, see the *Foundations* Web site.

Professionals agree that if you have serious problems in organizing your time, some form of stress management is important.

- You can seek help with this aspect of your life from your university health centre or from your doctor.
- Regular physical exercise, even walking, is one essential ingredient in stress management.
- Break large tasks down into smaller ones to make them easier to start and complete, devoting a regular bit of time each week to working on the larger task so that you chip away at it.
- Make a list of the tasks that you have completed, rather than focusing entirely on those that you need to do.
- Get a study partner with whom you can work well.

The aim throughout is to get started and to work toward completion. The story is told of the early French martyr St. Denys, who, after being beheaded outside Paris, bent over, put his head back on his shoulders, and walked back to Paris. Voltaire, the French enlightenment philosopher, commented on this legend that the first step was the hard one—a remark that applies to the recovering procrastinator.

Above all, you need to be realistic in setting out your academic goals and fixing your timetable to achieve your objectives. Your schedule is not a wish list but rather a map to help you chart your way to your goals. Your schedule will also change from week to week and month to month as the demands of your coursework change. So, you should be prepared to be flexible about what you can accomplish.

READING AND COMPREHENDING ASSIGNED TEXTS

From the first class, your professors start assigning readings: the quantity may seem overwhelming (a whole book in one week?), and a student often does not know what to read for—you may have a few frames of reference to relate different texts but, at the beginning of the course, may be at a loss about what is important. Students ask whether they have to know all of the detail in a text and, if not, how they should separate what is essential from what is not. These questions are all perfectly fair, and are going through the minds of most students in the course. Rest assured—in most courses, these frames of reference will emerge more fully throughout the term. So, do not give up at the beginning, but do all that you can to keep up.

Learning to read and understand assigned texts becomes a survival skill from the first week. We deal in Chapter 4 with reading and critical skills in more depth. Our concern here is to get you started with some methods that will help you through the first weeks.

In a large Psychology class at Harvard, students were told to take 10 minutes to read 20 pages of the textbook, a tall order in itself. Then, they had to shut the books and take a test in which they had to write out the main argument, describe the supporting arguments and evidence, and finally state the author's conclusions. Only about 10 percent were able to complete the last requirement. Most students began at the beginning and read as far as they could in the allotted time, but they failed to come close to completing the reading. Those who completed the last requirement had learned to read for an overview, to skim, and then to fill in the gaps.

These are essential survival skills in the first weeks of classes, and they can be broken down into a number of steps:

1. Look over the whole book, chapter, or article before you begin to read it. See how it is set out and what its divisions are (parts, chapters, sections, sub-headings, and so on). Sometimes, the table of contents is much abbreviated, so look over the parts or sections to see what each really contains.

2. Look over the sub-headings in the parts of the book, chapter, or article that you are going to read. If you will be reading it all, look at the other kinds of information, such as illustrations, graphs and diagrams, charts, and summaries.

3. Read at least part of the preface or all of an article's abstract or opening summary. Here, an author usually sets out his or her goals and a summary of the literature in the field, how this text relates to it, and how the argument is organized. You often get a useful summary of the whole reading in the preface of a book or the opening paragraph of a book or article.

4. Look to see whether the book, chapter, or article has a bibliography or list of works cited. Skimming it will help you learn which kinds of authors and authorities are referred to in the text and what they were writing about and will also give you a greater

sense of the field to contextualize your particular reading. In all honesty, this step will not make a lot of sense to you in your first few weeks in university or when moving into a new discipline or course of study. However, the habit is a good one to establish at the outset. As your knowledge of the course and the field broadens, you will begin to recognize citations from particular authors and key articles and will perceive their importance in the reading in establishing its frames of reference.

On a practical level, it helps to start off by scanning your assigned reading from the beginning to the end, even going quickly through an entire book to look at the chapter headings to see what is covered. You might want to modify this practice in the case of a novel or play, where you do not want to know the ending before your detailed reading. At the very least, having a sense of the structure of the entire novel (as well as any other kind of text) will help you immensely before undertaking a detailed reading. Of course, for reading poetry, the practice is quite different and might involve detailed attention to language, metaphors, and versification which takes time and frequent re-reading.

In most kinds of reading, however, after your survey or overview of the complete text, you move to a more careful read-through, marking your text with a pencil. You can number its stages in the margin, for instance, using a one-word summary for each. You can note any key definitions, examples, or technical words. In some texts, you will want to note parts of the narrative or important phrases. You might also mark those words or ideas that you do not understand to raise for clarification later. Try to avoid underlining page after page with a highlighter. The point is to select what you mark to help you understand what is being said.

Armed with this preliminary survey, you are ready for a more sustained and detailed approach to the assigned reading. We give further advice on critical reading practices in Chapter 4. In any case, doing the assigned readings before the lectures and seminars will give you an excellent preparation for taking part in them as a critical listener.

We turn now to the kinds of skills that make you into an effective note-taker in lectures and seminars.

CRITICAL LISTENING IN LECTURES

One of the most intimidating experiences is to be in a large lecture hall with a professor far away at the front lecturing in a fashion that is unfamiliar to you. If it makes you feel any better, most beginning lecturers face considerable anxiety before their first classes. The whole format of the formal lecture is strange and impersonal to most of us. In many ways, the format of a large lecture is difficult because it goes against most contemporary ways of processing information, such as advertising, news clips, or sound bites. It involves an expert delivering information and argument to a class of learners who usually have little chance to interrupt or ask questions. Lecturers have different personalities and styles and cover their material using very different approaches. Being aware of such differences will alert you to how they use different methods to indicate what is important.

Universities favour this method of teaching not only because it has been traditional for more than a thousand years but also because in these days of financial restraint, it is usually economical. Increasingly, universities are using new technology to save money, sometimes with a video replacing the lecturer who is in another room. Whatever method of lecturing your professors use, your best strategy is to get what you can from each lecture by being an active listener and note-taker. Both listening and note-taking are learned skills. These skills are vital to your success in the course, since you will need these notes later to complete the course readings, write your essays, and study for the tests and final examinations.

To develop critical listening skills in lectures and seminars, that is, to become an active listener, you need to choose where you sit in the classroom. Sitting in the middle and near the front positions you to see and hear best, with fewer distractions from your classmates. It also helps to be aware of the many activities that take place when you become an active listener: understanding what is being said, summarizing it for your notes, shifting attention between the lecturer and the notes, analyzing what has been said and evaluating it, and anticipating what will come next. Of course, you cannot undertake all of these activities all of the time with equal balance, but trying to stress two or three in any given lecture will help you improve your skills.

The Lecture

The structure of a lecture lays out its direction, the material to be covered, and, most importantly, the larger frame of ideas of a discipline to which the material in the lecture is related. Lectures in most disciplines are set up using a model that lays out a series of ideas or concepts with a related set of applications, examples, or elaborations.

Students may get lost in understanding the concepts and then find the examples confusing, considering them repetitious or unnecessary. Hence, one of the most difficult and important skills for students to acquire is to separate a lecture's main backbone—its main concepts—from the details that elaborate or illustrate each of those concepts. Both are crucial: the first gives the frame of ideas, and the examples are its application. Listening for the structure at the outset of a lecture and being able to differentiate between main ideas and details will help prevent you from getting lost. To help you make these distinctions from the first day of classes, in what follows, we break down the formal parts of a lecture along with the ways lecturers use language to persuade you or to emphasize their main points.

The Structure of a Typical Lecture

Some lecturers write out the structure of the lecture on the blackboard week by week and then follow it in the course of their remarks. Recording this outline at the beginning of the lecture, before the lecture actually starts, is a good way of preparing for the content of the next hour. Outlining the structure enables you to see the transitions and to anticipate where the lecture is going and, to some extent, how it will get there. Sometimes, there are key concepts or ideas in the outline. Finally, the outline will greatly help you in your short review of the lecture after it is over and in the more extensive review of your notes that you will have to undertake in preparing for your final examinations.

Other lecturers do not write an outline on the board, and so, you have to listen actively for the shape of the lecture as it proceeds. Many lecturers list or enumerate the items they are covering: "First... second... finally." Or they may say, "There are three reasons for such a reaction...," indicating a cause-and-effect relationship that you should be aware of as a critical listener. If you do not get the structure clearly when you are listening to it, you can try to note any of the transitions in the presentation and any ways in which points are enumerated, and then, after the lecture, take a few minutes to look over your notes and try to identify the structural elements, marking them in your notes (1, 2, 3; A, B, C; and so on).

Most lectures have several traditional features:

INTRODUCTION   An introduction might summarize last week's lecture, state the thesis for this week, outline a theme, or give some comments that might, in themselves, be considered an outline. It helps to be on time for the lecture and ready for this kind of comment when it occurs and to try to get down as much of it as possible in your notes. In particular, you should pay close attention to the emphasis laid on continuities between the present week's lecture and previous lectures. Such links indicate the patterns being developed over the course, allowing you to figure out on your own the answer to a question many passive listeners often ask, "What is important?" or the question dreaded by every teacher, "Will that be on the exam?"

BODY   The body of a lecture can take several forms:

- Setting out a range of materials under headings
- Explaining or defining the terms or concepts that will be used in the lecture and commenting on a reading systematically
- Making a series of points and illustrating them with references to the text or with examples
- Elaborating or expanding points or illustrations
- Rephrasing the argument to explain difficult concepts

CONCLUSION   The concluding remarks can be a flourish (some clever remark to end the lecture on a high point); a wrap-up or summary ("This week I have outlined ... and have shown that.... Next week I shall...."); a highlighting of the main points made; or an assignment of readings for the next week.

Being an active listener enables you to read the lecturer's mannerisms and body language for points of emphasis in the structure of the lecture. However, you should also be aware of the kinds of language signals that a lecturer uses to emphasize main concepts.

How Lecturers Emphasize Their Arguments

Lecturers usually use four major ways of stressing their key concepts:

REPETITION   A common complaint students make about lecturers is that they speak too quickly for them to take notes. While some lecturers are insensitive to students' needs and do speak too quickly, usually this complaint means that students have not learned to listen actively and to use paraphrase or synthesis in making notes. Lecturers also know that students cannot keep up with them in their note-taking and so repeat central ideas, rephrase them, or elaborate on them to give students a chance to catch up. The following expressions signal repetition:

Let me put that another way....

Once again....

In other words....

That is....

For example.... Another example....

As well.... Also.... In addition....

EMPHASIS   Lecturers tend to stress main points at the beginning or end of sections and to mark them off in their comments by some phrase or bodily signal, such as tapping the lectern, slowing down, changing the voice, or making a note on the blackboard. These points are those that the lecturer wishes to get across as central to the theme that is being developed, so you should try to get them down as clearly as you can. Signals of emphasis include the following:

> This is the first important point....
>
> Most importantly....
>
> The significant fact is....
>
> Specifically....

TRANSITIONS, TURNS, OR BRIDGES   In shifting from one topic to another or from one part of the argument to the next, lecturers usually signal their transitions clearly, but often without enumerating them ("second," "third," and so on). Such transitions indicate a change in direction, a turn in the argument, or a movement from one point to the next. Listening for and noting these transitions by some consistent mark in your note-taking will help you to identify the parts of the structure later on (many people use various kinds of arrows). Transitional signals include the following:

- Words that draw contrasts: *but, however, on the other hand, conversely, despite*
- Words that point to a new direction: *now, next, to continue*
- Words that draw cause-and-effect relationships: *hence, accordingly, consequently, therefore, because*

ELABORATION   Fuller and fuller explanations in a lecture are often hard for a student to comprehend. To a student, one example seems to be sufficient—or even too much: why go on and on? A student may complain that the example was all a digression or that the instructor did not get to the point. The student might well be right; or it may be that the student failed to catch the purpose of the elaboration.

Usually, a topic is explained at some length because it is important and, perhaps, difficult and so demands considerable attention from the lecturer. The point might be explained too briefly in the textbook and so might require fuller explanation. Or the definition might be best explained through comparisons and contrasts that indicate its complexity. Or the point might be controversial and, thus, need justification, support, or documentation.

Students often become confused when a lecturer elaborates a point by citing several examples or authorities, other scholars who have written on this topic. These authorities are often set up in disagreement with each other or with the lecturer. By this process, the lecturer is modelling the way that an academic argument works. There is no absolute right or wrong view on a particular point or topic, and when a point is controversial, lecturers or writers must position their view in relation to what others have written. By providing you with this range of different views, the lecturer is also mapping out places where you can find further information to help you formulate your own positions, perhaps different from what you are hearing in the lecture. A simpler form of this method of elaboration is to cite another scholar as an authority to back up the point. This use of authorities to support a point is already familiar to most students from having to back up their arguments with a source. On the other hand, a lecturer might cite a single author as a point of dis-agreement, arguing against that authority.

A lecturer often introduces an elaboration by means of examples with a comment, such as, "I want to elaborate the point I have just made"; or "I shall illustrate this point with four examples...." Ask yourself why these examples are being introduced and to illustrate what? Why is this example important? Such examples might be the interpretation of specific pas-sages in texts, the citation of statistics or graphs, the results of sociological surveys or psy-chological experiments or instances of historical data. So, you need to record three things: what the example is, its source or reference, and the point made about it. Then you are in a position to understand the reason for the elaboration.

Students usually expect a concept or point to be clarified immediately and hope that the example will do it. However, academic study often requires that concepts be laid out gradually, so they may not be understood more fully until later in the course. This way of conveying information uses a building-block approach to knowledge, in which learning is cumulative, not instantaneous, and so, this method goes against the modes of immediate gratification dominant in our consumer society. When you come to review your notes—soon after the lecture, in preparation for a seminar, or much later for a test or an examination—you will find that the examples, illustrations, and the references to authorities ground the lecturer's arguments in specifics that you can use effectively in your own writing. You are now progressing toward being an active listener.

Being an Active Listener

Learning how to be an active listener in lectures is an essential skill in getting through a course with good grades. For most of us, the form of the lecture is unlike any other public performance that we are familiar with, except, perhaps, for some, a sermon in a place of worship. To sit for one or two hours without making any noise, walking around, or switch-ing channels demands new skills.

The practice of watching TV and doing other tasks simultaneously, and similar prac-tices such as reading a newspaper while listening to music or, for that matter, watching three or four TV shows simultaneously by flipping from channel to channel have devel-oped skills in you that you can adapt to become a better listener and note-taker. Just as watching TV while reading a newspaper requires that you divide your attention between two tasks, so, too, does a lecture require that you learn to listen and record at the same time.

Being an active listener means that you approach the lecture positively as a reading exercise. You are, in fact, "reading" the lecture and making notes about your reading. Being an active listener means using all of your critical thinking abilities, including resisting accepted ideas; listening (or reading) for the structure, the ideas, and the concepts; and resisting the distractions of the lecturer's mannerisms, the classroom rustle, or anything in the content that puzzles you.

Coming Prepared

To get the most out of a lecture you need to be up and running before the lecture begins. You should have completed the required readings or lab work before the lecture. The course syllabus sets out the lecture topics or themes for the year, and often, the assign-ments will be specified, along with readings, page numbers, and so on. Even if you do not

TIPS Active Listening

1. Keep the lecture notes for each course in a separate notebook.

2. Date and identify the lecture clearly and number the pages of the lecture. Write down the lecture outline and any background readings. Use the same numbering scheme in your notes so that when you review, you know what point you have reached.

3. Maintain your concentration by making notes according to one of the following suggested methods.

4. Write on one side of the sheet only; use loose-leaf paper, which may be rearranged later, with inserts; and indent details and skip lines to separate topics.

5. Omit "a, an, the" and unnecessary adjectives and use abbreviations and other signs that help you get information and ideas down quickly.

6. Note in the margin or underline any words you do not understand and mark the concepts you need more information about.

7. Use an indent method, and number points.

have time to complete all of the reading in detail, you should learn to skim and read for general comprehension before the lecture. You should also bring the appropriate textbook to the lecture, especially if the lecturer customarily refers to passages or other materials for more detailed discussion and comment. You also will want to have your notebook ready, beginning each lecture on a new page. We outline several formats for note-taking during lectures in the next section.

PowerPoint and Other Multi-Media Presentations

For some academic activities, such as note-taking in lectures, focusing your attention on two tasks is not only desirable but also necessary. Some of your lectures will be illustrated with slides, over-head transparent projections, or, increasingly, with multi-media presentations using a computer and projection screen with a program, such as Microsoft PowerPoint. In the case of slides, it is important to identify them as you would any reference in a class, sketch the outline to help with identification (to be followed up later) and note the points made about it. Treat over-heads as you would any writing on the blackboard.

PowerPoint or other multi-media presentations, sometimes with audio or visual clips, depend upon a series of information slides or screens often with arguments presented in a summary form. Because such presentations use a kind of indent-outline method (see page 25) to arrange information, some note-taking preparation is already done for you. Almost certainly, your notes will have to be expanded because this method hits highlights and avoids subtle differences. Some screens might include charts or graphs, and sometimes instructors have hand-outs of the main images that you can annotate from the lecturer's further explanations. Beware of becoming lost in the technology. For further information, see the Internet sites at the *Foundations* Web site.

Note the Key Terms, Concepts, and Definitions

We have already commented on how noting definitions might indicate the structure of a lecture. Central terms and concepts are important not only for understanding a particular lecture but also for comprehending the general structure and goals of the entire course. Every discipline has its own key terms and specialized concepts. To a beginning student such language seems abstract and far removed from everyday language. This vocabulary, however, is one of the fundamental tools for undertaking further work in the field. Introductory courses, therefore, spend a lot of time putting into place these building blocks for further study. Understanding these terms and projecting ahead to how they will be useful to you will help you get through the many initial difficulties you may have.

Many students underline in their notes the key terms that a lecturer stresses and then mark them later in the margins for review, often expanded with a definition given in class. These notes can then be extended by adding definitions from the textbook, specialist dictionary, or some other source on the course. Raising questions about these key terms is an important way of ensuring that you understand them—during the lecture if there is an opportunity for questioning, after the lecture by speaking to the teacher, or during a seminar.

Definitions of key terms or explanations of central concepts in the course are important for comprehending both what the lecturer means and how these terms are being used in the course. Sometimes, a lecturer uses definitions to structure a lecture. Such definitions are usually not available or easily accessible in dictionaries but, rather, are specialist explanations given from the particular viewpoint of the course content. For instance, the term *hysteria* can have all sorts of popular meanings, but in a course on Freud's thought, it has a clinical and technical meaning that Freud (and probably your lecturer) is careful to define. Similarly, many literary terms, such as those defining various genres, such as *epic* or *sonnet,* or many historical movements, such as *totalitarianism* or *fascism,* or sociological models, such as *functionalism* or *post-modernism,* may be circulating in popular speech, but the usage in your course may be far more precise and focused. Some teachers explain definitions by means of different levels of usage (popular versus scholarly), technical terminology, example and illustration, or etymology (word derivations from source languages; see Chapter 5).

Note the Examples, Illustrations, or Page References

As we discussed above, many students get lost when the lecturer says "for example." That phrase, however, indicates that what is coming is intended to illustrate the theoretical or conceptual point just made or to provide evidence for a more general point. You may still be struggling to get down the point and are thrown off by the example with its concrete language or precise reference. To help you understand the theory or concept, you should make a note of the reference in a word or two. You may abbreviate the title of the book which the lecturer refers to and note the page reference, especially if it is a book on the course. Later, you can look up the illustration, elaborate it, and use it to understand the theory or concept.

In concluding an example, a lecturer often says something like, "By this example I have shown that...." Here, the lecturer is both repeating the point and summarizing the conclusion that the example illustrates. So, if you missed the point at the opening, you can get it here. Examples are intended to offer fuller explanations, not to while away the time pointlessly, and so, you should strive in your active listening to understand exactly why they are there and what they are illustrating.

Use Analytical Questions in Your Note-Taking

When your active listening has progressed appropriately, you will be able to question ideas as they are being advanced. This strategy is rather hard to master, since it depends both on understanding what is being argued in the lecture and on having confidence in your own position. You then can adopt some strategies in your note-taking to mark the places where you do not understand (writing a *?* in the margin), where you disagree (using the symbol *d/a* in the margin), or where you have to expand or explain later (marking *exp* in the margin). These points are also useful later to take up with your instructor. You can schedule an interview when you have gathered a number of questions.

Special Problems in Being an Active Listener

We have focused above on the importance of the structure of a lecture, and on four methods that lecturers use—repetition, emphasis, transitions, and elaborations. We have also outlined four methods of becoming an active listener—coming prepared, noting key terms, noting examples, and using a questioning approach in your note-taking. When you understand how these methods are used, you will be able to follow a lecture with far greater comprehension.

Other potential difficulties, however, might get in the way of clearer understanding, and it helps to be aware of some of them at the outset. For instance, you might have difficulties with a lecturer's accent, which might be unfamiliar to you. Give yourself time to become accustomed to it, and if you miss some crucial term, ask about it at the end of the lecture. Some lecturers might seem to you to be aloof or authoritarian, especially when they do not allow questions during a class. While some teachers really do not want questions during a lecture, others are just working hard to get their ideas across and do not want to be interrupted until their train of thought is finished, or they are trying to cover scheduled material in order to keep the course on track. In such cases, ask your question at a suitable point or after the class in office hours.

A lecturer might also use language that is more complex or abstract than you are used to. It seems intimidating, and so, you get bogged down with fears of missing out. Most students experience this problem at various points in their university careers. This complexity is often an aspect of a discipline's specialized language that you will soon get used to. Or the complexity might result from wider expectations about what a student should know in general, and you might have missed out on some aspect of that cultural knowledge that you will have to acquire. In any case, you need to be able to understand this complexity to succeed in the course. It might also be that a lecturer seems to be talking above you or is caught up in ideas that are too complex for you to grasp now. One solution here is to try to get down much of what is being said, even if you cannot completely follow it, and then go over it again later, trying to simplify it. Working through it with a friend in the same course or going back to the assigned readings to see how these ideas relate might also help. Bear in mind, a point worth repeating, that professors keep office hours when you can discuss your special concerns.

Some students find particular lecturers opinionated (sometimes just a term that refers to their hard-held viewpoint) or too political. Indeed, in some courses, teachers are adopting a particular political position to make a point or to stress a political interpretation, in which case you have to learn how that political position works and how it can be discussed. The first step to solving these problems is to approach your professor, indicating as clearly as you can your difficulties in comprehending the materials. Some of these matters are delicate and require tact and diplomacy to come up with workable solutions. Try to take as much responsibility for the problem as you can and try to avoid putting the professor on the defensive. In other words, do not initiate the discussion by blaming the professor entirely for the problem, even if you feel that is the case. No matter what the circumstances, such a strategy will probably not result in the solution that you need. In any case, maintaining your composure and persevering with the goal of remaining an active listener will have significant rewards later in the course.

What do you do if you think that your professor is being unreasonable, perhaps in course requirements? In fact, there is little that you can do because of the power imbalance between students and professors. Probably the best recourse is to decide exactly what it is that you can do to your best advantage, making strategic choices, and work at that. You could seek an interview to discuss any problems you might be having in comprehension, but it would be unwise in most instances to say anything about the workload. When speaking about your problems, be careful not to seem to be making accusations or attacking the professor; that is a battle you cannot win. If you have a teacher who marks assignments with only a few remarks before assigning a grade, you should realize that many such markers are over-burdened teaching assistants with heavy teaching and marking loads. Nevertheless, they also keep office hours, and you could make an appointment to discuss your assignment —perhaps, the opening of your essay—asking for advice about how to improve it or seeking clarification about the comments on the paper. If you have a teacher who misses an appointment, take it in your stride and simply book another. If a professor violates university policies (schedules tests outside the legal time limits, does not provide graded feedback within the university deadlines, and so on), then you can go to the chair or the dean with your complaints. If the problems you are having are not solvable despite your attempts or if you feel that raising such legitimate complaints will lead to reprisals, you may have to switch classes or tutorial sections or, as a last resort, consider dropping the course.

Other difficulties might arise, such as students who do not pull their weight in a group assignment. No doubt, they, too, are aware of this defect in themselves or they may be deliberately slacking off for reasons of their own. One way of helping out in such a situation is to divide up the work and have each person report back. Then, if the slacker is still not performing, you can ask the group how best that material can be covered. Turning the problem into a problem for the group, rather than having it as the slacker's problem or your own, is one way of beginning to move out of the difficulty.

DIFFERENT NOTE-TAKING METHODS

Many students beginning university have been accustomed to having detailed outlines or more complete notes written on the blackboard or provided in class hand-outs. While hand-outs are still sometimes used, most university teachers only use the blackboard for outlines or key terms, or they use overhead transparencies or projections with PowerPoint or another program. All students at the beginning of a course are somewhat in the dark about what to write down and, more often than not, feel their efforts to capture the important themes of the lecture are inadequate.

Increasingly, students use new digital recording devices or tape recorders, but then, they have to transcribe what they hear which means going through the lecture again. If you wish to use a recording device, you should seek permission from your instructor. Further, even with a tape-recorded transcription, it is helpful to use one of the five methods outlined below.

Most students eventually find that a combination of several methods works best. One aim is to avoid re-copying without synthesis. To synthesize a lecture means that you fill in the blanks in your notes, combine the main points to make a complete argument under appropriate headings, and summarize its conclusions at each stage. We give several widely recommended methods below. All of them involve dividing your page into sections where you add specific items in your review. All of them provide an opportunity to use the 5Rs of note-taking.

TIPS The 5Rs of Note-Taking

During the lecture, write down as much of the conceptual framework as you can. Write legibly and leave spaces for what you cannot get down. Then, take 15 minutes a night for each lecture to use the 5Rs.

1. *Record.* Soon after the lecture or in the 5R session that evening, fill in the blanks with what you missed, including missing concepts or phrases.

2. *Reduce.* Read through the notes, pick out key words, and put them in the left margin as a clue to what was covered.

3. *Recite.* Cover the "record" section; recall the substance of the lecture by going over the key words and recite it in your own words.

4. *Reflect.* Think about the content of the lecture and your notes; jot down at the end of the lecture notes any questions, problems of interpretation, and other illustrations or examples.

5. *Review.* Take 10 minutes each week for a quick review of that week's notes, looking particularly at the key words or concepts. Such concepts underlie the course's development.

The Indent-Outline Method

This method stresses the outline and structure of a lecture, with the most general points beginning at the left margin and the more specific sub-categories indented. You do not need to add numbers or letters, but you might find that useful, especially in the 5R stage when you go over the notes in the evening. At that point, with the help of a textbook or other sources, you might wish to fill in some of the details that you missed during the lecture. For instance, in the example we give below, you might want to correct the spelling of names, fill in dates, or add further information with the help of a textbook, reference book, or CD-ROM encyclopedia.

As our example, we take a typical lecture on a European History course on the rise of the Third Reich in Germany and the causes of World War II. Our example here is intended to demonstrate the method of note-taking, and a reader should not get bogged down in the historical details: the same method could be used for any other materials in any other course.

The lecturer's general outline on the blackboard might be as follows:

Third Reich in Germany and Causes of WWII

1. Aftermath of WWI: Treaty of Versailles and Weimar Republic

2. Rise of Hitler to writing of *Mein Kampf*

3. Development of National Socialism in Germany

4. Stock market crash of 1929 and world economy

5. Political pluralism in Germany: emergence of Hitler as Chancellor and President

6. Military, economic, and social policies of Third Reich: role of anti-Semitic laws

7. Territorial expansionism

8. Austria, Czechoslovakia, and reaction of Britain and Russia

9. Poland

The lecturer might begin with a brief introduction, explaining the outline, giving details about the readings, and so on. Then, the lecturer starts the body of the lecture with section one, on the aftermath of World War I. Having already written down the outline, you pick up with section one as follows:

1. The aftermath of WWI: general conditions

   – The treaty of Versailles, 1919: see Margaret MacMillan, *Paris 1919*

   Decisions of the Allies re

   Germany: 3 Issues:

   Debt and repayment obligations:

   resentment and inflation

   Military limitation to 100 000 in army

   Land—loss of Alsace-Lorraine to France and disputed territories

   – Italy

   Rise of Fascism from 1919

   Mussolini (1883–1945)

   – Russia

   Rise of Communism: from Revolution of 1917

   Lenin (1870–1924) and Stalin (1879–1953)

   – Weimar Republic (1918–1933)

   Political turmoil in Germany

   Relations with Allies

   Method of trying to repay debt

   Land constraints and problems

   Political failures

   Result is development of new political parties

The indent-outline method starts with the first topic from the lecturer's blackboard outline beginning at the left margin. Then, the four major stages of the first point, the Treaty of Versailles, Italy, Russia, and the Weimar Republic (Germany after WW I) are the major sub-topics, and so, each is indented the same amount. Under each of these sub-topics, further indentations indicate the more detailed information given for each.

For the first sub-topic, the lecturer might say: "The Treaty of Versailles was signed by the Allies, led by Britain and France in 1919. A new book by Margaret MacMillan, *Paris 1919,* has recently been on the non-fiction best-seller list, and you might consult it for further details. The Allies decided that three major requirements were to be imposed on Germany—the repayment of war debt, limitations to a standing army, and redistribution of land taken by Germany in World War I. I shall discuss each of these requirements briefly."

Hence, your summary includes relevant details. The lecturer refers to a contemporary source and, in an introductory course, is probably not urging you to read it. However, you can consult it if you wish and can certainly use it for getting the details that you might have missed. This kind of reference exemplifies the use of citing sources that we discussed above under a lecturer's methods of elaboration. At the end of the year, you will have a list of books that you can come back to to read over the summer or later in a more intensive course.

You might want to number the further points that the lecturer makes, or you might miss a detail, in which case, move on to the next topic and fill it in later. Then, the lecturer will turn to a brief consideration of Italy, perhaps in only two or three sentences. You note this change by indenting Italy to align roughly with the sub-heading for the Treaty of Versailles. After the rest of point 1, the lecturer turns to point 2, and your outline might be as follows:

2. Rise of Hitler to *Mein Kampf* (1925)

 – Adolf Hitler (1889–1945): see Kershaw's *Hitler*

 Served in German army in WWI (1914–18)

 Founder of National Socialist German Workers Party 1920

 Led Munich Beer Hall *putsch*, 1923—failure

 Imprisoned, and began writing *Mein Kampf* (= My Struggle) 1925

 Anti-Semitic propaganda and attacks on the Jews

Under point 2, only one sub-category is dealt with here, Adolf Hitler, with five events mentioned briefly. His biographical details will be resumed in section 3. Again, a lecturer might refer to recent debates about Hitler's biography and might refer to Ian Kershaw's two-volume study, *Hitler,* another book to add to your list.

The rest of the lecture proceeds through points 3 to 9. Assuming a lecture of 50 minutes, a lecturer has only about five minutes for each of the points to be covered and so will move through the material quickly, a necessary kind of compression in an introductory course. In more advanced courses, each of these points might be discussed over several lectures. One thing to keep in mind, however, is that within these quick surveys, there might be a particular topic dealt with briefly which you wish to pursue. For instance, Italy and the rise of Mussolini or Russia and the Revolution are both touched upon. If given an opportunity, you might want to write a term paper on one of those topics and might approach the professor about doing so.

By the indent-outline method, you will have a detailed plan of the lecture and the chief points made. Each point can be filled out with more argument, dates, or data in a paragraph or other notes during the lecture or later. Note that the indent-outline method does not use grammatical sentences but aims at recording key words and specific details. It does not record all that a lecturer says and may neglect shades of meaning or qualifications.

Advantages

- If the lecturer is logical and systematic, this method works well.
- Clear headings are easy to read, and space allows filling in details.
- Reading headings in order of indentation allows connections to be drawn.
- Indenting and analysis increase comprehension.

Disadvantages

- If the lecturer is unclear or lectures by associating diverse details or concepts or by explaining a text, this method is harder to use.
- It requires the ability to think ahead and anticipate where the next argument fits in, and so, it depends on your being well prepared with assigned readings.
- It requires alertness, analytical skills, and concentration.
- It is harder to indicate shades, nuances, or qualifications, though those can be indicated by use of the question mark or other short forms or can be filled in later.

The Line-Sentence Method

In this method, you use a new line for every new idea, topic, or fact of the blackboard outline as the lecture proceeds and number or letter each line or sentence of a section (the sentence does not have to be grammatically complete—you should abbreviate and omit unnecessary words). Leave a two-inch margin on the left side of the page so you can go back in the 5R stage to mark in the structure and divisions of the lecture and to add key words or other data.

For instance, using the same example as in the indent-outline method above, the first section of the lecture on the aftermath of World War I, the line-sentence method might look like this:

Third Reich in Germany and Causes of WW II

Aftermath of WW I: Treaty of Versailles and Weimar Republic

1. The aftermath of WW I: consider gen. Condit~s
2. Treaty of Versailles, 1919: cf. Margaret MacMillan, *Paris 1919*
3. Decisions of Allies re Germ. involve 3 issues: Debt & repay~t leads to resent & inflation; only 100 000 in army; loss of Alsace-Lorraine to France & other disputd land
4. Italy & rise of Fascism from 1919 & Mussolini (1883–1945)
5. Russia & rise of Comm~sm from Rev. of 1917 to Lenin (1870–1924) & Stalin (1879–1953)
6. Weimar Republic (1918–1933) with cont. political turmoil internally & re Allies; method of trying to repay debt & land constraints lead to problems & polit. failures
7. Result: development of new polit. parties

In this example we use abbreviations. You can follow our example or develop your own system (see Tips box on page 34).

Advantages

- This method gets down a lot of information efficiently when the teacher lectures fast in a sequence of points.
- It is particularly useful when you are uncertain about what is important in a lecture or how the parts fit together.
- If you have fallen behind in your readings and are unfamiliar with the material, this method lets you get down the content clearly, so that you can organize it and fill it out later.

Disadvantages

- You cannot determine the lecturer's structure as you hear it but only when you review it.
- It is difficult to distinguish between major and minor points from the numbered sentences.
- This method involves less critical thinking and analysis because following content and the development of an argument, as well as showing different emphases, is difficult.
- You will have to re-write to link related ideas.

The Cornell Method

Developed at Cornell University, this method involves review, organization and condensation of notes, and highlighting of key words for later study and reference using the 5Rs.

The *cue column* is sometimes called a *key-word column*. Some users also underline or asterisk (*) key terms in their note-taking or use another method to flag words or concepts that the lecturer stresses, as well as others that they do not understand or follow (see Figure 1.2).

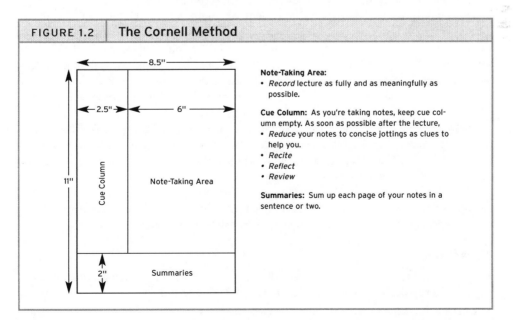

FIGURE 1.2 | **The Cornell Method**

8.5"

2.5" 6"

11"

Cue Column

Note-Taking Area

2" Summaries

Note-Taking Area:
- *Record* lecture as fully and as meaningfully as possible.

Cue Column: As you're taking notes, keep cue column empty. As soon as possible after the lecture,
- *Reduce* your notes to concise jottings as clues to help you.
- *Recite*
- *Reflect*
- *Review*

Summaries: Sum up each page of your notes in a sentence or two.

Advantages

- It requires no re-copying of notes.
- It fills in gaps in the lecture quickly.
- It involves immediate review and consolidation.
- It links lectures and preparation for exams.

Disadvantage

- It requires follow-up of 15 minutes a night for completion using the 5Rs. (Is this review not really an advantage?)

The Charting Method

The charting method depends on a graphic or visual representation, and it works best when your lecturer follows a chronological order that lets you set out a vertical or horizontal timeline. You then fill in the appropriate intervals on the timeline. If you can anticipate the kind of chart that will be used, it is helpful to come to the lecture with one partly prepared.

We could set out the same materials listed above as a chart on the causes of World War II (see Table 1.1). Three periods of time are set out in the left column under a time heading, and other categories are arranged across the chart. It helps to begin the chart by leaving space at the right-hand margin to add other categories as needed as the lecture proceeds. You can add dates, data, and other information later from your textbook or other readings.

Professors often provide such charts or sketch them on the blackboard, allowing you to fill them in. However, you can choose your own categories to make your own comparisons and contrasts. Often, this method works well in adapting lecture or reading notes into an outline for an essay.

Other kinds of arrangements of the charting method are possible. For instance, large contrasts between two opposing social conditions might usefully be laid out. To take an entirely different historical problem, a chart might set out the contrasts between urban and rural societies in North America. Three time periods—the colonial period (about 1750), the 19th century (1880), and the 20th century (1980)—are identified in the left-hand margin. Without filling in the details, the chart would then be divided in the middle between Rural and Urban to set out the major contrasts. Under each side might be columns devoted to Mexico, Canada, and the United States so that the details can be filled in (see Table 1.2).

Sometimes, students have no idea where this kind of chart will end and find themselves squeezing information into little spaces at the top or sides of a page. In any case, it is essential to select specific categories and then to arrange your note-taking by putting the concepts and information under your headings.

The charting method is also very useful in drawing together your summaries of large sections of a course in preparation for tests and examinations. You can choose appropriate categories and fill in the information as you undertake your review.

Advantages

- This method forces you to be analytical when you are listening to the lecture because you have to choose a category for each piece of information.
- The categories help you make comparisons and draw connections.
- The chart helps with efficient review.

TABLE 1.1		Example of the Charting Method				
Period of History	Act	Countries Involved	Major Events	Issues or Problems	Major Figure	Effects	Significance
1917-19	Treaty of Versailles	Allies → Germany	settlement of blame, debts, land	(same)		unworkable solution	
		Russia	Revolution of 1917	overthrow of Czar	Lenin	feudal → modern	rise of Communism
1920-29		Weimar Republic	war reparations	debt → inflation	von Hindenburg	resentment	helps Hitler
		Germany	Munich Putsch fails Hitler jailed	Germ. Workers Party	Hitler	anti-Versailles writes *Mein Kampf*	rise of Nazis
1930-39		Italy	overthrow of monarchy	re-militarization political instability	Mussolini		rise of Fascists
		Germany	Hitler loses election to von Hindenburg		Hitler	appointed Chancellor 1933 President 1934 Führer 1935	
				re-militarization	Hitler	territorial expansion anti-Semitism	leads to Holocaust

TABLE 1.2	Example of the Charting Method to Show Comparisons and Contrasts						
	RURAL				URBAN		
Hist. Period	MEXICO	CANADA	USA		MEXICO	CANADA	USA
1750		[fill in details here]				[fill in details here]	
1880							
1980							

Disadvantages

- You might categorize information incorrectly because your categories were not well chosen at first, and it is difficult to change them during a lecture once you are started; you should leave space at either end of your chart for new categories if needed, or you can revise your chart later.
- You might also have to force some materials into categories where they do not fit well, losing some subtlety.
- After you have selected some working categories for the first points of a lecture, you might have difficulty filling in subsequent points if a lecturer follows a different arrangement of information. In that case, either move to a different category instead of progressing systematically from left to right or abandon your chart for another note-taking method. Once you get this information down in the other format, you can return later to complete your chart.

The Concept-Mapping Method

The indent-outline, line-sentence, and Cornell methods of note-taking are linear and depend on your ability to perceive the linear arrangement of a lecture. The concept-mapping method, like the charting method, maps out the lecture in terms of a graphic or diagram and allows you to draw connections that you did not see before or that the lecturer may return to later in the lecture. Maps also can capture a lot of information on a single page and are excellent for showing relationships among concepts and data.

For instance, a map of the first point in the lecture on the causes of World War II might look like Figure 1.3.

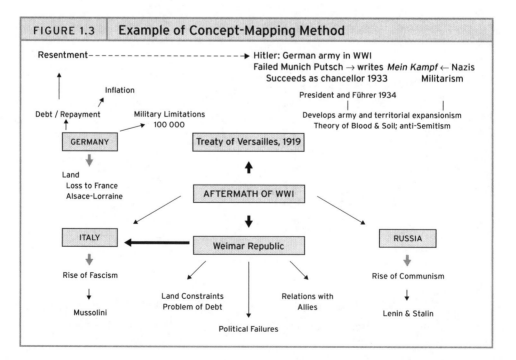

FIGURE 1.3 | **Example of Concept-Mapping Method**

The central topic is in the middle of the page, with the two major sub-heads above and below, with the other ideas radiating out from that as appropriate. Start in the middle of a page with the main topic and then branch out in any direction, drawing connections and lines as the lecture proceeds. A new page might be started for the second section of the topic in the outline, and so on. Some students find they draw one map for much of a lecture; others find that one map per section of the argument works better. Others use concept mapping as part of the "reduce" phase of the 5R summary.

A map can be used to re-organize and synthesize the lecture once you have taken it down in the indent-outline, line-sentence, or Cornell format. This re-organization is particularly useful to review for examinations.

Advantages

- This method allows you to perceive relationships and patterns that a linear method conceals.
- This method stresses critical thinking, since you are forced to find relationships and locate them graphically.
- All of the lecture, or a major part of it, is visible structurally on one page. You can later elaborate the map with better arrows, colour coding, further data, and links.
- Review is easy, since the key words are already there, and some students find the graphic format easier to remember, especially in relating ideas.

Disadvantages

- In drawing the map you focus on the grand plan and tend to neglect the details. It is more difficult to add the references and illustrations.
- For most students, this method is the most difficult, since it requires anticipating relationships among ideas while recording information that is being heard for the first time. It is perhaps best used in reviewing and summarizing your notes.

Taking Notes in Small Classes, Seminars, or Tutorials

All that we have said about lectures applies also to tutorials or to small classes where there is a good deal of discussion. The methods above can be modified usefully, especially because tutorials or seminars often do different sorts of work during class time. Because the atmosphere might be more informal and the instructor might not deliver a structured presentation, it is probable that the shape of the classroom discussion will be harder to grasp and record.

Many students feel that they have to take notes in a large lecture because that is where the information is being set out but that in tutorials, it is a different matter. How do you record the seminar discussion? In general, it is wise to take notes in tutorials as you would in lectures to try to see the structure of the seminar and how it is being shaped by questions and the discussion. Just as you should strive to grasp the structure in note-taking in a formal lecture, so, too, in a seminar do you need to perceive the teaching mode that is being used and how it is structured (perhaps introduction, then summary of the lecture, then student questions, before getting down to detailed readings or group work).

There might be as many as three or four different kinds of material or modes of teaching used: review of the lecture, close textual work, explanation and question/answer sessions about course concepts, discussion of a series of topics, review of assignments, critical thinking and writing exercises, or class presentations by students. Each of these modes requires a somewhat different approach to taking notes. At the very least, a student has to be aware of the differing shifts in teaching modes and materials. Try to indicate such shifts in your seminar notes and to record the important points.

When you understand the teaching model and something of the structure, you can begin to draw relationships among parts of the seminar. An outline of what the teacher wants to cover in the seminar might be written on the board to help you grasp the structure. You might find that the concept-mapping model works well here.

If your classmates give presentations (we discuss giving presentations in Chapter 3), they might provide hand-outs with an outline of what they are presenting, and you can add notes to those sheets. If there are no hand-outs, you should take notes during the presentation, paying attention to what is particularly strong in it (you can mark it as *G* for good or + in the margin), what you disagree with or want to question (mark *dis* for *disagree*), and what you want to question later (marked *?*).

In discussion classes, you can record the general topic and then, if you know the students' names, identify the key points they have made by their initials. It is as though you are recording the process of the discussion. Here, it is important to get the shifts or turns in the line of discussion and to note the conclusions reached, as well as the summary the teacher may make about that conclusion. Some students find that recording a discussion as though they were taking notes of a meeting to be circulated later helps them focus on what is important. Some classes designate one or two students each week to do just that— to record the discussion and circulate the record to all the students the next week.

In summary, two points need to be stressed about note-taking in seminars: first, keeping notes forces you to perceive the structure in the way that information is being conveyed, and second, keeping notes forces you to pay attention.

TIPS   Using Abbreviations in Note-Taking

1. Invent your own shorthand tricks—after all, your notes are for your eyes only.

2. Use conventional symbols: $ (money), & (and), # (number), w/ (with), ∴ (therefore).

3. Abbreviate common words in the field: total. (totalitarian), indiv. (individual), cons. (conservative). Omit final letters: intro (introduction) hist (history). Use ~ to indicate *ion*, *tion*, or *ism*: confus~ (confusion), rela~ (relation), terror~ (terrorism).

4. Omit vowels: prblm (problem), gvt (government), bckgrd (background). Abbreviate authors' names or titles of books in context: AS (Adam Smith), SF (Sigmund Freud), AW (Alice Walker); WN (*Wealth of Nations*), ID (*Interpretation of Dreams*), CP (*The Color Purple*).

5. Use *g* to represent *ing:* mrkg (marking).

6. Omit unimportant words, such as *a, an, the,* or verb forms.

7. See suggestions on abbreviations from the University of North Dakota: **www.und.nodak.edu/dept/ULC/rf-abbrv.htm**

Some Final Advice on Note-Taking

It is never a good idea to hand over your notes to another student. If you must lend them, photocopy your originals yourself and give away the copy. As well, you should take enough paper to class for the lecture; but leave your lecture notes at home unless they are being discussed in class or you have points to raise from them. Then if you lose them, you will not have lost an entire set of notes.

If you have a lecturer who you find talks too fast, it helps to use a two-page system, in which you write the main part of the lecture on the right-hand side and leave the left blank. During lulls in the lecture, you can fill in the gaps on the left-hand page at the appropriate place, and immediately after the lecture, go back over the lecture to fill in what you can recall.

What about re-typing your lecture notes on the computer? Some authorities think this task is a waste of time, but others think it is useful, especially if your handwriting is bad. You might find that you can expand your notes well when you re-type and later can add other information to the computer file when undertaking a review. You also can paraphrase and organize the lecture more efficiently. If you combine this strategy with the 5R method, you might find it useful during the "revise" stage.

There are many useful abbreviations and shortcuts that experienced note-takers use that you could adapt for your own purposes. It is important to use abbreviations that you will remember so that your notes will not be gibberish.

Finally, it sometimes helps to get together with other students to compare and discuss your lecture notes or to study with a friend who also takes good notes. See what you can learn from each other, both about the methods of taking notes and about the course.

CHAPTER SUMMARY

This first chapter has introduced you to the fundamental skills and practices that you need to survive the first weeks and months at university. Perhaps you will have had some unsettling times, like any student, or have felt overwhelmed by work and anxious about your upcoming deadlines, but you are now empowered to look realistically at your own study habits and have been given help in building on your strengths.

• You have begun to develop your skills in concentration, and have worked on consolidating your time, balancing the various aspects of your life, including work, family, recreation, and study.

• You have worked through some of your assigned texts and are starting to understand what your teachers are asking of you.

• Your note-taking skills have improved from a fairly rudimentary stage to become more capable, and you are continuing to develop this expertise.

• You are starting to take part in seminars and are getting ready for your first presentations.

Having used this chapter effectively to change gears and move up to speed in your first weeks or months or to re-learn skills that were under-developed in your first year of study, you also need to be aware of the changing expectations involved in university studies. What you have already learned in Chapter 1 remains fundamental and basic, and you will continue to use these skills. But these skills are also building blocks for more advanced strategies in critical thinking, reading, and writing, to which we turn in the following chapters.

FURTHER READINGS

Albrecht, Karl. *Brain Power*. New York: Prentice-Hall, 1980.

Burka, Jane, and Lenora Yuen. *Procrastination: Why You Do It, What to Do about It.* Reading, MA: Addison Wesley, 1983.

Fiore, Neil. *The Now Habit: Overcoming Procrastination with Guilt-Free Play*. Los Angeles: Jeremy Tarcher, 1989.

Fleet, Joan, Fiona Goodchild, and Richard Zajchowski. *Learning for Success: Effective Strategies for Students*. Toronto: Harcourt Brace Canada, 1999.

Jarvis, Peter. *Adult and Continuing Education. Theory and Practice*. London: Routledge, 1995.

Pauk, Walter. *How to Study in College*. 5th ed. Boston: Houghton Mifflin, 1993.

Roberts, Susan M. *Living without Procrastination: How to Stop Postponing Your Life*. Oakland, CA: New Harbinger, 1995.

chapter two

Changing Expectations

In Chapter 2, we discuss seven important areas where new developments have taken place that are changing student interaction with university life. In returning to university after some time away, perhaps even an entire summer off for work or travel, or in moving to university from high school, students will find that they are facing a different environment. Some of these developments have a relatively long history, but all are areas where universities are undergoing changes in what they expect from students. Some areas of change—such as ways to document your sources to avoid charges of plagiarism and how to use computers following the principles of critical thinking, reading, and writing—will be dealt with in more detail in subsequent chapters.

LEARNING OBJECTIVES

Here, we discuss the impact of these changing expectations to prepare you for challenges in your first few months:

- How can you cope with the new demands on your memory and how can your memory be improved?
- What are the expectations regarding university customs and policy?
- What are the changing expectations in the case of inclusive language?

- What are the problems in relation to academic honesty in the era of the Internet, such as the dangers of plagiarism?

- How can you best combine your use of computers with critical thinking?

- What are the different learning styles, and how do your aptitudes fit with university work? How can they be adapted and developed for different tasks and demands?

- What are the changes in traditional classroom teaching and learning, especially resulting from the electronic classroom, correspondence courses using e-mail, and distance learning?

IMPROVING YOUR MEMORY AND LEARNING ABILITIES

Numerous psychological studies on memory and forgetfulness show that we tend to forget quickly the material that we have learned recently. Then, with regard to what we do remember, the rate of forgetting slows down over time so that we all recall some events from much earlier in our lives in considerable detail, more, perhaps, than recent events. Such studies depend on the theory that memory works by making links between pieces of information. Facts are fitted into mental frameworks, structures, or maps and then are related to other facts. Stocking these frameworks with information and useful relationships among kinds of information helps strengthen your memory. In fact, most people can do a great deal to improve their memories. Some material needs to be retained for a short time (and short-term memory is sufficient for that), but other kinds need to be retained by long-term memory. Hence, the problem is knowing how to learn material the first time so that it will be better remembered and then ensuring that the rate of forgetting is slowed down.

The act of remembering is characterized by three *r* words: *recognizing, recalling,* and *retaining.*

- When you *recognize* something, you can identify or associate it with something that you already know: you can pick it out from among similar items. The emphasis on this part of remembering is on the actual object or idea that you recognize, rather than on analysis, evaluation, or description of it or your reaction to it.

- To *recall* something is to pull it back into your mind, to reproduce it in some measure. Here, the stress is on what you can do as part of your response to a prompting.

- *Retention* is the capability of holding that recognition and recollection in your mind. If you retain a memory, you are defeating the forces of forgetfulness. These functions of the human brain require practice to work well and even more practice to work better.

Two main methods are often used to help train and exercise memory:

- *Organization* as a mental activity groups the information into categories, smaller portions, or major and minor emphases and so helps you classify information and perform more apt associations.

- *Association* relates new information to what you already know in order to create a new meaning, thereby helping both recognition and recollection.

Such comments may be useful, but how do you train your memory? One advantage of using critical thinking practices is that the materials and concepts of the course—the intellectual structures and frameworks in which the course can be placed—are already known to you. Hence, it is a lot easier to fit into the course frameworks the smaller details, such as data, individual readings, and concepts. You already have done some of the work required to aid your remembering—you have organized the components of your course.

It is within this context that a major part of learning and memory comes into play for most students. You are expected to understand the concepts and materials of the course and to be able to discuss them in essays and examinations. To do that, you have to recall them, not necessarily in detail but in the general ways in which they fit into the intellectual frameworks of the course. You have to discuss them in that context, demonstrating your competence. You are not usually expected to recall the exact words of the lectures or the texts you studied, but you are expected to understand the concepts and to be able to reproduce their arguments and analyze them in your own words.

In some coursework, you will need to recall specific details precisely. Biology students have to recall thousands of names of parts of the body, and law students have to memorize

---

TIPS   Improving Your Memory

1. Be clear about what you have to remember, beginning with the larger structures, concepts, or ideas and only move to the details once these larger patterns are in place in your memory. Beginning with the details will soon have you lost and will prevent your grasping the structures they fit into.

2. Make sure that what you are setting out to remember is in the form in which you want to remember it. That is, learn it right the first time. It is far easier to do so than to unlearn what is wrong and re-learn it.

3. Try using a cassette or mini-disc recorder when memorizing, so you can repeat the information.

4. Alternatively, write out the information and then learn it from the written draft.

5. Practise memorizing. With practice, more and more can be memorized; most of us have our minds filled with details that we do not need urgently, such as many phone numbers, but even that can help you extend the range of your memory.

6. Memorize passages, formulas, or information as a whole, rather than line by line or item by item. Memorizing passages from texts, especially poetry, in which the rhythms and rhymes aid recall, is comparatively easy. This skill provides a permanent acquisition: what is well memorized will stay with you to be of use later for recollection and pleasure.

7. If you have to memorize words, definitions, or rules exactly, mark them that way in your lecture notes or texts. Some people find it helpful to write words or definitions on sticky-notes to post them around their house or to use flash cards to review in spare moments. This method often works well for learning new concepts or specialized vocabulary.

details of specific legal cases; students in theatre, mathematics, and foreign languages also have to memorize many details. Indeed, most students have to learn some passages from texts in detail, some dates, some historical figures, some vocabulary and concepts, and so on.

This more specialized and particular use of memory can often be frightening. However, you will feel less overwhelmed if you reflect on what you have already memorized: you probably know the names of dozens of singers and their songs in detail or the phone numbers of many of your friends, and you memorize all of that without effort because you want to learn it or it just appears to implant itself in your brain. Hence, you know that you have the ability for precise memory as well as the more general ability to relate concepts and ideas to your own understanding processes. Still, that nagging question remains: "How can I remember it all better?" For further suggestions on improving your memory, see Chapter 2 on the *Foundations* Web page.

All of that said, the most valuable suggestion for improving your memory is to exercise your mind by consciously trying to recall what you have heard in lectures and have read in the course. The 5Rs method of note-taking discussed in Chapter 1 can be adapted here. As you do that more frequently, building on what you have learned, you will find that you become more successful in remembering.

TIPS   Using Mnemonics

Mnemonics is the name given to memory helpers, to ways of recalling specific data, often through some set of associations. For instance, in a musical scale, the names for the staff lines in the treble clef are "each good boy does fine," each first letter referring to the line "EGBDF." Or in biology, to remember the orders of classification for living organisms, the phrase "kings play cards on fairly good soft velvet" recalls the classification of "kingdom, phylum, class, family, genus, species, and variety." Another form of mnemonics is the poem or ditty: "Thirty days hath September...." Use mnemonics to recall lists or data of any kind.

EXPECTATIONS ABOUT UNIVERSITY CUSTOMS AND POLICY

We all use differing kinds of behaviour to meet what is expected in various circumstances: we talk differently in front of our grandparents than we do among our closest friends, and language that passes in the college pub would probably not go down well in the local place of worship. At university, there are few formal codes of conduct—most accepted ways of behaviour are not written down. They are almost invisible and are explained only when they are infringed upon. Of course, universities and their members must abide by federal, provincial, and municipal laws, but as special communities, they also formulate their own laws, regulations, customs, and expectations that govern how the social and learning aspects of the university work. Some of these procedures are found in the student calendar, and it is your responsibility to read and follow them. They outline the kinds of behaviour that are unprofessional or disruptive, and they state those that warrant intervention by university authorities, such as threats of violence, harassment, or discrimination in contravention of human rights or conduct codes, and theft or the destruction of property.

Unwritten customs include the tolerance of others' views and cultural and ethnic differences. Student conduct in the classroom and seminar should involve mutual respect and shared responsibility for maintaining the academic goals of the course. That means listening to others, avoiding offensive language, especially language that is racially or gender biased, and refraining from intolerant words or actions.

INCLUSIVE AND APPROPRIATE LANGUAGE

Universities, like other public institutions and most areas of life, require that you follow the expectations and conventions of inclusiveness and appropriateness in the language you use. We consider here two areas, the use of stereotyping language and the inappropriate use of humour and jokes.

Inclusive Language: Gender, Sexual, Racial, and Religious Stereotyping

Universities and colleges and most businesses and professional practices now avoid stereotypical language for gender and race. It is unacceptable for speakers and writers today to refer to *man* as though the collective noun included the whole of humanity, as in the phrase "man has struggled for 200 years with the problems of poverty." The silliness of this patriarchal usage is demonstrated if the sentence is changed to "man has struggled for 200 years with the problems of gender bias and equality." Formal academic prose should reflect current standards of treating all people with respect and hence should avoid such expressions as *chairman* or *policeman* or other words with *-man,* in favour of alternative forms, such as *chair* or *police officer;* it should avoid conveying the assumption that all authors, critics, politicians, historians, or theologians are men or are white and Anglo-Saxon; and it should avoid adopting a tone that assumes all readers are male and white. Some writers redress the historic gender imbalance in language by self-consciously using feminine pronouns in their prose, by alternating them with male pronouns, or by using the form *s/he.* This field is one in which language is undergoing rapid modification, and it will likely be some time before the usage becomes more settled.

Such is the state of what is generally called *inclusive language.* A particular problem involves the use of pronouns. The earlier practice of using only male pronouns, *he, him,* and *his,* has changed significantly to avoid the exclusion of women. You can re-write a sentence to put it into the plural or can use *he* or *she* or *his* or *her.* It is also preferable to avoid the use of such forms as *he/she* or *his/her.* In your writing, you should also strive for a broad representation of geographical, ethnic, and gender roles, instead of using stereotypes, such as a New Brunswick fisherman, a suburban housewife, or a western farmer, unless the analysis of a particular social issue requires such focus. Further, members of a group or profession are not necessarily all of one gender: not all nurses or kindergarten teachers are women, and not all police officers are male, so avoid suggesting that. Use terms that are not exclusive in describing professions: *mail carrier,* rather than *mailman.* In another area of concern, be specific, whenever possible, in referring to a particular ethnic or national group, to a Liberian, rather than an African, or a Sri Lankan, rather than an

Asian. On the matter of physical or mental disabilities, make no mention of them if they are not relevant to the discussion; if it is pertinent to do so, refer to the person before the disability ("Jean Smith who uses a wheel chair," rather than "the wheel-chair bound Jean Smith"; or, "that person who is visually impaired," rather than "that blind person").

A more troubling and difficult aspect of stereotyping involves the use of derogatory terms for gender, sexual orientation, and racial and religious groups. The university community encourages diversity and open thought; therefore, the use of derogatory terms that are threatening to many people is unacceptable. Using derogatory terms, such as *bitches* to refer to women, *fags* to refer to gays, or *ginos* to refer to Italians (to take but a few instances), is not only impolite but often is an infringement on the speech codes set down in your university. Whatever the political and ideological implications of these speech codes, they are in place and usually will be enforced. Probably, many infringements are made from ignorance, rather than with the intention of direct confrontation, and if you make such an error, you should not be afraid to apologize and amend your practice. When in doubt, it is wise to err on the side of caution. You should not hesitate to ask for advice regarding this controversial and changing area of language usage.

Ethnic groups should be referred to in the terms that they themselves use. Terms that have been used in the past to denigrate particular groups are unacceptable unless you are directly quoting these terms from a particular source, perhaps in an essay on racial prejudice. For instance, terms like *nigger* or *Jap* are, of course, absolutely unacceptable, as they reflect racist usage. Terms like *negro* and *Indian* are also not accepted usage; the preferred terms now are *African Canadian* (or *American*) and *First Nations*. Other terms like *Black* and *Native Canadian* (or *American*) are still in transition, and, while controversial, are generally acceptable.

In your own comments in class and in writing your assignments, you should try to follow your university's practices and the codes that are set out in your department or course. Some instructors are only now learning to change their ways; others can be fierce about infringements, so you are far better off to avoid gender and racial stereotyping of any kind in your classroom comments and written assignments. For further treatment and examples of inclusive language, see the *Foundations* Web site.

Humour and Jokes

Humour and jokes often violate acceptable language expectations by turning a particular physical trait, a stereotypical action, or a characteristic into the butt of someone's remarks. Hence, all that we have said about inclusive language above applies also to the use of jokes. As well, there is a possible danger of infringing on the university's regulations regarding appropriate conduct.

Humour in the classroom is often a welcome diversion, both to your fellow students and to your instructor. But you need to assess the level and tone of the humour or joke and respect the criteria for general civility and tolerance.

You also need to exercise caution in using jokes in your essays and assignments. You decide early on about the tone and pitch of your paper. If you are serious, engaged, and challenged by it, your reader will take you on the same terms. If you are flippant, dismissive, or superficial, that will also be the reaction of your reader to your position. In this context, the use of humour and irony is a particular problem. On the whole, such attempts should probably be avoided. Humour in an academic essay is very difficult to control because it involves a destabilization of the rhetoric and the audience. Attempts to be humorous often backfire, resulting in a collapse of the reader's sympathy with your argument because such attempts assume a common ideological position, even a chumminess, within which the joke will be shared. Beginning writers often miscalculate the quality of their humour in academic writing.

The same thing applies to parenthetical asides inserted into a paper, often with the addition of slang, or as moments of direct and confiding address to the reader: *Sez you. As though you didn't know! You thought I'd forget this, didn't you? Ha! ha!* Such interjections break the flow of your thought, the rhetorical seriousness of your style, and the reader's attention. They assert an informal conversational tone and friendliness in the place of persuasive argument. Students often use such interjections in examinations, but more often than not such phrases put off a reader. At best, they will be ignored; at worst, they might be seen as offensive and will be held against you as an attempt to curry favour or to avoid taking the exercise seriously.

THE DANGERS OF PLAGIARISM

Most beginning students who are charged with plagiarism have fallen into this trap because they do not understand the conventions of making references to sources consulted—in some of their high school work they were assigned the task of simply looking up sources for a particular topic and copying them out. In university, this practice, if it involves handing in such work without references, constitutes plagiarism. Plagiarism is a serious academic offence. It involves presenting other people's work as your own without acknowledgment. Sometimes, carelessness in making your reading notes leads you to use other people's words or ideas as your own. Recording direct quotations from any of your sources when taking notes avoids this problem. As a protection against charges of plagiarism, keep your notes and drafts until you have received a final grade in the course.

A more serious offence is when students deliberately plagiarize. Instructors can quickly detect such theft by shifts in level of argumentation, word choices that are inconsistent with other parts of the essay, or complex stylistic features. New computer programs have been developed to detect plagiarism from online sources, and their use is becoming commonplace among university instructors. The penalties for plagiarism are severe, ranging from failure in the assignment, failure in the course, or suspension from the university. When you are uncertain about documenting your sources, consult your instructor. We will discuss plagiarism extensively in Chapter 9, where we demonstrate the proper methods for documenting sources; at this point, as part of your survival skills, you need to be aware that because of services that sell essays and because of the Internet, plagiarism is perceived by university teachers and administrators to be increasing and that steps are being taken to stop it.

Different disciplines follow widely accepted conventions to document or refer to sources (books, essays, and Web sites). The social sciences use the conventions of the American Psychological Association (APA style), called the author-date system: refer to your sources within your essay with the name of the author, the date of publication, and a page reference, gathering all sources into a "Reference List" at the end of your essay. The humanities use the conventions of the Modern Language Association (MLA style), the author-page system: refer to your sources within your essay with the name of the author and a page number after your citation, gathering the full bibliographic data into a "Works Cited" list at the end of your essay. Both the APA style and the MLA style have conventions for printed and online sources. Specific details about formatting different types of sources are given in *Foundations* or in other handbooks on writing; there are also various online sites now available that give these formatting conventions in detail. Your instructors will give you advice about what conventions to follow in your course (see Chapter 9).

COMPUTERS AND CRITICAL THINKING

In the 21st century, some computer expertise is necessary for any student who wishes to think, read, and write critically. The ways in which computer technology affects modes of critical thinking are complex and controversial areas of debate. Over 40 years ago, Marshall McLuhan re-defined the world as the "global village"; it now must be re-defined again as the "global chip," as all parts of the world can be linked to communicate simultaneously. All parts of this world use multi-media with audio and visual clips and graphics. When you use a computer and gain access to the Internet, you become a part of this vast electronic network of communicators, with its greatly varying skills, assumptions, and purposes. However, using your computer effectively requires specialized knowledge and newly directed methods of critical thinking to find and evaluate computer-available data.

Many courses require access to computers and software programs, but most professors assume students will use computers at least for writing assignments, and we discuss using computers for writing essays in Part IV of this text. Almost all university students have some computer skills, but most are unaware of methods of using available technologies to improve their university work. *Foundations* assumes basic computer skills throughout but also builds on your present strengths to equip you for advanced writing and research on the computer.

All students will continue for at least some decades to use a mixture of print and electronic media for their reading, research, and writing of class assignments and research essays. Because of this combined use of print and electronic media, in our discussion of critical thinking, we do not separate traditional methods of critical thinking, reading, and writing from new ways of thinking about communicating ideas. Although we draw distinctions in Part III between research in print and electronic media, we believe that both require the use of critical thinking. Critical thinking uses methods of induction and deduction, cause and effect, and a sequencing of ideas (see Chapter 6). Such skills are vital tools in effectively using your computer. The principles of critical reading (see Chapter 4) will help you assess the usefulness of the data that you discover. We also outline methods to find, select, and quote the research material that you find on the Web and explain how to cite it in your bibliographical records (see Chapters 7 and 9).

Your university library has a computerized catalogue that you can use in the library or at home via the Internet. Increasingly, many courses require that students undertake work on the Internet, either by conducting research on the Web or by conferencing, e-mail, or other interclassroom communication. Furthermore, universities are developing distance education that makes courses available on the Internet.

Much of the Web information is trivial or of narrow appeal, but there is also a great deal that is useful and important, and it is becoming increasingly vital in academic work.

TIPS Basic Computer Advice

1. Use a surge-protector; back up your files regularly, especially your data files. At some point, your hard drive will crash.

2. Use an anti-virus program. If you use others' disks or your own disks in the library or even in downloading files from the Internet, you are imperilling your system. Your university probably already has an onsite licence for one of the popular anti-virus programs: McAfee, Norton AntiVirus, Dr. Solomon's, and so on. Install it now, use it, and keep the virus program updated.

3. If you lend your disks to another student, you run two major risks: (a) when they are returned, you could be infected with a virus, so check it out before using it; and (b) you have no control over how anyone else might use your work.

4. Consult your instructors, your university's computer help desk, the library, and your friends for advice on how to make your use of your computer effective and enjoyable. The many facilities each university provides are there for your use. You have already helped pay for the facilities in your fees, so take advantage of them.

5. If you run into problems, first consult your manuals and then the online help. Then, a knowledgeable friend can help if it is not a hardware or major software problem. The Internet user-group information, the university computer help desk for students, a computer retailer, and private service agencies are other sources of help and information. If a deadline approaches and your problem is not yet solved, take your back-up disks to a friend or to the university computer lab and print your essay or other work, writing a note to your instructor explaining your difficulty.

6. Some specialized sites for computer information are given on the *Foundations* Web site.

Two questions immediately arise: how can you find what you want? How can you evaluate what you find? We discuss these questions extensively in Chapter 7, but for now, a few preliminary answers are in order.

To find information, you can use different Web browsers to access the Web and a large variety of search engines that perform different tasks. To evaluate what you find, you need to use the methods of critical thinking. In many ways, the rapid technological developments that allow information to be distributed more quickly and easily have made critical reading and thinking even more important. The Web provides information from diverse sources, many of which have no monitoring procedures or accountability, so large questions about the reliability of information become crucial to avoid problems of false information, or of plagiarism if you use the material you find as your own. While it is important to think critically about all aspects of your reading and research in more traditional formats, such as the lecture, textbook, and academic monograph or journal article, the Internet, with its instant access to Web pages, discussion groups, and e-mail, makes these demands for critical skills all the more urgent.

LEARNING STYLES

Learning styles refers to the fact that people's aptitudes for learning anything, from a song, to swimming the backstroke, to an abstract idea, differ widely but can be classified. Knowing something about your own dominant learning style can help you to adjust better to university work and find ways of improving the other learning styles that you will have to use. As with other skills, practice in doing anything, including working on a learning style, is a key to understanding it. The Chinese sage, Confucius, who lived about 550 B.C.E., wrote: "If I hear it, I forget. If I see it, I remember. If I do it, I understand." In a sense, he was anticipating much modern study on learning styles.

Many different methods are used to assess learning styles, but experts agree that if you are tested, you should work with a counsellor to assess the results and to understand that the test is a guide to some patterns in the way your mind processes information and not an iron-clad determinant of your personality. You can work on some learning styles to improve them and will undoubtedly find that your learning styles change over time.

One analyst, Howard Gardner, a Harvard University professor of education, suggests in *Frames of Mind* that most people have various balances of eight kinds of intelligence: *kinesthetic* (or physical), *musical, spatial* (visual), *interpersonal* (the ability to understand others), *intrapersonal* (the ability to understand oneself), *naturalist* (the ability to recognize fine distinctions and patterns in the natural world), *logical,* and *linguistic.* He argues, as do the authors of each theory of learning types, that each kind of intelligence can be enhanced through learning and practice.

Other views include those of David Kolb and Roger Fry, who argue that experiential learning is the most helpful learning route for many people, moving in a circle from a concrete experience to observation and reflection, then to forming abstract concepts, and finally to a testing stage in a new situation. Such a process is perhaps found less in the content of a university lecture or textbook than in the experience of hearing the lecture and taking notes on it (as a concrete experience) or reading a textbook to understand it for the next class. Most helpfully, however, Kolb and Fry propose that the learning circle can begin at any point so that a student can bring any particular learning style to bear while developing other styles.

Probably the most widely used assessment of personality traits that is useful in understanding learning styles is the Myers-Briggs Type Indicator. Thousands of university students have taken this personality evaluation, and it has also been used extensively by businesses and corporations. From studies of student tests data, many kinds of new teaching and learning methods have been developed. This test uses four pairs of categories to assess learning styles:

1. **extrovert/introvert** indicates whether a person prefers to direct attention to the external world of people and things or the internal world of ideas and concepts.

2. **sensing/intuiting** indicates whether a person perceives the world through directly observing or experiencing the surrounding external world or through impressions and imagining possibilities.

3. **thinking/feeling** indicates that one makes decisions on the bases of different criteria. When people operate in a thinking mode, they tend to make decisions on the bases of guidelines or rational choices, while making decisions in a feeling mode is based on a value system or individual preferences or opinions.

4. **judging/perceiving** indicates how people react to the external world so that judging people prefer to have things orderly and established, and they form and express decisions to bring things to a close, while perceivers tend to prefer things to be spontaneous, flexible, and open ended.

Of course, people combine such tendencies in all sorts of ways throughout their lives. According to studies of students by Charles C. Schroeder and others, at least half of entering students understand their world by sensing or experiencing it and prefer direct concrete experiences in their learning situations. They like a moderate to high degree of structure, as well as a sequential or linear mode of presentation of material. To them, complex or abstract ideas are difficult, at least at first, until they learn the practical reasons for their existence, and they tend to move from practice to theory. Clearly, much traditional learning in university that begins with theory before its application is difficult for such learning types, and they have to work hard to learn new techniques. For such students, learning situations that stress active engagement are helpful, such as group work or small group projects that involve talking through a problem—perhaps in tutorials as well as in-class presentations, field work, developing simulations or case studies, and so on.

On the other hand, students who tend toward the intuitive learning type consider the world or a particular problem with respect to its possibilities. They perceive the world abstractly and are comfortable with alternatives or contradictions existing together. Hence, they prefer an open-ended discussion of concepts or ideas and can tolerate a high amount of difference, ambiguity, or lack of closure. To them, independent work comes easily, and they respond well to traditional modes of university teaching that put an emphasis on general concepts, models, or abstractions, moving from theory to practice.

This book assumes that most students, if they wish, can use university facilities to find out about their basic learning styles and preferences and can become aware of the kinds of styles that they should develop for more advanced work. Throughout, we address issues that affect different learning styles, and we set out boxes, charts, and discussions to stress these different styles, aware that most students will have to practise those styles they are least familiar with—those that meet the demands of university work—in order to progress effectively.

DIFFERENT CLASSROOM FORMATS, THE E-WIRED CLASSROOM, AND DISTANCE LEARNING

All over the world, universities have gone online and are offering courses on the Internet. The choice is dazzling and makes it possible for anyone with a computer to log on to a university site and begin to sample what is there, and perhaps enrol for extra courses that might count toward a degree (though be sure to check with your registrar first about possible difficulties). In Britain, the Open University first experimented with distance learning, offering courses on the radio and TV and making big-name teachers and scholars available to lead eager adult learners through courses from Art History to Zoology. In Canada, too, TVO (Television Ontario) made courses available for credit to enrolled students who signed up for the ancillary course readings and opted to have their work marked and graded.

Universities have embraced the World Wide Web as a friend and ally, putting up hundreds of courses with multi-media presentations, self-assessment questionnaires, student-paced learning modules, and interactive dialogues. At the same time, traditional classrooms have experimented with different formats and technologies, changing expectations and demands on critical thinking. Further, new developments in electronic classrooms and distance learning pose other new challenges. There has been a sudden expansion of wireless connection to the Internet, as universities make residences, student lounges, and libraries active with wi-fi (wireless connection for computers, usually laptops with the required technology). Some campuses, in the next few years, will be moving quickly in this direction to make Internet learning and communication fast, easy, and almost omnipresent.

Different Classroom Formats

Most classrooms continue to rely upon the lecture format, with a short period of student questions; the seminar that is teacher focused and is, in large measure, a kind of mini-lecture; or the more informal faculty-led question-and-answer procedure, sometimes called the Socratic method, named after the Greek philosopher Socrates (d. 399 B.C.E.). At the same time, these conventional lectures and seminars are being balanced with many different kinds of teaching formats. In the traditional classroom space, there are all sorts of variations enacted, for instance, labs being widely offered in humanities and social science subject areas. They have long been conventional in creative writing and theatre courses but are now used in history, religion, and sociology courses, too, sometimes working on a particular problem, with resources at hand and sometimes setting out different learning possibilities, such as problem-based learning or simulations.

Problem-based learning (PBL) consists of carefully designed problems of a complex nature that require either a single student or a team working together over a period of time to be solved. They began in the 1970s at the McMaster University faculty of medicine and are now being widely used for courses in social work, sociology, geography, and throughout the humanities and social sciences. The problem is usually highly realistic, may involve some fieldwork, and is intended to open up large and overlapping areas in the field of study. Faculty become resources and facilitators. For students, the process demands the acquisition of knowledge, critical skills, and a high degree of self-directed learning and problem-solving ability. Usually, the end results are highly rewarding because the model builds team support, motivation, and a sense of accomplishment.

Simulations use some of the same techniques. They customarily use a model of a specific system, mechanical, social, biological, or political. For instance, a particular sample national state with a presupposed military coup could be the subject of study. The class could divide into teams and work through all of the institutional and international choices that might come up. Similar kinds of projects work in psychology and sociology courses, sometimes using game theory or various kinds of psychodrama. Such formats involve different cognitive skills and learning styles and may help students who have difficulties with traditional classroom settings. Like problem-based learning, such courses require considerable self-motivation and co-operation, so being aware of your own learning styles and ability to work without supervision are important.

Other formats include the old convention of the debate, sometimes heightened with legal trappings so that the classroom becomes a courtroom—common practice, of course, in many law courses. In small group work, a larger class is broken up into smaller groups, each being assigned a particular aspect of an issue, text, or problem to work on, with one of the groups designated to take notes and report back in the wrap-up at the end of the class. Or the group work could take half of the time and the wrap-up the rest.

Such seminar group work puts some useful pressure on all students to have the readings or other preparation completed in order to support the group. If the group work is a surprise, however, many students will feel frustrated that they are ill prepared. Another form of this procedure involves co-operative work in teacher-assigned teams between classes, with the next class being the reporting-in session. Such teams depend upon co-operative learning and often bring very good results to students who respond well to self-motivation and learning from and with peers. Larger teams can also be set up as a learning team, either self-selected or teacher selected (more effective), to work on a longer or larger project over several weeks. Here, the benefits of sustained co-operative learning are increased, though the cost in time and sometimes the inconvenience of meeting at late hours because of people's busy schedules are a liability.

The pros and cons of different models of teaching in the classroom are set out in Table 2.1.

TABLE 2.1	Classroom Teaching and Learning Models	
	Strengths	Weaknesses
Lecture -traditional	delivers information orally; authoritative, hierarchical	hard for many students to record; aural; unmodifiable by listener
Lecture -audiovisual	oral and visual: appeals to wider learning styles	visual elements hard to record; difficult to stay alert
Seminar -traditional	hierarchical/peer mix	hard to take notes; uneven content
Small group work simulations	collaborative, involving real-life application of theory; teaches teamwork	random degree of preparation time consuming, long preparation, differing levels of commitment
Learning team	diverse strengths, perspectives	different abilities and strengths
Student-led projects	peer level; faculty as resources	hard to focus on goals
Peer-to-peer tutoring	one-on-one learning	hard to assess
Fieldwork	application of theory; varieties of learning styles are exercised	time consuming, may involve off-campus work, travel
E-wired seminars -e-mail with instuctor	not tied to a schedule, may supplement traditional seminar	hard to deal with complex questions; requires good writing skills
-peer-to-peer -moderated	directed at student's level supervised and guided peer learning	no guidance or supervision may be above or below your level
Computer lab modules	self-directed, learn at your own speed; can modify content; appeals to different learning styles	depends on self-motivation; easy to procrastinate (getting there); easy to be side tracked (once there); requires technical skills

The E-Wired Classroom and Distance Learning

Many classrooms are now equipped with wiring for multiple computer terminals, and some campuses are already "wired for wireless" communication. Other classrooms have desks that will accommodate laptops for in-class work on relevant software or course content. But besides the classroom, there are larger points to be made about the kinds of courses that are taught with technological or computer assistance.

Computer-enriched or computer-delivered courses are now widely used. The first tends to take place only on the home campus, and the second may take place in campus computer labs but increasingly is taught to students off-campus. Distance learning is one of the hot items on universities' development plans. Most universities see them as a major initiative for the future, using technology to reach more students effectively. While this field is evolving rapidly, some provisional conclusions can be drawn about the different ways that universities are using instructional technology. We introduce you to some different formats of instruction that you might be considering to enrol in. Not every format is for everyone, and you should consider the strengths and weaknesses of each along with your resources before you enrol.

First, some universities and courses use technology to *enhance* learning. Such courses continue to use the traditional lecture/seminar modes of instruction (either on a weekly basis or at a few set times throughout the term) and to put major emphasis on a course kit with other readings, a textbook, and so on. In addition, the enhancement consists of having a Web page that may contain the syllabus, a bibliography, links to other Web sites, some instructional sheets, copies of assignments, and other such items. In most courses with enhanced technology, students communicate with the instructor face to face at the lectures or seminars but, in addition, can contact them by telephone at set times each week to discuss their readings or assignments or can be in touch by e-mail. This e-mail contact is called "asynchronous." That is, it occurs outside real time, or there is a gap in time between the sending of your e-mail and your instructor's response. Such courses depend, to a very high degree, on self-motivation, and since there might be little contact between students and the instructor, if the course meets infrequently as a whole, there is only opportunity for contact by telephone or e-mail on a one-to-one basis.

The electronically active classroom ("e-wired") can take several forms. At its most basic, the instructor continues to teach a class in real time (synchronous) but has all of the students' e-mail addresses and can send out particular instructions to all, course information, assignments, or comment on essays, and they can contact the instructor with any questions or comments (asynchronous learning stage). Fundamentally, however, this model is hierarchical and is based on one-to-one communication between the teacher and the student. However, it makes clear the expectations of the course and explains the requirements. This mode of delivery can also be combined with work in groups or teams.

This instructor-centred model using enhanced technology can be extended by the addition of peer-to-peer communication whereby any student can discuss anything with any other student, without faculty intervention. This communication is unmonitored and will be as effective or as distracting—or even unused—as the students wish to make it. A monitored list, watched over by the course director, can link the discussion and direct it more effectively, and all students can see and participate in the course of the discussion. Each of these procedures is the subject of a great deal of discussion as a teaching and learning model, and it is certainly possible that you will have one or more of these courses in your career.

A more intensive computer course can make use of one of the learning or technology labs at your university. In this case, the whole class may meet from time to time for specific instruction that is pertinent to the whole class, usually at the beginning when the software or other parts of the course are introduced. Then, students are left on their own to complete the assignments in their own time.

Second, some courses and entire universities are committed to using technology to *deliver* learning. Courses taught by this method are dominantly in electronic media, sometimes using multi-media, and, while they may also rely on printed course kits or readings, their chief source is electronic information. Such courses are known as distance education courses or distributed learning courses. Contact with the instructor might be either by e-mail—the basis of all of these electronic modes of delivery of course materials—or through Web conferencing in real time ("synchronous") in a "virtual classroom." Such courses allow students with very different skills and backgrounds to proceed at their own pace and to be widely dispersed geographically. They also allow students with very different learning skills to use a variety of those skills. Sometimes, students submit class assignments electronically, often for the whole class to share and sometimes, as is the case with a "written" electronic paper or other assignment, for the instructor alone.

TIPS   Success in Distance Learning Courses

1. While distance and online courses allow you to avoid problems in scheduling and let you proceed at your own pace, remember that you are responsible for your self-learning and will often have to find your own way through difficult material.

2. Read all of the course syllabus before you register in order to become familiar with the course design and requirements from the start. If you cannot come near to completing the schedule on time, re-think registering.

3. If the course makes use of the Internet, you will need to be able to use a variety of search engines and database managers with some ability. The course description should make you aware of these requirements.

4. Identify the tools you need before you start—word processor skills, access to graphics, video or other programs or equipment, database software, and any print media. How close is your nearest library, and/or can the Internet be a sufficient substitute?

5. Be realistic in your own goals and expectations, but also be clear about how your time and application fit with the weekly schedule of coursework and assignments.

6. Stay in touch with your instructor. Make regular contact by phone or e-mail, and ask whether you can send questions, outlines, or drafts in connection with readings or assignments. It is important to get feedback that you are making good progress and are keeping on track before the first mid-term test.

7. Remember your audience when you are in touch with your instructor or other students in your course. Good communication skills and being clear about what you are writing will mean that you are taken seriously.

8. Prepare your assignments well in advance of the due date, especially if they involve different media, such as print along with electronic text, video, graphics, audio, or Internet sites. All sorts of unexpected things can, and usually do, go wrong when you have to rely on technological sources. Keep copies of everything that you submit.

Further, some classes might be set up to correspond with each other through a discussion group using Usenet and a dedicated listserv (see Chapter 3). Often, such groups, while monitored by faculty, will be largely student centred and student controlled. They might also be multi-sensory, relying on audio and visual enhancements to make the e-learning field almost a virtual classroom. Wider in scope is Web conferencing, and again numerous sites are available, some of which might be recommended for your courses. For a list of the variety of these, and access to many different kinds of resources and facilities, see the Think-of-It Web site (**www.thinkofit.com/pubs.htm**). What becomes clear very quickly is that the exploding dimensions of the classroom into cyberspace can take on a huge variety of configurations. Some make use of desktop video to make simple written and visual communication possible from one person to another (called point-to-point connection), while others make use of audio, including real voice connection, or software that lets your computer do the voice translation. Whatever the resources you are presented with in any class—and they are certain to be full of changing expectations as these systems and their use in higher education change—you will need to use all of your critical skills to learn to use them to your advantage.

CHAPTER SUMMARY

Chapter 2 has introduced you to some of the changing expectations that universities are now asking of students. Along with the practices that you have used to survive the first weeks and months at university, you are becoming acquainted with these new expectations and learning environments:

- Your memory is still not where you would like it to be, but you are working on improvements.
- You have been introduced to university customs and expectations and are clear about using inclusive language.
- You are aware of the dangers of plagiarism.
- You are beginning to use your computer more effectively.
- You have been working on adapting your learning styles to the new university setting.
- You now have greater knowledge of changing formats for courses and have a basis for thinking critically about where you might best fit in.

At each point in Part I, we have emphasized critical thinking about your own habits and practices. For instance, we have proposed that you assess your study habits and identify those habits that are impeding your progress, breaking them down into smaller aspects, isolating them, and working on improving each one, much as a person works on an exercise program. We have also tried to introduce you to the changing expectations of university life that you may not have been aware of. You will quickly become acclimatized to these expectations. We now move to more advanced aspects of university studies—the development and implementation of critical thinking and reading skills.

FURTHER READINGS

Albrecht, Karl. *Brain Power*. New York: Prentice-Hall, 1980.

Gardner, Howard. *Frames of Mind: The Theory of Multiple Intelligences*. 10th ed. New York: Basic Books, 1993.

Jarvis, Peter. *Adult and Continuing Education. Theory and Practice*. London: Routledge, 1995.

Kolb, D. A. *Experiential Learning*. Englewood Cliffs, NJ: Prentice Hall, 1984.

Kolb, D. A., and Roger Fry. "Toward an Applied Theory of Experiential Learning." In *Theories of Group Process*. Ed. C. Cooper. London: John Wiley, 1975.

Maciuba-Koppel, Darlene. *The Web-Writer's Guide* [e-book].Woburn, MA: Elsevier Science, 2002.

Pauk, Walter. *How to Study in College*. 5th ed. Boston: Houghton Mifflin, 1993.

Quenk, Naomi L. *Essentials of Myers-Briggs Type Indicator Assessment*. New York: John Wiley & Sons, 1999.

Yates, Frances A. *The Art of Memory*. Chicago: U of Chicago P, 1966.

Critical Thinking and Reading

chapter three

Implementing a Critical Attitude

Part II involves a shift in focus, another change in gears. These four chapters are all devoted to critical thinking and reading and begin our discussion of critical writing.

Chapter 3 concentrates on developing skills to move from merely stating your opinions without basis to formulating reasoned arguments. A critical frame of mind is the foundation for analytical thinking, and this chapter illustrates the ways to assess your audience and present your analysis effectively. To function effectively in lectures and seminars, you need to assess the demands of your course materials and your assignments. This chapter stresses different approaches to your course readings and writing projects by getting you started on implementing a critical attitude.

LEARNING OBJECTIVES

In Chapter 3, we address the following questions:

- What is a critical attitude? How can you be critical without being negative or sarcastic?
- How does a position based on critical thinking differ from your opinion?
- How do you stress your own analysis of readings and assignments?
- How do you use critical thinking skills in written and oral presentations?

- How do you understand the concepts and terminology of instructions and assignments?
- How can you apply critical thinking to learning environments changed by technology?

CRITICAL ATTITUDE: FROM NEGATIVE COMPLAINT TO ACADEMIC FRAME OF MIND

The American philosopher Richard Paul defines a critical attitude as "thinking about your thinking while you are thinking in order to make your thinking better: more clear, more accurate, or more defensible" (**www.criticalthinking.org**). In the most basic terms, critical thinking involves being able to move from asserting opinions to formulating a position; from passively receiving ideas, arguments, and readings to actively engaging with them.

A critical attitude means developing a reasoned position for what you are arguing, not attacking an opponent. Of course, sometimes, you will want to differ from accepted positions or views, but to be critical means that you can give reasons for and against for your position, that you are aware of the assumptions underlying what you are considering, that you can question it and analyze it according to some coherent method, and that you are able to summarize your results in a way that will be clear to your readers or listeners. The first step toward critical thinking is adopting and developing a critical attitude. To begin that process, we shall undertake an exercise in critical thinking, examining two terms, *critical* and *attitude*, moving from some of their popular meanings to the ways that they are used in Paul's sense.

Critical is frequently misunderstood or, rather, understood in senses different from our meaning. Its most common usage is negative, usually meaning always finding fault or complaining. Another usage refers to what is important, and so students often take that to mean that it is also difficult to understand. Even more seriously, if a friend has a car accident and is taken to hospital and reported as "critical," he is in a crisis that might go either way, to life or death.

This last use of the term points to another aspect of the word's meaning: *critical* refers to what is indispensable, and hence, the critical care unit gives treatment to your friend that is crucial in his life-threatening condition. Our use of the term builds on this transition—from critical as complaining, to critical as life-threatening, to critical as indispensable in meeting an emergency, to critical as referring to something important in any subject area—leading eventually to critical as a reasoned disposition of the mind. Fundamentally, critical thinking means finding what is most important in solving the intellectual problem that you are faced with; it means evaluating and using what you find as a mental skill. This skill is a learned accomplishment; developing a critical attitude, therefore, means finding a way of establishing an enquiring, reflective, and evaluative frame of mind, one called for in academic work but also, as we shall see, in demand by employers.

Turning *critical* from a negative complaint to a positive attribute requires thinking about it differently from the way the word is used in everyday speech, and the same work must be done with our second term, *attitude*. One of the authors of *Foundations* recently heard a parent in a park chastising his child, "Get rid of that attitude! You've had nothing but an attitude since you got up this morning!" We are all familiar with calling any bad behaviour an "attitude," in what dictionary definitions call colloquial or everyday usage. A person engaged in such behaviour is referred to as aggressive or uncooperative and responds by being resentful or antagonistic. That child, and most of the rest of us when we are told we have an attitude, hear an authority figure telling us we are misbehaving. If friends say you have an attitude, people at your own level are probably telling you that you are acting in a way that offends them personally. Alternatively, a good attitude, as seen from the position of an authority figure, is behaving properly, following the rules, and conforming to expectations, or on the level of peers, it means being friendly or happy.

A bad attitude (in the sense above) has been extended by writers to attack whole societies. For instance, in Mark Twain's *Adventures of Huckleberry Finn* and J. D. Salinger's *The Catcher in the Rye,* the two adolescent male heroes are scathingly critical of the adult world. According to the norms of the adults in their societies, both heroes have bad attitudes, but their acting up is the authors' literary strategy to call into question the hypocrisy and contradictions of those authority figures and the accepted social conventions. A more recent book, *Generation X* by Douglas Coupland, depicts people in their early thirties who also have a bad attitude: they criticize contemporary society by being ironic, making fun of everything in their culture. This making fun is another literary strategy that enables the author to be subversive to the culture he is writing in.

Perhaps you are more familiar with popular movies that have done similar things, such as *Fast Times at Ridgemont High, Ferris Bueller's Day Off, Risky Business,* or *Clueless.* These movies adopt a critical attitude toward adult authority by having the stars (Sean Penn, Matthew Broderick, Tom Cruise, and Alicia Silverstone, respectively) play rebellious adolescents with a bad attitude. This bad attitude provokes a response from authorities within the film (parents, teachers, and police), as in the novels above, that strategically reveals their hypocrisy or lack of fairness.

The critical attitude that we want you to think about for academic work adopts part of the strategies of these movies. A critical attitude stresses the importance of questioning and evaluating accepted norms and received ideas. It also exposes the weaknesses in the general assumptions and assertions being examined, revealing their fallacies and inconsistencies. Unlike these movies about adolescents' acting up, however, what we mean by *critical* does not end in chaos or disaster nor does it rely on another of the movies' conventions—turning the authority figures into cartoon-like buffoons. Our sense of adopting a critical attitude means having an outlook that evaluates and weighs alternative positions but that does not dismiss or ridicule.

Another meaning for *attitude* has developed lately, which undoubtedly you are familiar with. It means taking on a new identity or pose, a kind of style, appearance, or way of holding the body. Such a meaning derives from the use of attitude as a descriptive term in paintings, plays, or movies, where a figure adopts a specific pose that indicates identifiable social characteristics, for instance, the attitude of a grovelling beggar, rubbing hands together or that of the damsel in distress tied to the railroad tracks or cringing on the ledge of a high building. So, too, is *attitude* a pose in contemporary usage. One of the author's daughters has described *attitude* as a person of one ethnicity taking on the pose of another, "a white guy trying to be black" and, in the process, "making a fool of himself." But some of the attitudinizing is necessary in specific social settings. So, in certain kinds of dances, according to her, you have to take on an appropriate attitude, "a defiant face in hip-hop," or "preppy snootiness in ballet." Whether she is right or not about the particulars is not the point; this notion of attitude involves the adoption of specific identity categories to suit particular roles. On the one hand, these categories are not fixed, but on the other hand, they are relatively stable because they are set out according to recognizable cultural norms.

In university, the cultural norms also call for the adoption of an attitude in this everyday sense. For instance, students often try to appear casual and nonchalant, as though not caring what anyone thinks about them when they actually do. But there is a further meaning to *attitude* that we have already hinted at and want to stress here. It is also part of the cultural norm of the university. Adopting this attitude is to take on the role of being a serious student, engaged in academic work as an intellectual-in-training, behaving or adopting the pose (in a serious sense) of acting as a professional in ways appropriate to your stage of study.

In all sorts of ways, your external appearance and physical pose communicate important messages about your intellectual attitude, just as they do in broader social situations and as they do in paintings and movies. They are short-hand indicators that say something about how you are using the skills in critical thinking that you are learning. Even such seemingly trivial things as your arrival time for class, how and where you sit, how alert you are—all apparently inconsequential—are noticeable. Your professors notice when students sneak into the back corner seat without books or pens. On the other hand, arriving with a lively and engaged attitude will also be noticed. However, adopting a critical attitude means much more than these rather obvious external appearances.

In university study, a critical attitude produces an alternative mental state, an intellectual position, one that can be clearly set out, defended, and applied. Instead of simply defying authority, as in the films we mentioned, *critical* in this sense tries to break down the logic of a particular argument, isolate its component parts, and extend its range to solve problems and develop new forms of knowledge. (See Table 3.1.)

The Conference Board of Canada has recently reported that having and using a critical attitude is one of the most important "employability skills" a person can have. Employers across the country stress the significance of being able to "assess situations and identify problems" so as to be "innovative in exploring possible solutions" ("Employability Skills 2000+"). However, a critical attitude here refers to the disposition of mind needed for academic work, and it is the cultivation of that attitude that the rest of this chapter is devoted to. Such an attitude involves taking charge of your own learning as it is provided by your courses and teachers and making it your own.

FROM FACT AND OPINION TO ARGUMENTS BASED ON A CRITICAL ATTITUDE

In this section, we engage in a further exercise in critical thinking, this time on the level of argument, moving from positions that assert facts and opinions as though they were beyond question to establishing a reasoned position.

Fact and Opinion

It is often assumed that there are only two kinds of argument, those based on fact and those based on opinion. Arguments of fact, common in elementary levels of science, have only one right answer: for example, the boiling point of water is 100°C. In arguments of fact,

TABLE 3.1	Non-Critical and Critical Thinking	
	Non-Critical Thinking	Critical Thinking
View of Knowledge	• sees everything in right/wrong, true/false opposites • knowledge is closed, single, definite • knowledge is limited to one level, often superficial • knowledge is restricted to one field, discipline, with no overlaps	• sees everything as graduated, shaded, blending from one to another • knowledge is open, diverse, undecided • knowledge operates on several or multiple levels, often discovered at complex levels • knowledge extends over related fields, and is subject to examination by several disciplines with many overlaps
View of Thinking	• suspends rational thought to seize on statement or conclusion • inconsistent in use of evidence, support • focuses on learning *what* to think to please audience • limited frame or frames of reference and small selection of materials, some relevant, some not • thinking is only linear from A to B to C, yielding a simplistic structure for your argument • can only cope with simple thinking without subordinate ideas • avoids complications or qualifications which interfere with linear argument	• uses rational thought to build arguments to conclusion • consistent in use of evidence, support • focuses on learning *how* to think to make and defend argument or case • multiple frames of reference and wide selection of materials and broad view of their relevance • thinking is networked or woven strands to complement linear or intricate structures • can cope with all kinds of thinking from simple to complex and uses subordinate and complementary ideas • uses complications and qualifications to extend argument
Strategies of Thinking	• moves quickly to closure, with push to resist questions • unformulated or unstated thesis that states the obvious • implicit thesis defended by weak evidence, data, authorities • tends to unjustifiable assertions often unfounded or without grounds • resists different opinions, brushes aside opposing arguments • may resort to opinion, assertion, emotional appeal • uses vague and imprecise language, not suitable to topic and ignoring audience	• suspends closure, even at the end, preferring to leave open questions • clear thesis arrived at soon in argument that points to way through materials • thesis defended by strong evidence, data, authorities • tends to exploratory probing of a problem or question, with supporting grounds • balances differing opinions, takes opposing arguments into account • uses facts, persuasion, appeals on basis of rational argument • uses precise and articulate language, suited to topic and audience

Adapted from the U-Study Guide of the University of Saskatchewan. Reproduced by Off-Campus Library Services, Golden Gate University: /internet.ggu.edu/university_library/critical/critnoncrit.html#knowledge

then, there is generally agreed-upon knowledge within which specific questions have only one right answer; that is, the right answer is conditioned by the accepted knowledge in the relevant field or discipline. Such facts can be defended by an appeal to a scientific rule or other such authority. Matters of opinion, on the other hand, depend on human preferences, convictions, or personal beliefs about an individual's choices, and they, too, are often supposed to need no supporting evidence, as, for example, in the assertion, "I like to wear blue jeans instead of dress pants." In matters of opinion, the position asserted is governed by a personal preference—what a person prefers or believes cannot be disagreed with, except by a contrary opinion or a demand that such an opinion be clarified or supported.

However, if we begin to take apart the opinion and look at the conditions of this preference in relation to different circumstances, then we begin to move to a third kind of argument. This move involves questions for which the answers are neither right nor wrong and are not matters of personal preference or conviction but are based on positions established as better or worse. If you are going for an interview for employment at a bank, then the matter of dress moves from your mere opinion ("I like to wear ...") to a set of appropriate choices governed by other circumstances. If you want the job at the bank, it would be better not to wear jeans to the interview.

Moving from Holding an Opinion to Establishing a Position

An opinion, then, is an assertion of personal preference that may have grounds, though they are rarely stated. An argument makes a claim to intellectual validity based upon the coherence of its structure and the logic of its arrangement. One key to making a distinction between opinion and argument is to ask if the position taken can be disagreed with. If it cannot, it is an assertion or opinion; if it can, then it has moved toward an argument. By disagreeing with a position, we do not mean dismissing it or replacing it with another opinion. An argument involves making a judgment on the basis of critical thinking, taking a reasoned position on the material being discussed. Moving from opinion to reasoned position in the instance of choice of dress involves taking account of the conditions within which the choice is made. These conditions can be argued about in a form outside of personal preference. Your preference or opinion has to be placed in the context of dress codes, social expectations, and appropriate behaviour. Your choice of what to wear, then, should not be a matter of opinion or preference, but a matter of reasoned judgment, whereby you weigh the implications of your choices. Of course, you may not want the job in the bank, in which case wearing jeans to the interview probably would be a reasonable position.

The example of appropriate dress at the bank interview may seem unconnected to the kinds of critical judgments you are asked to make in academic work. However, just as you need to be aware of the implications of what you wear in applying for a job, so, too, do you need to be aware of how you use your opinions and preferences in adopting a reasoned position in your essay or class presentation. To substitute for a reasoned judgment, as many students do, the view that your opinion on this text is as good as anyone else's is not critical thinking. The opposite tack—to take at face value everything you read, being completely intimidated or overwhelmed by the authority of someone else's assertions—is not critical thinking either. A critical attitude depends on arranging your ideas in arguments that are clear, logical, and convincing (see Figure 3.1).

The arguments you make are set into a course and discipline where conventions of knowledge and power positions are already established. You cannot hope to challenge their knowledge or power by either simple facts or personal opinion. Nevertheless, you can challenge their knowledge and power by means of a rational argument. To argue effectively means that you may disagree with *some* of these conventions or positions. You need not

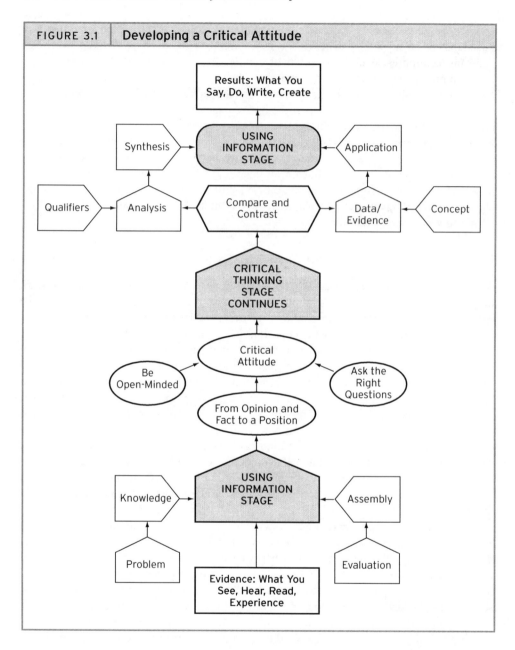

FIGURE 3.1 | **Developing a Critical Attitude**

agree with them entirely. However, in challenging or opposing them, you cannot ignore the existence of their established knowledge or dismiss their power in an offhand manner.

Indeed, the assumptions of a course often are based on precisely this relationship between the conventions and positions of power as they exist in the classroom and the knowledge that the discipline defends. At the same time, you are frequently encouraged by faculty to criticize established knowledge and power positions. Philosophers sometimes claim that well-established disciplines (such as History and English, for instance) embody their accepted schemes of knowledge as though they were absolutely accepted truths, like those in the sciences (philosophers call these truth systems). They go on to explain that the power of these disciplines in an institution like a university is guaranteed by the acceptance of those truth claims. For instance, a discipline may claim that certain wars or political figures are important, or certain authors are great, or certain books are classics—not on the basis of fact or opinion but on the basis of the power of the discipline in asserting such knowledge as commonplace, as though it cannot be questioned. So, patriarchal literature and history dominated the disciplines of English and History as unquestionable knowledge and unchallenged power until the middle of the 20th century. That frame of reference, of course, has been held up to radical challenge, not on the basis of opinion but by the arguments of thinkers who have taken opposing frames of reference. Feminist scholars, for instance, have demonstrated that women's history, experience, and narratives effectively challenge the accepted norms of patriarchal literature and history.

Of course, from your position as an undergraduate, you can hardly expect to launch such radical challenges to the established systems of knowledge and positions of power; however, you can learn to construct reasonable arguments and establish your position within these established frames of reference. Chapter 6 addresses in detail the ways to do that. In the next section, we consider key strategies to present your position, first by considering the task, purpose, or objectives of a course or a particular assignment and, second, by considering the audience that you are addressing.

ANALYZING THE OBJECTIVES OF YOUR ASSIGNMENT

In considering in some detail the purposes or objectives of a specific assignment or, for that matter, those of the whole course, you provide yourself with the grounds upon which you can make all sorts of strategic decisions based on critical thinking. In this section, we discuss four preliminary procedures to enable you to break down the elements of your assignment and to reassemble them using a well-formulated argument and pertinent applications.

Stressing Your Own Analysis

Your attitude toward the course materials, your classmates, and the teacher relates to matters of critical thinking. Virtually any course can be open to methods of critical thinking, and in many courses, the instructor will encourage a questioning attitude toward the course materials. In some courses, however, there appears to be a body of material that the professor simply has to cover, perhaps more or less without question. In still other courses, the professor may take a set position that discourages disagreement, and in such a course, a questioning attitude might prompt a negative response. If we assume that a course encourages critical thinking, an analytical and questioning attitude of mind, and an openness to legitimate student enquiry, then positioning yourself with regard to the course content, lectures, and texts is vital.

When faced with a lot of information written by experts in a particular field, however, you often may be overwhelmed and feel helpless—there seems to be no opportunity for your own voice to be heard or for you to find a fresh critical attitude. The first step is to analyze the terms of your assignment so that you are very clear about what you are being asked to do (for instance, *outline, summarize,* or *compare and contrast*), and what materials you should draw upon. The second step in developing your own analysis is to make distinctions within the particular readings among the assumptions behind the readings, the concepts the author is using to structure his or her analysis, and the data or examples to which the concepts are being applied. Now you can move to the third step, positioning yourself in relation to that reading, problem, or material. There are many ways that you can form an analysis:

- **Exposition and examples** involve describing an argument in terms of its parts and conclusions, illustrating each stage by examples.
- **Concept and application** involve formulating a basic idea about your material, either already stated in the reading or perhaps derived from other course material and applying it to the assignment, noting ways in which the concept needs to be qualified.
- **Compare and contrast** involve selecting key ideas, passages, or issues from the material to show similarities and differences—to be successful, this method must organize the points of comparison and contrast on the basis of importance, relevance to other course materials, assumptions, or other conceptual frameworks that serve as bridges between the ideas, passages, or issues. You can check out your proposed approach with your instructor.

Whether in oral or written presentations, Internet discussion groups, or reading journals, in stressing your own analysis, it is important not to hide behind banal assertions, such as "It is obvious," "It is clear," "The author reveals," or "It is evident from the text." In each of these instances, you are asserting something without demonstrating it. You need to change the phrasing to say what you are arguing: "From the evidence of ... I shall demonstrate how...."

You also need to say what you mean or exactly what you want to be heard. When you refer to yourself or to your own ideas, you should be direct and unapologetic but unobtrusive: "Bradley is wrong, I believe, to exclude *Antony and Cleopatra* from consideration in his *Shakespearean Tragedy*." Here, the direct personal opinion is more acceptable when embedded in the sentence. First person or "I" references may sometimes be generalized to apply to others, and "we" phrases can be used sparingly to involve your readers in your argument. Like the "I" references, they are better when included inside the sentence, rather than at the beginning.

Using Different Approaches for Different Assignments

Different kinds of writing require different approaches or a combination of approaches.

- A **concept essay** requires you to write about a specific concept in the course, often applying it to one or more texts or examples from the course to demonstrate your ability to use the concept.
- A **single-book essay** usually requires you to use a particular theme or idea in your paper and to read and analyze the text in light of that notion, citing appropriate evidence.
- A **comparative essay** requires you to do the same with one or more ideas or texts, and it involves greater problems in organization.
- A **research essay** requires that you undertake library work on your topic and, after analyzing and arranging your materials into an argument, apply that research to your topic in a coherent and clear way.

Most university assignments require a combination of these different kinds of writing. Some courses include writing assignments that ask you for reaction, opinion, expression of feelings, or interaction with other students. For example, you may be asked to keep a reading diary or journal of reactions to texts on the course or to engage with other students by networking through computers and exchanging opinions about course material. Such writing implicitly asks you to suspend judgment and to defer critical evaluation in favour of impressions and reactions. These assignments give weight to your opinions and feelings, but they also conceal a contradiction. On the one hand, you are being invited to offer your own opinions and to state your feelings—on the other hand, your work will be judged and evaluated. Your opinions and reactions are as good as anybody else's, but they will be evaluated according to criteria that might well be concealed or unstated. The methods of critical argument and analysis we have outlined can still be used in such assignments to provide the basis upon which you establish your opinions and reactions.

Speaking and Writing to the Assignment

One of the most powerful misconceptions about a written or oral presentation is that it is a free expression of an individual's ideas and feelings about a particular subject. In reality, most assignments are done under particular limitations: the due date, the scope of the topic, or the time of the meeting when the minutes or brief you were to prepare has to be presented. Failure to comply with or address these requirements often leads to drastic devaluation of your work, leaving you with little recourse for appeal because you simply did not follow the requirements.

The academic or analytical essay, in a simpler form, is the kind of work that many academic faculty members undertake in writing scholarly articles. As a genre, the very nature of the critical essay is to question and to challenge fundamental attitudes, a position that the university as an institution is supposed to foster.

Usually, the instructor assigns your essay topic. Occasionally, however, you will have to formulate a topic yourself as part of the assignment. In either case, it is essential to become aware of the scope of the topic, of its terms and limitations. In preparing to write an essay on an assigned topic, you will usually undertake some systematic reading, perhaps augmented with library research. Sometimes, you will begin with an impression, later developed into a hypothesis that has to be proved from some passages in the text under consideration. You might also begin with a problem or contradiction that the text or issue raises, or with an idea that needs to be developed, again with specific citation and documentation. In any case, you will eventually develop several hypotheses about the text or problem, and as you "assay" or test these hypotheses, you will begin to construct the thesis of the essay, the central argument that is to be made in the course of the essay. In traditional rhetoric, this development of the kinds of arguments to be used in defending the thesis is called the discovery stage.

Almost all academic work is done according to specific instructions about the topic and scope of your paper, the kind of essay you are to write, the number of texts you are to use, and so on. It is impossible to overstate the importance of considering carefully the terms of your assignment. Neglecting this step leads not only to mechanical mistakes in formatting or to dealing with too few texts but also to the more general criticism—which we have all received at one time or another—that we failed to answer the question or to address the topic. In what follows, we outline steps to ensure that you examine closely the terms of an assignment. These steps can be applied to any assigned work in university courses. In chapters that follow, we discuss in detail how to research and write academic papers; however, at this point, which we might call the pre-writing stage, it is important to assess the terms and requirements of an assignment in order to position yourself effectively.

The first step upon receiving the assignment is to separate this subject matter from the formal requirements. If the assignment says to write on "at least two texts from the course syllabus," or to hand in a paper of "six to eight pages," or whatever, then you need to comply with these instructions. At this stage of assessing the assignment, you need not decide exactly how you will follow some of these specifications—for instance, you may consider four texts from the course as a basis upon which to narrow your final choice of two. Your work at this stage may be recuperated later in at least two ways: (1) the broader your range in thinking about the topic, the more you will have to work with in choosing the most effective texts and examples from which to make your argument, and (2) specific examples from texts that you do not select can be used as points of illustration, comparison, and contrast throughout your argument, not only clarifying it but also demonstrating a more extensive reading knowledge of the course materials. But in the end, you must follow the formal requirements unless given permission to do otherwise.

The second step upon receiving an assignment is to look at its terms to figure out what kinds of skills you are being asked to demonstrate. Most undergraduate essays follow a format of stating or assuming an abstract concept, a theme, a mode of character analysis, an historiographical principle, a psychological phenomenon, and so on and then asking you to apply that concept to a limited number of texts or documents. In some cases, it is clear from the instructions and from the mode of presentation in the course that this concept or analytical principle is really not open to question; in other cases, the terms of the question and the mode of the course encourage questioning, qualification, and perhaps even the rejection of these concepts. In either case, the essential skill that you will be asked to demonstrate usually involves moving between these two levels—the principle and the application.

The third step is to consider carefully the ways in which the organizing concepts or abstract principles, or themes or topics, are framed or expressed in the assignment. We give examples below to show what we mean here. Key words or operative terms in the assignment indicate the scope of your topic. A common strategy instructors use in framing an assignment is to give a quotation that states a definite position about a topic. This quotation or statement accomplishes two things: (1) it directs and limits the topic, and (2) it establishes a firm position to be qualified, or agreed or disagreed with. This quotation is often followed by a statement of qualification or by a series of questions that reflect on the quotation in a supposedly neutral way. The important tasks here are to find the key concepts and to draw relationships between the position stated in the quotation and the qualifications introduced in the following statement; you then will be able to state your own position regarding the topic. At the pre-writing stage, you need not have a specific position already formulated, but you should have a clear sense of the range of possibilities within the assignment.

Assignment Examples

In considering the following two examples of assignments, you should not get bogged down in the specifics of their content but, rather, try to understand the principles we are stressing. At the pre-writing stage, you should think about the operative terms of the question, the limitation of the topic, the resources that you have or need to work within these limits, and the research that will be required. Then, you can take preliminary steps in planning the time available to ensure that you do not neglect any phase in the writing process.

EXAMPLE 1:

Here is a typical essay question that might be assigned in a course on Victorian literature:

Quotation

> "Themes of anxiety, disillusion, and despair are prevalent in all the works of Thomas Hardy."

Instructor's Commentary: Re-directing the Quotation, or Setting the Groundwork for the Argument

This critical evaluation was conventional until the 1980s; however, recent commentators have qualified themes of despair in Hardy's works by noting his strategies of maintaining hope and even optimism in the face of cosmic gloom.

Formal Requirements

Write an essay of eight to ten pages in which you discuss at least one poem and a novel in relation to despair and optimism.

This assignment example specifies consideration of an author within a range of operative terms that can be summarized as moving between hope and despair. The qualifications indicate that recent commentators have re-assessed the earlier conventional position.

In establishing your position, therefore, you must consider two areas: (1) the *themes* of despair and hope in Hardy's works, and (2) the ways in which critics reading Hardy *have changed* their emphases. Within these limitations, wide possibilities are open to you in forming and arguing your position. However, in order to do so, *you will have to address both levels of the question: the themes and the critical readings.* Hence, in considering the research necessary, you will have to have adequate knowledge of Hardy's work as well as of the critics' positions. Finally, you are governed by the limitation of length, by the choice of critics, and by the choice of a novel and a poem. You will likely have enough material for a much longer paper and, thus, will have to select the best examples to use in the most effective arguments. The choice of critics, novels, and poems again opens possibilities for you. Although your choice will likely be determined by the readings in the course, expanding this range will add depth and persuasiveness to your position.

The assignment also leaves open the possibility for at least two fundamental disagreements: (1) that themes other than despair and hope are "prevalent," and (2) that the critics' positions have not fundamentally changed since the 1980s. While these levels of disagreement are logically possible from the terms of the question, they should be used with caution, as to address them requires considerable expertise. In any case, you can see the point: an assignment's instructions, when read with a critical attitude, open up numerous possibilities for you to position yourself within a set of logical options.

EXAMPLE 2:

Here is a typical essay question that might be assigned in a course on Canadian history:

Generalization or Assertion

Canadian society changed radically in the period from 1880 to 1920.

Instructor's Commentary: Re-directing the Statement, or Setting the Groundwork for the Argument

Through a consideration of immigration, urbanization, and industrialization, discuss the benefits and disadvantages of these changes.

Formal Requirements

An essay of 10 to 12 pages.

The second assignment example posits "change" in a specific historical period as a given and then goes on to specify three areas to consider in explaining the change. The topic introduces the possibility of making some judgment about the value of each area in explaining the change, but it does not require you to do so (as in the Hardy assignment, concerning "recent commentators"). Your range of choice in disagreeing with the statement is much more limited than in the first example. To disagree by arguing that there was little or no change or that there were other more important categories than the three specified changes the assignment in ways that you probably should check with your instructor.

You establish your position in this assignment with the instructor's qualification that these changes are to be explained as *benefits* or *disadvantages*. These qualitative terms force you to ask the question, *For whom were they benefits or disadvantages?* In answering this question, you are required to establish a reasoned position; therefore, your thinking and research should be directed to examining a range of possibilities within the specific areas indicated. Note that the instructions do not require an *either/or logic:* that is, the changes could be *both* benefits to some *and* disadvantages to others.

Finally, the formal requirements do not specify the materials you are to consider: statistics, economic or demographic analyses, secondary sources or scholarly positions, and so on. The course materials are an obvious place to start. *After* you have done some preliminary reading and have some specific questions to ask about other kinds of sources you might use, there are two strategies to pursue. (1) You might consult your instructor; often, however, an instructor will not specify method or materials, leaving you to your own devices. (2) The other possibility, then, is to consider how this kind of problem was dealt with in the course readings, lectures, and source materials and then to use one of those methods.

These two examples and our critical reading of the assignments in the pre-writing stage do not exhaust the possible kinds of assignments. Assignments may vary the order of the steps we have outlined, omit a step, or conceal the assumptions of the topic. The important thing here is to establish the limits and possibilities of the writing process in the pre-writing stage by reading the assigned topic critically. It is also important to observe that the same methods can be used in analyzing questions on examinations.

Another approach to assigning essay topics might require you to formulate your own topic. This kind of exercise also requires considerable thinking at the pre-writing stage. An effective way to formulate your strategy is to follow the same principles outlined in our reading of the two assignments above. That is, you pick a topic that interests you from the course, formulate a statement concerning it, introduce some qualifications that indicate a range of possibilities, and select the materials for analysis to conform to the length of the assignment. In much advanced undergraduate work, such as honours theses or in post-graduate work up to the Ph.D. dissertation, you can follow the same procedures.

CONSIDERING YOUR AUDIENCE

We have now considered in some detail one of the key strategic aspects of performing effectively in academic work—the ability to position yourself in relation to the possibilities and objectives of what you are being asked to do in your coursework. We now turn to another strategic point, the consideration of your audience. Such considerations are crucial in judging various aspects of your mode of address, such as word choice, the level of argument, and many other decisions that constantly come up as you are writing or preparing a class presentation.

Considering Your Audience in Written Assignments

Your audience for written assignments in university courses is usually limited to one reader, your instructor. You can assume that he or she has read the books and knows the concepts of the course, so you do not have to waste time on plot outlines or explaining concepts as though you were writing the paper for a different audience. You should not "dumb down" your arguments and style to the level of a reader who is ignorant of your topic.

Finding the right "voice" is not an easy thing for many students. Generally, it is a good policy to adopt the style of the kinds of books and articles that the instructors recommend in the course. Just as importantly, you should be judicious about not writing in the mode of sensationalist journalism or book blurbs in an analytical essay. Such phrases as "wonderful book," "splendidly written," "excellent economic [or military] strategy" most often indicate empty assertions based on hollow clichés—critical thinking involves reading and writing that challenge or question such clichés and engages with the terms and arguments of the course's reading and lectures. Most university instructors will be put off by such undemonstrated and extravagant assertions.

You are demonstrating your academic skills and are being evaluated for your use of academic skills, and so, you should strive for an appropriate pitch directed to your audience. Consideration of your audience does not mean tailoring your arguments to what you think your instructor might agree with; rather, it means being conscious of the language and strategies of argument appropriate to the level and purpose of your assignment.

In writing other than academic essays, a different consideration of audience is necessary: you should take into account the background knowledge of your audience on a particular topic, their expectations, the appropriate degree of difficulty in concepts and diction, and the specific mode of presentation effective for that audience. For instance, if you were writing a journalistic piece for the student newspaper, you would have to consider your audience and lower the level of assumed knowledge—they would not have the specialized knowledge of the particular course that you studied.

Writing an academic essay to defend a thesis, present information, analyze an argument, or criticize a text or document is a skill you learn. In Parts III and IV of *Foundations,* we take you through the research, planning, and writing stages of written assignments. If you can write an academic assignment well, you will get good grades because your arguments will be taken seriously. If you write poorly, with weak punctuation, faults in standard English grammar, spelling mistakes, and feeble use of examples, logic, and quotations, you will receive low grades. The skills learned in writing an essay, in analyzing and presenting your ideas, can be exported to any course and are essential after university. At every stage in the preparation of arguments, it is necessary to make choices about how to write effectively for the audience and about how to write as though one were an expert.

Considering Your Audience in Class Presentations

Many courses require you to make seminar presentations to your classmates. Making an oral presentation in a smaller class is an important skill, useful later in life when you have to summarize your ideas to make them convincing for others. For many students, presenting is an extremely intimidating experience: it is normal that you should feel anxious and nervous. Such feelings are common and to be expected, so make them work for you. The nervous tension is like that of an athlete before a game or a musician or actor before a performance. These presentations give you a chance to demonstrate, in an isolated instance, your grasp of the course materials and your ability to work with them.

Classroom presentations raise questions about the appropriate audience and your position with regard to that audience. Your purpose in class presentations is usually to present information, arguments, and interpretations and to provide a basis for discussion. Often, you determine the focus of the topic, within the week's readings and any additional readings you select and within the guidelines for presentations that have been distributed or discussed in class. You should follow any specific instructions scrupulously. You should undertake your preparation and presentation in close discussion with group members if you are working as a team. After you have thought about the topic well in advance of the presentation and have looked up some of the information about it, you need to discuss your approach with your instructor.

Different courses and disciplines will have different expectations about what is to be done in a classroom presentation. An instructor might want a summary of the week's readings or a summary followed by some form of analysis of readings, data, arguments or positions, or problems. You are usually expected to assume that everyone in the class has read the assigned material. Many students have been taught to assume that their audience knows nothing, that the material has to be explained from the ground up, or that the audience is made up of literate but non-specialist readers or listeners who are unfamiliar with the course materials. Such a view is often manifested at the beginning of a class presentation or an essay when a nervous student explains what the book is and who the author is—facts already evident to the whole class from the syllabus. On the other hand, however, you have to accept the fact, especially if your presentation is toward the end of the term, that most of your classmates will not have completed or even begun the readings on which your presentation is based. While it is best to pretend that they have read it, resist asking factual questions about obvious details of the readings. Such questions are often used by instructors to gauge whether a class has been keeping up with their assigned readings. You are not, however, in that position of authority and should not put your classmates in such an awkward position. They will be embarrassed or hostile. So, help them out by avoiding such questions on matters of fact and help them follow along your line of enquiry.

You need to ask yourself, "To whom am I speaking?" The answer is, usually to your fellow students. However, while you can assume that the rest of the class has some familiarity with the material (and you, like the seminar leader, must assume that all have done the assigned readings), you cannot expect that they will know the definitions of technical terms or difficult concepts or that they will have the background information that you have acquired in preparing for your presentation. Hence, you should speak with some authority and assurance, but from your reading, you will also be aware that you have selected only several aspects of the material to highlight and that your treatment, while comprehensive, is not exhaustive. That is not to say that you are seeking an edge over your classmates or that you are engaging in intellectual bullying or mental aggression. Instead, you, along with your classmates, will be expected to raise questions about what you do not understand, to have a position on the course readings and lectures up to that point, and to be able to articulate the course's goals, methods, and interim conclusions.

Your preparation involves getting ready for the actual presentation, part of the work that many students do not allow enough time for. Your rehearsal of the presentation should include going over it in detail by yourself in front of a mirror or with a friend. If you will be speaking from notes, rather than a completed text, use them. However, do not follow notes slavishly, and even in rehearsing from a text that is fully written out, practise looking up and speaking to your imaginary audience. You need to watch your timing during practice, but probably, you will go faster in class (because of nervousness) than in the rehearsal.

A class presentation should have a planned, coherent structure. This structure is important not only because it gives your presentation a shape and direction but also because it allows you to put controls on the time allotted for your presentation. Your structure (unless the instructions indicate otherwise) should probably be based on the same principles as a written essay (discussed in Chapters 10 and 11). It should have an introduction; a thesis statement that ties together the specifics of what and how you will be presenting; a body, divided up into separate sections, in which you make your case; and a conclusion in which you can summarize and perhaps suggest further questions to pursue following your line of reasoning.

During the presentation put some energy and conviction into your voice and manner. That is not to say that you should be overly dramatic—no pounding of the table—but be enthusiastic; since what you are presenting is important to you, make it important to the class, too. Be aware of your body language, your voice, and your eyes: do not be afraid to use your hands and arms, vary your voice, and look at your audience. Be sure also to keep within your time limit, but do not rush: people want to take in what you are saying. Remember not to speak too fast: if you find yourself doing so, take a few deep breaths to slow down.

Dealing with questions and interruptions during a presentation is often a problem. Try to find out from your teacher beforehand if interruptions take away from your time. Answer questions clearly and completely, but do not get distracted into side issues. If there are several questions, you can group them together. You could ask another student to be a recorder for you to jot down the questions and then respond to them later. If there is something that you do not want to respond to then (perhaps you are in the middle of a complicated point), you could say, "That is a good question, but I wonder if we could consider it just a little later or at the end of the presentation." Then, do not forget to return to it.

As the presentation is in progress or at the end, the students and the instructor might ask you to define your terms, to explain further difficult concepts, or to clarify your method: "Why did you choose to do this?" and "Why did you do it this way?" You must be prepared to field these questions. It is best to relate the presentation to the details of the texts or assignments for the week—for example, by stressing the application of the week's methods to the material to be read by considering some of the issues that the lecture or the readings raised. You can stress two or three particular questions that you bring to the topic, text, or problem, such as an application of theory to different materials: "I have argued that … and have shown how such-and-such can be applied to three examples. Now, how do you think the same argument can be applied to something quite different, for example…." Or you could see how the class responds to extending the argument by asking: "If you had to push the argument in this or that direction, how might that be done?" Such questions challenge the class to push the topic further and give directions about how to proceed, how to open up the topic, or how to raise some further questions at the end to prompt further discussion. Make sure you have considered ways to get the class started in asking these questions. That is, be prepared to give them the opening steps of an answer if you are met with silence.

A hand-out with some of the data (dates, names, key points, technical information, terms), thesis statement, outline, and a short bibliography is useful. Alternatively, you could write an outline of your presentation on the blackboard or on an overhead sheet beforehand. Secondary reading may or may not be required, but it may be helpful; the presentation should be based on your careful reading, thinking, and preparation.

In large classes or seminars, where the discussion time is limited, your presentation is one of the best opportunities you have to display your skills in organization, argument, and response to questions on a topic on which you are something of an authority. It is a good chance to demonstrate your understanding of course materials, to formulate a coherent position, and to address these materials at a level appropriate to your audience.

It helps to learn from others' experiences, so if you can avoid making the first one or two presentations of the term you will see how they go and what the professor's expectations are; however, if you are assigned one of the first few presentations, you should keep in mind that most professors make allowances for inexperienced presenters. Finally, get some feedback from your classmates about how it went so that you can build on your strengths. Your instructor should also be able to give you some tips about improvements you can make and will probably be willing to discuss what you said and how you said it. Make an office appointment for later when you have had time yourself to reflect on your presentation.

CRITICAL ATTITUDES IN ELECTRONIC LEARNING ENVIRONMENTS

In Chapter 1, we discussed how to take notes in small classes, seminars, or tutorials. In fact, you will find that most of these classes will continue to use traditional course requirements, such as assigned readings, preparation for tutorials by coming with a set of responses to the readings, class presentations, essays, and so on. Some of your classes will also be linked in various ways using computers and e-mail or discussion groups, either for group work or for commenting on each other's work in ways that we discussed in Chapter 2. We comment in this section on some of those technologies for use in a variety of different classroom situations. In each of them you will be able to contribute best when you are aware that your contribution to the discussion—whether to your professor, an e-mail correspondent, or a group—is being evaluated by your readers. They are your audience, and all that we have said above about writing and presenting to your audience also applies in communicating using new technologies.

E-Mail

At the most basic level, your key connection with electronic learning, or e-learning as it is called, is your e-mail. Through e-mail, you can connect with your instructor in a regular class or routinely, sometimes as part of the requirements for a course, in an electronic-based course, such as those in distance learning. By this means also, you will be able to communicate with other students in your classes, exchanging messages, information, Web sites, and attachments (documents, graphics, Web pages, software, and so on).

Since most students already have their own e-mail addresses, we do not go into the details of how to do that here. Suffice it to say that you can get free e-mail through your Web browser or through your home university—consult your computer help desk. Instead, here, we are concerned with how a critical attitude can help you make best use of your electronic communications.

Many students are familiar with chat lines in which people talk with one another about any number of things, sometimes just to get acquainted or pass the time, and sometimes to find out information about a particular subject. It is common for all sorts of abbreviations to creep into those conversations, such as "How r u?" or "lol" (laughing out loud). While such shorthand is useful for quick and informal chat, it is not an appropriate medium to use in communicating with your instructor or fellow students. While e-mail is less formal than writing an essay, you can go overboard: such abbreviations, in fact, can be very annoying to both instructors and students and might greatly interfere with your presentation of yourself.

TIPS Sending E-Mail

1. E-mail is convenient, fast, and easy. But it is not necessarily private. You should be aware that you have no control over who is accessing the mail at the receiver's end of the line.

2. Good manners on the Net ("netiquette"):
   - Do not type everything in capital letters: it is considered to represent shouting and so is aggressive and rude.
   - Do not type everything in lower case letters either: that is considered mumbling.
   - Follow standard English conventions of spelling and punctuation.
   - Except for personal correspondence, keep e-mail messages brief.
   - It is also a convention to acknowledge receipt of an e-mail message, even with a simple "Thanks" or "Got it. Bye," indicating to the sender that the message got through and that you are logging off for now in this exchange.
   - The worst negative action on e-mail is flaming—sending e-mail that is overly argumentative, hostile, or even abusive.

3. If your file is too large for e-mail, you can compress it (or de-compress a message you have received) with file compression software installed on your computer, such as PKZIP from **www.pkware.com/** or WinZip from **www.winzip.com**.

You will also need an e-mail communications software program, such as Pine, Eudora, or your browser's e-mail facility, such as Hotmail (see **www.hotmail.com**). Consult the vendor's Web sites or the help boxes in your browser. You might also consult your university's computer help desk or ISP (internet service provider) for assistance in enabling your browser to receive your e-mail.

Some university classes circulate e-mail addresses for the purposes of keeping in touch or for joint classroom projects. Some set up the whole class as a distribution list (in which some or all messages can be posted to the class), following the procedures for a particular e-mail program as used by the distribution list manager. Not all members of the class, however, need to use the same e-mail software.

Some courses, especially distance learning courses and correspondence courses, ask that you submit your assignments by e-mail. In that case, you need to pay particular attention to the instructions that come with your assignment. That will include such details as whether it is to be included in your e-mail as an attachment, what format it is to be in so that your reader can easily process it on a word processor, whether it is acceptable to paste the assignment into the e-mail itself, and any other details. Above all, it is incumbent on you to keep a reliable copy of your assignment. Sometimes, e-mails do not get delivered, and you might have to re-send it. It might also be that you have to send your assignments to a central distributor at the university offering the distance learning course, and again, their technical details have to be followed to the letter to ensure that your work is received and processed correctly.

Some helpful sites for e-mail information are the following:

- A Beginner's Guide to Effective E-Mail: **www.webfoot.com/advice/email.top.html**
- E-Mail Etiquette: **www.iwillfollow.com/email.htm**

Other Web Environments

Newsgroups and discussion groups of many different kinds are available for classes to use if their topics relate to course material. Individuals can also access them. These include *HyperNews* discussion groups that are available on almost topic, making Web page information available in hypertext format. *Listservs* are e-mail discussion groups which you can subscribe to. They might be proposed in a course, or you might wish to explore them for your own interest. *Usenet Newsgroups* are public discussion groups or online forums on a huge number of topics. For detailed discussion of each of these technologies, their advantages and limitations, and how to access them, see the *Foundations* Web site.

Finally, the Internet has many interest groups that are accessible directly on the Internet itself through your Web browser. For instance, there are discussion groups maintained by the major word processors that allow users to correspond about the virtues and defects of their programs or to seek advice about how to overcome difficulties. There are also user groups for all kinds of medical conditions, for specific kinds of pets, for historical events (such as the military history of World War II), for popular culture (such as *Star Trek*), and so on. These user groups are normally located not by searching for the discussion group but by activating a link to them on a Web page that you have already found. Such discussions contain a lot of trivial information as well as some useful contributions. The trick here, as with all newsgroups and listservs, not to mention Web pages in general, is to evaluate what you find and to adopt and use your critical attitude.

CHAPTER SUMMARY

In Chapter 3, we have covered what you need to know and practise about developing a critical attitude. In a sense, we have stressed what it is to be self-conscious and self-reflexive about your position in the university classroom, about how you present yourself. With this self-reflexive or critical attitude, you are now becoming proficient in the following areas:

- You are now able to implement a critical attitude that knows the differences between an opinion and a position.
- You can stress your own analysis, rather than only relying upon others or repeating the analysis of authorities.
- You are well prepared to read the instructions of an assignment critically, can assess your audience, and can address that audience in written and classroom presentations.
- You are aware of and are beginning to use new computer environments and technologies of communication and information sharing in the university.

Having become self-reflexive about your position, you can now turn to ways of applying those new critical attitudes to more sophisticated reading skills, strategies that will be presented in the next chapter.

FURTHER READINGS

Bowell, Tracy, and Gary Kemp. *Critical Thinking: A Concise Guide*. London: Routledge, 2002.

Browne, M. Neil, and Stuart M. Keeley. *Asking the Right Questions: A Guide to Critical Thinking*. Upper Saddle River, NJ: Prentice-Hall, 1998.

Dussart, Georges. *Biosciences on the Internet: A Student's Guide*. Chichester, NY: John Wiley, 2002.

Fallon, Thomas. *The Internet Today*. Upper Saddle River, NJ: Prentice Hall, 2001.

Fisher, Alec. *Critical Thinking: An Introduction*. Cambridge: Cambridge UP, 2001.

Fleet, Joan, Fiona Goodchild, and Richard Zajchowski. *Learning for Success: Skills and Strategies for Canadian Students*. 2nd ed. Toronto: Harcourt Brace, 1994.

Gordon, Jeffrey. *The University in Your Life*. Madison, WI: Brown and Benchmark, 1996.

Inch, Edward S., and Barbara Warnick. *Critical Thinking and Communication: The Use of Reason in Argument*. 3rd ed. Boston: Allyn and Bacon, 1998.

Lieb, Anthony. *Speaking for Success: The Canadian Guide*. Toronto: Harcourt Brace, 1993.

Porter, Burton F. *The Voice of Reason: Fundamentals of Critical Thinking*. New York: Oxford UP, 2002.

Ruggiero, Vincent Ryan. *The Art of Thinking: A Guide to Critical and Creative Thought*. New York: Longman, 1998.

chapter four

Developing Critical Reading Strategies

From your first class, you are aware of the pressure on you to read faster and better. You hear your professor's instructions, "Read the first two chapters of the textbook and the first two articles in the Course Kit, and be prepared to discuss them at the next class." No other instructions. In what way are you supposed to read them? Discuss them? Will there be a surprise quiz? How do you begin?

To benefit most from university courses, you must cultivate ways of becoming an active and efficient reader. From the start, teachers expect their students not only to keep up with course readings but also to be engaged and thoughtful in their comprehension of them.

LEARNING OBJECTIVES

This chapter introduces effective strategies for reading in different kinds of courses and for assignments and answers questions about how to develop more advanced reading skills:

- How can you increase your reading comprehension?

- How does the way you were taught to read still influence how you read now?

- How do you skim texts for an overview? When is this skill acceptable?

- How can you prepare outlines and summaries of your readings?

- How do you draw links with other readings in this particular course or with other courses?
- How can you annotate your readings?
- How can you learn to increase your reading speed?
- What do you do if you suspect you have a reading disability?
- How can you combine analysis with reading for content and information?
- How do you annotate e-texts on your computer?
- What different reading skills should you develop to read in different disciplines?
- How can you read film, TV, and other media critically?

WHAT IS CRITICAL READING?

Reading is a process of acquiring meaning from a text, whether it is printed, electronic, musical, or visual (architecture, artwork, film, or video). Reading such texts involves a reader in the acquisition of vocabulary, factual knowledge, and relational meaning. *Critical reading* at its simplest involves reading any text with interest, comprehension, and a questioning frame of mind. You look not only for what an author is saying but also for the links in argument, the bridges from one point to another, the patterns of words and thoughts, and the stated and unstated assumptions. You will be reading to question the validity of the argument, and so, you will be engaged in ongoing analysis. And when you are done, you will be able to summarize the main points of the argument and to offer a critique of it, stating its strong and weak points. Best of all, this reading process will happen with increasingly greater efficiency and ease as you become more accustomed to practising it. Then you will find that far from being intimidated by your weekly reading assignments, you will be well prepared to begin them and to carry them out effectively.

Many recent studies on the preparedness of students for university work indicate that the most serious problem that students have is an inability to read critically in the way we have described. These skills of critical reading are not widely taught, and many students either do not know they have problems or lack an interest in improving their reading on their own, but by working through this chapter, you will see that help is at hand.

Above all, critical reading is an integral part of critical thinking. When you have learned how to exercise these skills, your reading and thinking will become part of the same learning process and your work will improve.

HOW DID YOU LEARN TO READ? THE CONTROVERSY ABOUT TEACHING READING SKILLS

You probably learned to read in elementary school either by recognizing whole words (the whole language method), by sounding out your ABCs (the phonics method), or by a combination of both. The linking of reading to spelling and writing has roots that go back to such books as Solomon Lowe's *Critical Spelling-book* (1755).

The merits of different methods of teaching reading have been heatedly debated by educational experts over many years but recently have achieved a balance that combines both methods. In our view the neglecting of phonics training over this period has hampered university students in reading complicated texts and coping with technical terminology. For more detail on this topic, see the *Foundations* Web site.

In Chapter 5, we discuss ways of expanding your reading skills by building a critical vocabulary and using words with knowledge and precision. The rest of this chapter proposes practical ways of using and improving your reading skills.

PRACTICAL READING STRATEGIES

Whether you are reading a book for a course or for pleasure, in an area of knowledge that you are studying in detail or about which you know little, at an introductory or advanced level, there are some basic approaches to reading that will greatly increase your comprehension and your pleasure. We summarize some introductory reading strategies here and later discuss several more intensive methods and modes of reading in different subject areas.

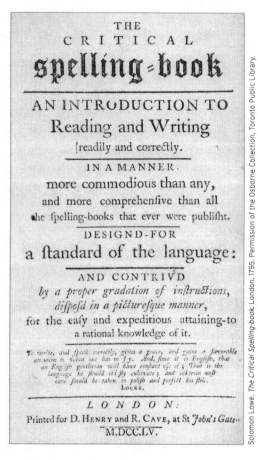

Solomon Lowe. *The Critical Spelling-book.* London, 1755. Permission of the Osborne Collection, Toronto Public Library.

Strategies to Increase Comprehension and Retention

Most reading assignments are remarkably similar in all courses. You are expected to read the number of assigned pages, understand them (in the sense of knowing what they mean, what they are saying, and how they are saying it), and be able to respond to them with some comprehension. In all likelihood, you are also expected to be able to retain the points of the reading for later work in the course—to understand the lecture or seminar better, to build on the information you already have, or to extend the dimensions of the topic. But how are you to begin?

We list nine preliminary strategies to increase your comprehension and retention of what you read. These strategies are intended to get you started in becoming a more engaged reader. You can adapt them or add to them as you become more self-reflexive about the reading process. The general thrust of these strategies is to have you begin to consider a reading as a dialogue in which you participate with the text in constructing meaning.

Distinguishing Primary from Secondary Readings

In many disciplines, such as English, history, and philosophy, a distinction is drawn between *primary* and *secondary* works or texts. It is important for you to know the differences between these two orders of classification. In the simplest terms, a primary work is the text to be analyzed; a secondary text is the analysis, summary, or interpretation of the primary text. Secondary readings that are devoted to a specific topic of research are often called monographs (Greek *monos,* alone; *graphein,* to write; written on one particular subject).

In other words, a primary text in literature is a work of fiction, poetry, a play, or other writing by an author whom you are studying. The designation primary refers to a work's status as a first-line object of study. Then, works by critics about such novels or poems are called secondary because they interpret or analyze the primary texts. In history and political science, a primary text might be treaties, speeches, letters, records of cabinet discussions, diaries, government documents, or public records (such as records of graveyards for the names of immigrants in a statistical survey). Secondary works in history are written by historians who interpret the past by analyzing or summarizing it. In philosophy, primary texts are the works written by important philosophers in the history of the field, such as Plato or Berkeley's *Dialogues,* Descartes or Rousseau's *Discourses,* and Bacon or Derrida's *Essays.* Secondary texts in philosophy are commentaries on such writers or on the kinds of issues they raise.

Often, you only have access to primary sources indirectly through references in the secondary works. You could go back to look at those primary sources to question or reassess them. Two further points should be made. Many primary works, such as works of literature, philosophical treatises, diaries and letters of famous people, government records, and important political documents, are readily available in published sources or on the Internet. Further, most introductory courses (particularly in the fields of history, political science, economics, philosophy, sociology, and others) use textbooks, which, by and large, are summary and commentary on a discipline's major ideas, set out in an order that is either thematic or chronological. Such texts usually insert into this commentary some excerpts from primary works. So, for instance, an introductory textbook in political science would probably have a chapter on Karl Marx into which might be inserted excerpts from his most famous works, the *Communist Manifesto* and *Capital.* The fact that these primary works of Marx are commentaries on and interpretations of previous political philosophers and analysis of data taken from government records does not matter: Marx's importance within the discipline makes these works primary documents.

Many recent critical reading practices developed over the past 30 or 40 years, stressing such words as *intertextuality, deconstruction, discourse analysis,* or *post-structuralism,* challenge or reject the distinction between primary and secondary works. This challenge is based on theories of language and history that presuppose that all texts are both reinterpretations of previous texts and are, in a sense, primary as cultural documents on their own right and within their own historical context. Despite these challenges, however, the distinction between primary and secondary works is fundamental at introductory levels, and fundamental in developing a critical strategy. Somewhere in your first two years of study you will undoubtedly need to make this distinction.

Skimming for an Overview or Preview

Experienced academic readers skim books all the time, and they have learned to skim with efficiency and purpose. They avoid the temptation that many inexperienced readers fall into, of beginning to read from page one with as much attention as possible and continuing until they are too tired to persevere or have to give up from frustration. Reading is a process of several stages. An experienced critical reader will often go through the entire contents of a book or article from beginning to end several times, separating major concepts or the organization of the argument from the data, examples, or specific details that are used as evidence. In the first few stages, experienced critical readers do not get bogged down in the details of the evidence or minute qualifications. Instead, they go for an overview; that is, they skim a text several times for its general shape and argument, before moving, if ever, to the details. Skimming by such methods is not an open permission to avoid close reading or to ignore the details of evidence or argument: it is a means of locating that material so that it can be followed up later, if necessary.

Other readers want particular information from a book and go immediately to the index to see if the topic is included there. If not, they quickly check related terms and might look over the "works cited" list or bibliography to see if an author who customarily deals with such a topic is listed. If so, that name is looked up in the index, and that section of the book is consulted. Such a process is very fast and highly efficient, but it requires precision in your choice of topic and some knowledge of a few related topics or terms.

Even glancing over a book from start to finish because you have no time for more systematic reading can be useful. If you are looking it over because you have budgeted your time poorly and just need to have some acquaintance with the text before class, knowing how to use skimming skills will help you. Skimming, however, is not a substitute for careful and systematic reading. However, for many books, it is all you will have time to do. Skimming a book, if done purposefully, can give a vital overview, or it can be a preview to a more systematic and analytical reading.

Skimming means that you look over a whole book or article to determine the general organization and contents. Reviewing the table of contents in a book or the sub-headings in a chapter or an article is the quickest way to determine what the text covers. Perhaps you are used to skipping, rather than skimming, the boldfaced or italicized passages that highlight the organization of a section of a book. In skimming, it is important not only to notice these signals but also to see how they fit together. Often, there is a point being made in the arrangement of chapter headings or sub-headings: perhaps they are set out chronologically, conceptually, or cumulatively. Authors want you to be able to recognize the way that their ideas are put together, so skimming such headings for clues gives you an important preview of the argument. Sometimes, the book's purpose and argument are outlined in the preface or introduction in a little more detail. Sometimes, there are comments there, too, about a book's intended audience or about the situation for which the author is writing.

Skimming can also mean that you move from chapter titles and headings to some of the content of the chapters. Many experienced readers look at the opening of chapters or the first paragraphs of an article, where authors often summarize their goals and positions. The final chapter and the last paragraphs often summarize the argument again or place it in a wider perspective. Reading over these sections quickly will enable you to comprehend the book's or article's range and methods. Then, you can narrow your focus in skimming the chapters or sections that are particularly interesting or relevant to you. When you look them over, you can read the opening and closing sentences of paragraphs to get the gist of the argument, noting any lists of points set off by numbers or paragraphs that enumerate them: "First ... second ... and third," or "The four most important causes of the...."

Key words are also important to this overview—*reasons, causes, results, effects,* and so on. The argument may also be organized to balance both sides of a question, so you should be alert to signals of arguments for and against (such as the use of "On the one hand ... on the other hand...."). Italicized type is sometimes used in definitions, which can be a great help to you in understanding how important concepts are being used. The repetition of arguments in slightly different terms or as summaries (sometimes with such a phrase as "In other words ...") will help you comprehend the main concepts. Finally, if there is a glossary at the end of the article or book, it will introduce you to technical terms and special meanings. For instance, in *Foundations,* each chapter begins and ends with lists of questions and goals. Skimming the beginning and end of every chapter, then, will give you an idea of the entire contents of the book. After you have completed your skimming of a text, you will know how the argument is organized and where it is proceeding and can then go back for more concentrated reading, from which you will reap much greater understanding and pleasure.

TIPS Skimming

1. Note the author and what angle the title takes on the field of study.

2. Study the table of contents or headings to discover the range and coherence of the materials covered. Note boldfaced sub-headings.

3. Survey the preface or introduction to find a summary of the book's argument and audience.

4. Scan the opening chapter and/or paragraphs for a summary of the argument.

5. Scan the last chapter and/or paragraphs for a summary of the argument and a discussion of its implications.

6. Zero in on the main topic or section that concerns you, and read the opening and closing sentences in each paragraph. Do not get distracted and read what is in between. You are looking for the general shape of the discussion.

7. Go back and note any itemized or numbered lists or places where key stages are stressed.

8. Note key phrases, such as *the main point, the chief reason, three issues,* or *the key idea.*

9. Note points of transition in the argument by key words: *in contrast, on the other hand, however,* and so on.

10. Note words and definitions that are set in italics or bold type.

11. Scan the index for terms or concepts relevant to your topic, and check the references for other pertinent books.

Reading Actively

To read actively means that you approach any reading with a positive attitude as well as a critical attitude (see Chapter 3). Do not regard your reading of an article, textbook, or other assignment as a duty that just has to be done, as a boring imposition, or as a waste of your time—such attitudes ensure that you will get little from what you read. Instead, regard each reading as a helper or tutor in the course, improving your understanding and assisting your success.

To read actively also means that you set a goal for yourself in your reading, usually focusing on where you are in the course and the questions raised about the text in lectures and seminars. Without such goals, you have little idea of what to concentrate on, and everything you read tends to have the same value. You are unable to focus on major themes or ideas and often miss important connections. The organization of a textbook, novel, or journal article with its headings and divisions is a help in focusing your goals. For instance, you can turn a heading into a question by using appropriate interrogatives, such as who, what, where, when, or how. Scan a few paragraphs for some interim answers. Then, take the detail a step further by inverting the first sentences of opening paragraphs into questions to get at the main points.

Reading actively also involves thinking critically as you read, assessing your attention span and focus, noting difficulties and problems, questioning the argument, and determining what is crucial and what is less important.

TIPS   Being an Active Reader

1. To get a clear overview of an argument, read the first and last sentences of each paragraph. See the Tips box on skimming above.

2. Look for the indications in the text of important information, such as when a paragraph begins with a phrase that highlights it (e.g., *most importantly*).

3. Note any unfamiliar words, and look them up in a dictionary. Keep a record of them as you build your vocabulary.

4. Learn the basic Latin prefixes of words so that you can begin to understand even unfamiliar words, such as *ante-* (before), *contra-* (against), *extra-* (outside), and *post-* (after). (See Chapter 5.)

5. Turn headings or opening sentences of paragraphs into questions, and look for answers in what follows.

Reading for the Literal

The only way to understand a text and to build your vocabulary, critical concepts, and cultural knowledge is to use a good dictionary, the course's reading aids, and other reference books. We deal with developing your vocabulary and with dictionaries in Chapter 5. To get to the literal level of any reading, you need to develop specific reading skills that we address later in this chapter. But you should also draw on other materials that will aid your comprehension of what a text means at this most basic level, namely, the accumulative meaning of the words on the page as they lay out an argument or develop a narrative.

For instance, having a few reference books of your own is an excellent investment, such as a reference guide to your major field of study (both Oxford and Cambridge publish such

"Guides" or "Companions"). You might also consider buying a CD-ROM encyclopedia to consult for unfamiliar names, historical events, places, and so on. In most cases, you do not need the latest version unless you are looking for statistics or very recent events. Reputable CD-ROM encyclopedias that are only a few years old are very inexpensive. You also will want to have easy access through the Internet to standard references for quick help when you are reading—to check a word meaning, a historical fact, some definition, or whatever you are unclear about. Such references might include the *Encyclopaedia Britannica* (**www.britannica.com**) or the Virtual Reference Desk (**www.refdesk.com**). You will want to bookmark these Web addresses (URLs) in your "Favorites" for fast access, along with others that you find useful. These points may seem obvious and even trivial; however, many students do not bother to use such simple practices to help them get the information they need for a text's literal meaning, and so, they bypass the first stage of understanding—the words and references on the page.

Reading for the Context

Among other things, critical reading involves locating the text in its own time of writing and in the context of your own reading. That is, you need to establish, at least in a preliminary way, an understanding of the text's position in history (including its cultural role and the author's credentials or biography) and of the text's position in the field in the present. You could do so by looking up reviews of this book or article in specialized journals, such as those that summarize a year's work in a field—that would at least indicate how some knowledgeable reviewers evaluate the work in relation to other scholarship. However, other information is right in front of you.

For instance, you can begin by looking at the back of the title page. This publication page sets out the publisher's details, but it also may include information about the book and the author. It will tell when the book was published, its publication history (such as earlier editions), and perhaps give the author's birth and death dates. This page also includes information about how the book is catalogued, often including the subject headings that classify it in the Library of Congress system used in most university libraries. With this information, you can search the subject headings in your university library for other books on the same subject.

You also bring all kinds of assumptions from your present context into the reading of any text. A critical reading strategy helps you become aware of and question these assumptions. We discuss reading for the context in more detail on page 101.

Preparing Outlines and Summaries

An outline is a map of a text: it lists or enumerates the main features or points in an argument, narrative, or exposition, indicating its main parts, divisions, and sub-divisions. The divisions may be marked off by numbers or letters, perhaps by using the indent-outline method (see Chapter 1). Frequently, the best way of making an outline is to do it on the computer, using your word processor's paragraph or outline functions. To make a useful outline of an article, chapter, or whole book, or of an argument, narrative, poem, or other document, you need to be aware of its general shape or structure. You should distinguish between the main line of argument and supporting ideas, illustrations, and examples, or, in narrative, between the main plot and the sub-plots or digressions.

A summary begins with an outline but moves from a list of words or points to a whole new text in your own words. This step requires creating an overview or synthesis of the text. If you use the text's actual words, you should be certain to put them in quotation marks and indicate the page references to avoid using them later as your own ideas by mistake and, thus, laying yourself open to charges of plagiarism.

Outlines and summaries are particularly useful in preparing readings for class, since they give you a written overview, providing a kind of written form of what you covered in the skimming phase. But they are also helpful in annotating books or articles that you will return to or for keeping a record of a reading that you want to document and file away. For a discussion of various ways to organize your reading notes into files on your computer, see Chapter 7.

Drawing Connections with Other Readings

As you are reading week by week in a course, you should draw relationships with previous readings by situating them within the course. This process will give you a map of the entire course, into which you can fit individual readings. As well, you might want to draw relationships with other readings in other courses, in which similar issues or historical contexts are addressed. You can do so by making quick references in your lecture notes to this or that reading, or by noting in the reading a reference to the lecture or to the topic to which you want to draw a connection.

Reading with the SQ3R Method

One widely used reading strategy is the SQ3R method, first proposed in 1946 by F. P. Robinson in *Effective Study* (1970, 4th edition), which stands for "Survey, Question, and then apply the three Rs to answer your questions: Read, Recite, and Review." This method has three stages. In the first, you survey the whole contents of the book or article you are examining, and in the second you question it. The third stage involves the three R responses to your question: read, recite, and review. In detail, the system looks like this:

1. **Survey** the whole contents of an assigned book or article when you begin it. Start with the title and what area of knowledge it points to. Include the preface, introduction, table of contents, bibliography, and index. Try to get a sense of the ideas and argument of the whole text. Read the introduction to an article or chapter, its conclusion, and the headings throughout—spend only a minute or two on this process. This stage is similar to what we describe as skimming.

2. **Question.** While you are surveying, frame a question about the introduction or first main point to increase your concentration and to develop a critical attitude. Your question can be on the level of organization or content. For instance, "What does the author argue were the main factors in Hitler's rise to power?" Or, your question may position the book's argument in relation to other works in the field. For instance, "How does this particular author modify or disagree with other explanations for Hitler's rise to power?" The second question is more difficult to formulate; however, the purpose of this stage of reading is to create a device to make you an active reader, to focus your attention as you read, and to alert you to the ways that your question is answered or modified. See if this question is answered in the paragraphs or pages that immediately follow. If you wish, you can write out your questions.

3. **3 Rs.** Finally, apply the 3 Rs:

   - **Read** to the end of the first section, trying to find answers to your questions. If you are unsuccessful, consider again the questions you asked and re-formulate them.

   - **Recite** the answer. When you finish the section, look away and try to recite the answers to your questions. Now is the time to take brief notes or underline key passages. Complete the entire chapter like this, adding to your notes. You can repeat the same procedures for other sections in the book you are surveying.

   - **Review** the argument. Re-inforce your reading by periodically recalling the main points in each section and the questions and answers you formulated in the previous stages.

Other Reading Strategies

The SQ3R method is particularly useful in reading books that have a sustained argument, but it is less successful for literary works. When reading fiction, for instance, you can follow the survey stage for the whole text and then approach each chapter as a unit in the development of the entire text. While reading, you can keep in mind some of the following traditional aspects of prose fiction:

- What can be said about the setting?
- What is its time period? Its location? Its atmosphere?
- Who is speaking, and to whom?
- What are the main events?

Some students find it helpful to write two- or three-sentence synopses, or just points to be recalled, at the end of each chapter to summarize the plot line, the characters and their interactions, to note the main events, and to pose any questions. You might also like to make your own index to the book, especially of the terms that are particularly important for the course in which you read it. Then, when you finish the book you already have it summarized, making it far more accessible for class discussions and examinations.

The same method can be used to summarize in a running fashion the content of any book you are reading. In addition, you can extend your questioning of a text to a deeper level by asking how it is constructed:

- What are its parts?
- What is its subject area or literary genre?
- What are its analytical or stylistic features?
- What does it mean, and how does it construct that meaning?

The assumptions of the text or author can also be questioned in such a reading:

- What are the theoretical assumptions of this text?
- What theory of human nature, art, or history, or other large concepts does this text assume?
- What is its audience?
- How does it deal with controversial issues of race, gender, and class?
- What are its political and social assumptions?
- On what does it rely for proof and evidence?

- Are its truth claims appeals to religious belief, morality, scientific or statistical evidence, or common sense?
- How can the text be opened up to contrary readings?

Critical reading involves planning a strategy before you begin reading any text; that is, you need to have a purpose to address the different kinds of readings that are required in university courses. Not all assigned reading is of the same level of difficulty. The techniques that follow present different critical reading skills for difficult kinds of material.

Techniques for Reading Challenging Texts

Sometimes, you will not find that the preliminary practical strategies outlined above are of sufficient help: you need more rigorous methods to apply to those readings that you find more difficult. We outline two different approaches in this section, one dealing with a demanding article or chapter and one dealing with a difficult book.

Reading an Article or a Chapter Effectively

Most courses have weekly reading assignments, consisting of chapters from a textbook, a selection from a course kit, or an article located in the university's periodical or reserve collection, where your instructor has deposited it for short-term loan. If you own the textbook or the course kit, you are free to mark it up as you choose for best comprehension (see the section on annotatiing on page 86). If it is a library book or is on deposit there, you cannot mark it and must use other reading strategies. One possibility, of course, is to photocopy the article. In any of these instances, there are specific strategies that make your critical reading of such an assignment more productive. First, you should note the name of the author and the title of the article. You will likely not have time to return to this reading, so you need to make adequate notes that you can look over before your class, assignment, and any examinations; the author's name and the title of the article will help you to locate other works by the same author, and the title will indicate the general topic. A quick read through or skimming of an article acquaints you with the author's thesis, general argument, and main points and prepares you for a more systematic reading.

Second, from this overview, you should try to re-formulate the author's thesis and argument by answering such questions as the following:

- What is the main point that the author is making?
- What question or issue is the author examining, and what does he or she conclude about it?
- What principle is being examined in this article?
- What evidence and methods are used to support it?

You might find some of this information set out clearly in the first or concluding paragraph.

Third, you are now ready for a careful reading of the whole article. You want to come away from a detailed and systematic reading with a clear sense of the author's argument, including evidence, data, and conclusions, and with a sense of how the argument is organized into major and minor arguments. Above all, you need to understand the relationship between the author's ideas or concepts and the facts or data that are used to support them.

It is important to note key transitions in the argument, along with the author's outlines, summaries, and conclusions. You should circle any words you do not understand and look them up in your dictionary.

Most readers find that it is important for their understanding at this third stage to make notes, either in the text by means of annotation if the document is your own copy or in a notebook if you are using a library copy. Underlining or copying out the thesis statement, numbering the stages in an argument, writing key definitions in the margins, and writing in questions or queries all help with understanding. You might also want to outline the main argument in your own words and perhaps summarize the conclusions of the article. Above all, you should clearly mark out or make a note about the divisions of the article—the introduction, the main points of the body of the essay (numbered, if possible), and the conclusion. Within this skeleton outline, you can go back and refine the analysis of the major points by noting the concepts, ideas, or principles and the evidence to support them, the minor parts of the argument, and so on.

Finally, you can move to some evaluation by asking and answering such questions as the following:

- Are you convinced by the argument?
- Do the data and evidence support the argument and conclusions?
- For whom is the author writing this article?
- What are the author's assumptions about the audience and the subject of the article?
- Do you see implications beyond the article's conclusions?
- How does this article relate to the rest of the course and the other readings?

Reading a Difficult Book

Many books that you will read at university are written by specialists in a field. They usually write with the assumption that their readers are other specialists, rather than undergraduates, though in your more advanced courses, you are becoming something of an expert yourself. A relatively small number of the books and articles that are assigned or that you will come across in your research are written as introductions to a field (like this book) or for the general public. That kind of book is normally found in a good public library. To use a book in your study and research you need to approach it as though you were an intelligent reader, though not necessarily a specialist in the field.

First, the skimming approach outlined above is most useful to you in reading a difficult book. You have probably already begun the process of skimming just by looking over the book in the library, checking the title, contents, and general range of the work. Now, you can skim more systematically.

Second, you should get down to the reading of the book, refusing to become bogged down in passages that you do not understand but also refusing to just let them drift by. If you do not understand something that seems crucial, it is a good idea to note the location and return to it later after you have read further. Chances are, you will later understand it far more readily. Looking up all of the footnotes and references will slow you down. The purpose of this initial reading is to acquaint you with the argument in general and with some detail.

Third, after the first quick reading, you can return to the same chapters or passages and read them more carefully. In all probability, you will already have fallen into this habit in your skimming stage as you were attracted or challenged by part of the argument and stopped there to get it in detail before moving on. In this penultimate stage, you will likely want to make some notes for future reference. In any case, you will likely not have time to go back to the book again and so will have to rely on the notes that you make now. You should be certain to copy any direct quotations accurately (including the punctuation) and to make a careful note of the reference (author, title, place of publication, publisher, date, and page numbers).

Finally, you can skim over the book again to make certain that you have all of the information from it that you need and that you have the arguments and data copied down accurately.

Annotating

In general, careful and speedy annotation is fundamental to each of these strategies. Mechanical highlighting of page after page, either continuously or in a random fashion without any thought-out strategic principles, makes little sense. It is better to annotate in pencil, marking clearly the points that you want to record from the text.

Annotating Readings for Lectures and Seminars

If a particular passage is to be discussed in a lecture or seminar to illustrate specific points of argument or rhetoric, you should mark and annotate it. Many critical readers annotate their own books (not library books) by using some of the following methods:

- Underlining key words, phrases, or sentences
- Writing brief comments or questions about difficult passages in the margins
- Marking important sections of the text
- Drawing connections between ideas through numbering ideas in sequence
- Drawing arrows
- Using question marks or other shorthand annotations to indicate concepts you do not understand or points that are particularly important for your reading

Many readers make indexes of important words or concepts inside the back cover. Others annotate monographs by writing an outline or summary (see above) or a statement of the thesis and conclusions at the end of a chapter. Similarly, they annotate fiction by writing a brief summary of the action, setting, and characters at the end of a chapter. Such practices give you important ways of quickly reviewing your entire reading list at the end of the course.

Annotation Styles in Different Subject Areas

It may seem obvious, but it needs to be pointed out that different subject areas use different kinds of writing styles and so demand different kinds of reading practices. Science subjects depend on classification and process, stress problem-solving methods, may introduce instructions on experiments, and summarize evidence and statistics. In the social sciences, definitions of concepts shape the argument, which proceeds with details and illustrations as evidence. Kinds of argument include comparison and contrast, cause and effect, and complicated arguments that move through the addition of layer after layer. In humanities subjects, some texts are constructed analytically, like those in the social sciences. Others are read for the narrative, as in fiction. But here, too, a reader can use critical thinking and analytical tools to question the narrative. Making reading notes is like making lecture notes, and some of the same methods can be followed. The concept-mapping and indent-outline methods are particularly helpful (see Chapter 1).

TIPS Annotating Your Own Copy of a Book

1. Mark up your text appropriately if it is your own copy. *Do not mark up library copies*—other readers' purposes might be quite different from yours. Underlining in your personal copy is useful for the *most significant* passages, but underlining or highlighting whole pages simply means that you know how to run your hand, not your mind, over the page. It is better to throw away your highlighter and use a pencil to add quick comments.

2. Draw connections and relationships between ideas in the text.

3. Number the stages of the argument in the margins to keep track of them.

4. Take some notes on what you read, choosing a method appropriate to the book and the assignment.

5. If you record quotations, record them accurately and note the source. Save time by doing it now, rather than later, when another reader may have borrowed the book from the library. Be careful not to incorporate these quotations into your essays without acknowledgment.

Reading and Annotating E-Texts on the Computer

Some courses use e-texts (electronic texts) that are either put onto a course site especially for that course, or that are more generally available through one of the big sites that attempt to make a huge body of e-texts available. Such sites include Gutenberg, which covers major documents in philosophy, history, and literature from the ancient world to the modern age (**http://gutenberg.net/**). Students may find that it is easier for them to use e-texts for their courses than the ones that are assigned for a course. However, you need to be aware that if you use an e-text it might not be the same edition as the one used in class, and you should check with your teacher to be certain that e-texts are acceptable.

You can download the text to your computer, clean it up (see Chapter 7), and save it. Then, you can make your own annotations directly in the text. To have your e-text with you in class, you can either print off the required chapters in hard copy or can bring your laptop to class. If it is on the hard drive you can add comments during class to the text as it is being discussed. Again, it is wise to check that the use of a laptop in class is acceptable.

Annotation of e-texts can take several forms:

- **Use brackets.** Setting off your comments from the text with square brackets [...] identifies which comments are yours. The problem with this method is that it is hard to differentiate your comments from the text itself.

- **Add comments** at the end of the chapter or section. You can set these off from the e-text by spacing and then adding comments, such as outlines or summaries (see above), questions about the text, or your own remarks.

- **Mark your annotation typographically** from the e-text. Use the computer's *italics* or **bold** functions to mark your comments off from the rest of the e-text. That makes the comments quick to find and easy to read. You can also skim a text fairly efficiently by referring to your comments entered this way.

- **Use colour.** All word processors can change the colour of what you type. You can enter your comments in blue or red, or choose different colours for different purposes, for comments, definitions, and questions. To activate colour, consult the help function of your word processor.

- **Use footnotes or comments.** Some readers find that it is clearest to them if they leave the e-text intact and add their own comments at the bottom of the page in a footnote (use the word processor's footnote function), as endnotes, or as comments (use the word processor's comment function). These methods mark off your notes from the e-text physically but keep the annotations adjacent to the text they are commenting on (footnotes or comments) or gather them together at the end of a chapter or document (endnotes). One potential problem is differentiating your notes from those that an author might have used. Most readers find that using this method for texts that are already footnoted or endnoted is too confusing and so opt for another choice.

- **Add annotations in a different document.** This process is also simple to use and efficient. Just divide your screen horizontally, and have the e-text in the upper half of the screen, and your comments in the bottom half. As you scroll through the reading, use your mouse to switch to your annotation screen and there you can add your comments, identifying the computerized page number or other reference. You can also move text from the top to the annotation screen by blocking and copying it, thereby having your references already incorporated into your own annotation pages. Mark any passages so moved with quotation marks and add the reference to keep the cited passages separate from your own comments or summaries.

Finally, be certain that, if you want to use e-texts, you are willing to spend your time in front of your computer reading them. That is usually fine for an article that you are asked to look up, but it might be wearisome for a substantial book. However, having the comments already entered in the computer can be a great advantage in preparing to write an assignment or essay.

POWER READING

Speed reading is a tremendous asset in courses with a heavy load of assigned texts, but it is a valuable skill for anybody. Most universities provide advice on speed reading, and some give classes in it or recommend books. A number of self-help books on this topic will be available in your university bookstore. Different kinds of books and articles make different kinds of demands on your time and energy. A philosophy textbook or one in computer science or mathematics requires that you understand each step of the argument, and very likely requires re-reading as you are progressing. On the other hand, some books can be read very quickly. You would not attempt to read a magazine article at the dentist's office with the same attention that you give to your psychology course. For some self-testing reading programs on the Internet, see the Regents' Testing page at the Georgia State University, which uses American national magazines to test and assess reading speed and comprehension, along with a self-analysis of your results (**www.gsu.edu/~wwwrtp**). (See Box 4.1 and Tips.)

For a longer discussion of power reading, see the *Foundations* Web page.

| BOX 4.1 | How to Calculate Your Reading Speed |

To determine your reading speed in words per minute (WPM), read something that you enjoy for exactly 10 minutes. Note precisely where you stop at the end of the time. Then make the calculations as in the following example:

Determine the word density of your reading sample:

1. Calculate the number of lines per page in your sample   (e.g.) 36
   (count the lines on three pages and average them)
2. Calculate the number of words per line   11
   (count the words on several lines and average them)

Determine your WPM rate:

1. Count the number of pages you have read   7
2. Multiply the page total by the number of lines per page   252
   ($7 \times 36 = 252$)
3. Add the extra number of lines beyond the pages read and total them   259
   (7 lines + 252 = 259)
4. Multiply the line total by the average of words per line   2849
   ($259 \times 11 = 2849$)
5. Divide the total number of words by the reading time   285
   ($2849 \div 10 = 285$)

Your reading speed = 285 WPM

The overall WPM value is affected by round-off error. Average university students read between 250 and 350 WPM of fiction and non-technical writing. A good score is about double that, and some people can read four times that speed. Checking your speed over several weeks should show steady improvement in your WPM rate.

TIPS Improving Power Reading

1. Twice a day read something you enjoy for 10 minutes without stopping. Time yourself to within 30 seconds.
2. Record your reading rate (words per minute, WPM) and chart your progress for a week. Recording and charting are essential if you wish to make real progress.
3. Push yourself gently as you read. If your mind wanders, get it back on track.
4. Wait until you have finished reading to look up unfamiliar words.
5. To improve comprehension, recite the chapter after closing the book. See how many specific details you can recall. Use the SQ3R method.
6. Sign up to use one of the speed reading computer programs in the academic skills centre of your university for an hour twice a week. It will help you boost your rate.
7. Set reading rate goals for yourself. A 10-percent increase in your reading rate over the previous record is a good guide for charting your improvement.

Source: Adapted from Student Academic Services, California Polytechnic State University: sas.calpoly.edu/asc/ssl/ personal.reading.imprvmnt.html.

READING PROBLEMS, DISABILITIES, AND REMEDIES

Almost all students find some of the readings they are assigned difficult. So do professors. But some students discover that they regularly have difficulty completing assigned readings or seriously misunderstand them. Some of these problems may result from an undiagnosed medical condition or a learning disability. The first step you should take if you suspect that this might be the case is to ensure that you are not experiencing vision difficulties that could be treated by a routine check-up.

Reading disabilities are one aspect of more general learning disabilities, which might have physiological causes (eye–brain co-ordination or eye–hand co-ordination) or psychological causes (brought on by financial difficulties, home or work environment, family problems, and so on). Many of these difficulties are evident from the first stages of learning to read and write and are now diagnosed much earlier than in the past. Often, reading and writing problems are diagnosed as *dyslexia*. Originally, the term meant a dysfunction of reading ability, but it now is applied to a wide range of difficulties in short-term memory retention and eye–hand co-ordination. It is often marked by reversing or transposing letters (R as Я or Milton as Mitlon), syllables, numbers, ideas, sequences, and so on. American government data indicate that about 15 percent of the school population (one child in seven) is dyslexic (see the Web page of the Davis Dyslexia Association at **www.dyslexia.com**).

If you know that you have a serious reading disability, you should follow the procedures that address your particular difficulty. If you suspect that you have a reading disability (or some other kind of learning disability that impedes your reading and comprehension), you can have that checked at your university health services or student services centre. Many universities have a special office for students with disabilities that routinely tests for such problems and offers assistance to cope with the problem, including computer assistance, reading recovery programs, individual tutoring, writing assistance, and special arrangements for taking examinations. Much information, including preliminary self-help checklists, is also available on the Internet. A number of such sites are linked on a Web site maintained by SNOW (Special Needs Opportunity Windows) at the University of Toronto (**snow.utoronto.ca/Learn2/resources/readisab.html**).

LEVELS OF READING: MORE ADVANCED READING STRATEGIES

In this section, we take an apparently trivial example of a text, a well-known fairy tale that has recently received a great deal of critical attention, to show how reading the story with an awareness of different levels of comprehension and understanding can yield increasingly valuable results. The illustrations suggest ways in which those levels can be interpreted visually. At each level, we have added applications to other kinds of texts in other disciplines. The reading model we propose here is laid out to be cumulative, from the simple to the complex, and is a tool for raising self-awareness about reading techniques that open a text up to critical thinking. More sophisticated methods are added to each level. This model is not to be understood as the only proper or legitimate way to read—keep in mind, as we have said, that it is a tool to illustrate different levels of reading.

Literal Level: Reading for Content

When you were a small child, you likely read the fairy tale *Little Red Riding Hood* in some simplified version or in a collection of children's stories. You were caught up in the narrative, with its repetitions and violence, and were probably slightly frightened, too, especially by the three scenes usually illustrated: the girl being sent by her mother to her grandmother's cottage, the girl's encounter with the wolf in the woods, and the girl's meeting with the wolf in bed in the grandmother's cottage. If you were asked what the story was "about," you could provide a summary of its content on the literal level.

It is at this level that many students remain when reading works of fiction; even many students in English and the humanities do not read at a more intensive level. It is comparatively easy to test for literal comprehension at this first level by asking "What happened?" in each of a narrative's sections. Problems arise only over difficult words, complicated relationships, or complex plots. Nevertheless, a reading at the literal level for comprehension of content is vital to further levels of understanding.

When the same approach is carried over to non-fiction, to course texts or kits, to critical or scholarly articles, however, this method becomes shakier, and literal comprehension becomes more difficult. What must be followed now is not a plot, but an argument, and the normal supports for a plot (such as characters, setting, dialogue, and action) are missing. To make the content accessible at this stage, you can still ask, "What happened?" Your answers will be something like, "First this point is made on this evidence, then this, then this," each of them being stages in the case that is being made, corresponding to the key scenes or events in the fairy tale.

Sometimes, of course, a reading for content at the literal level is followed by another leading question: How did you like the story you read? This question evokes an appreciative or affective response, since it involves the reader or auditor in a reaction on the basis of likes or dislikes, how the text is appreciated by or affected the reader. Responses at this level can be mere knee-jerk reactions and are difficult to evaluate, compare, or discuss (they are like the opinions, rather than the positions that we discussed in Chapter 3). Critical reading practices require that such responses be assessed and positioned by asking for the basis or criteria used in a statement of likes or dislikes:

- Can the response be identified as instinctual (such as an immediate reaction to pain), commonplace (such as reactions often attributed to human nature, like the fear of snakes), emotive (based on fiercely held personal opinions), prejudicial (based on political or social preferences, hatreds, or aversions), or careless (such as an off-the-cuff viewpoint with little or no investment)?
- What fields of knowledge are the responses based on?
- What are the grounds for these value judgments?
- Are the criteria aesthetic? That is, are they based on theories or principles of beauty or some other value category, usually defined in each discipline?
- If they are not aesthetic, can the criteria be related to other fields or systems of evaluation, such as historical, moral, or logical positions?

Until there are some criteria in place that can be discussed and compared, there is no basis for appreciation except individual taste or opinion. To carry an appreciative response to a level of evaluation involves moving from a reactive phase to more intensive levels of reading.

Formal Level: Reading for Content and Form

When you first became familiar with the story of *Little Red Riding Hood* you knew that whoever was reading it to you could prepare you by the almost-magical opening words, "Once upon a time, there lived in a certain village a pretty little girl that ... everybody called Little Red Riding Hood." It was the phrase "Once upon a time" that signalled to you that the story was a fairy tale and that it was about to begin. You already knew what happened in the story, but you increasingly took pleasure in the way that the story was told, in the warnings of the mother to avoid strangers, in the trip through the dark woods, in the arrival at the grandmother's cottage, and the five exclamations about the new appearance of the grandmother:

> "What big arms you have, grandmother!" she said to her. "The better to hug you with, my child." "What big legs you have, grandmother!" "The better to run with, my child." "What big ears you have, grandmother!" "The better to hear you with, my child." "What big eyes you have, grandmother!" "The better to see you with, my child." "What big teeth you have, grandmother!" "The better to eat you with!"
>
> (Zipes *Beauties* 59. All subsequent citations are from this edition unless otherwise noted).

How the story is told concerns its form, the shape that it takes, and what words are used. How the story is told deals with the patterning of the story, its repetitions, familiar phrases, the intensifying pace of the story, the shifts in scene, and so on. All of these elements constitute its form, and reading at this level comprises a formal analysis of *Little Red Riding Hood*, a consideration of answers to the question, "How is the story told?"

The Blue Beard Picture Book. London, 1875. Illus. Walter Crane. VII. Permission of the Osborne Collection, Toronto Public Library.

As it turns out, the story of *Little Red Riding Hood* closely follows the chronological events as they might have taken place in real time. There is a close correspondence between the story as it might be set down as a historical event (first this actually happened, and then that), and the way that the story is told or read to you. But in many stories, there is not so close a correspondence. The real-time story is broken up by anticipations and flashbacks, and the events are re-arranged so that there has to be some fill-in of other details. Sometimes, they are signalled by a well-known phrase, such as "meanwhile, back at the ranch," a common device in old-fashioned Westerns. It is customary to call the story as it is told the "narrative," and the way its action is put together is called the "plot."

Various phrases mark off the divisions in the plot, sometimes referring to physical locations and sometimes to shifts in time. Such temporal and spatial markers occur throughout *Little Red Riding Hood:*

> "*One day* ... she [her mother] ... said to Little Red Riding Hood...." "Little Red Riding Hood departed *at once* to visit her grandmother, *who lived in another village*." "In passing *through the forest*, she met old neighbor wolf." "The wolf *began* to run *as fast as he could....* It did not take the wolf long to arrive *at the grandmother's house*" (58–59).

Such markers of changes in time and place are common in every story and help to give the story its form, moving the pace of events or the "action" along in such a way that a reader can follow it.

As well as plot and action, traditional formal analysis examines the ways that character is portrayed (motivation, kinds of characters, such as wise old guides or threatening villains, character traits, and so on), how the setting contributes to the story, and how the language is used (the choice of words or diction, the use of imagery, literary devices, and figures of speech such as metaphor and symbol, and other stylistic characteristics, such as repetitions, rhymes, and so on).

A formal reading also brings together the literal reading with the consideration of the story's form in another way. The phrase "once upon a time" at the beginning of a story and "They lived happily ever after" at the end mark the story as a fairy tale. Such conventional phrases signal that the story belongs to a family of stories that are similar, that can be linked together because of their formal characteristics. They might be quite different in content (as *Cinderella* is different from *Little Red Riding Hood*), but they share formal marks, such as the beginnings and endings, the repetition of questions and answers, various threats (the wicked sisters and the wolf), and the arrival of a saviour figure (the prince and the woodcutter) to turn the plot from disaster to its happy ending. The family of stories is called its *genre* or its *kind*. Literary conventions have accumulated over time that help to draw connections between one story and another so that they can be identified as fairy stories, detective stories (such as the Sherlock Holmes stories, or the detective Poirot tales), sword-and-sorcery fantasy stories (like the Harry Potter stories and those by J. R. R. Tolkien), and so on. In poetry, some genres are well known and established, such as the sonnet and the epic, while others are less familiar, such as the ode. An awareness of the formal marks of your text can indicate a great deal about how the text is functioning and how it can be linked to other texts and can prepare you to look for other details that will follow if the conventions of the genre are maintained.

The major contribution of this traditional literary criticism to the formal level of reading has been its concentration on what is called "close reading," paying attention to the words on the page (the literal level) and how they are working together to accomplish what the text is trying to say. This practice has now been dominant in teaching literature for over 60 years and arose from a group of writers and critics in the United States and England called the "New Critics" (including Robert Penn Warren, Cleanth Brooks, and others). Their close reading of poetry was applied to fiction and has been extended to all kinds of writing. This method examines language for its images and metaphors, its diction, and the ways that the conventional elements in a genre are assembled to impact on the reader. Such close reading tended to stress the words on the page, rather than the hidden presence of the author. Since the New Critics, from the 1960s on, several other types of formalist criticism, such as deconstruction and narratology, have radically challenged such assumptions. We return to some of the implications of these challenges in the next section. Despite these challenges, the modified formalist principles of the New Critics continue to function widely.

Reading at the formal level can be applied, like reading at the literal level, to any subject area and is by no means restricted to the fairy tale or to literature. In philosophy, from ancient times, one of the chief genres of introducing the conflict of arguments was through the device of the debate. Hence, it is no surprise that Plato's philosophy is set down in "dialogues." His most famous treatise, *The Republic,* is a dialogue between Socrates and his friends that at first raises the topic of the nature of justice, but it does so through a dialogue, questions which Socrates poses (giving rise to the name of the "Socratic method" of teaching), by which he uses the expected answers of his friends to pose more and more searching questions, exposing the limitations of their answers, and pushing their thinking to new levels. Another genre used in philosophy and in political science is the utopia, the depiction of an ideal society that implicitly or explicitly criticizes the author's real society. This genre takes its name from the philosopher Sir Thomas More and his depiction of an imaginary island, *Utopia,* that criticizes the 16th-century English society.

Similarly, reading at the formal level can greatly illuminate the reading of history. Many history texts are re-tellings of past events (whether biographies, war histories, accounts of national policies and politics, and so on), but they necessarily rely upon all kinds of historical documents, including a wide variety of genres: personal letters and memoirs, treaties, documents of all kinds, public records, government acts, speeches, and so on. Each of these is a particular genre and follows or deviates in important ways from the conventions that are traditional in describing that form. A formal level of reading examines the genres of such documents and seeks to understand how their meaning can be read from their formal structure. Furthermore, some historians have become interested in the ways that historians "tell" their history or write their narratives about the past. For instance, Hayden White's ground-breaking work *Metahistory* (1973) discusses ways in which formal levels of reading can be applied to a wide variety of historical texts.

Such diverse uses of formal levels of reading suggest that active readers become increasingly aware of the ways that language and narrative function in all of the texts that they read. Close reading, combined with attention to the kinds of discourse being used and to the forms of narrative techniques in any text, makes this level of reading accessible and useful to readers who are advancing in their levels of sophistication. The formal level of reading suggests, further, that knowledge of a text's formal qualities is far from regarding it as a mere assembly of parts but leads to an understanding of how it works, thereby pointing to the next level—the expository which combines content and form to produce meaning.

Expository Level: Reading for Content, Form, and Meaning

You might be asked a different question, such as "What does *Little Red Riding Hood* mean?" You are then forced to explain in your own words what you have read about. You have to assess what you understand the story to mean and relate what you read as content at the literal level to what you think that content means in a larger sense. You are being asked to generalize and abstract from the content and form to its significance, to explain it, and to translate its content and form into meaning. At this level, you are giving what is often called an exposition or explication. At this point, you move from what the story has said and how it says it to see how the literal and formal levels combine to produce more complex meanings. That is, you have moved well beyond thinking that meaning is limited to what is read at the literal level to seeing how meaning is also determined by the shaping of the text at the formal level.

Your interpretation of the fairy tale might be quite simple, based, perhaps, on what you have been taught: "Don't talk to strangers," or "Stay out of danger," or "Don't go alone to visit your grandmother." Many versions of the tale exploit such meanings. Illustrations of the opening scene often suggest a direct moral meaning as a conventional mother sends a potentially rebellious daughter into a world of temptations with warnings and a cautionary shake of her finger. It is at this third expository level that reading becomes evaluative. Your responses are moving well beyond the affective or appreciative response, or the summary of the literal content, and you can begin to see how a text is making its meaning effective. You are evaluating the means by which its conceptual and rhetorical controls are put into place.

While such responses may seem trivial when applied to fairy tales, the same process can be applied to any work of fiction or to a scholarly or critical article on any topic. The move from content at the literal level and how the text is shaped at the formal level to meaning at an interpretive level does not usually happen, however, at a single reading. Many works benefit from repeated readings even at the literal level. However, to some degree, reading at the literal and formal levels, along with the expository level, usually takes place simultaneously. This simultaneous reading is especially true with fairy tales, since most readers have internalized the ways in which they construct meaning. For instance, at a literal level, the fairy tales signify that animals, such as wolves and little pigs, can talk and are motivated by what are human concerns. All readers beyond a very early age know that these modes of conduct are not literally true. However, because of the conventions of the genre of fairy tale, the reader accepts their anthropomorphic conduct on an expository level as part of a fable, moral, or lesson. Furthermore, the shape of the tale usually builds in stages of danger to a climactic threat where the hero or heroine is rescued. Again, the formal principles of the tale, familiar to readers because they are so conventional, allows the literal level (the wolf about to eat the little girl) to be read simultaneously at the formal level (the final danger from which she is about to be saved). That is, this expository level is established by both the literal content as well as structural relations within the text. To take another example, the meaning or moral of fairy tales is conditioned by an author's comments, which traditionally come at the beginning and after the end of the tale.

Ludwig Bechstein. *Märchenbuch*. Leipzig, 1857. Illus. Ludwig Richter. 200. Collections of the authors.

The version of *Little Red Riding Hood* you were reading was probably based on *Le Petit Chaperon Rouge* ("Little Red-Cap") by Charles Perrault. It was first published in his *Histoires ou Contes du temps passé avec des Moralitez* ("Stories or Tales of Times Past, with Moralities," 1697). The collection's subtitle gave its name to an entire genre of children's stories: *Contes de Ma Mère l'Oye* ("Tales of My Mother Goose"). Perrault's version begins:

> Once upon a time there was a little village girl, the prettiest in the world. Her mother doted on her, and her grandmother even more. This good woman made her a little red hood which suited her so well that wherever she went, she was called Little Red Riding Hood.
>
> One day, after her mother had baked some biscuits, she said to Little Red Riding Hood, "Go see how your grandmother's feeling. I've heard that she's ill. You can take her some biscuits and this small pot of butter." Little Red Riding Hood departed at once to visit her grandmother, who

lived in another village. In passing through the forest she met old neighbor wolf, who had a great desire to eat her. But he did not dare because of some woodcutters who were in the forest. Instead he asked her where she was going. The poor child, who did not know that it is dangerous to stop and listen to a wolf, said to him, "I'm going to see my grandmother, and I'm bringing her some biscuits with a small pot of butter that my mother's sending her" (Zipes *Beauties* 58).

At the end of the story are the "moralities" that Perrault promised in his title. At the beginning of the story, the meaning or morality is suggested in the phrase "who did not know that it is dangerous to stop and listen to a wolf." At the end of the tale, outside the formal structure of the narrative, however, he wrote this meaning out in verse, another formal structure, so that the reader did not need to stop at the literal level of the story but could move to the expository level under his guidance:

MORAL

One sees here that young children,   For some are winning and have sharp minds.
Especially pretty girls,   Some are loud, smooth, or mild.
Who're bred as pure as pearls,   Others appear plain kind or unriled.
Should question words addressed by men.   They follow young ladies wherever they go,
Or they may serve one day as feast   Right into the halls of their very own homes.
For a wolf or other beast.   Alas for those girls who've refused the truth:
I say a wolf since not all are wild   The sweetest tongue has the sharpest tooth (60).
Or are indeed the same in kind.

At this stage of our example, the literal content of the text remains unchanged, but the meaning is conditioned by the structure and details of the tale and its form. In fact, it is the morality verse that is structurally controlling the meaning of the entire text.

So it is with any text. At the expository level, you place the content, form, and meaning together so that the arrangement of the content points to the meaning. Content and form are, in fact, constructing an argument. In the fairy tale, the argument is the moral injunction that little girls should not talk to strangers. Every parent knows the importance of this maxim in making children street-smart. But the fairy tale cannot be reduced only to a moral lesson, even if the author wants it to be so. Similarly, any other work, any textbook or article, cannot be reduced to the literal level alone. For instance, to consider a contemporary problem in another area, say history or political science, "Why in this article are the causes of the First Iraqi War put in this order? Why is this cause put first, and this cause second?" The meaning would be different if two causes, such as the liberation of Kuwait and the protection of the oil supply for the West, were put in reverse order. So, at the expository level, *content* (the events or points in a case) + *form* (Why *this* order?) = *meaning* (What is the argument?).

Comparative Level: Reading for Associations and Implications

Almost all reading at the analytical level involves comparisons. Part of the context for evaluating any work involves comparing it with other works in the same field. This new biography of Hitler or Jane Austen involves comparison with earlier biographies. The recent analysis of the nature of evil by Claudia Card (*The Atrocity Paradigm: A Theory of Evil,* 2002) can be compared with that of C.E.M. Joad (*God and Evil,* 1947) and that of Augustine (*City of God,* c. 400). One argument is compared with another, one set of historical facts with another (the First Iraqi War of 1991 with the Second of 2003), and so on.

It might be that you were not familiar with Perrault's version and his morality but know the version told by the Brothers Grimm:

> There was once a sweet little maid, much beloved by everybody, but most of all by her grand-mother, who never knew how to make enough of her. Once she sent her a little cap of red velvet, and as it was very becoming to her, and she never wore anything else, people called her Little Red-cap. One day her mother said to her, "Come, Little Red-cap, here are some cakes and a flask of wine for you to take to grandmother: she is weak and ill, and they will do her good. Make haste and start before it grows hot, and walk properly and nicely, and don't run, or you might fall and break the flask of wine, and there would be none left for grandmother. And when you go into her room, don't forget to say, Good morning, instead of staring about you" (Grimm 132).

The version by the Brothers Grimm (1812–1815) begins with a conventional, pretty young woman, often depicted in illustrations. It continues with Red-cap's telling the wolf the location of her grandmother's cottage and his advice that she take longer to get there by gathering flowers on the way (so that he might get there before her and eat her grand-mother whole). In the Grimm version, the wolf eats Red-cap, too, and it is only the timely arrival of the woodcutter that saves both the eaten victims, who step forth fully clad and alive when he slices open the wolf.

When you take on a more systematic reading and study of *Little Red Riding Hood,* you become aware that the story has many analogues, or parallel versions. Until recently, it was believed that Perrault invented the tale and that the Brothers Grimm had transcribed one of the oral versions; we now know from the research of Marianne Rumpf, Marc Soriano, and others that the tale is medieval and that it was still popular in France in the 17th century, partly because Europe was in the last stages of witch hunting and there was widespread fear of werewolves. Furthermore, research into the manuscript of the Brothers Grimm shows that they modified their version considerably.

Grimm, Jakob, and Wilhelm Grimm. *Grimm's Fairy Tales.* London, 1900. Illus. Eddie J. Andrews. Facing 26. Permission of the Osborne Collection, Toronto Public Library.

Grimm, Jakob, and Wilhelm Grimm. *The Fairy Tales of the Brothers Grimm.* London, 1909. Illus. Arthur Rackham. Facing 116. Permission of the Osborne Collection, Toronto Public Library.

Further study of the story, therefore, would involve the reading of its analogues (parallel or similar versions from related or even very different literary traditions). Such readings are conducted not only to bring out the parallels but also to examine the roots of the story—here, in its instruction about the appropriate roles for working-class and bourgeois children, about parental warnings concerning sexual exploits, and about conventional gender roles (some of the interpretations of which we will outline at the next level of reading). Hence, with fairy tales, as with many forms of writing, a comparative reading of variants of the tale will involve not only a comparison of near contemporary versions but will also consider how the history of those versions has yielded modern re-writings.

The story has associations with rural or village life, and it reflects the values and habits of a peasant community that was closely connected to nature. These associations can be questioned when the story is re-told in the 21st century or in an urban setting. The implications of the story in the warnings against the wolf, the responsibilities of parents and grandparents, and the ability of the child to follow instructions are all part of the comparative reading level that places the narrative in its own time and in other times when it is reproduced. One way of illuminating such questions is to see whether other versions of the tale stress some of those aspects of present-day life that were called into question in earlier versions.

For instance, in an effort to modernize the tale, James Finn Garner published this version:

> There once was a young person named Red Riding Hood who lived with her mother on the edge of a large wood. One day her mother asked her to take a basket of fresh fruit and mineral water to her grandmother's house—not because this was womyn's work, mind you, but because the deed was generous and helped engender a feeling of community. Furthermore, her grandmother was not sick, but rather was in full physical and mental health and was fully capable of taking care of herself as a mature adult.

The Book of Nursery Tales, London, 1845. Third series. Frontispiece. Permission of the Osborne Collection, Toronto Public Library.

> So Red Riding Hood set off with her basket through the woods. Many people believed that the forest was a foreboding and dangerous place and never set foot in it. Red Riding Hood, however, was so confident in her own budding sexuality that such obvious Freudian imagery did not intimidate her.
>
> On the way to Grandma's house, Red Riding Hood was accosted by a Wolf, who asked her what was in her basket. She replied, "Some healthful snacks for my grandmother, who is certainly capable of taking care of herself as a mature adult" (1–2).

Other versions draw on ecological, sociological, and other implications and associations by carrying the reading even further, such as "Politically Correct Red Riding Hood" by Stan Greenberg posted on numerous sites on the Web:

There once was a young person named Little Red Riding Hood who lived on the edge of a large forest full of endangered owls and rare plants that would probably provide a cure for cancer if only someone took the time to study them. Red Riding Hood lived with a nurture giver whom she sometimes referred to as "mother," although she didn't mean to imply by this term that she would have thought less of the person if a close biological link did not in fact exist. Nor did she intend to denigrate the equal value of non-traditional households, although she was sorry if this was the impression conveyed. One day her mother asked her to take a basket of organically grown fruit and mineral water to her grandmother's house. "But mother, won't this be stealing work from the unionized people who have struggled for years to earn the right to carry all packages between various people in the woods?" Red Riding Hood's mother assured her that she had called the union boss and gotten a special compassionate mission exemption form.

In both these modern versions, the writers have used a comparative reading. They accept the fact that fairy tales are meant to teach children, which, as we have seen, was established in Perrault's making explicit the morality of the tale after the conclusion of his version. The particular moral of the 17th century, however, is updated to the context of the late 20th century. Hence, both modern writers satirize various contemporary political movements by adapting Perrault's morality to fit their own contemporary context. A comparative reading makes each of these moves apparent.

In a different contemporary context, one reading of the version by the Brothers Grimm has resulted in a case of censorship. As recently as 1989, an illustrated edition of *Little Red Riding Hood* was banned in two California school districts. The fact that the story involved Red Riding Hood's taking "this piece of cake and bottle of wine" to her grandmother raised to the school boards a concern about the approval of alcohol use in the story.

Such a comparative level of reading can be applied to many other kinds of writing and, indeed, other media. For instance, many students are interested in the ways that a piece of writing is transformed from one medium to another, as when films are made of well-known books, such as film versions of Alice Walker's novel *The Color Purple* or Toni Morrison's *Beloved,* or the re-making in film of previous television icons, such as *The Brady Bunch* and *Charlie's Angels.* There are many other examples, some very controversial, such as the re-workings of children's classics by Walt Disney Studios, or the many film versions of Mary Shelley's *Frankenstein.* Other re-workings include taking a piece of fiction as a model for a text in another medium, as is done with Francis Ford Coppola's *Apocalypse Now* for Joseph Conrad's *Heart of Darkness.* Reading such texts at the comparative level (as well as at the other levels) is a productive exercise.

The scope of such a reading can go further, however, so that a particular reading stressing social analysis or historical background, a reading level to which we now turn, can draw on different disciplinary materials or different historical contexts. In fact, many readings at the analytical level necessarily avail themselves of the comparative level at the same time. That is, they combine the analytical level of reading with the comparison of data or events, versions, or treatments from other sources, linking them together and drawing implications for such associations. Two studies of the American Revolution, for instance, can be read comparatively, or one can be read with prior knowledge of the other so that throughout a critical reading at the comparative level there are grounds for questioning assumptions, assertions, and analysis of similar data. These kinds of comparative approaches to historical, social, economic, intellectual, or scientific data lead to the modifications of historical or scientific theories; therefore, this reading method is an important part of critical reading strategies.

Analytical Level: Reading for Contexts

At an analytical level of interpretation, you read texts in relation to various contexts in which the text has appeared and been studied. You already have the words of the text at the literal level under your control, and you have some knowledge of the form and meaning of the text, of the ways that its argument is put together. You also have a reading practice that lets you compare it with other texts. But in what contexts were they written, and in what contexts have they been read or are being read today? To answer such questions, you need to have knowledge of the contexts in which a text was produced, as well as the contexts in which others before you have read it and in which you are reading it.

For the fairy tale, you might know something about the intellectual context of the 17th century from your general knowledge, or you might know about the use of moral tags as advice from adults to children about appropriate kinds of behaviour necessary to fit into society. When you make an interpretation you necessarily draw on other kinds of information to contextualize any reading within your own resources. Whether or not those are adequate depends on your stock of information and concepts as a developing reader. In your reading of the fairy story—or any other text—you have to be able to recognize where you have to undertake further reading to fill in the gaps in your knowledge about its various contexts.

Fairy tales were transformed by Perrault and others in late 17th-century France and have been read in a particular historical context—the decline of the aristocracy and the rise of the middle class. In this transformation, the fairy tales were re-told or translated from their form as oral tales from the peasantry or oral tales from the nurseries of the aristocracy (told by governesses and wet nurses who took care of the children) into written tales for the middle class. As such, they acted as educational tools to teach middle-class children how to behave and to warn them of dangers (see Zipes *Beauties* 1–12, *Trials* 1–15, 25–37).

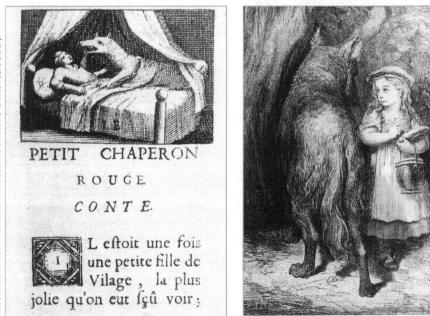

Charles Perrault. *Histoires ou Contes du temps passé, avec des moralitez.* Amsterdam, 1721. Illus. Charles Perrault. I. Permission of the Osborne Collection, Toronto Public Library.

Charles Perrault. *Les Contes de Perrault.* Paris, 1862. Illus. Gustave Doré. IV. Collections of the authors.

At the analytical level, reading for such contexts may also involve drawing on the methodologies and systems of other disciplines. This intellectual context often means that you can apply the methods of one discipline to another. For instance, you might put your reading of *Little Red Riding Hood* into the context of psychology, gender studies, or other courses in social analysis. While some influential psychoanalytical interpretations of the story have considered the mother to be the superego and the child's adventure as learning to conform to parental values (Bettelheim 181), many modern interpretations consider the story a rape narrative, moving from domestic order to transgression in the wood and punishment by rape. Most illustrations suggest the power of the wolf by making him larger than the girl and showing him touching her, intimately sizing her up, and casting knowing glances, a convention from at least the time of the illustrations of Gustave Doré (1862). A key moment in this reading is the violent double action of the bedroom scene in Perrault's version, in which the wolf first rapes the grandmother before forcing or beguiling the girl to undress and get into bed.

> Upon seeing her enter, the wolf hid himself under the bedcovers and said to her, "Put the biscuits and the pot of butter on the bin and come lie down beside me." Little Red Riding Hood undressed and got into the bed, where she was quite astonished to see how her grandmother appeared in her nightgown. "What big arms you have, grandmother!" she said to her. "The better to hug you with, my child" (Zipes *Beauties* 59).

Susan Brownmiller reads the story from a contemporary feminist perspective in the context of sexual intimidation and violence against children, drawing out the associations and implications at the analytical level and commenting on the details. She concludes: "Red Riding Hood is a parable of rape. There are frightening male figures abroad in the woods—we call them wolves, among other names—and females are helpless before them. Better stick close to the path, better not be adventurous. If you are lucky, a good *friendly* male may be able to save you from certain disaster" (343–44).

A number of modern versions of the story seek to draw out further feminist potential. For instance, Marcia Lieberman writes on all of the volumes of Andrew Lang's collections of fairy tales (including *The Blue Fairy Book,* 1889, containing part of the Perrault version of *Little Red Riding Hood*). She argues that the happily-ever-after endings have "been made the repositories of the dreams, hopes, and fantasies of generations of girls," each awaiting their Prince Charming (383–395)—and so, she challenges Bruno Bettelheim's theory that the fairy tales are gender-free stories that help children of both sexes solve problems and come to maturation and self-definition. Whether or not you agree with her analysis, the point is that her reading is based on placing the meaning of the story in the context of the role of fairy tales in the 17th century in educating children. This analytical level relates the well-known content of the story (the literal level) and its formulaic ending (the formal level) to a new meaning. Her exposition (our third level) does not depend only on the poetic "morality" of the tale or on its structural organization leading to its moral argument, though these aspects are important. Lieberman re-reads the story in the political and social context of 17th-century France; her analysis allows her to conclude that the story was used to socialize children, particularly girls in conventional behaviour. The validity of her argument can be tested on its own merits and depends on the ways she establishes how this socialization to conventional behaviour relates to her feminist analysis.

Other analytical readings of the story include Marxist interpretations, which consider how fairy tales have been used in the process of socialization, especially in legitimizing the vested interests of capitalist societies by relying on conditions of servitude and standards of courtly conduct watered down to bourgeois respectability. To resist such bourgeois readings, Catherine Storr re-locates Red Riding Hood in contemporary urban settings in "Polly and the Wolf" (1955) and a number of other re-tellings, such as "Clever Polly and the Stupid Wolf" (1995). The wolf cannot get to the grandmother's house easily, and so, he takes the bus when the train fails. The child takes whiskey for her grandmother and is wily and street-smart, taking along her boyfriend, who is called Hunter. The American poet Anne Sexton has re-told 17 traditional German fairy tales (from the Brothers Grimm) as psychological studies in her book *Transformations* (1971).

Charles Perrault. *Les Contes de Perrault.* Paris, 1862. Illus. Gustave Doré. xxiii. Collections of the authors.

An analytical reading of any text combines the literal, formal, and expository levels, along with the comparative level, and takes them one stage further. Analytical reading places *argument* (form + content = meaning) first in a comparative frame, moving between texts written at different times or from different perspec-

Charles Perrault. Les Contes de Perrault. *Paris, 1862. Illus. Gustave Doré. xix. Collections of the authors.*

tives. Then, it places the arguments in larger frames or *contexts*. We suppose that from your perspective, the most elemental context of reading is the necessity of getting your work done for your next seminar or, better, understanding it in some relationship to your course. But a more advanced application gives context a wider scope and, as with other levels of reading, is applicable to other disciplines.

For instance, for a sociological article on the relation of school absenteeism to employment patterns, that context might involve relating this study to others on single-parent capacity to control teen-age behaviour, teen-age cultural and social norms, peer pressure, availability of school-sponsored sport and cultural activities, and so on. In other words, data and interpretations from other disciplines and sub-disciplines provide a context in which to evaluate your reading. In history, analytical reading for context might involve putting a historical event, like the First Iraqi War of 1991, in a larger historical framework, such as Middle East politics, American imperialism, the financial policy of the oil cartel, and so on. Or a philosophical text, say, on the emergence of idealism in the 19th century, can be read analytically through the context of cultural norms and social aspirations during the same period or through other competing philosophical positions—the first a context involving different disciplines and the second a wider contextual frame within the same discipline.

That is, analytical readings can consider the context of an author's other works, a larger historical or conceptual field (What are a text's historical conditions, assumptions, and temporalities? What are its conceptual conditions or intellectual relationships?), or its relationship to other fields or disciplines.

Summary: Putting It All Together

All that has been said in these sections on the five levels of reading *Little Red Riding Hood* is applicable to other kinds of readings (as we have shown). To extend the brief examples from other disciplines that we discussed above, we shall give two instances of how to apply the five levels of critical reading to disciplines in which many of the levels appear to be inapplicable. The first example moves on the general level of a discipline, sociology. Our second applies the five levels to a specific reading, a chapter of a psychology textbook. We have chosen these examples in disciplines in which beginning students often have trouble moving beyond the content of their readings to levels that allow them to read critically.

In sociology, the particular problem in your reading is often to identify and understand the evidence, arguments, and conclusions that result from research on the structure of human society. While historians might be more interested in the history of social institutions, sociologists are interested in how they relate to each other, how human beings in social situations behave and interact, and what influences that behaviour and interaction. Sociology, like some kinds of psychology, often depends upon surveys to gather its data. Because of this tendency, the temptation of a reader is to stay on the literal level and simply try to figure out what the data are about. But considering the five levels of reading opens up this literal level to other kinds of questions. In your reading, note the kinds of surveys undertaken and evaluate the design of the survey or experiment by asking questions based upon critical thinking: What kinds of questions were used to gather the information? What was the sampling method? What provisions were made for the correction of errors? How were the results compiled? What methods were used for the analysis of results? How do the conclusions follow the design? Is the survey reliable statistically?

In analyzing the argument on its own terms (the literal and formal levels), consider the validity of the application of data to the thesis and conclusions (the expository level). Using the information that the author supplies, ask what you know about the author's theoretical model. Does the writer make clear a position about the kind of sociology that functions in the article (comparative level), about a political or social stance, or about the advantages or limitations of the theoretical model (analytical level)? What are the guarantees that your reading is itself free from bias, especially with regard to race, gender, class, and economic status? Of course, one or the other of these conditions might be the particular focus of the study you are reading, but be alert to the issues that each raises and compare them with other readings in your course.

To read sociology critically, you have to move from the presentations of data (from surveys, government documents, or other sources) to its analysis. That is, in reading at the comparative and analytical levels, you first have to move through the literal level for content, the formal level for shape or structure, and the expository level for argument. Reading at the comparative and analytical levels means that you have to compare this reading with others in the course or others on similar topics, as well as assessing the context of the writer. What are the biases that display or conceal the writer's position, and how are they accounted for? For instance, in writing about teen-age pregnancy, you may be reading relevant articles on the kinds of abortion practices available and used, as well as the support services for women. Despite the supposed neutral stance of the social scientist, an article might contain evidence of biased attitudes, depending on whether it is written from a pro-life or pro-choice position. Similarly, articles on gun violence and street gangs written by the gun lobby would be different from those supporting the national gun registry of the federal government. How do the authors make their positions clear (comparative level)? How adequately or accurately do they represent contradictory positions (analytical level)?

The five levels of reading can also be applied productively to a specific reading in a social science discipline. For instance, if in a psychology course you were assigned the chapter "Language Development" in *Child Development: An Introduction* by John Santrock and Steven Yussen, your reading for content at the literal level would be a matter of simple comprehension of what the words mean. A number of technical terms about language (*morphology, phonology, syntax, surface,* and *deep structure*) as well as some words concerning areas of the brain associated with language learning (*Broca's area* and *Wernicke's area*) are used. While a number of definitions are given in the chapter, other terms (*biological evolution* and *abstract speech,* for example) are not explained, and some other words might be unfamiliar to some readers (*traversed, brain hemisphere, ingenious,* and so on). So, in sorting out the technical language with a dictionary or encyclopedia, the acquisition of content at the literal level might take some time and work for a reader inexperienced in the field.

If, however, you are a more experienced reader with some knowledge of the field, your reading for form as well as content moves you to a level of exposition: you are reading to follow the development of the ideas (the argument), and you are seeking to link the content to the larger meanings that are being presented. In this chapter of the textbook, you will perceive that the argument is arranged (formal level) first to examine the definition and systems of rules of language and then to consider how language is acquired. It is this latter part of the discussion that takes up the most space in the chapter (eight out of ten sub-divisions). At the same time, as an experienced reader, you are attempting to understand the concepts as they are presented (content level), to place those concepts into the argument that the authors are making and to explain that argument (expository level), to relate that argument to the more general argument that the article and the book are making (comparative level), and perhaps to contextualize it in relation to other theories of language acquisition (analytical level).

You would have observed that the chapter's content is divided into sub-sections, each with a heading and sub-categories. The headings summarize what each sub-section contains and help keep the reader on track. So, your comprehension of the major part of the chapter places its main points in sequence. It argues that in the process of biological evolution, humans have developed sophisticated means of acquiring language, and some thinkers, such as Noam Chomsky, argue that human brains are pre-wired, so to speak, with a language acquisition device (LAD), by which he means a predisposition or innate capability to acquire language. Other positions concerning language, which supplement the biological argument, stress the cultural context of language, and at least two schools of thought dispute the precise ways in which language is acquired: the psychological behaviourists and those who stress cognitive interaction. The final section of the chapter places these arguments into the context of other developmental processes, examining language acquisition in infancy, early childhood, and late childhood.

By reading at the comparative level, you can assess these different views in the light of your other knowledge. In one sense, this linking of language acquisition to other kinds of development (motor, visual recognition, and physical development) raises questions about the extent to which the developmental model is inherent or imposed. At the analytical level, the research into the acquisition of more than one language simultaneously or at least by late childhood before the onset of puberty may be set in the context of bi-lingualism, a major issue in education in Canada and the United States. Santrock and Yussen raise some of the socio-economic dimensions of the problem in the largely unilingual United States, but these could be extended. For instance, the highly criticized bi-lingual education in Spanish and English in some states bordering Mexico has greatly complicated education, with both supporters and detractors arguing that bi-lingual education socializes Spanish-speaking Americans to a servant class. In Canada, bi-lingualism is an educational and political issue related to the nation's two official languages, and multi-lingual education and heritage language funding crises raise additional questions about language acquisition.

Of course, the distinctions we draw between levels are somewhat artificial. No one actually reads all the time with a self-conscious awareness of the levels as isolated stages. Any reading practice tends to synthesize the levels, but with increasing practice and familiarity, you can implement these levels with impressive results. Hence, the reading of this chapter with awareness of the various interfunctioning reading levels can open up a reading for content at the literal level to various kinds of questions in a critical reading.

These five levels of reading can be applied to almost everything that you read at university. One of the problems is that you likely try to read only for the content at the literal level; you are not quite certain what content you are supposed to get from the assignment and even less certain about what points are going to be raised in class unless there have been reading guides or in-class instructions about how to proceed. As a result, you often remain on the first or literal level, taking what is presented at its face value, whether in fiction, a scholarly article, or a book. Dominated by the urge to gain some command over the material, you resist all temptations to question, analyze, or summarize.

As you gain more experience by using the suggestions in this chapter, you will be able to incorporate these apparently separate levels in your first or second reading through the text. You will then have prepared yourself well for classroom discussions, writing assignments, and greater enjoyment of your reading and studies. These levels of reading are not restricted to the written word. Increasingly, university courses include other media in their curricula.

SPECIALIZED STRATEGIES FOR CRITICAL READING IN PARTICULAR DISCIPLINES: READING MULTI-MEDIA

Critical Reading in Particular Disciplines

As we have shown, each discipline makes its particular demands on you as a reader. In the discussion of the various levels of reading, we have concentrated on the example of a fairy tale but have not considered it extensively in relation to its own discipline, literature, myth, and folklore. Instead, we have generalized our comments, showing how one fairy tale can be read in increasingly complex ways. At the same time, we have made reference to the reading practices that *Little Red Riding Hood* has prompted in other disciplines and methodologies: feminist readings of the fairy tale in sociology, Marxist readings in cultural studies and history, studies in ethics and education in relation to the tale's moralities. We have also extended these brief specific comments to more general examples in contemporary politics and social policy. In our summary, we considered how they might be applied to reading practices in sociology and psychology.

Each discipline has its own specialized vocabulary and conventions of setting out its own system of knowledge. Scholars writing in each field know the conventions and tend to follow them. We conclude this chapter on critical reading by showing how similar techniques can be applied to one further field, reading films, television, and multi-media (video games, computer animations, music videos, and so on) as texts. We have chosen to discuss this field because it is one of the newest disciplines and because mass media dominate our culture with their presence and influence. Further, it is one of the most difficult areas to which critical reading practices can be applied because multi-media tend to position readers as passive consumers of entertainment who have already learned to read these texts uncritically, in the manner that the producers and advertisers want them to. Therefore, this section will give you some analytical tools to begin reading against the grain, that is, as an active reader.

Reading Multi-media

Reading multi-media critically means that you use critical responses in viewing and analyzing films, TV, and other media productions similar to those used in reading texts in other media. At the very least, these readings involve drawing a distinction between subjective responses ("I like this or dislike that") and reasoned positions ("This works in the film because of that and by this method"). Hence, the language and logic of films, to speak of one medium, their content and form, can be subjected to exposition, comparison, and analysis. Similarly, TV has been subjected to detailed analysis of film techniques, genres (soaps, serials, and reality TV, for instance), audience participation and response, and so on. And, as in the case of fairy tales, these modes of analysis have been part of the discussion of the role of TV in the education of children and the programming of sex and violence. Part of this analysis is also devoted to the use of TV advertising (audience, market strategy, use of big name brands and sponsors), the limitations of one-minute clips in news broadcasts, the technology of music videos, and the social role of video game arcades or stores in malls, among many other topics.

Our comments on reading multi-media concentrate on movies, but the methods can also be applied to all other multi-media formats. To undertake a critical analysis usually requires more than a single viewing, so it is often a good idea to videotape a movie or TV show or to get a video or DVD of a first-run movie. A first viewing is needed to comprehend the content of the film or TV program at the literal level, and the large structural elements at the formal level. A further viewing, or perhaps just the first one if the structure is not complex, allows you to read the content and form with greater attention, concentrating on the details of the storyline, the re-arrangement of chronology in terms of plotting, the use of characters, setting, dialogue, rising and falling action, and so on. Subsequent viewings for study enable you to analyze other formal aspects, such as the use of conventional subject matter (which helps you to identify a film's genre), the history of the medium (such as the history of documentary films), transitions between scenes and shots, noting shifts in camera work, specific dialogue, details of the setting, symbolic elements, parallels from shot to shot in composition and framing, and various problems in the film, such as unexplained gaps in scene, dialogue, or detail.

Film Genres

Genre Studies have also had an impact on film study and criticism. Comparative analysis enables you to compare a film or TV program with others in the same genre or with the history of a genre or the medium in general. The conventions whereby films are classified according to accepted types are fairly well established. In your local video store, for instance, films are classified according to such genres as war, adventure, horror, musical, drama, classic, children, adult, and so on, often without much clear information about what makes a film fit into one category or an other. To what extent are the literary terms we have been using applicable to film? Do film genres have institutionally sanctioned criteria concerning narrative, plot lines, and expected audience identification and reaction? You might consider, for instance, the wide critical literature available on the horror/slasher films or on the *Frankenstein* industry, with the cross-over between romance and horror.

Film History

Film history is linked to the origins of photography (about the middle of the 19th century), the introduction of the moving image about 1900, as well as the addition of recorded sound in the 1930s. From a historical perspective, media are usually discussed in relation to the different media, historical periods—often decades—national film industries, and the films of individual directors and actors.

Just as contemporary culture is dominated by multi-media, so are the media deeply involved in the construction and interpretation of contemporary history. Reading a moving image (film or video) from a historical perspective involves reading at all five levels, especially at the analytical level because it requires an assessment of context. That context involves the history in which the moving image was produced, and the history of that production, and the history of how that production has been viewed by audiences. John E. O'Connor in *Image as Artifact* raises three kinds of questions about these contexts that historians ask about any moving-image document:

- **Content questions:** How is a reading for content at what we call the literal level determined by the technical devices and editing techniques that have their own history? More generally, how is the content related to the specific social milieu that it represents, or the time and place in which the document was made?

- **Production questions:** How does a reading at the analytical level explain the broad socio-political and cultural contexts of the film? How do the biographical details concerning the actors, directors, producers, and others associated with making the film influence its production? For instance, the fan sites for the recent *Lord of the Rings* series give much detail about the production aspects, special effects, and biographical details of those involved in the film, but how far is that detail promotional? How far is it too conditioned by the film's socio-political and cultural contexts?

- **Reception questions:** Again, how does a reading at the analytical level open up questions about an audience's reaction to a film? What effect did the moving image have on its first audience? How far was that effect determined by its social setting and how far by marketing strategies behind the film? A comparative reading might push these historical questions to ask how this reception has changed over time. Has this film been re-made to meet new times and audiences? Has it influenced other films or media?

Analytical readings of film history help explain the ways in which the media have come to dominate world culture from the 20th century on. The media have been used by, and have helped make, huge multi-national corporations that extend into all areas of life (like the Disney corporation); have set before the public the concept of star and popularity that has led to some actors becoming national leaders; have developed and extended the reign of technology in domestic and public life; and have been the expression and determinant for national cultures (as in Soviet film of the 1920s and 1930s, and the whole history of American film). All such analytical readings depend, however, not only on reading the context of film history but also on literal and formal analysis of content and the details of film making.

Annotating Narrative in Films and TV

Many students take notes while viewing a film for critical reading (possibly not at the first viewing but often at the second or third). When you are using a film as one of the sources for one of your writing assignments, detailed notes or annotation are a necessity. You might make notes about scene changes, sequencing of action, invisible characters, sound effects, and various other aspects that we discuss below. In assessing these aspects of a film, you can also draw parallels with other disciplines. For instance, some TV talk shows present teens in crisis who are brought into a case interview situation. In this context, the host acts as therapist, and the audience as onlookers, participants, commentators, and, sometimes, cheerleaders. You can make comparisons between the blending of this genre with the disciplines of sociology, psychology, and social work, where the roles of experts and clients transform into mass entertainment. Other shows can be read as interpretations of history (such as differences between national coverage of the Second Iraqi War by the CBC and by the American networks).

Social Discourse, Chronology, and Film Narrative

Criticisms of film and TV program narrative have often discussed plot as a major element but have also drawn on the analysis of various kinds of social discourse (the relations between language and its socio-cultural dimensions, and hence the various *languages* in a film and their connections to the social hierarchy), examining how they are put together into a narrative. Some film writers refer to the relation between social discourse and narrative as *narrative discourse*. The analysis of social discourse involves examining how language in a film—not only the spoken language but also the languages of setting, society, character portrayal, especially in action and psychological interrelations, and so on—has social, functional, or interactive uses in particular situations, contexts, or institutional settings. For instance, a patient speaks of the condition of her body differently from how her doctor would, and such "discourses" are placed in a hierarchical order of power and authority. A woman's opinion is disregarded in the hospital in favour of the doctor's, but among her friends, her opinion might be given increased importance. A quite different set of discourses is set into a very different narrative and group of power relations in the novel and film of Michael Ondaatje's *The English Patient*.

At the same time, increasing attention has been placed in film studies on the story itself. Media studies often borrow the term *narratology* from literary studies for examining narrative. Narratology clarifies the distinction we mentioned earlier between the chronological story and the way that it is re-arranged as a plot. Rather than considering the narrative as a fictional representation of life, narratology pays particular attention to the formal ways in which the narrative is put together as a structure, and therefore, it is especially appropriate for use at the formal level of reading of films. The chronological story, often called the *histoire* (derived from French critics, such as Gérard Genette, who developed this field first in relation to fiction), is the sequence of events as they occur in a chronological order. In a literary, historical, or film text, they are re-arranged, being read into a plot (that is, what narratology calls the "narrative" in fiction or plot in drama or film). A film's narrative, then, is the sequence of events as they actually appear in the film, re-arranged from their real-time occurrence or chronology. Further readings in this field are suggested at the end of the chapter.

This distinction between the chronological "story" and the re-arrangement of that story in terms of plot (formal level of reading) and its context (in narrative discourse as it relates to the socio-cultural setting and its institutions) is widely exploited in the production and analysis of films. Films rarely represent events or actions in the sequence in which they would occur in the real world. For instance, Roman Polanski's film *The Pianist* tells a story of the Warsaw ghetto and the holocaust of World War II, but almost from the periphery, as events are foreshortened or lengthened, with gaps and omissions of narrative and of time in the concentration on the life of the pianist of the title. However, even that life is not told in a strict chronological sequence. So it is with virtually all other films. Some, such as *Catch-22,* based on Joseph Heller's novel, take particular delight in re-arranging the events so that they are full of flashbacks and flashforwards.

One exception is the documentary film, of World War II, for example, which attempts to present a narrative that makes breaks in space but tries to avoid breaks in time so that a fairly strict sequence, often of cause and effect, is maintained. But close analysis will reveal that documentary films do jump in time and do pause over particular events or emphasize people who are foregrounded as important. In most films, then, the *histoire* never exists. A supposed chronology might underlie the film's frame-by-frame sequence, but viewers see only portions of the *histoire* re-arranged in the film as narrative.

Narrative Framing

Films customarily frame and balance scenes or narrative episodes or set an important scene within the frame of another scene that occurs before or perhaps after it, often in a slightly different form. Hence, the study of framing devices is partly an application of a formal reading to perceive the frames. However, it also is expository (asking why the content of this frame is used structurally to contain that scene) as well as analytical (asking how the context of this frame—institutionally or socially, perhaps—comments on the meaning of the framed scene or sequence). Hence, the study of frames is the analysis of how certain scenes are enclosed and why.

For instance, films usually use the formal frame of the title and cast at the beginning and end with the credits. This formal discourse of the film is a long-standing one in film history and is probably rooted in the drama, in which printed texts from at least the 16th century contained the *dramatis personae* at the beginning, and at the end the word *finis* signals the end, the dropping of the curtain. But this convention is paralleled by the formal words that we pointed to as helping to determine the genre of the fairy story, moving from "Once upon a time" to "happily ever after." In modern and contemporary films, however, the title and cast are often overlaid visually and sonically onto scenes from the film or opening background shots.

In *Apocalypse Now,* for instance, the opening and closing shots and the credits are different in various versions of the film, but they provide important implications, contexts, and conclusions, and a comparative and analytical reading of the film would want to examine each version and assess the different functions of each change. The 70-mm version of the film concludes with Willard's leading Lance back to the patrol boat, while the tribesmen and soldiers drop their weapons and a cleansing rain falls on all but Willard. Added to the 35-mm video version are the credits, which appear over the shots of an air attack destroying Kurtz's compound with napalm. What is the effect of the framing of the sound overlay of "This is the End" by The Doors?

In *Marat/Sade,* set in an insane asylum, the opening and closing credits are the title and credits entered a word at a time in silence. An expository reading would ask, "What is the effect of this stress on the linear and visual sequence of written text?" It would want to determine how that narrative framing prepares for the static anonymity of the supposedly insane actors about to enact the history of the French Revolution and to carry out their own revolution against the asylum's authorities. A different kind of formal narrative framing is used in James Whale's *Frankenstein,* in which one of the actors steps through a curtain (as on a stage) to warn the audience, even before the credits, that Boris Karloff as the monster will horrify them. The narrative frame worked: he did horrify, and ambulances rushed people to hospitals all over North America after the film premiered in 1931. Such historical detail, of course, provides another context for an analytical reading in audience reception.

Time and Space

Time and space are manipulated in films with significant visual clues. In older films (here, Whale's *Frankenstein* and *Bride of Frankenstein* are particularly useful films), the allusions to time and space are verbal as well as visual (the dialogue "Where is Henry?" anticipates a scene shift to where Henry is, in his lab). A cliché drawn from the captions used in silent films points to this shift in scene: "Meanwhile, back at the ranch...." Later films provide important transitions to the modern use of various kinds of cuts to indicate shifts and juxtapositions in time and space. *Anachronies* (or sequences out of normal temporal logic) and sequences that violate normal spatial logic (a coined term might be *anatopies*) are familiar to contemporary viewers of films, who have learned to read this new grammar partly from video clips and music videos. In music videos, the sound sequence is sustained and continuous, but the visuals shift in time and space, partly according to the lyrics and partly according to the separate (and possibly only tangentially connected) narrative in the visuals. Woody Allen has experimented a good deal with these shifts in time and space in such films as *Annie Hall* and *Manhattan,* as have many other modern film makers.

Focalization

Focalization in films is the vantage point or orientation from which events are "seen" or from which they are brought into focus. Focalization is the perspective from which scenes are narrated visually. In fact, the focus and perspective derive from the camera's lens, but film viewers have already learned to read the camera's eye in a far more complex way so that it suggests that the vantage point is elsewhere within the scene or even in the head of one of the characters. Determining that location is the subject of focalization. The term *focalization* was elaborated in the last 40 years in the analysis of narrative fiction and refers to a broader range than the more restricted narrator's point-of-view, by asking "Who sees?" and "Who speaks?" From information in the film, in the way that scenes are shot or directed, viewers are informed about whose "eye" is seeing or who is narrating the scene. Sometimes, that focalization is accomplished by the lens of the camera in a kind of objective scrutiny (external focalizer) and sometimes by a character or by a voice-over, when a character speaks but is not seen, or in a dialogue when the focalization shifts from one to the other character (internal focalizers). Hence, the study of focalization is another strategy in the formal and expository levels of reading that enable a film reader to begin to determine meaning on the basis of multiple patterns of focalization, especially in key scenes where detailed work is especially effective.

Metanarrative

Metanarrative or *metafiction* (again the film term is derived from the analysis of narrative fiction) draws attention to the self-reflexive way in which texts reproduce their own process of making. That is, during the process of narrating a sequence of events, a film may interject sequences about the making of that episode. Two recent TV series, for instance, *Malcolm in the Middle* and *Bernie Mac,* both employ metanarrative when the main character pauses in the middle of the action to address the audience directly (a variant of the soliloquy in drama). Usually, at this point, the main character rationalizes his actions and suggests probable outcomes according to his distorted logic. Inevitably, the logic blows up in his face, and a different outcome follows in which he is made a fool of. Metanarrative is used here in at least two ways. First, by stepping out of the level of fictional time and space to address the audience directly, the character introduces to the action a completely different level of time and space. Second, by commenting on the action up to that point and predicting probable outcomes according to his logic, the character calls attention to another level of plotting, that done by the screen writers who are using this device to poke fun at the main character's pretensions and their own craft.

In another sense, metanarrative is always wrapped up in its own art forms and conventions and cannot easily achieve objectivity or avoid being conditioned by its medium. For instance, it is difficult for committed peace activists to be objective in making a film about a munitions factory, being already implicated in the reality that they are trying to represent. Metanarrative draws attention to this very complicity, asserting that not only is such a work not objective, but it is reproducing its own identification with the subject of the film. Michael Moore continually makes this point in his allusions to the camera crew and their film work in *Bowling for Columbine*.

Metanarrative often goes a step further, incorporating into a film something of the process of making a film—perhaps even another film. For example, *Apocalypse Now* draws attention to the process of making the film itself (sometimes called metafilm), when an assault on a village includes Francis Ford Coppola himself making a different film on the same set, for an American news cast (or perhaps shooting material that will not be used in the movie?). In fact, we learn from other sources that he was making a film about the making of *Apocalypse Now,* released several years after *Apocalypse Now*. The role of the photographer later in the movie, played by Dennis Hopper, is another reference to the notion of the image photographing itself. The self-consciousness of the filmic techniques is foregrounded in Alain Resnais' *Night and Fog,* in which the focalization (then and now) is juxtaposed with documentary footage of the Auschwitz death camp. On the other hand, the notion of metanarrative in *Marat/Sade* is more narrowly focused on the notion of the drama of making a drama.

Reading for this self-reflexivity is a kind of comparative level of reading that requires you to be aware of the ways in which a film is sometimes parodying itself and the genre. At the end of *Blazing Saddles,* for instance, the heroes go into a movie house to watch a Western that is, in fact, the film that they are in. The beginning of every episode of *The Simpsons* makes a similar self-reflexive gesture. Such gestures amount to the stretching and breaking of conventional reading patterns, especially the comparatively solid notion of frames. The idea of fixed frames in contemporary life that make it possible to understand meanings and to function easily are quickly disappearing, or at least, the notion that such frames are fixed is being questioned. The conventional frames of morality, social behaviour and expectations, canons of respectability, and so on are under intense pressure and often break apart. Metanarrative exploits this fragmentation and turns the lens back on itself, questioning the solidity of the frame. "Happily ever after" does not apply, and contemporary films, TV, music videos, and other media break the frames like those we discussed above, resisting the kinds of closure or resolution that end a scene or a film, a device exploited by the films of Alfred Hitchcock, such as *The Birds* and *Psycho*.

Signification and Film Syntax

In the last three decades, critics of films and film theorists have been much influenced by the work of Ferdinand de Saussure and other structuralists and post-structuralists. To them the notion of the film sign (or signification) and of the grammar and logic of a film (or its syntax and structure) are very important analytical tools. In spoken and written language, according to Saussure, a *signifier* is the word or sound (*tree,* for instance), while a *signified* is the concept that the word evokes (the concept of tree). Together, these elements constitute a linguistic sign, the building block of language and communication. The signifier in film is usually considered the image (or even a single frame). But the signified is more difficult to define and to isolate from the signifier in films.

While a film is not a language, it functions *like* a language, with its significance, scenes, sequences, and syntax. Signs function within this order and make sense within the logic of the film, and their signifieds work there, not independently of other connotations that the signifieds have in other language systems (such as English) but in concert with those associations and conventions. One of the commonest conventions is *metonymy*, often used in films, as in literary or other texts, to indicate the part standing for the whole so that the spinning of train wheels indicates travel; the flipping of calendar pages the passing of time; the hand on the forehead thinking; and marching feet an army.

The syntax of films (the way their language of frames is assembled, and the rules by which those frames are put in order with fades, cuts, flashbacks, and so on) has also changed as the technology has changed, so, as film readers, we have learned the way the new film language works: we can read the syntax and can accept all sorts of shifts in perspective and cuts that earlier viewers could not accept. In earlier films, links in the plot had to be explained either through captions in silent movies or through sequences that allowed for the shifts (which is one reason that some earlier films seem particularly slow). The syntax, then, usually involves the modifications to time and space and the conventions of film making that allow for those categories of "reality" to be indicated.

The modification of space is referred to as *mise en scène* (French for "put into the scene"): the positioning of the actors in the setting, the angles and lenses of the cameras—all that takes place on the movie sound set or an actual location. Composition, meaning the arrangement of the details of the scene as a visual composition (including planes, perspective, balance of objects, angles, and so on), is an essential part of the *mise en scène*. In *Marat/Sade,* for instance, the love scene between Corday and Duperret, in which they are sitting on a bench, with golden light coming through the sheet behind them, gives to the scene all of the traditional romantic connotations of two lovers in a park at sunset. The composition of the scene underlines those associations. However, these associations are undercut by the irony of the attempted seduction that continually overtakes the romantic love song that Corday sings and by the actual words of her song. The various kinds of shots contribute to the effect of the *mise en scène*. The modification of time is called *montage* (French for "putting together"), the cutting that takes place in the editing room to juxtapose different shots and to interpose different time conditions.

Understanding Technical Terms

Technical terms, such as cuts, shots, *mise en scène,* and *montage,* as well as many others, are often used in film production, criticism, and analysis to describe the formal structure of scenes, camera work, and editing and are useful to you in your critical reading of films and other media. We indicate below some printed and Web sources for readily available glossaries that explain these terms and provide well-illustrated detail, often with frames and clips from films. A short film glossary is found in the materials on Chapter 4 on the *Foundations* Web site.

CHAPTER SUMMARY

In Chapter 4, you have learned how to become a proficient reader, active and able to read different kinds of course materials with different kinds of skills. You are able now to skim effectively, as well as undertake close readings. You have now developed some annotation methods that will help you avoid having to re-read materials before you write tests on them. Even your more advanced reading techniques, based on the five levels that we have discussed, are becoming part of your academic resources. Perhaps you have also tested and increased your reading speed. And finally, you are now able to re-direct appropriate reading strategies from printed texts to different kinds of course material and to different disciplines. As a critical reader you have been able to address many of your earlier concerns about how to cope with a substantial reading load in most courses:

- Your reading comprehension has been greatly advanced beyond the limitations you had carried over from your early reader training.
- You have learned that skimming is not a bad habit but a necessary critical skill.
- You are now able to annotate your readings, prepare outlines and summaries, and you can link your readings to lecture notes and other course materials.
- You have the information you need to assess your reading speed and know of ways of improving it.
- From being a reader concerned only with content, you have become a critical reader, able to understand texts at different levels.

- You are also able to export your reading skills to different kinds of texts, to computer texts, multi-media, and materials in a variety of disciplines.

In this chapter, we have outlined reading skills as a cumulative process, from basic techniques to more complex strategies. Do not worry if you have not grasped everything in some of the more complex methods: at this stage, however, you should work to master techniques of skimming and reading for basic comprehension. All of them are useful to you now, but all of them also need working on in your later years of university study and through life-long learning. In the next chapter, we move from reading techniques to an even more basic level of critical reading—words or vocabulary.

FURTHER READINGS

Reading Debates: Phonics and Whole Language Methods

Adams, Marilyn. *Beginning to Read: Thinking and Learning about Print*. Washington: Sponsored by the Office of Educational Research and Improvement of the U.S. Department of Education, 1990.

Anderson, Richard, Elfrieda Hiebert, Judy Scott, and Ian Wilkinson. *Becoming a Nation of Readers*. Washington: Sponsored by the National Academy of Education, National Institute of Education, and Center for the Study of Reading, 1985.

Chall, Jeanne S. *Learning to Read: The Great Debate*. 3rd ed. Fort Worth, TX: Harcourt Brace, 1996.

Hiebert, Elfrieda H., David Peterson, Barbara Taylor, Virginia Richardson, and Scott G. Paris. *Every Child a Reader*. Ann Arbor, MI: CIERA (Center for the Improvement of Early Reading Achievement), U of Michigan School of Education, 1998.

Snow, Catherine, Susan Burns, and Peg Griffin. *Preventing Reading Difficulties in Young Children*. Washington: Sponsored by the Office of Special Education Programs, the Office of Educational Research, the National Institute on Child Health and Human Development, and the National Research Council of the National Academy of Science, 1998.

Critical Reading Practice

Benner, Patricia Ann. *Breakthroughs in Critical Reading Skills*. Chicago: Contemporary Books, 1996.

Cheek, Earl H., and Martha D. Collins. *Strategies for Reading Success*. Columbus, OH: Merrill, 1985.

Knight, Theodore O. *Mastering College Reading*. Chicago: Irwin, 1995.

Phillips, Anne Dye, and Peter Elias Sotiriou. *Steps to Reading Proficiency*. 2nd ed. Belmont, CA: Wadsworth, 1987.

Wright, Larry. *Critical Thinking: An Introduction to Analytical Reading and Reasoning*. New York: Oxford UP, 2001.

Zipes, Jack David, trans. *Beauties, Beasts, and Enchantment: Classic French Fairy Tales*. New York: New American Library, 1989.

———, ed. *The Trials and Tribulations of Little Red Riding Hood*. New York: Routledge, 1993.

Speed Reading

Berg, Howard S., and Marcus Conyers. *Speed Reading: The Easy Way*. New York: Barrons, 1998.

Buzan, Tony. *Use Your Head*. London: BBC Books, 1995.

Carver, Ronald P. "Speed Readers Don't Read; They Skim." *Psychology Today,* August 1972: 22–30.

Dudley, Geoffrey A. *Speed Reading*. London: Thomson, 1977.

Frank, Steven. *Speed Reading Secrets*. Holbrook, MA: Backpack Books, 1998.

Robinson, Francis P. *Effective Study*. 4th ed. New York: Harper & Row, 1970.

Smith, Nila Banton. *Speed Reading Made Easy*. New York: Time Warner, 1966.

Film, Television, and Media Studies

Allen, Robert C., ed. *Channels of Discourse, Reassembled: Television and Contemporary Criticism*. Chapel Hill, NC: U of North Carolina P, 1992.

Bordwell, David, and Kristin Thompson. *Film Art: An Introduction*. New York: McGraw-Hill, 2001.

Braudy, Leo, ed. *Film Theory and Criticism*. New York: Oxford UP, 1998.

Budd, Mike, Steve Craig, and Clay Steinman. *Consuming Environments: Television and Commercial Culture*. New Brunswick, NJ: Rutgers UP, 1999.

Burnett, Ron, ed. *Explorations in Film Theory*. Bloomington, IN: U of Indiana P, 1991.

Cook, David A. *A History of Narrative Film*. New York: Norton, 1996.

Edgerton, Gary R., and Peter C. Rollins, eds. *Television Histories: Shaping Collective Memory in the Media Age*. Lexington, KY: U of Kentucky P, 2001.

Hayward, Susan. *Cinema Studies: The Key Concepts*. New York: Routledge, 2000.

Hill, John, and Pamela Church Gibson, eds. *The Oxford Guide to Film Studies*. Oxford: Oxford UP, 1998.

Marris, P., and Sue Thornham, eds. *Media Studies: A Reader*. New York: New York UP, 2000.

Monaco, James. *How to Read a Film: The World of Movies, Media, and Multimedia: Language, History, Theory*. New York: Oxford UP, 2000.

Nelmes, Jill, ed. *An Introduction to Film Studies*. New York: Routledge, 1999.

Newcombe, Horace, ed. *Television, the Critical View*. New York: Oxford UP, 2000.

Pearson, Roberta E., and Philip Simpson, eds. *Critical Dictionary of Film and Television Theory*. New York: Routledge, 2001.

Vande Berg, Leah R., Lawrence A. Wenner, and Bruce E. Gronbeck, eds. *Critical Approaches to Television*. Boston: Houghton Mifflin, 1998.

chapter five

Building a Critical Vocabulary

University work depends upon your ability to use words critically. Chapter 5 gives a range of strategies to develop your vocabulary, from information on reference books to practical advice on ways to extend your mastery of language.

LEARNING OBJECTIVES

In this chapter, we address the following questions:

- How do you extend and improve your vocabulary through effective reading strategies?

- What kinds of dictionaries are most useful to you for different purposes?

- How do you select and use your desk dictionary?

- What are specialized dictionaries, and how do you use them?

- What dictionary resources are available on the Web?

- How can you use word origins to understand complex vocabulary better?

- How can you increase your vocabulary by being aware of parts of speech, roots, prefixes, and suffixes?

The matters introduced in this chapter, like the previous chapter on critical reading, are not to be digested and put into practice in one sitting or one week. Extending your vocabulary, making it become an effective tool in reading and writing, is a life-long project.

EXTENDING YOUR VOCABULARY

From earliest childhood, we make sounds, at first babbling to indicate happiness or crying to indicate needs, but by the age of three years, we are well on our way to learning a basic vocabulary, and by the age of six years, we have a vocabulary of between 5000 and 8000 words. By the early teen years for many people that number has increased fourfold to 30 or 40 000 words. The average adult has a vocabulary of about 50 000 words. These numbers can seem intimidating, since most people have no idea how many words they know or can control. But the problem is much greater, as Hunter Breland and his colleagues report in *The College Board Vocabulary Study:*

> A large vocabulary is difficult to acquire and maintain because many important words occur infrequently in a language. [One study] found that only about 3000 words occurred more than 10 times per million words of running text and only about 10 000 words occurred more than once per million words of running text. If a college student is to maintain a vocabulary of 50 000 words, four-fifths of those words will be encountered relatively infrequently in normal reading and, thus, must be stored in memory for long periods of time (Breland, Jones, and Jenkins 2).

The College Board study attempts to indicate the levels of expertise that advanced high school and first-year university students have with a core vocabulary and how well they fare in defining more difficult words. Many teachers are aware that their students have a limited grasp of many of the words that are used in lectures and readings for courses. The incidence of vocabulary failure increases dramatically when the materials are either technical or literary. Students have considerable difficulty with the vocabulary on any page of a novel by Charles Dickens or a play by Shakespeare. In a recent classroom exercise, the authors found that second-year students could not comprehend the meaning of many fairly common words in a short essay by a Victorian novelist. In one sample, out of a class of 30 students, 10 or more admitted they could not understand the meaning of the following words: *adduced, allegory, burlesque, cockney, postulates,* and *sonata.* Five or more could not identify the following: *assail, breadth, consorting, embodiment, engendering, mastery, vitality.* In a lead article on homework in *Time* magazine, the following words occurred on one page, almost all of which would cause difficulty for many university students: *acclimates, almanac, bolster, confound, diorama, gauge, loquacious, ratcheted, requisite, rigor, rote, scant, decade,* and *sonata* (Ratnesar 38).

Some philosophers and psychologists think that our ability to know anything is directly related to the size and functioning of our vocabulary. Without language, we might still be able to think, but without an adequate vocabulary, we cannot organize or communicate what we know. What, then, can you do to build a more effective vocabulary? One easy answer is to read more effectively. *The College Board Vocabulary Study* estimates that children learn between 800 and 1200 words a year from their reading. You should aim to learn at least double that number of words during each year of your university study. As your vocabulary increases, you will read faster and more accurately, and you will be able to communicate your ideas more effectively.

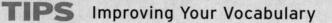

TIPS   Improving Your Vocabulary

1. Carry a pocket dictionary with you, and use it frequently to check words you are uncertain about.

2. Keep a vocabulary book and enter unfamiliar words as you read.

3. At the end of a week, go through your vocabulary book, write out the 10 most important words for the week with brief definitions on sticky-notes, and put them on your mirror.

4. Use an association method (*mnemonics,* or memory jogging) to help you learn the words.

5. Go over the words each night as you brush your teeth, and check the meanings in the morning. When you are certain you know them, replace the sticky-notes with new ones.

6. Learn to recognize the roots of words, especially if you know any languages other than English.

7. Learn some basic prefixes and suffixes to see how the meanings of words are modified.

The most effective tactic for vocabulary building is to be methodical. You should mark unfamiliar words in your reading (many students use a small *x* in their own books, or note words from library books in their own vocabulary books). You can figure out definitions from the context and note them down, or you can look up a number of words in your dictionary at the end of a reading period. If you are power reading, you should not pause to look up words, since that will slow you down, but should remember to look them up at the end of your reading session. You can keep your own reading dictionary as a file in your computer and add words as you come across them. In the evening, you can add to the dictionary words that you jotted down during the day in your reading or at lectures. In this way, you maintain a continuous review. Each week you should set aside some time to review the words more systematically, focusing on a page or on several letters. Above all, keeping a good dictionary at your desk or accessing a good dictionary on the Web should be a routine part of your study habits.

In the sections that follow, we discuss what you can learn from a dictionary, what kinds of dictionaries you will use regularly, and what kinds you will need only from time to time. We also suggest ways to build vocabulary through knowledge of word sources (in other languages, or through root words in English) and word parts (such as prefixes and suffixes). But first, it is important to distinguish between dictionary meanings and definitions (denotation) and contextual associations (connotation).

DENOTATION AND CONNOTATION

The meaning of any word is the result of a long process of social agreements and language usage stretching back through several thousand years of language history. Meaning is not inherent in words but is the result of usage and agreements so that any word, say *tree,* is used in English to designate specific phenomena, in this case both evergreen and deciduous plants with a large, single trunk and many branches. The ancestry of the word can be traced to the Anglo-Saxon word *treo* and to similar words in other Scandinavian languages (Icelandic *tre;* Danish *træ;* Swedish *trä*). The word also is allied to the Russian *drevo* (the letters *t* and *d* being variants in some languages), all from the Greek *drus* (an oak tree) and the Sanskrit *dru* (a tree). Other languages derive their word for *tree* from different language roots, so the French *arbre,* the Italian *albero,* and the Spanish *arbol* may be traced back to the Latin *arbor* (also used in English). The sound and shape of a word is determined by its difference from other words and by its likeness to other words in its family (such as plurals, adjectives, and adverbs).

This long process of the development and changing of words and their meanings results in both fairly precise definitions and also more general associations. Precise definitions are called *denotations,* and associations of words with other words and implications are called *connotations.* That is, denotation is what the word means according to dictionary definitions, while connotation is what a word suggests by usage and context, particularly the associations connected to the word. Many students remember the difference by aligning the first letter of each with its major basis of meaning as bold-faced below:

denotation = **d**ictionary **d**efinition

connotation = **c**ontextual or associational meaning

Denotation

Denotation is the explicit meaning as determined by a dictionary. A dictionary summarizes the root of the word and gives the literal and established meanings for a term, often providing information about how usage has modified the definition over time. Such denotations will help you understand the subtle differences in meanings between words that might seem alike or that might even have the same definition in a thesaurus or shorter word guide but that have, in fact, very different shades of meaning. However, dictionaries, especially concise or desktop dictionaries, often define by listing synonyms, which, when examined more closely for their definitions in a larger dictionary, can be shown to have quite different shades of meaning.

For instance, in a popular dictionary published at the beginning of the 20th century, *Chambers's Twentieth Century Dictionary,* the word *thin* is said to mean "having little thickness: slim: lean," and so on. So, it might be appropriate to speak of a particular book or a person as *thin*. It would also be proper to speak of the same person as slim, but if the book were spoken of as slim, that would mean that its contents were slight or not intellectually challenging. Indeed, to speak of the person as *lean* would suggest that, as with bacon, there is little fat or only muscle, meanings that are not involved in the word *thin*. That is, the synonyms are not always perfect matches in more abbreviated dictionaries. To get the fuller definitions, you have to use the larger dictionaries. Other synonyms, such as those given as possible alternatives for *thin* in a thesaurus, such as *slender, bony, gaunt, flimsy, trim, narrow,* or *slim,* raise many more problems of appropriateness and push denotation back to the level of connotation, where the implications of particular words and their use in context come into play.

One of the frustrations of using a dictionary, especially the brief paperback dictionary that many students find useful to carry to class but continue to use when doing more advanced academic work, is precisely this problem of synonyms. When you are uncertain of the denotation of a word, you might look the word up in a dictionary, only to be faced with a series of synonyms that are equally mystifying. Such is especially the case with technical or scientific terms ("*Cumin:* an umbelliferous plant common in Egypt"; "*Pecten:* a genus of molluscs"). The denotation of many words can be confusing. For instance, the word *pedant* is defined in *Chambers's* as "one who makes a vain display of learning," but the word *vain* might present further problems, since the meanings given for it include "unsatisfying: fruitless: unreal: silly: conceited: showy: vacant: worthless"—all of which do not apply equally to the word *pedant.* The denotations *conceited* and *showy* best apply to the kind of "display of learning" that a pedant would exhibit, though a reader seeking enlightenment would have to dig further to find a way through this thicket.

Still, the problem remains. Often, an essay topic introduces problems in terminology, perhaps derived from the course, from the text examined, or from the pertinent critical commentaries. To clarify procedures and method, such terms should be defined, since they might be open to confusion or misunderstanding. Most students think that they can solve the central problem of the interpretation by finding a short dictionary definition. However, such a denotative meaning might be too short, wrong, or insufficiently focused on the materials of a course. It is often best to use course materials to arrive at such definitions. For instance, a course might use the concepts of gender, race, and class to discuss important readings. An essay on a topic that requires consideration of ways that gender codes function in some of the readings might require that notions of masculinity, femininity, and gender and genderism be discussed. Many short dictionaries will not define such terms helpfully for developing a comprehensive argument. It would be better to use a specialized dictionary or encyclopedia, such as Maggie Humm's *Dictionary of Feminist Theory* or Lisa Tuttle's *Encyclopedia of Feminism.* But perhaps the best approach would be to use the definitions of the course.

Connotation

Connotation refers to the associations of a word, drawn partly from how a word is used in a sentence, partly from the other associations that a word has in related or even different uses and partly from the social context or discourse in which the word is used. The word *horse,* for instance, signifies a quadruped that eats grain, but that definition can be applied to many other animals—for instance, to a mule, an ox, or a cow—as well as to different types of horses—broncos, ponies, colts, steeds, and so on, each with different connotations.

Similarly, the word *car* can mean very different things in different contexts. It can mean the new car in advertising: it can suggest freedom and power as it drives over empty highways in desert sunsets or over rocky mountain terrain that no sensible driver would ever traverse. Or it can mean family values, as mom, dad, three kids, and a dog get in the car with their stuff and head for the family cottage. Or it can mean the getaway car associated with a bank hold-up, the problem for the city planners, the ecological nightmare, and so on. The connotations of *car,* then, depend on the associations that refer to the way of life of the user, the conventional codes associated with the word in a culture in general, and the use of the word in a particular context. Furthermore, other words for *car* that carry the same denotation (or dictionary meaning) might have very different connotations. For instance, many car-rental firms advertise "rent a car," and others, somewhat downscale, advertise "rent a wreck," with roughly the same denotation but with the distinct connotation of a car in less reliable shape and at a more modest rate. The terms *automobile, auto,* and *motorcar* all suggest a more archaic period, probably before the 1950s. The term *vehicle* is a generic category much loved by government licensing bureaus, and the term *wheels* is slang from the 1960s and earlier.

Such connotations have attached to them all kinds of social values, both positive and negative. For instance, in the three categories of odour, human weight, and mistakes, it is possible to draw up words that indicate roughly the same meaning but that have very different positive and negative connotations.

Category	Negative	Positive
odour	smell	scent
weight	skinny	slender
mistake	screw-up	slip

In another example, the term *buck* denotes the male of the deer, goat, hare, and rabbit, especially the male of the fallow deer. In a recent legal judgment in Ontario in the case of a dominatrix known as Madame de Sade, the judge acknowledged that there was "overkill" on the part of the 15 officers who entered her premises to investigate and possibly arrest her. There was, according to the judge, no reason to submit her to a body search, and "she was not well done by." However, he excused the rowdiness of officers who donned wigs and had mock whip fights as the understandable actions of "young bucks" exposed to an unusual environment (Levy A6). Here, the connotation of "young bucks" has aroused the rage of many people because it is a way of excusing police actions in the name of stereotypical gender roles. The comments are widely seen as sexist. The term "bucks" carries with it the connotation of aggressive pranksterism, or of the good-natured, wholesome sport of males having mildly sexual fun—when the context demands something quite different. So, the judge's use of the phrase, his connotation, excuses the officers on the basis of their youthful masculinity; to justice watchers, feminists, and people concerned about the implications of legal language, the term has the connotation of excusing conduct on the basis of sexism.

Connotations also carry social codes and values and can be read for their political power and ideological content. For instance, when a newspaper reports on a strike, the two opposing sides refer to the same stage in their proceedings by different terms that emphasize their political positions. Hence, the union leaders stress the "strike demands," while the CEOs stress the "management offer," and these values are set in order on the basis of their relative positions in the dominant power hierarchies of the opposing sides:

To the CEOs:

Negative connotations	Positive connotations
strike demands	management offer
bargaining position	settlement process

To the union leaders:

Negative connotations	Positive connotations
management offer	strike demands
settlement process	bargaining position

The best source for information on denotation and connotation is your major resource for words, your dictionary, to which we now turn.

DICTIONARIES AND WHAT THEY TELL YOU

Dictionaries come in many shapes, sizes, and ranges; they can be encyclopedic and make claims of recording all of the words in a language, or they can be brief word lists with simple definitions; they can be devoted to a particular topic (dictionaries of metals, chemical formulae, literary terms) or directed to a particular audience (dictionaries for new learners of a language, for high school students, and so on). Some knowledge of how most dictionaries work is a useful tool in becoming a better reader. The preface in a dictionary explains the conventions used, the ordering of the alphabet and the system used in the word entries, and the special marks and abbreviations that indicate pronunciation, usage, and derivation. Entries in dictionaries usually include abbreviations (either as a part of the main word list or in a special section of abbreviations at the back of the book). Hyphenated words or compound words are also included (for example, *lynx-eyed*). Some dictionaries also include foreign words or phrases that are often used in English, such as *fait accompli, gesundheit,* or *homo sapiens,* though, again, they may be listed at the back of the book. Some desk and student dictionaries (such as *The Canadian Oxford Dictionary*) include encyclopedic entries, such as short biographical and geographical identifications as well as illustrations.

You may use a good dictionary regularly for conventional spellings and meanings (such as *The Concise Oxford Dictionary, The American Heritage Dictionary, The Random House College Dictionary,* or *Webster's Ninth New Collegiate Dictionary*). But it is recommended that you consult *The Oxford English Dictionary (OED)* in 20 volumes for detailed historical commentary on words when you need technical or literary definitions.

TIPS Dictionary "Dos" and "Don'ts"

1. Do use your dictionary to learn the meaning and use of unfamiliar words.
2. Do not use general dictionaries to reduce complex terms to simplistic definitions. An essay on the Holocaust or Totalitarianism might need complex definitions of terms. Simple dictionary definitions are not helpful in beginning an essay.
3. Do define technical terms in a course (such as *fantasy, romance, horror, obsession,* or *monster*) through course readings or lectures, specialized subject dictionaries, or the *OED*.

Spelling and Syllabification

The usual spelling (or *orthography*) of a word is given first, and variants are usually noted, such as differences between British and American spellings. The entry word also shows capitalization. The word is divided into syllables, an easy way to determine where the word should be hyphenated at the end of a line. Different principles for dividing words into syllables are used in Britain and Canada and in the United States. In Britain and Canada, words are divided according to derivation so that the smallest meaning-parts of words (morphemes) make up the bases of syllables (for instance, *know-ledge*). In the United States, words are divided into syllables according to pronunciation (for instance, *knowl-*

edge). Such differences have important implications for both phonics in learning to read through familiarization with conventional syllables and for learning to spell. In both systems, however, the same general rules for dividing words apply (see the Tips box below). Modern newspapers use computer dictionaries to divide words, but often, the divisions are arbitrary and make nonsense words or comical splits, such as *bar-bed, forest-all, mans-laughter, men-swear, ong-oing, real-locations, roman-tic, sung-lasses, superb-owl, wee-knights, line-age* (culled from recent issues of *The Globe and Mail*).

Pronunciation

After the word heading, the pronunciation is given, often in parentheses, and variants and annotations may indicate special uses or regional differences. Some dictionaries use respellings to indicate the pronunciation of each syllable according to a phonic method. Others use special typographical symbols or diacritical marks, explained either at the bottom of the page in brief form or in a more detailed form at the beginning of the book. Increasingly, the International Phonetic Alphabet is being used, and older dictionaries that are reprinted often convert older systems to this international standard.

TIPS Syllabification and Hyphenation

Syllables

- Words are divided after a vowel *(a, e, i, o, u)* so that the next syllable begins with a consonant.
- Where a single vowel is a syllable in the middle of a word, the word is split after the syllabic vowel (e.g., *physi-cal, he-si-tant;* not *phy-si-cal* or *hesit-ant* or *hes-i-tant*).
- Double consonants are usually separated in syllables *(mil-len-ni-um).*
- Two consonants are usually separated *(ad-ver-si-ty).*
- Single-syllable words are not divided.
- Prefixes and suffixes (such as *con-, pre-, mis-, -tion,* or *-ing*) are single syllables, and it is preferable to break the word after a prefix or before a suffix, rather than elsewhere.

Hyphens

- Do not leave one or two letters at the end of a line before a hyphen.
- Do not put fewer than three letters on the next line.
- Do not divide the last word in a paragraph or the last word on a page.

Parts of Speech

After the indication of pronunciation, the part of speech is identified by means of an abbreviation. Many of these abbreviations are obvious: *n.* (noun), *adj.* (adjective), *adv.* (adverb), *conj.* (conjunction), *interj.* (interjection), *prep.* (preposition), *pron.* (pronoun), and *v.*

(verb). Some dictionaries (chiefly the *Oxford* series) use the abbreviation *sb.* (substantive) for nouns. If you do not recognize any others, you may identify them in the list of abbreviations in the front matter of the dictionary. When a word functions as more than one part of speech, for instance, as both a noun and a verb (such as *fly,* which can be used to mean both a winged insect and moving through the air), the meanings for one part of speech are given together before the meanings for the other. Some dictionaries list the nouns first (the *Oxford* series, for instance), while others list verbs first.

From this point, dictionaries differ in the order of information given, though usually they provide similar kinds of information.

Etymology

All dictionaries, except for the smallest pocket dictionaries, provide some explanation of a word's origins, sometimes before the definitions (as in the *Oxford* and *Webster's* dictionaries), sometimes after. For students, these explanations of word origins are often puzzling because of unfamiliar abbreviations, typographical symbols, and foreign words. This information is often very useful in indicating shades of meaning and in pointing to a word's history. Usually, a dictionary will use an opening symbol such as < or — to indicate that the word in English is "from, taken from, or derived from" a word in another language, indicated by an abbreviation identified in the preface. Some dictionaries (such as *The Shorter Oxford*) give Greek roots in Greek, so some knowledge of the Greek alphabet is necessary to read these words; other dictionaries usually transliterate other language scripts (the Cyrillic alphabet for Russian, Arabic, and so on) into the Latin alphabet.

Restrictions of Usage

Dictionaries usually indicate any usage limitations, either in time (old, rare, obsolete, or archaic usage: e.g., *avaunt* or *aroint* to mean "begone") or by different classes of society, language groups, regional communities, or forms of discourse. Hence, some uses are informal or colloquial (such as abbreviated verb forms, *I'll, can't, couldn't,* which are acceptable in conversation though not in formal writing), others are slang *(butt, rip off, screw)* or vulgar. Vulgar usage may refer to semiliterate usage *(ain't)* or to terms with sexual or scatological references that are not generally acceptable in formal public discourse *(ass, shit).* Some words that formerly were vulgarisms, especially swear words, have now moved up to slang or informal words in the conventional hierarchy of acceptable usage *(Hell! Damn!).* Some words belong to a local dialect (*crick* for creek), and some may be poetic usage (*aweary* for "weary," *even* for "evening"). Some dictionaries explain any peculiar uses of a word in detail. Any use of a word in a specialized field of knowledge is also indicated (for instance, *med.* for medical, *chem.* for chemical, or *nav.* for naval terminology).

Definitions

The list of meanings is the reason most people use a dictionary. Users of a dictionary should be aware that the meanings are not set out randomly but according to one of two organizational principles: some dictionaries give meanings in chronological order *(Oxford* and *Webster's),* beginning with the meaning that entered the language at the earliest date;

others try to give the most common meaning first, followed by more minor meanings and specialized ones, and grouping related meanings close together *(Random House* and *American Heritage)*. This latter method of organization eliminates much of the history of a word, but it gives faster access to the most common meaning. In either method, the meanings of a word are grouped according to the part of speech. That is, all of the uses for a noun are given first (for instance, *fly* as a noun would include the insect, a baseball hit into the air, a flap in clothing to cover buttons or a zipper in trousers, a fish hook used in fishing for trout, the space backstage and above the stage where the scenery can be hoisted and stored on ropes, and a light, double-seated coach drawn by a horse); the meanings for the verb follow (to move through the air on wings, to flee, to cause to fly, as *to fly a kite,* and so on). Meanings are usually given by a brief statement, in a phrase or a single word. More complex meanings have expanded definitions, sometimes with an indication of special idiomatic usage, such as which preposition follows a particular word (for example, *adhere* may be defined as "stick fast [*to*]"; or particular uses of the verb *to read* might need fuller explanation: *to read into something* means to read more meaning into something than the text warrants; *to read out of* means to expel, as to expel from a political party). Most desk and reference dictionaries also include definitions that illustrate a particular sense with a phrase or sentence, adding a level of connotation to the denotative meaning. Dictionaries based on historical principles date these examples and indicate the sources.

TIPS Using the Dictionary

1. **Derived forms.** Dictionaries list words derived from the main entry word (for instance, *read* is followed by definitions for *readability, readable, reader, readership,* and *reading*).

2. **Compound and combination words.** Dictionaries often define compound words that use the main word together with another word, with or without a hyphen (*reading-desk, livingroom*). Combination words combine two words together into one idea (*reading room, income tax*).

3. **Related words.** Dictionaries usually indicate by *cf.* (Latin, *confere*, compare) words that are closely related, deriving from the same root, though their subsequent history has been different. For instance, *fancy* is an abbreviation of *fantasy,* and *essay* (trying or testing, an attempt, a short composition on any subject) and *assay* (a testing of the virtues or qualities of a thing or person) are related because both are adopted from the Old French *assai,* and *essai,* from the Latin *exagere* and *exigere* (to weigh, examine, or test).

4. **Synonyms and antonyms.** *Synonyms* are words with meanings close to the entry word, though no two words are exact synonyms. Many dictionaries (the *Thorndike-Barnhart High School Dictionary,* for instance) provide extended discussions of synonyms to explain usage and shadings of meaning. *Antonyms* are words that are opposite in meaning to the entry word. A *thesaurus* is a book or collection of words or information, but the term is usually applied to a work that lists synonyms systematically.

Usage Notes

Particular phrases might have special meanings, might be used in special circumstances, or might be undergoing changing usage. Some dictionaries indicate which word is generally accepted or preferred when there is a confusion between words (such as *accept* and *except* or *disinterested* and *uninterested*), when a word takes a particular preposition *(adherent to),* or in other instances of idioms or conventional practice.

There are many sites on the Web related to dictionaries. Some consist of English and foreign language dictionaries, and others provide introductions to dictionary work and links to other sites. A general site is Dictionary.com (**www.dictionary.reference.com/**).

For general information on dictionaries by the major publishers, see the publishers' Web sites, as, for instance, that of Longman (**www.longman-elt.com/dictionaries/**).

KINDS OF DICTIONARIES

Dictionaries that university students use are generally of five different kinds:

- Pocket dictionaries
- Desk dictionaries
- Reference dictionaries
- Foreign language dictionaries
- Special subject dictionaries

A comparison of entries for the word *critical* in several of these kinds of dictionaries allows us to set out a number of important distinguishing features and differences in the meanings of the word, which is the most important topic of this book. (See the *Foundations* Web site.)

Pocket Dictionaries

Mass-market paperback dictionaries can be carried to class and are useful on a daily basis for quickly identifying meanings that you are unfamiliar with. You usually cannot consult them during lectures, since you will be too busy taking notes; in lectures, you should write down words that sound unfamiliar and asterisk or otherwise mark them in the margins to be checked once you get home and revise your notes. Pocket dictionaries usually cost between 10 and 15 dollars. All have about 100 000 word entries and additional user help, such as lists of abbreviations. Suitable choices are the following:

American Heritage Dictionary. 3rd ed. New York: Laureleaf, 1995. 60 000 word entries.

The Merriam-Webster Dictionary. Springfield, IL: Merriam-Webster, 1995.
   70 000 word entries.

The New American Webster Handy College Dictionary. Ed. Philip D. Morehead. New York: Signet, 1995. 115 000 word entries.

Oxford American Dictionary. Ed. Eugene Erlich and Stuart Berg Flexner. New York: Avon, 1983. 70 000 word entries.

Pocket Oxford Dictionary and Thesaurus: American Edition. Ed. Frank R. Abate. New York: Oxford UP, 1999. 50 000 word entries.

Pocket Oxford Dictionary of Current English. 8th ed. Ed. Della Thompson. Oxford: Clarendon,
    1996. 140 000 word entries.

Be wary of brief pocket dictionaries that do not give full enough definitions or etymologies. Pocket dictionaries often provide definitions only by means of synonyms, the
meaning of which may be no clearer than the original word. A user then has to look up several words until a meaning that is understood is reached, and by that point, all of the shades
of meaning will be lost.

Desk Dictionaries

Most dictionary publishers produce a substantial dictionary that is not as complete as a reference work, but far more complete than the pocket dictionary. It should at least contain
more than single-word definitions and word origins. Your instructors might recommend a
desk dictionary, and a variety will be available in your university bookstore. Examples of
desk dictionaries that will continue to be useful long after university include the following:

The American Heritage Dictionary of the English Language. 4th ed. Boston: Houghton Mifflin,
    2000. 350 000 word entries.

The Canadian Oxford Dictionary. Ed. Katherine Barber. Toronto: Oxford UP, 1998. 130 000 word entries.

The Concise Oxford Dictionary of Current English. 10th ed. Ed. Judy Pearsall. Oxford: Clarendon,
    1999. 150 000 word entries.

The Merriam-Webster's Collegiate Dictionary. 10th ed. Springfield, IL: Merriam-Webster, 1998.
    215 000 word entries.

Webster's New World College Dictionary. 4th ed. New York: Macmillan, 2000. 150 000 word entries.

Webster's Ninth New Collegiate Dictionary. Springfield, IL: Merriam-Webster, 1987. 160 000
    word entries.

Even larger desk dictionaries include the following:

The Random House Dictionary of the English Language. 2nd ed. Ed. Stuart Berg Flexner. New
    York: Random House, 1987. 315 000 word entries.

The World Book Dictionary. 2 vols. Ed. Clarence L. Barnhart and Robert K. Barnhart. Chicago:
    World Book, 1988. 225 000 word entries.

For a comparison of how desk dictionaries deal with definitions, especially the word
critical, see the *Foundations* Web site.

Some desk dictionaries also include "encyclopedic" information that extends beyond
word definitions. For instance, they often list countries and major cities and towns (information found more completely in a gazetteer) with some details about location, population, and features. They also often include famous people, with birth and death dates and
brief biographical notes (information usually found in biographical dictionaries); time
charts; lists of abbreviations; diagrams of such items as the geological ages or the relationship of language groups; tables of weights and measures; special signs and symbols;
forms of address; and common phrases from other languages.

Some of the introductions to these dictionaries are available on the Web, as is that for
Merriam-Webster's Collegiate Dictionary, 10th edition (**www.m-w.com/pronguid.htm**).

Reference Dictionaries

Reference dictionaries are comprehensive in their coverage of a language and attempt to record usage exhaustively (usually including archaic or obsolete usage). Some of them also attempt to record the history of usage, especially by citing quotations, rather than examples coined by the authors of the dictionaries.

Among such reference dictionaries are the great dictionaries published by the Oxford University Press, originally edited by Sir James A.H. Murray, and *Webster's Third International,* published by Merriam-Webster. The publishing of the *Oxford English Dictionary,* commonly known as the *OED,* began in 1884 and was completed in 1928 in 12 volumes. It was corrected and re-issued in 1933 and then re-issued again (1971–1987) as *The Compact Edition of the Oxford English Dictionary* in three volumes as a micrographic reprint of the 1933 edition and the four volumes of supplements. The second edition was published in 20 volumes (Ed. J.A. Simpson and E.S.C. Weiner) in 1989. Yet another edition, the *New Oxford English Dictionary* (*NOED*) is in progress. A CD-ROM version is also published and is available in most university libraries; often, it can be accessed online if you have a university modem account as a registered user.

The advantage in using the *OED* is that it lists in chronological order the earliest recorded uses of every word so that you can study a word according to its meanings and different uses over time, with precise references to specific texts. However, the *OED* does not cover standard vocabulary completely: it is limited in its treatment of scientific and technological terms, slang, dialect, and English usage outside the British Isles. An abbreviation of the multi-volume dictionary, the *Shorter Oxford English Dictionary,* reduces the space given to obsolete and archaic terms and to citations, while retaining the historical approach to the English language found in the larger edition. The pronunciation is marked by a more complex method of notation, explained in detail in the introduction and set out on each page in abbreviated form. The word sources are given in the original languages and orthography.

The *New Shorter Oxford English Dictionary on Historical Principles* reduces the *New Oxford Dictionary* to two volumes. It places far greater stress on scientific usage and on contemporary citation. Many of the older historical citations have been reduced or eliminated. It includes specific instances of usage, gives quotations from authors, and identifies and dates the source.

The equivalent American dictionary is the *Dictionary of American English on Historical Principles* in four volumes, which deals with words that originated in the United States, with a cut-off date of 1900. Other related dictionaries extend the range to recent times. The comprehensive American dictionary, however, is *Webster's Third New International Dictionary.* It lists definitions in historical order and gives illustrative quotations, chiefly from 20th-century sources. It is particularly useful for American usage, spelling, pronunciation, and abbreviations. It does not include any proper names and has omitted usage labels (such as *vulgar, slang,* and *colloquial*), although it has been much criticized for abandoning its duty to specify proper usage. Students who want to find out whether a usage is appropriate for formal prose should consult another dictionary, such as one of the desktop dictionaries.

The major reference dictionaries include the following:

Dictionary of American English on Historical Principles. 4 vols. Ed. William A. Craigie and James R. Hulbert. Chicago: U of Chicago P, 1938–1944. Word entries end at 1900.

New Shorter Oxford English Dictionary on Historical Principles. 2 vols. Ed. Lesley Brown. Oxford: Clarendon, 1993. 500 000 words under 98 000 word entries, with 83 000 quotations.

Oxford English Dictionary. 12 vols. Ed. James A.H. Murray. Oxford: Clarendon, [1884–1928] 1933. About 478 000 words based on several million quotations.

Oxford English Dictionary. 2nd ed. 20 vols. Ed. J.A. Simpson and E.S.C. Weiner. Oxford: Clarendon, 1989. 600 000 word entries.

Shorter Oxford English Dictionary on Historical Principles. 3rd ed. Ed. C.T. Onions. Oxford: Clarendon, 1973. 170 000 word entries.

Webster's Third New International Dictionary. Ed. Philip Babcock Gove. Springfield, IL: Merriam-Webster, 1993. 450 000 word entries.

See also the Web site associated with the *OED:* **www.oed.com/**.
Your university may have an online version accessible to members of your university.

Foreign Language Dictionaries

Often, you will come across words or phrases in another language in your reading or research. Sometimes, the context is sufficient to provide an explanation, or there may be a translation given in the text or in a footnote. But at other times, it is necessary to consult a foreign language dictionary. These dictionaries are of two kinds. First, foreign language dictionaries are written for native or bi-lingual speakers of the language, with all of the information, including definitions, given in the foreign language. These are the basic dictionaries of any given language. The second kind consists of bi-lingual dictionaries, among which the most commonly used are those that translate from the original language into English and from English into the original language. Some examples of both types of foreign language dictionaries are the following:

Grand Larousse de la langue française. 7 vols. Ed. Louis Guilbert, René Lagane, and Georges Niobey. Paris: Larousse, 1971–1978. One of the standard French-only dictionaries.

Grand dictionnaire français-anglais, anglais-français. Paris: Larousse, 1993. (Bi-lingual)

Collins-Sansoni Italian Dictionary. Ed. Vladimiro Macchi. Firenze: Sansoni Editore, 1981. (Bi-lingual)

Collins Spanish-English/English-Spanish Dictionary. Ed. Colin Smith. London: Collins, 1988. (Bi-lingual)

Collins German-English/English-German Dictionary. Ed. Peter Terrell. London: Collins, 1988. (Bi-lingual)

On the Web, a number of dictionary sites have direct or linked access to major English and foreign language dictionaries. Some sites have dictionaries that allow searching through the dictionary page by page, while others offer immediate translation of a word from one language to another. See the sites at the *Foundations* Web site.

Special Subject Dictionaries

Almost every subject has a special dictionary of the terms that are particular to that topic. There are dictionaries for almost every nation, historical period, major field of study, and interest group. There are dictionaries on law, dogs, Marxist thought, computer terminology, and so on, available in both printed and electronic forms. We strongly recommend that you survey the special subject dictionaries in your university library reference room, look up others on the Web, and note in particular those that are relevant to your major. The following useful dictionaries for university students are a mere sampling of several fields:

Black, Henry Campbell. *Black's Law Dictionary: Definitions of the Terms and Phrases of American and English Jurisprudence, Ancient and Modern*. 7th ed. Ed. Bryan A. Garner. St. Paul, MN: West, 1999.

Blackwell Dictionary of Twentieth-Century Social Thought. Ed. William Outhwaite and Tom Bottomore. Oxford: Blackwell, 1993.

A Dictionary of Marxist Thought. 2nd ed. Ed. Tom Bottomore. Oxford: Blackwell, 1991.

Dictionary of Slang and Unconventional English. 8th ed. Ed. Eric Partridge; rev. Paul Beale. New York: Macmillan, 1984.

Dorling Kindersley Ultimate Visual Dictionary. London: Dorling Kindersley, 1994.

New Dictionary of American Slang. Ed. Robert L. Chapman. New York: Harper, 1986.

New Grove Dictionary of Music and Musicians. 29 vols. Ed. Stanley Sadie. New York: Grove's Dictionaries, 2001.

New Palgrave: A Dictionary of Economics. Ed. John Eatwell, Murray Milgate, and Peter Newman. New York: Stockton, 1987.

Oxford Dictionary of English Etymology. Ed. C.T. Onions, G.W.S. Friedrichsen, and R.W. Burchfield. Oxford: Clarendon, 1969.

Special interest dictionaries of English are available that explain particular difficulties in meaning, connotation, and pronunciation for ESL students:

Collins Cobuild English Dictionary. 2nd ed. Ed. John Sinclair. New York: HarperCollins, 1995. Provides extensive information on usage and idioms and adds complete sentences as examples to definitions.

Oxford ESL Dictionary for Students of American English. Ed. A.S. Hornby. Oxford: Oxford UP, 1991.

ETYMOLOGY, OR THE ORIGIN OF WORDS

Word Sources

Words contain within their structure—within their parts or syllables, shape, sound, and use—the whole history of the language from which they come and, in an important sense, the history of the people who use them. Because words have histories that are, at least in part, embedded in their shape, sound, and meaning, they contain the records of the languages with which they interacted, and they record the important contacts between peoples of different languages over many thousands of years. Philologists (from the Greek, *philos,* loving, and *logos,* word, discourse, account, or study), or historical linguists, are those who study the history of language and its use. One of the branches of philology is etymology (from the Greek, *etymos,* true sense), the investigation of the derivation and original meaning of words. Knowing the etymology of a word means that you will have a clearer sense of its meaning, and certainly of its history. Many words in English are derived from other languages and reflect periods when English-speaking peoples interacted with the speakers of other languages to such a degree that there was significant borrowing and sharing of words; gradually, words from one language were adopted and perhaps adapted by the borrowing language. For a fuller discussion of this transformation of the English language and its implications for current vocabulary, see the *Foundations* Web site.

Some knowledge of another language, therefore, is very helpful to a reader of English, partly owing to the awareness of how another language works in its grammar and syntax, but especially its vocabulary. You can begin to trace for yourself some of the etymological roots of English words. A dictionary that includes etymologies, or word origins, is a great asset in building your vocabulary. You should make it a point when consulting a dictionary to note the word origins and to try to fit them together with other words that you know. Even students who have little or no knowledge of another language can pick up clues from the English words themselves about what the parts of words mean. In the next sections, we show how knowledge of the parts of words—their roots, prefixes, and suffixes—can help expand your vocabulary and deepen your reading comprehension.

The Roots of Words

An English word consists of three possible parts, though not all parts will be present in every word. The parts are the root, the prefix, and the suffix.

The root is the part of the word that contains the basic meaning or denotation of the word. It is the base form of a word from which other forms of words are derived. That is, the root of a word is the basic morpheme (the smallest form of a word that conveys meaning). Some linguists call this part of a word the *stem,* though technically the stem is the part of a word to which prefixes and suffixes can be added. This root in English can often be traced to a different kind of root—to its etymological source in another language—and some linguists use the term *root* to refer both to the smallest meaning-part in an English word and also to the word's etymological source in another language.

A prefix is a word element that is placed in front of the root word, and a suffix (there may be more than one) is an element placed after the root. A prefix changes or modifies the meaning of the root element to make a new word. A suffix also changes the meaning, but it changes the grammatical function of a word or its use, as well. Suffixes tell us whether the word is a noun, an adjective, or a verb, and convey the comparative degree of an adjective: for example, *smaller, smallest.* Two suffixes may be added to a root to create a word, as in *uncritically.*

Unscientifically can be broken down into the following parts:

English Root

Science

Prefix

Un- [from the Old English *un-* or *on-*] expresses a negative meaning of the following root.

Suffixes

1. *-ific* > *-fic* making, causing, or producing [from the Latin suffix *-ficus,* making or doing, from the Latin verb *facere,* to make or do]
2. *-al* of the kind of, pertaining to [modelled on the ending of the Latin adjective in *-alis*]
3. *-ly* befitting, characteristic of [from Old English *-lic,* like]; also grammatical function of the adverb

Etymological Root

Latin: *scientia*

From another root, Lat. *sciens,* knowing, the present participle of the Latin verb, *scire,* to know.

In the *OED,* the prefix *un-* has 22 columns dealing with the history of the prefix alone, independent of any root words to which it is attached. There follow 373 pages of definitions of words that use the prefix *un-.*

Dictionaries normally give the roots of words, both in the sense of the English stem and the etymological root from other languages. Most dictionaries that are larger than the concise or pocket dictionaries also list prefixes and suffixes among their meanings. In the *OED,* the commentaries on these prefixes and suffixes are extensive. Many common English words are made up of combinations of roots from other languages; thus, one of the best ways to develop your knowledge of English roots is to take a course in another language. Some of these etymological roots are used as English roots (for instance, *amiable* and *amatory* are words both deriving from the Latin *amo, amare,* I love, to love), or as prefixes (*advent,* from the Latin *ad,* to or toward, and *venire,* to come).

Prefixes and Suffixes

Old English had numerous prefixes and suffixes. During the period when the language was first developing, they were combined with root words to form new words by combinations. With the coming of the Normans, English was influenced by more French and Latin forms, and the number of prefixes and suffixes that were used to make new words declined. Indeed, many of the old prefixes and suffixes began to disappear as the language changed. For instance, the Old English prefix *for-* was attached to verbs and verbal forms to change the meaning of the root to which it was attached (like all prefixes). *For-* intensified the meaning of the verb to which it was attached, or it could add the notion of negativity or destructiveness to the verb. Formerly widely used, this prefix began to be used much less frequently after about 1050. In modern English, the Old English prefix appears in only a few verbs:

forbear, forbid, fordo (to destroy), forget, forgive, forsake, forswear, forlorn (participle)

Similarly, the prefix *with-*, meaning "against," largely disappeared, except for such words as *withdraw* and *withhold.*

A number of Old and Middle English suffixes have survived, such as *-ness* (the state of being, as in *blessedness*), *-ful* (full of, as in *cheerful*), *-less* (without, as in *homeless*), *-some* (causing, as in *awesome*), *-ish* (resembling, as in *childish*) and others.

Many Latin prefixes and suffixes were added to the English language during the Middle English period, but many more after the Normans arrived in England after 1066 through French derivations from Latin. Many Latin prefixes give directions, such as toward (*in-, epi-, ad-*), away from (*ab-, ex-*), above (*super-*), below (*sub-*), or indicate time and age (*pre-, post-*).

A suffix tells how a word is being used, with respect to its meaning and to how it is being used in the syntax or grammatical structure. For instance, words ending in the suffix *-ly* are adverbs, while those ending in the suffixes *-tion* and *-ment* are nouns. Hence, suffixes can help in identifying word functions or parts of speech in sentences. In the word *uncritically,* the parts can be divided as follows:

un	-	**critic**	-	**al**	-	**ly**
prefix		root		suffix 1		suffix 2
negativizes				*makes the root into an adjective*		*makes the root into an adverb*

The same principle operates with other words. For instance, in the word *fatalists,* there are three suffixes added to the root, *fate.* The first two work by changing the root's grammatical category: *-al* turns the root into an adjective, and *-ist* turns it back into a noun, indicating the condition of one who is determined by fate. The final suffix, the letter *-s,* does not change the grammatical category, but simply indicates the plural of the noun. It is often spoken of as an *inflection,* a suffix that indicates such grammatical relations as singular/plural (cat > cats), possessive (girl's), tenses (walk > walked) and comparisons (small > smaller > smallest) (Traugott and Pratt 91). For further examples of prefixes and suffixes and their derivations, see the *Foundations* Web site.

Words are the vital instruments of thought. Increasing your vocabulary by any of the methods outlined above will increase your ability in critical thinking, reading, and writing. Knowledge of how words are formed from other languages, how they are related through their roots and prefixes and suffixes in English, and how they function in communicating meaning, is a lifetime learning project.

Some linguists think that language is a marker of rational creatures. Human language is a complex and intricate part of human life, allowing us to communicate with both ease and difficulty. But it is also a storehouse that yields its treasures only gradually. Vocabulary, as Raymond Williams says, is "a shared body of words and meanings in our most general discussions ... of the practices and institutions which we group as *culture* and *society*" (15). In this chapter, we have been concerned with the range of words available to you as a reader and writer, but to have a *critical* vocabulary, you can use words to formulate ideas and to analyze the culture and society that you are studying. We have proposed numerous ways of making the world of words not only accessible but also relevant to your whole university work.

CHAPTER SUMMARY

Chapter 5 has given you strategies to develop your critical vocabulary:

- How to differentiate between connotation and denotation and how to be aware of subtle shifts in language use that position an argument through the associations that words call into play.
- How to select and use different kinds of dictionaries for different tasks as well as how to crack what seems to be their secret code—to read dictionary entries and abbreviations for the wealth of information they contain.
- How the origins of words and the history of the language play a vital role in using vocabulary effectively.
- How you can become a critical reader by identifying the uses of words in sentences and the meanings of commonly used prefixes and suffixes.

During your university years, you have an unparalleled opportunity to develop your vocabulary; once you leave university, you will probably never have the time to devote to extended reading and study. In the next chapter, we discuss ways of using your vocabulary in arguments.

FURTHER READINGS

Vocabulary

Black, John W. *The Use of Words in Context: The Vocabulary of College Students.* New York: Plenum Press, 1985.

Espey, William R. *Thou Improper, Thou Uncommon Noun: An Etymology of Words that Once Were Names.* New York: Clarkson N. Potter, 1978.

———. *Another Almanac of Words at Play.* New York: Clarkson N. Potter, 1980.

Funk, Wilfred, and Norman Lewis. *30 Days to a More Powerful Vocabulary.* New York: Pocket Books, 1971.

Nurnberg, Maxwell, and Morris Rosenblum. *All About Words: An Adult Approach to Vocabulary Building.* New York: Mentor-New American Library, 1966.

Safire, William. "On Language." Weekly column in the *New York Times Magazine.*

———. *You Could Look It Up.* New York: Times Books, 1988.

Silverthorn, J.E., Devern J. Perry, and John W. Oberly. *College Vocabulary Building.* 5th ed. Cincinnati, OH: South Western, 1971.

Stockwell, Robert P., and Donka Minakova. *English Words: History and Structure.* New York: Cambridge UP, 2001.

Williams, Raymond. *Keywords: A Vocabulary of Culture and Society.* London: Fontana, 1981.

Language

Baugh, Albert C., and Thomas Cable. *A History of the English Language.* 5th ed. Englewood Cliffs, NJ: Prentice-Hall, 2002.

Byrne, Mary. *Eureka! A Dictionary of Latin and Greek Elements in English Words.* Newton Abbot: David and Charles, 1987.

Crystal, David. *The Cambridge Encyclopedia of Language.* Cambridge: Cambridge UP, 1995.

Danner, Horace G., and Roger Noel. *An Introduction to an Academic Vocabulary: Word Clusters from Latin, Greek, and German: A Vade Mecum for the Serious Student.* 2nd ed. Lanham, MD: UP of America, 1990.

Hughes, Geoffrey. *A History of English Words.* Oxford: Blackwell, 2000.

Knowles, Gerald. *A Cultural History of the English Language.* New York: St. Martin's Press, 1997.

McCrum, Robert, William Cran, and Robert MacNeil. *The Story of English.* London: Faber and Faber; BBC Books, 1988.

Pei, Mario. *The Story of Language.* Rev. ed. Toronto: Mentor-New American Library, 1966.

Pyles, Thomas, and John Algeo. *The Origins and Development of the English Language.* 4th ed. New York: Harcourt Brace, 1993.

Shipley, Joseph T. *In Praise of English: The Growth and Use of Language.* New York: Times Books, 1977.

Stevenson, Victor, ed. *Words: The Evolution of Western Languages.* London: Methuen, 1983.

Traugott, Elizabeth Closs, and Mary Louise Pratt. *Linguistics for Students of Literature.* New York: Harcourt Brace, 1980.

chapter six

Arguing and Assessing a Position

In Chapter 3, we discussed ways of adopting and extending a critical attitude, showing how to move from an unsubstantiated opinion to a reasoned position. In Chapter 6, we show how arguments work, how their parts are put together, and how they can be understood and critiqued. This chapter highlights the two basic methods of arguing a position —induction and deduction. The most common logical mistakes (or fallacies) for each method are explained to help you to avoid them in your own arguments and to provide you with analytical tools for evaluating the arguments of others.

LEARNING OBJECTIVES

We address the following questions:

- How can you make an argument that follows logically?
- How can you recognize an argument and its parts?
- How can you recognize and use the two fundamental methods of formulating an argument—induction and deduction?
- What are the strengths and weaknesses of each of these methods?
- How can you avoid mistakes in your own arguments and recognize logical faults in the arguments of others?

In this chapter, we stress that academic argument is not a shouting match or an attempt to demolish an opposing viewpoint. Rather, it is a form of dialogue or debate which extends fields of knowledge and that depends upon widely accepted conventions and methods.

THE GROUNDWORK FOR ESTABLISHING A LOGICAL POSITION

An academic argument involving critical thinking is not a contest or a confrontation that you try to win by destroying your opponent. Nor is it a series of assertions in which two opposing sets of opinions are left up in the air with the oversimplified conclusion, "Well, that's just my opinion"—the implication being that all opinions are equal and the reader can take it or leave it. Critical thinking involves breaking down a position into its various components, separating assumptions from hypotheses and premises from evidence. Strategies of argument allow you to critique other positions and help you to formulate your own in a manner that will move or persuade your reader.

Students are often puzzled about how they can state a position that they want to explore or defend, for either an essay or a presentation, and they are at a loss about how to gather information to support it and how to marshal that information toward a conclusion: in short, how to make an argument. If your assignment is to write an essay on the reasons for Canadian Confederation or on the political implications of the films of Roman Polanski, you very likely will begin by assembling your data or other evidence to support one of these general topics. Usually, you do not have a clear case that you want to argue, that you can put into a single sentence, until you have most of your supporting evidence in place. When that is gathered together, you can start to formulate what you are trying to prove, what you are proposing or laying claim to.

What Is a Logical Argument?

While some kinds of "creative" assignments will be performative (as, indeed, are all essays and classroom presentations at some level), academic essays rely on conventional marshalling of arguments and evidence and so are open to the kinds of traditional faults and fallacies that have been specified by logicians. Readers will hope to find in an academic essay that the arguments follow logically one after another, rather than jumping about from one point to another only tangentially related point. You should be able to control the logical sequencing of arguments partly through building paragraphs from topic sentences through to their conclusion, with a bridge to the next paragraph. Another control comes from a clear and articulate style, which will allow arguments to come forward in a clear and unambiguous way. But, in addition, there are informal and formal requirements to be met with respect to the logic of arguments. For instance, it is not logical to assert at the end of an essay a position that has not been introduced and demonstrated earlier in the paper. Nor can the dismissal of a particular position as rubbish be substituted for analysis and demonstration of *why* that position is rubbish. Similarly, when evidence does not support a thesis, when you argue beside the point, when you look at only some of the evidence, or when you distort the evidence, the logic is weak, often faulty, and there is a poor match between the position that is in the process of being developed and the marshalling of evidence.

Ideas must always be set out in a coherent fashion, usually proceeding from the strongest point to the weakest, or the reverse, which is a more difficult procedure. Generalizations will be supported or qualified by relevant evidence. For an argument to be convincing, the relationship between generalizations or assertions and supporting evidence must be considered carefully. Many students have the most trouble at exactly this point: they either cannot qualify a generalization in the face of contradictory evidence and ignore the exception, or they suppress that evidence and continue to assert a generalization. Evidence will be reliable and pertinent if you take into account any contradictory evidence (for instance, by considering both sides of a question or by examining a text carefully for contrary evidence) or if you can modify your generalization (perhaps by claiming that it applies in most cases or in these specific cases, but not in others). Your argument will be much less convincing if it is apparent that you are trying to play up to your professors with flattery or by overstating agreements with points made in lectures or class, basing your argument on bias or prejudice, or oversimplifying a complex topic.

An academic argument, then, is not a contest of absolute rights and wrongs but is a structured statement of a position that moves logically to persuade an audience of your views.

Supports, Claims, and Warrants

In *An Introduction to Reasoning* and his other works, Stephen Toulmin identifies two stages in developing an argument—the *support* stage and the *claim* stage.

The *support* stage answers the questions, "What have you got to go on?" and "What are you relying on to make your case?" That is, you are setting out the grounds for your argument in order to convince your audience that your claim is sound. Support can be of two kinds, either through evidence (facts, statistics, expert opinion, or statements by authorities) or by appeals to your audience's motives (their emotions, their special interests, or their worries or fears). It is sometimes advisable to introduce into your support stage contrary evidence, or reservations that might have already been expressed about the validity of your evidence. Here, you have an opportunity to rebut or contradict possible opposing arguments in advance, thereby strengthening your case.

The *claim* stage answers the question, "What are you trying to prove?" That is, the statement of your claim really is the conclusion which you want your audience to agree with. When such a statement is placed at the beginning of your argument, it is called a thesis statement. The claims are of three kinds: (1) claims of fact (they assert a condition which is based on data or facts); (2) claims of value (they assert that x or y is better than z on the basis of personal taste, aesthetic criteria, or moral principles); and (3) claims of policy (they assert specific policies, often social policies, that will solve specific policies and that usually include *should, must,* or *ought* to indicate what is practicable or feasible). Sometimes, a claim includes specific limitations or qualifications that must be met before it can be accepted.

Often hidden from this relationship of support or grounds to your claim are the assumptions which you rely upon. Toulmin calls this bridge between support and claim a *warrant.* It authorizes the application of the support to the claim and answers the question, "How did you get there?" This warrant guarantees the reliability of a claim. That is, a warrant is what is assumed or taken for granted; it is a general principle that reflects common observations or general experience. If a warrant is expressed or stated, it is said to be *explicit,* and if

FIGURE 6.1	The Stages of an Argument

ARGUMENT

An argument is a statement or statements offering support for a claim. More generally, an argument is a set of statements that attempts to persuade a reader or listener to accept a claim on the basis of reason and logic, though it may also include appeals on the basis of emotions.

SUPPORT

"What have you got to go on?"

= all the materials used to convince the audience that the claim is sound.
- Support by evidence: facts, statistics, experts, authorities.
- Support by motivational appeals: emotions, interests.

CLAIM

"What are you trying to prove?"

= thesis statement of what is to be argued and how, or the conclusion that says what you have argued or demonstrated.
- Claims of fact: assert conditions based on facts, data.
- Claims of value: assert x or y is better than z on basis of aesthetic taste or morality.
- Claims of policy: assert specific policies that will solve problems usually with *should, must, ought* to indicate what is feasible.

QUALIFIER

Sets limits or qualifications on the claim, asserting that it can only be valid if it is accepted with such and such qualifications.

WARRANT

"How did you get there?"

= the assumption(s) which connects the support to the claim and so guarantees its reliability. A warrant is what is assumed, or taken for granted, a general principle that reflects observations or general experience. A warrant may be expressed or stated (explicit) or unstated (implicit).
- Warrant based on authority: depends on the reliability of the source.
- Substantive warrant: based on beliefs of the arguer about the reliability of the factual evidence.
- Warrant of motivation: based on the needs and values of the audience.

REBUTTAL

Presents the other side of the support, or contrary evidence, or a different motivational appeal.
- Reservation = less intense form of rebuttal.

BACKING

A subsidiary category may establish the warrant, backing it up by other arguments, such as by cause and effect.

Terms drawn from Toulmin, Rieke, and Janik 29-128.

unstated, *implicit*. Like claims, there are three kinds of warrants: (1) warrants that are based on some kind of authority; (2) substantive warrants based on the beliefs of the arguer about the reliability of the factual evidence; and (3) warrants of motivation, based on the needs and values of the audience. These relationships are set out in Figure 6.1.

Experts in the analysis of these terms of argument try to make such terms as clear as possible: they define argumentation as "the whole activity of making claims, challenging them, backing them up by producing reasons, criticizing those reasons, rebutting those criticisms, and so on"; they also define argument as "the sequence of interlinked claims and reasons that, between them, establish the content and force of the position for which a particular speaker is arguing" (Toulmin, Rieke, and Janik 14). Hence, they define an argument as a statement or statements offering support for a claim.

TWO FUNDAMENTAL METHODS OF ARGUING A POSITION

When we make an argument, we need to be able to assemble our supporting evidence to justify the claim or conclusion we reach. We want to do so on the basis of assumptions or general principles that warrant us to make these connections between our evidence and our conclusion. But what method can we use to construct our argument?

Many generations of thinkers have identified two different methods of argument (see Figure 6.2). The first provides a high degree of probability that the conclusion is justified, and it is called the *inductive* method. For instance, I might argue: "Because I am 25 years old, I have a long life ahead of me." This inductive argument depends upon assumptions about human life expectations and that no sudden accident or deadly disease will carry me away. But this argument remains only probable, both statistically and with respect to my present circumstances, because you might not know that I am a skydiver with a (to me unknown) weak heart, important but hidden qualifications to my claim. Nevertheless, this argument remains probable.

The second method requires that the assertions or propositions of the argument, if they are placed in a logical order, will guarantee that the conclusion is true, and it is called the *deductive* method. For instance, I might argue: "On my farm, there are 30 head of cattle in one field, and 10 in another. No other field has any cattle. Therefore, there are 40 cattle on my farm." This conclusion depends on the truth of the earlier statements and the fact that they are put together logically, and since they are, its truth is guaranteed.

Some accounts of *inductive reasoning* maintain that it argues from specific instances to general principles, and deductive reasoning from the general to the specific. That is, the inductive method uses informal logic to move from data to a general claim or probability, while the deductive method states a conclusion and then shows how that conclusion was reached by logical steps (or it can state a truth claim that all would agree upon and then builds on that to reach the inevitable conclusion). Most university assignments involve an inductive method, moving from the gathering of data to some kind of general statement, assertion, or hypothesis. The applications, illustrations, or examples justify the claim. Inductive arguments take many forms, including formulating a hypothesis and supporting it with evidence, arguing on the basis of cause and effect, or arguing by drawing analogies between two different kinds of materials, each of which we address below.

Deductive reasoning moves from detail to arrive at a general principle or truth claim. Such deductive arguments, at their simplest level, are based on formal logic and are composed

FIGURE 6.2 | Inductive and Deductive Reasoning

TWO METHODS OF ARGUMENT

DEDUCTIVE REASONING

Arguer thinks the premises guarantee the truth of the conclusion.

1. Premises, conclusions, statements, or beliefs may be either true or false but are not valid or sound; only deductive arguments can be valid or sound.
2. Deductive arguments proceed from a general axiomatic premise to a claim about a specific instance.
3. It begins with a generally accepted principle, law, or rule.
4. Its simplest form is a syllogism, made up of three stages, a major premise, a minor premise, and a conclusion.
5. It depends upon formal logic.
6. Its conclusion is valid if the syllogism is put together correctly, according to the rules of logic.
7. Its conclusion is guaranteed to be true if the premises are true.

Deductive Arguments use Formal Logic

Deductive Arguments use Form of Syllogism

Only Deductive Arguments can be Valid or Sound and Make Truth Claims

INDUCTIVE REASONING

Arguer thinks the premises provide evidence for the probability of the conclusion.

1. Inductive arguments may be strong or weak, plausible or implausible.
2. Inductive arguments proceed from specific observations/facts to a general conclusion about the whole.
3. It begins with experience or direct observation.
4. Its typical forms are a scientific demonstration, police report, or legal case.
5. It depends upon informal logic.
6. Its conclusion is an inference based on the premises.
7. Its conclusion is probable, never certain.

Inductive Argument using Hypothesis and Evidence

Inductive Argument using Cause and Effect

Inductive Argument using Analogy

STATISTICS

- All modes of induction may use statistical data.
- The more samples, the greater the plausibility of the hypothesis (induction by enumeration). But the instances or samples should be representative of the whole.
- If you use a sampling method, the sample must be representative based on statistical sampling procedures.

of statements that are either true or false, each statement being called a premise. Two premises are followed by a conclusion in a deductive argument that sets out all of its parts:

> All people are mortal.
>
> Shakespeare was a person.
>
> Therefore, Shakespeare was mortal.

Such a deductive argument is called a *syllogism* and has three parts: (1) a general claim or axiomatic statement (the *major premise*), (2) a more focused claim in which a new term is introduced (the *minor premise*), and (3) a *conclusion* that properly combines the elements of the premises.

In your studies, you will encounter many courses that require both inductive and deductive reasoning (see Figure 6.3). Many science, social science, and humanities courses depend at first on inductive reasoning, assembling various kinds of evidence, building up a body of data, collecting problems or specific instances, and then drawing a conclusion or general principle from them that has a high degree of probability. Then, a deductive phase can begin, in which the conclusion of the inductive phase is tested by application to

---

FIGURE 6.3	**How to Identify Arguments**

In both inductive and deductive arguments, statements contain clues that help you identify the parts and processes of an argument, the premises and the resulting conclusion. One way of locating arguments is to find words which indicate that an argument is lurking nearby. When people draw conclusions from evidence or the statements of an argument (the premises), they are said to *infer* conclusions. An *inference*, then, is the process of drawing a conclusion from premises. *Inference indicators* are the words that indicate that an argument is being made, moving from premises to the conclusion. There are two kinds of inference indicators: (1) those that indicate that what follows is a premise, and (2) those that indicate that what follows is a conclusion. Marking them will help you identify the parts of an argument.

Inference Indicators of a Premise	**Inference Indicators of a Conclusion**
Words that signal that what follows is a statement that makes general claim, or a premise (that will eventually point to a conclusion):	Words that signal that what follows is a claim or conclusion, the end point to which the argument has been leading (based on some premises stated shortly before):

after all...	as proved by...	allows us to infer that...	as a result...
assuming that...	because...	consequently...	demonstrates that...
can be concluded from...	can be shown by... for...	entails that...	hence...
for the reason that...	given that...	implies that...	in conclusion...
inasmuch as...	in view of the fact	in short...	it follows that...
deduced from...	that...	proves that...	shows that...
is implied by...	is proved by...	so...	therefore...
is shown by...	it follows from...	thus...	is proved by...
since...		we can conclude that...	

Adapted from Arthur K. Bierman and Robin N. Assali, *The Critical Thinking Handbook*. Upper Saddle River, NJ: Prentice Hall, 1996, 33–34.

other cases. Some other courses proceed by examining examples each week, such as different texts (say, works of fiction) or concepts, without fitting them from the outset into an argument based on some critical or theoretical principle and without drawing connections between them. It might be that the final examination requires you to pull these examples together to an explicit conclusion, stating some general principle that was implicit in the course from the beginning.

Many courses that stress critical thinking also put considerable emphasis on deductive reasoning. Such a course typically has a thesis or principle argument (functioning like a major premise), which is being tested or examined throughout the year, and each part of the course extends the argument of that premise by inferring other lines of argument that flow from it. Within that overall deductive argument, the individual lectures, seminars, and assignments also tend to stress the deductive method. The lectures are cast as arguments based on principles that are set out at the beginning of the year and that are elaborated as the course proceeds, building on the details and adding to the definitions and concepts to make a coherent deductive argument. In each lecture, a minor premise is set out and is linked to the main argument about the course materials or concepts to draw a conclusion. If you understand that the lecturers are using this method consciously, you will see that they are not just setting out examples or moving randomly from topic to topic.

In your own writing, you will often use an inductive method during your research as you gather examples to see whether there is any method of classifying them that will lead to a general principle under which they can be grouped as an argument. It is this principle that you will then be able to re-shape into a thesis statement, the general position on which to build your argument, which will then follow a deductive method. Your thesis statement will move not through instances to support it but from one position you are taking to a second position, and perhaps a third and fourth, all linked together in a chain of deductions. To develop a reasoned position in a classroom presentation, essay, or examination is a considerable achievement.

THE ROLE OF LOGIC

To be convincing as well as valid, an argument must follow logical principles. However, many arguments manage to convince readers and listeners without being particularly logical or even in spite of committing one or more well-known logical faults. Often, it is because of the faults that the argument convinces unthinking people. Politicians are particularly expert in evading questions, appealing to popular opinion, or equivocating. Student essays often try to employ similar tactics. However, critical thinking depends on using arguments that are both convincing and sound.

Critical thinking primarily makes use of *informal logic*. That is, it applies the principles of logical concepts to the analysis of such bodies of knowledge as the materials studied in a course or the writing of assignments. Informal logic, then, is a kind of practical reasoning about the world. Since the 1970s, informal logic has been the subject of much scholarly interest, as thinkers have tried to apply it to a wealth of examples of the mass media. Such studies have concentrated on the ways that communication is established between the media and its audiences, on how persuasive language and images are used to convince an audience of the validity of the media's arguments, and on the ways that logical connections are broken in arguments that appear in the media (often through fallacies or errors in logic in informal reasoning).

Another kind of logic, *formal logic,* is used to analyze the specific statements in an argument that are presented as a syllogism. In formal logic, the rules that have to do with the logical forms of arguments are stripped to their essential elements and are put into a coherent pattern according to conventional rules.

Arguments depend on statements, assertions, or declarations that are connected to reach a conclusion. A declaration expresses what logicians call a *proposition,* a concept that is distinct from the sentence that expresses it. So, the declarative statement "Mag loves Jim" expresses the same proposition as "Jim is loved by Mag."

People use language in different kinds of sentences, to give commands or to ask questions. But propositions are different in that they are declarative or assertive: they make assertions that are either true or false. Truth claims enter at the beginning of an argument, often unstated, when you make an assertion that you are about to defend. You may make a proposition, for instance, to the effect that the fundamental cause of the French Revolution was economic, or that all of Hardy's poems are pessimistic, or that the moon is made of Swiss cheese. Each of these statements or propositions can be defended or denied, but if it is asserted as a fact, a truth claim is being made about it at the beginning of your argument. Your audience might disagree, but they will have to withhold their judgment about the validity of your truth claim until you finish your argument. Here, what is called *traditional logic* can serve a useful purpose in indicating the *validity* of your arguments (whether the arguments are put together correctly according to the rules of formal logic), and a knowledge of informal fallacies will often expose the gaps where an oppositional reading of a truth claim may be launched. Furthermore, a knowledge of basic principles of formal logic will help you in formulating your own arguments.

To illustrate this point about different kinds of arguments, we provide an imaginary dialogue that might have occurred near a cave about a million years ago:

> Thog: "I've noticed that every time I throw a stone up in the air it comes down. And so, if I shoot an arrow in the air now, it must come down, too."
>
> Nootun: "That's because of the law that everything that goes up comes down. If you shoot the arrow up, it comes down."

Thog is using *inductive reasoning,* arguing a case of probability, though he does not know it, from his experience and previous examples to reach a general conclusion. Nootun, on the other hand, is using *deductive reasoning,* arguing that the general law is a necessary conclusion, guaranteed to be accurate, and then is moving to the specific. Thog is making a prediction about what will probably happen, on the basis of his observation, while Nootun is asserting what is certain. Or, to take a different example:

> Thog: "I've noticed that every time there is a drought, we get rain. And so, now, in this drought, we will get rain."
>
> Nootun: "That's because the rainmaker does his dance and says his prayers. So, now, in this drought, we will get rain."

In this instance, the argument of Thog is again based on *inductive reasoning,* but unlike the first example, it is not founded on an observation that all people would accept. In many droughts, there is no rain. And if Thog has a science teacher, the teacher might have to explain that that is why we have deserts. Nevertheless, Thog is still making an inductive argument, but it is flawed statistically because it is based on too few examples and does not consider any contrary evidence. Nootun is using *deductive reasoning* again, stating what to him is a principle or axiomatic truth (when the rainmaker does his ritual, it rains) and a necessary conclusion, but his logic, too, is flawed because the rain may not be the necessary effect of the ritual. Thog and Nootun are stating their arguments pretty well. Both of them are making important arguments; neither way is inherently better or worse than the other. Each starts from a different basis, a different kind of argument, to reach different kinds of conclusions.

INDUCTIVE REASONING

Inductive reasoning, as in Thog's arguments, begins with observation, experience, evidence, or facts. Then, it compares all of these data, and after showing what the facts have in common—their similarities—or how they progress from one to another, it draws conclusions that are probable consequences of his reasoning. This is the process of induction.

The inductive method draws conclusions out of the facts or evidence that have been presented on the basis of some point of comparison or similarity. This drawing-out process is called *implication*. That is, the implications of the evidence are elicited to provide the basis for a conclusion. Induction, then, moves from the implications of particular details to a general principle or conclusion. The conclusion is then tested against the evidence, and new evidence starts the process off again.

The inductive method does not lead to any claims for absolute proof but, rather, if the propositions are true, only to what is highly probable. For the method to be absolutely or conclusively valid, *all* of the examples would have to be considered, a practical impossibility. Normally, however, only a number of examples are chosen, and from them a generalization is made that is probable and usually convincing. But if a contrary example can be found, then the concluding generalization has to be modified. Hence, the inductive method can lead to conclusions that are probable, and the grounds on which that assertion can be made are either strong (or *cogent*) or weak.

Plausible inductive reasoning should be distinguished from stating a position and using one example to back it up as evidence, such as saying, "The schools are in terrible shape. I know that because my brother is fourteen and cannot spell yet." In this instance, you are trying to prove your point by using only your brother's poor spelling to validate the weak claim that your position can be maintained. The schools might, indeed, be bad, and doubtless your brother is a poor speller, but the reasons might have nothing to do with the school. You might be drawing a false relation of cause and effect, or your sample might be far too small, an error in statistics (see the fallacy of the hasty conclusion on page 160). You would presumably have to draw on a much wider and more varied sample. This kind of weak inductive reasoning, however, is a common fault among television talk show hosts and politicians, who frequently generalize from one instance to a principle, misrelate cause and effect, use examples to elaborate a point, rather than argue a position, or draw false analogies. Instead of using induction to advance argument, they tend to draw false conclusions and misleading inferences by generalizing from too few samples, by reading the evidence selectively, or by misrepresenting it.

Strong inductive reasoning seeks to move from an accumulation of evidence to a probable conclusion. This method is often used in criminal procedures by the police and by lawyers in gathering the evidence to make a case (along with deduction in linking the parts of their arguments together). It is also the basis of the scientific method, in which the experimenter states a hypothesis, then proceeds through the experiment to examine all of the data to come up with a conclusion based on the evidence; one contrary piece of evidence means that the conclusion has to be modified. The scientific method then uses deduction to state the principle, to apply it to other specifics, and to draw a valid conclusion about it. In this way, the scientific method uses both inductive and deductive reasoning.

There are three major forms of inductive argument: (1) by means of hypothesis and evidence, (2) by means of cause and effect, and (3) by means of analogy.

Inductive Argument by Means of Hypothesis and Evidence

This argument is presented as a hypothesis, followed by evidence to support it, leading to a general conclusion. In fact, however, the evidence is often gathered before the hypothesis is stated or according to some working hypothesis that might have to be refined on the basis of further evidence.

The scientific experiment is one example of the argument made on the basis of hypothesis and evidence. A series of experiments and observations leads to the formulation of a hypothesis that accounts for the evidence. That generalization is then claimed to be the conclusion of the experiment. This hypothesis and evidence method is also used extensively (often with other forms of argument) in law cases, and it involves making a claim or stating a thesis that you are going to test by means of facts, statistics, examples, evidence, or the opinions of experts. The lawyer builds the case on the basis of induction. Similarly, in detective fiction, the sleuth sifts through the evidence to find elements that can be compared and that point inevitably to the criminal: Sherlock Holmes in Conan Doyle's fiction is a master of inductive reasoning; Inspector Clouseau in the *Pink Panther* series is a failure in induction because he misses the points of comparison in the evidence, just as he fails in common sense, as when he asks the hotel clerk, "Does your dog bite?" The clerk responds "No," but Clouseau is still bitten. The clerk then explains: "That is not my dog."

Most students use inductive reasoning in essays by making a thesis statement in the opening paragraph, supporting it with a series of examples (historical data, readings of specific passages in a text, comments on specific concepts, demographic patterns in sociology, and so on) more or less associated with the topic and reaching a conclusion in which the thesis is re-affirmed in somewhat different wording than in the opening paragraph. In fact, however, many of these essays use examples to illustrate or elaborate, or even to describe the claim made in the thesis, rather than to make an argument that actually defends the thesis. Such an argument is a weak form of inductive reasoning.

For instance, in a literary analysis, arguing that a character was often angry with his wife and children and then listing and quoting from the text seven or eight instances of his anger will certainly support your case. However, the argument is not functioning at a very sophisticated level because you are only concluding something about his disposition from its external manifestations. The statement that he is angry is self-evident to anyone who has read the book: listing numerous examples of the obvious does not constitute a demonstration of proof for a thesis, though it is backing up a character trait here. It cites a series of instances as examples and concludes with some generalizing comment on the basis of the examples. That comment is then turned into a thesis statement and is placed at the beginning of the essay. However, this thesis is a self-evident truth or axiom. It is really a premise for a better argument—that the character is angry *because of* industrial exploitation, or the deaths of other children, or because of his deep-seated feelings of guilt, or whatever. Such an argument would require a subtler thesis statement and would depend upon more complex matters as evidence, not just those that support the self-evident fact of his rage. That is, you will have to argue a better thesis on the basis of evidence, rather than the listing of instances of the obvious.

Evidence here is not merely a listing of instances, or a one-dimensional application of facts to prove a limited case over and over. This one-dimensional application is one of the most common errors that beginning students make in constructing arguments. Furthermore, your own first-hand experience usually falls into the field of opinion and is discounted or even dismissed as weak or unreliable evidence. The strength of your argument using the inductive method depends largely on three factors:

1. The formulation of your thesis
2. The way in which you organize your evidence into categories related to your thesis
3. How the evidence in each of the categories is put together to support the categories

In more rigorously argued essays, the examples cited are, in fact, evidence, and they are arranged in some justifiable order, moving from stronger to weaker, or the reverse in order, to make a point. Hence, the thesis is well supported, and the paper takes the form of a more coherent inductive argument, much like that of the scientific experiment. The examples follow one another in a linked chain and rely on one another in important ways. The comparison of the evidence involves carefully assessing the points of similarity and noting which points are important and which are less so. Therefore, the similarities in the evidence and the linking of them together point with increasing probability to the claims of your thesis. To test your argument, you need to ask yourself why that order of your points appears as it does. If you cannot explain why the points follow in that order, each tied to the previous point, then you are not arguing logically and might be setting out examples without apparent connections.

A minor form of induction, proving a point or stage in an argument by means of an example, is also frequently used by students, often with good effect. When a claim is made, for instance, about the interpretation of a particular passage of a text, and then some evidence is provided to support that interpretation, the proof is exemplified and validated, at least for this one instance. However, a marker can legitimately ask in the margin whether there is any contrary evidence.

When the evidence does not support the claims of the thesis, the conclusion is unconvincing and implausible. That is, it fails to convince a reader. Reasons for failures in inductive arguments concerning thesis and evidence can include the following:

- The thesis is not clearly formulated.
- The thesis is not sufficiently qualified on the basis of your evidence.
- An opinion or unsubstantiated position is mistaken for a fact or authoritative support.
- An error concerning fact is represented as a truth.
- A position that has been discredited is represented as true.
- The evidence is based on errors of fact or interpretation or is drawn from an unreliable source (such as a disproved scientific position). The evidence must be presented in your argument without distorting or twisting it to make it fit your case.
- The evidence is not substantial enough to warrant a generalization. A poll conducted using only two people is invalid. Two hundred people would be better, but many

thousands would make a much better case. Proving a case from a work of fiction means that one example can support a focused or limited argument, but more evidence might be needed to make a more general case. On the other hand, it is possible to give too many examples as evidence to support a claim that has already been proven.

- The evidence is unrepresentative. To be valid, the evidence must be fair, balanced, and representative of the case you are arguing. If you conduct a poll among people who are ignorant of the subject, you cannot make any claim for its validity unless your argument is related to something about the ignorance of people concerning this subject.

- The evidence is irrelevant to your hypothesis. If you argue that in a survey in your class of 100 students' study habits, the half who listened to music while they studied did significantly worse than those who did not, your evidence is not necessarily relevant. Many other factors might have been involved: the need to work, the number of courses taken, students' abilities, other claims on their time, familiarity with the subject matter, and so on. The evidence of listening to music is not relevant to performance unless both halves of the class are equivalent in other respects except for their music-listening habits.

- Sweeping claims are made for your evidence in either your thesis or conclusion. This mistake often occurs when students make universal claims about their evidence, using such words as *all, always, certainly, everywhere,* and *never*. Instead, a more qualified position, allowing for exceptions or special conditions, is more reasonable, as in arguments using such words as *a few, many, may, often, perhaps, possibly, probably,* and *usually*.

Inductive Argument on the Basis of Cause and Effect

The second common kind of inductive reasoning is used to show causal relationships among events so that a specific cause can be claimed to have a particular effect or the reverse. This kind of argument draws a connection between one assertion and another by saying that cause A produces effect B: for example, if enough heat is applied to water, it boils. It is assumed that there is regularity and uniformity in the physical universe and that, on the basis of many observations, this cause (heat) has this effect (water boils). For the water to boil, the heat is both a necessary and a sufficient condition or cause.

When we move away from physical phenomena (and even in them, there may be variations that depend on other conditions in either the cause or the effect) to consider the causes and effects in historical events, in interpersonal relationships, in psychological experiments, or in works of fiction, the notion of a single and unambiguous cause for a single effect becomes much more difficult, if not impossible, to determine and may be irrelevant. In such cases, the induction depends on even more careful observation of examples or instances, and on the very careful comparison of points of likeness.

Drawing out the implications of cause-and-effect arguments, however, can be very difficult. Sometimes, the causes are remote, complicated, and complex; sometimes, they are immediate, direct, and singular. For instance, the cause of a person's ill health may be some bad fish, or it could be a complicated set of heart and lung problems. Trying to determine the effects of specific causes can produce a variety of alternatives. For instance, much medical practice consists of determining the proper causes for effects (symptoms) and prescribing appropriate remedies. In the field of psychoanalysis, Freud's study of hysteria in the case of *Dora* is based on exactly this issue: Dora's physical symptoms of a cough, loss of voice, and a limp were not, in his analysis, the result of a physical malfunction; instead, he argued, they were caused by psychic disorders resulting from events earlier in her life that she had suppressed into her unconscious and that were outwardly manifested in the changed conditions of her body. Freud's method is that of induction, to trace the effects to their remote causes in her earlier life.

The probable relationship between a cause-and-effect induction collapses in the following cases:

- **Post hoc.** Merely because one event follows another, the first is claimed to cause the second, or there is no demonstrated relationship between the cause and the effect: for example, *Nettie went to Africa and therefore Celie fell in love with Shug;* or*, I took Tylenol and a day later my migraine went away.* Technically, this fallacy is called the "After this and therefore because of this" fault, often given in its Latin form: *post hoc ergo propter hoc.* Other versions include the claim that when two events occur together, they are causally related (*cum hoc ergo propter hoc*). The reverse is that there is no case for the claimed cause (*non causa pro causa*) because the claim that one event caused another was based on insufficient evidence or there was, in fact, no causal relationship.
- **Wrong direction.** There is a wrong direction in the causality sequence or antecedent effect, or causality takes a wrong direction; the effect occurs before the cause, as when the door slams before the wind blows. Either the cause and effect are in the wrong order, or there must be a cause other than the wind.
- **Oversimplification.** A complex cause or effect is too simplistically drawn. To assert that World War II had a single cause (for instance, the rise of Hitler's Germany) or that the Stock Market Crash of 1929 had a single effect (the Great Depression) is an oversimplification.

Inductive Argument by Means of Analogy

When various points of evidence are gathered in an inductive argument, they have to be compared, and the aim of that comparison is to find some points of similarity so that a generalization or conclusion can be drawn. That process often involves drawing an *analogy* between one set of evidence and another. At its simplest level, an analogy suggests that one object and its characteristic or effect can be compared with another object and its characteristic. Such a ratio or equivalence is common in speech and might not be used in argument. For instance, a writer might draw an analogy between the dying of a human body and the last days of a political regime. Such an analogy is descriptive, but it is not part of an argument. A more developed analogy can be used to persuade an audience that some things that are similar in some respects are probably also similar in some other respect: apes and humans are alike in characteristics A, B, and C. It is probable that they are also alike in characteristic D. Or one may draw an analogy between a well-known instance and a less-understood one, using the familiar and accepted points concerning the first to make a probable explanation of the latter.

One of the most famous of these analogies is the argument for the existence of God, called the argument from design, used by William Paley in his *Natural Theology* (1802). Paley argues that if you were walking on the beach and found a watch and examined it, you would have to assume that because the watch has parts that move in a certain fixed, orderly, and complex way, the watch had a maker (the watchmaker). Further, the watch was not made randomly but with a function and a purpose (to tell time). Paley then draws an analogy to the universe. Like the watch, the universe moves in a certain fixed, orderly, and complex way and similarly must have a maker as well as a purpose. Analogy here is a vital part of Paley's argument based on induction in the rest of his book, where he draws upon example after example of complex designs in the external world, each of them an analogy to this fundamental one at the beginning of his discussion. The point about analogies that makes them work in an inductive argument is that the common characteristics must be drawn out and expanded, and as with cause and effect arguments, their common characteristics must be relevant.

Analogies, like other kinds of inductive evidence, are strengthened when there is an increased number of points of similarity (the watch is like the universe in more ways than one: it moves in a fixed, orderly, and complex way) and diminished when there is an increased number of differences. An analogy is also strengthened when the comparison involves many instances, rather than just one or two.

Analogical arguments fail in the following cases:

- **False or faulty analogy.** An analogy is faulty when the two events or objects that are being compared are alike in a number of irrelevant respects but differ in the one relevant respect on which the analogy must depend. For instance, Jim and Sam are both from New Brunswick. Both have been in jail for misdemeanours. The one without a college degree has been able to get a good job in computer technology, and therefore, the one with a degree will get a job there, too. Put another way, the false analogy claims that two situations, A and B, are alike in many ways, and because situation A has the property X, so must situation B. But in the case of Jim and Sam, property X is fundamentally different from the similarities upon which the analogy is based. Oscar Wilde's witticisms frequently depend on false analogy, as in the following examples from Lady Bracknell in the first act of *The Importance of Being Earnest:* "Ignorance is like a delicate exotic fruit; touch it, and the bloom is gone"; "To be born or, at any rate, bred in a handbag, whether it had handles or not, seems to me to display a contempt for the ordinary decencies of family life that remind one of the worst excesses of the French Revolution. And I presume you know what that unfortunate movement led to?"

- **Extended analogy.** Inductive comparison using analogy fails when it is assumed that because two situations are referred to in the same context, often the context of a proposed general rule, they are analogies. For instance, in a discussion of instituting laws on censorship, it is a faulty extended analogy to claim that censoring adult sites on the Internet is analogous to censoring books in high school libraries.

DEDUCTIVE REASONING

When Nootun made his argument to Thog about the law that everything that goes up must come down and about the rituals of the rainmaker bringing rain, he was stating an axiomatic truth as his first principle. You could silently agree with him, or you could argue with him about the truth or falsity of his assertions, but in both cases, he began with a principle.

Deductive reasoning begins with some kind of position that can be defended or argued, often an *axiom,* or a self-evident truth, such as Nootun's statement that what goes up must come down. This opening declaration is called the first, or major, premise. Deductive reasoning then adds a second, or minor premise, in order to draw out the implications (in this form of reasoning, they are called *inferences*) of the argument to apply them to a specific situation or set of data: an arrow is something that goes up. That is, a deductive argument moves from the general principle to the detail. Then, it draws a conclusion: the arrow must come down.

Truth and Validity in Deductive Arguments

One of the problems students face when they are developing an argument is whether their argument is solid, or sound. Will it hold up to closer examination? In short, is it a valid argument? And what does it mean to call something valid? Is something that is valid also always true?

Like many other concepts in this book, such as *critical* and *attitude,* as discussed in Chapter 3, the notions of truth and validity have both popular and technical meanings. To say that something is true might derive from your religious belief, be based on the sacred scriptures of a religion, or might rely on the teachings of a religious leader—and that would be grounds for your asserting that something is eternally and unchangingly true in all circumstances and for all time. That would amount to what some philosophers call a universal truth claim.

Consider Nootun's assertion that what goes up must come down. Such a statement seems to be making a universal truth claim, and we could defend it by saying that the claim is based on the scientific laws of gravity. However, is such a statement true in all circumstances? A space shuttle is launched and goes up. Must it come down? According to Nootun's law, it must, but suppose it explodes, or lands on Mars and cannot re-launch. In these circumstances the law is tested, and from the evidence, it cannot apply to these examples. Is it, therefore, not true?

To answer such questions, philosophers, especially those who study logic, draw important distinctions between truth claims and the issue of whether an argument is valid. For our purposes in this book, we are introducing and are laying out some fundamentals of this complex topic (see more detailed treatments in Further Readings). Philosophers try to restrict the terms *truth* and *falsehood* to propositions, never to arguments, and they want to keep the terms *valid* and *invalid* to apply only to deductive arguments and never to propositions. Logicians say that a deductive argument is "valid" when it is put together according to the rules of logic, when each of its premises is properly stated and proceeds toward drawing a conclusion that is based on the preceding propositions. Deductive arguments also make truth claims, beginning with the first premise, which is often a statement of an axiomatic or generally accepted truth, such as Nootun's law. This truth claim is one that you can agree with or not, but it cannot be disputed in terms of the validity of the argument until it is put in relation to the second premise and the conclusion.

If the argument is also put together correctly, then it is both true and valid, as in the following argument, a syllogism used frequently in logic textbooks:

All humans are mortal.	(*major premise–axiomatic truth claim*)
Socrates is a human.	(*minor premise–self-evident truth claim*)
Therefore, Socrates is mortal.	(*conclusion–conclusion is framed as truth claim*)

In this argument, both of the premises are true, and the argument is valid. However, it is possible to have a valid argument with false propositions, as in the following syllogism:

All whales have four legs.	(*major premise—false claim*)
All fourlegged creatures have tails.	(*minor premise—false claim*)
Therefore, all whales have tails.	(*conclusion—conclusion is framed as a truth claim and is true despite two false premises*)

In this argument, the first and second premises are false, though the conclusion is true. The argument is put together correctly, however, and so it is valid. If its premises were also true, it would be both true and valid.

A conditional argument depends on a stated conditional "if" or "when" concept:

When it snows the streets get slippery.	(*major premise—axiomatic truth claim*)
It is snowing.	(*minor premise—truth claim* [*observation*])
The streets are getting slippery.	(*conclusion—conclusion as truth claim*)

However, arguments that begin with a false statement, whether or not it can be considered metaphoric, might be valid in their terms and arrangement, but untrue:

All humans are baboons.	When it snows, balls of fire drop everywhere.
Socrates is a human.	It is snowing.
Socrates is a baboon.	Balls of fire are dropping everywhere.

It is also possible to have all of the premises and the conclusion true but the argument invalid:

If this squeegee kid owned all of the money in the IMF, he would be wealthy.

This squeegee kid does not own all of the money in the IMF.

This squeegee kid is not wealthy.

The premises and the conclusion to this argument are true, but the argument is invalid because it does not draw a correct inference from the premises as they are stated. The premises would remain true even if the squeegee kid were to inherit a lot of money from a regular customer who died, but the conclusion then would become false. For instance, if the terms were changed, this point would be even clearer:

If Bill Gates owned all of the money in the IMF, he would be wealthy.

Bill Gates does not own all of the money in the IMF.

Therefore, Bill Gates is not wealthy.

Thus, there can be invalid arguments with true conclusions and valid arguments with false conclusions. When an argument is both true and valid, it is spoken of as being *sound*. When it is an invalid argument (even with a true conclusion) or has a false conclusion, it is referred to as being *unsound*. Hence, the logic of a sound deductive argument allows a conclusion to be drawn as a certainty. On the other hand, as we have said, inductive arguments, moving from examples toward conclusions, always posit a high degree of probability, but never certainty. For further explanations of this relationship between arguments and their validity, truth claims, and soundness, see Peter Suber's "Truth of Statements, Validity of Reasoning" (**www.earlham.edu/~peters/courses/log/tru-val.htm**).

Many of the texts we read in courses, especially literary texts, are based on a major premise that is untrue. But rather than being called a false truth claim, such texts are often described as *fictions,* as assertions that, though false in fact, can be accepted as potentially true or as true for the purposes of representation in a text. For instance, when Dickens begins *Great Expectations* by saying, "So, I called myself Pip and came to be called Pip," he is beginning a fiction, an invented narrative that purports to tell the "true" story of a boy's growth to manhood. It represents the data of the story as true, but, in fact, it is false: such a person has never existed.

Even texts loosely based on historical narratives take one aspect of that historical narrative and fictionalize it so that it is untrue in point of fact. When Dickens begins his account of the French Revolution (a "true" historical event) in *A Tale of Two Cities,* his opening paragraph sets out a series of oppositions: "It was the best of times; it was the worst of times...." The truth of either part of the statement can be debated. The argument that Dickens advances in the narrative draws out the inferences of that statement and applies them to the cases of two men, Charles Darnay and Sydney Carton, at first the best and worst of men. However, the story that Dickens tells of their love affairs and their involvement in international intrigue and French politics is an invented fiction and is not a true story.

More pertinent to deductive arguments are those texts (both print and visual, as in films) that take some element of the external world and distort it as one of the axioms for creating the fictional world, as in science fiction, fairy tales, much children's literature, and fantasy. Often, this major premise is not stated overtly but, rather, is implied, especially in the journey or transition from the represented real world to a representation of an alternative world. What follows in the narrative, however, unravels this false premise according to a logic that is entirely valid in its own terms, that is, according to the alternative world. In the alternative world, then, the false premise is accepted as true. For instance, in Lewis Carroll's *Through the Looking-Glass* a major premise is that everything works backwards. Within the alternative world of Looking-Glass Land, this premise (false in the real world) is both true and valid. The premise is implied in the moment of transition, when Alice steps through the mirror. There are, of course, many other major premises that are advanced—for instance, Looking-Glass Land is constructed as a chess game.

In fact, however, propositions deal with the smaller parts of arguments, with the formal coherence between one statement and the next logically dependent statement and on the conclusion that can be drawn from the related propositions. It is only when we look at the major concepts of an intellectual position, say in abnormal psychology, or the causes of the collapse of Napoleon's march on Russia, or the logic of Looking-Glass Land as an alternative world that we can see how a false assumption or assertion in the major premise can be carried forward logically to set out a coherent argument and how the validity of the argument as a whole depends on the logical connections of the parts of the deductive argument.

Rules for Syllogisms

Most courses do not have either the time or the need to examine in detail all of the arguments that go into making a reasoned position or a deductive argument. However, it is important to see exactly how that reasoning can be applied, especially in crucial turns in an argument. Hence, it is useful to consider in a brief form how propositions work.

A number of formal rules govern the way deductive arguments work, a matter that can become a complicated study in itself. The most common errors, or fallacies, in students' arguments are suppressing the first stage of the argument (not stating the premise), using an opinion instead of an axiomatic truth for the first or major premise, and using too few or too many terms in the syllogism. Each of these difficulties is dealt with in textbooks on logic, often in very technical language. Here, we give a summary of the rules for syllogisms and note a few fallacies. The discussion is not intended to be exhaustive, but it describes the main points that can be examined in greater detail in the suggested readings and Web pages. Put simply, trying to find the formal logical steps in your thinking can help you formulate your arguments with much greater precision and effectiveness.

The logic used in deductive reasoning is concerned with the relationships among propositions, how they can be arranged as major and minor premises to make arguments with valid conclusions. When two or more premises are arranged together, they are intended to provide support for the conclusion. The term *inference* describes the relationship of moving logically from proposition to proposition so that the end of one premise leads into the next by inference. The validity of the argument depends on its logical integrity or coherence, not on its truth claims, as we demonstrated above. It is possible for the propositions to be true and the conclusion to be invalid (because the logic is invalid) and for the propositions to be false and the conclusion valid.

A deductive argument is composed of several declarative statements that verbalize the position or concept being argued. According to traditional formal logic, every deductive argument can be set out in a logical form made up of propositions or declarative statements leading to a conclusion, a form called a *syllogism* (Greek, *syn,* together; *logizesthai,* to reckon > *logos,* speech, word, reason). A syllogism is composed of three propositions that contain three simple terms. Each of the three terms occurs in two of the three propositions. The first two propositions are the major and minor premises, and the last, which follows from them, is the conclusion. The standard form of a syllogism follows a specific pattern:

All A are X.	All university students receive grades.	(*major premise*)
B is A.	I am a university student.	(*minor premise*)
Therefore, B is X.	Therefore, I receive grades.	(*conclusion*)

Both the major and the minor terms appear in the conclusion, and it is in the conclusion that you can locate the parts of the syllogism. The subject term of the conclusion of the syllogism (B, or "I") is the minor term of the syllogism as a whole. The major term of the syllogism (X, or "grades") is the predicate of the conclusion. The third term (A, or "university student"), one that does not appear in the conclusion but only in the two premises, is known as the middle term. The proposition that connects the major term and the middle term is the major premise, while that connecting the minor term and the middle term is the minor premise.

Normally, every deductive argument can be reduced to its logical components, the premises of a syllogism. In fact, however, most arguments abbreviate a syllogism, stating only one of its premises and its conclusion, especially in complicated arguments. Such an abbreviated syllogism (called an *enthymeme*) leaves out part of the argument, stating only a fragment of it and the conclusion that allows them to proceed to the next point; for example, *all physicians are university graduates, and so all members of the Canadian Medical Association must be university graduates.* Normally, you would accept such a statement as almost self-evident, but if you wish to test its validity, you have to supply the missing premise to the syllogism:

> All physicians are university graduates.
>
> [All members of the Canadian Medical Association are physicians.]
>
> So, all members of the Canadian Medical Association must be university graduates.

One of the most difficult tasks for a student in considering the formal validity of categorical syllogisms is finding the major and minor premises and stating them so that they make a syllogism that is faithful to the terms of the argument and so that its validity or invalidity can be recognized. The key is to find the conclusion of the argument and to begin there. As stated above, the major and minor terms of the argument both appear in the conclusion, for example, *Socrates is mortal.* The word *Socrates* is the subject of the conclusion, and therefore it is the minor term. *Mortal* is the predicate, and therefore it is the major term. The remaining term, found elsewhere in the sentence just before the conclusion, is the middle term, in this case, *human.* Hence the syllogism is:

> All humans are mortal.
>
> Socrates is a human.
>
> Therefore, Socrates is mortal.

For further information on syllogisms, see the *Foundations* Web site.

FALLACIES OR ERRORS IN THE LOGIC OF ARGUMENTS

How can I judge whether my argument makes any sense, and how can I find the gaps in it? A reasoned or logical argument moves between its levels, that is, between hypothesis and evidence, or between premises and conclusions, in a sound manner. By a sound manner we mean that the links between the levels of the argument must avoid fallacies or mistakes in reasoning. *Fallacies* are logical faults that invalidate the relationships between the parts of an argument. In logic, there are two kinds of fallacies—informal and formal.

Fallacies in Informal Arguments

Informal fallacies are faults in inductive arguments based either on appeals to emotions or audience reactions that have nothing to do with the point being argued or on mistakes in logical connections. An example of a fallacy based on an appeal to emotion is to attack the speaker of an argument on personal (and irrelevant) grounds: *Jean Chrétien's policy on the Second Gulf War, keeping Canadian troops out of the war, was wrong because he was too old to be prime minister.* Formal fallacies are faults in deductive reasoning that do not follow the rules of the syllogism: fallacies can occur at each level of the syllogism. The major premise might not be an axiomatic truth. The minor premise might introduce too many terms, or the conclusion might not draw the proper inferences from the premises. Books or Web sites that deal with fallacies should be consulted to help you to detect fallacies in other arguments and avoid them in your own. The essential first step in assessing any argument is to become aware of the links between an argument's parts and to test the logic of those connections.

A fallacy is a form of reasoning that should not be persuasive, though it often is. It depends on mistakes in logic, whether formal in propositions, or informal in thought or language forms. There are many more common mistakes in reasoning or argument than those we have listed above after the various forms of argument. Many are technical faults in the ordering of propositions (formal fallacies in formal logic), while others are usually called informal fallacies because they do not depend on the strict form or formal structure of the syllogism. Some informal fallacies have special names, usually their Latin names. The following list divides other common informal fallacies (in addition to those noted above) into two kinds, those that are based on an appeal to emotion and those that are based on mistakes in logical connection. This list is, by no means, complete, but if you are interested, there is an extensive compilation by Stephen Downes on the Internet, with many apt and current Canadian examples and with many links to other similar Web sites (**www.datanation.com/fallacies**).

Fallacies Based on the Appeal to Emotion or Audience Reactions

These fallacies distract the reader or audience by appealing to emotions or other psychological factors. You should be aware of these fallacies in testing your own arguments as well as in judging someone else's.

- The **argument or attack against the person** (Latin, *argumentum ad hominem*) is the most common of all of the appeals on the basis of emotion, rather than logical arguments. It is usually an attempt to win an argument by attacking the personal characteristics of an adversary, often in a derisive or abusive way. Characteristically, instead of attacking the logic of the arguments presented, the arguer committing this fallacy attacks the person making the argument—criticizing character (as in discrediting honesty or sexual activity or orientation), labelling, or name calling. Sometimes, this particular kind of argument against the person is called the *genetic fallacy,* since it attacks the source of an argument, rather than the argument itself. Or the attack on the person may make the point that a particular position on one subject should be adopted by the adversary merely because of the adversary's special circumstance, for example, *Paul Martin's position on agricultural reform is wrong for the country because he has had a major interest in a shipping industry; Professor Smith's lectures are incoherent because he is dishevelled and dresses poorly*. Other forms of the attack on the person include guilt by association. This form is often used in political attack, perhaps the most famous being McCarthyism in the United States in the 1950s, when Senator Joseph McCarthy accused a number of civil servants, actors, and writers of being communists because of their friendships.
- A variant of this argument is the **"you too" fallacy** (Latin, *tu quoque*), when the action is deemed acceptable because the other party has also committed it, as when it is argued that a professor cannot deal harshly with a plagiarism case because he, too, had been convicted for the same offence, or, more generally, when it is argued, "You've told a lie" and the response is, "You are a liar, too." A more minor version, creating

misgivings, is to dismiss the arguer and the source of the argument by dredging up old, even unsubstantiated, charges against the arguer, as in alleging old rumours of prostitution charges against a rape victim.

- Another form is **to ridicule, mock, or laugh at the person** who is making the argument, rather than deal with the argument made.

- The **appeal to force** (Latin, *argumentum ad baculum*), meaning to physical force, violence, or threats to cause someone to accept a conclusion, is often a last resort when an argument is slipping away and rage takes over. When all other arguments have failed, you make your point by punching your opponent. Governments bring in the army. The appeal is based on the notion that "might makes right" and is appealed to by the political lobbyist who reminds a politician of how many voters are annoyed with a particular position.

- The **appeal to the people,** the audience, a majority, or popularity (Latin, *argumentum ad populum*), is the attempt to win over the readers or audience by claiming a position is true because it is widely held, rather than appealing to facts and established positions or making logical connections. This appeal to the people, the crowd, or the gallery also often involves the appeal to pity or an attack on the person. Shakespeare's Marc Antony uses this kind of fallacious argument in the funeral oration over Julius Caesar's body (combined with irony). This fallacy is much beloved of television commercial writers and evangelists.

- A variant of this fallacy is the **argument from numbers** (Latin, *argumentum ad numerum*), or the bandwagon effect, which states that because many people hold a position, it must be correct: *Because six million Canadians smoke, it must be good for you.*

- The **appeal to false authority** (Latin, *argumentum ad verecundiam*) arises when the authority appealed to is being adduced for evidence outside his or her field of expertise, just because he or she is an expert somewhere. Advertisers use this fallacy as a stock-in-trade: *Drive a Ford because a member of the Toronto Blue Jays says it is the safest car.* A variation of this fallacy is the appeal to anonymous authority: *A well-known government spokesperson says...,* or *Many scientists have claimed that eating broccoli prolongs life.*

- The **appeal to pity** (Latin, *argumentum ad misericordiam*) is an argument based on emotional sympathy. The many TV appeals to support children in the developing world exploit this fallacy: *The hunger of children in the Third World means that we should always leave our plates clean (or adopt a child, or support a particular charity).* In courts of law, the argument on the basis of pity is often made to provide an extenuating circumstance for a breach of law: *I am poor and hungry, and that is why I stole the bread.*

- The **appeal to consequences** or the **appeal to intimidation** is used when the audience is warned of unacceptable consequences to follow unless the argument is accepted: *Unless you buy this burglar alarm, your house will be broken into and your children will be murdered in their sleep.*

- The **appeal to the holy cow** uses any concept, person, thing, or event that, in any given cultural context, is good and is immune to criticism, such as a national flag to a group of patriotic citizens, or the Queen to members of the Canadian Monarchists League.

- Variants of this fallacy include the **appeal to tradition** (Latin, *argumentum ad antiquitatem*), which means arguing that because something has always been done this way, it is the best way (a favourite of city councils and local politicians who do not want to re-think a matter) or that older is better. A variant is the **appeal to modernity** (Latin, *argumentum ad novitatem*), that the newest is the best, the claim of most software vendors wanting you to upgrade to the most recent version, despite the possibility that the bugs have not been worked out.

Fallacies of Mistaken Logical Connection

Logical arguments connect assertions and propositions together in ways that move from evidence to principles, or from premises to conclusions. When the evidence is faulty in inductive reasoning, or the premises are false or poorly constructed or ordered in deductive reasoning, many faults in logical connection can occur. A number of these faults are used consciously by speakers and writers to skip over some embarrassing evidence, to raise a false argument to distract the audience, or to persuade the audience by some rhetorical (but illogical) trick. For instance, when a politician is asked a direct question about some unpopular social policy and responds by saying, "I have this to say about that" and then speaks of something altogether different, perhaps something very popular, this rhetorical ploy (changing the subject) is also an error in logic (dodging the issue), even though it might be an astute tactic. This fault is also called not answering the question, not facing the problem, or answering a question that was not asked—and this fault, like those that follow, exhibits weak or faulty links between evidence and proof.

- The **hasty conclusion or generalization** consists of jumping to a conclusion before you have proved it or to a generalization on the basis of too small or partial a sampling: *Fifty English fans rioted at the game between Manchester United and Chelsea, and therefore the English are a violent and lawless people.*

- A variant is the **sweeping generalization** (the fallacy of accident), in which a general rule is applied to a particular situation in which it does not fit, or when an exception should be made or when the context appropriate to the rule is ignored: *The law says you must drive past this school at 40 kph, so even though you are rushing your wife, who is in labour, to the hospital, you should not have driven faster than 40 kph.* Another variant is the inappropriate generalization (the fallacy of converse accident, the reverse of the fallacy of accident), in which the exception to the general rule is applied to cases where the generalization should apply: *Because Michelle, who was in the hospital, got an extension on her essay submission, all members of the class should have extensions.*

- **Fallacy of belaboured repetition** (Latin, *argumentum ad nauseam*) applies when an assertion is repeated, rather than proved; the arguer believes that the more times a position is stated, the more likely it is to be true: *I've told you before and I tell you again that he is a habitual liar. He lies all the time. He is always telling lies. He lies, he lies, he lies.*

- **Fallacy of composition** applies to an argument in which what is true of the parts is argued also to be true of the whole: *Each of the parts of a machine is light; therefore, the whole machine is light.*

- **Fallacy of division** applies to the reverse of the fallacy of composition by stating that what is true of the whole is also true of the parts: *Yale University is excellent; Jane Bloggs is a student at Yale; therefore, Jane Bloggs is excellent.*

- The **appeal to ignorance** (Latin, *argumentum ad ignorantiam*) argues that a position is true simply because it has never been proved false, or the reverse: *There must be people on Mars because no one has ever proved there are no people on Mars;* or, *There must be ghosts because they have not been disproved.*

- **Fallacy of many questions** (Latin, *plurium interrogationum*) occurs when two or more questions are made into one, as in the question "Have you stopped beating your dog?" Answering either yes or no admits to the beating. The fallacy is sometimes called the complex question; it is a frequent device in Sophocles' *Oedipus the King*. This fallacy reduces the complex question into a simple either/or.

- **Begging the question** (Latin, *petitio principii*) uses as a premise the same proposition as is used in the conclusion. Usually, this circular argument begins with an assumption that you (and perhaps everyone) might think is true, and after some arguments, you conclude that it is true. Often, the basic premise (or first argument) is hidden, is not stated, and so cannot easily be challenged: *Shakespeare is a greater writer than Agatha Christie because people of good taste prefer Shakespeare. And people of good taste are defined by reading Shakespeare.*

- **Assuming or asserting a position without demonstrating it** occurs when a statement asserts a case without evidence, a frequent problem in students' essays: *It is obvious that Alice hates all of the characters at the Mad Hatter's Tea Party.* Politicians frequently use this fallacy to their advantage in hiding behind "government policy" or concealed economics: *Tuition fees must rise because there is no money for universities and colleges* (the statement that there is no money is an assertion that is not demonstrated or that can be challenged). Readers will often mark such a statement as a defective argument that is not demonstrated with the letters Q. E. D. (Latin, *quod erat demonstrandum,* what must be shown—and is lacking).

- **Self-contradiction** occurs when two contradictory premises are joined together to make a claim: *Only after he kills himself in a car accident will he realize that he should not drink and drive.*

- The **false analogy** draws a comparison between two items on the basis of a supposedly common characteristic when, in fact, the items differ on precisely the point or context of the comparison. False analogies compare things that do not fit the case you are arguing: *Universities are like shopping malls. In shopping malls, customers can enter any store and buy what they want and leave with it, and so it is with students at universities.* The analogy here could be unpacked usefully, and by pointing out differences between universities and shopping malls many cogent critical arguments could be developed. Although students do have choices and pay for services at universities, paying for a course does not mean passing it. There are many requirements and contractual rules that apply at a university; therefore, the argument draws a false analogy.

- The **vicious circle** (Latin, *circulus in demonstrando*) occurs when an argument proceeds to a self-contradictory conclusion, as in the famous paradox of Epimenides the Cretan: "All Cretans are liars." If he includes himself in the statement, then the statement is a lie, and therefore, some Cretans are not liars and Epimenides may be speaking the truth. And yet he cannot be speaking the truth if he is included in his own statement that all Cretans are liars. Some logicians place this fallacy among the formal fallacies related to standard syllogisms.

- The **irrelevant conclusion** (Latin, *ignoratio elenchi,* ignoring the point) sets out to prove one thing and ends up proving another or may draw a conclusion that is irrelevant or beside the point of the argument: *Closing hospitals is necessary financially to keep the health care system running. Saved money can be spent elsewhere in the system. Therefore, health care will be improved.* This argument begins with the goal of keeping the system running by saving money and ends with asserting that health care will be improved; there is no necessary connection between closing hospitals and improving health care. On the face of it, this argument also appears to be contradictory.

- The **red herring** throws the argument off track or diverts the audience by introducing irrelevant issues or questions: *Why should we worry about the raising of tuition fees when Pakistan and India are developing nuclear bombs?*

- The **domino fallacy** alleges that if one item in an argument can be dislodged, the whole structure of the argument will collapse: *In this course on feminist literature, this novel is not about women. Therefore, the whole argument of the course is invalid.* But it is usually the case that the parts of many arguments will stand independently; the fall of one is not necessarily tied to the fall of all. Sometimes, this fallacy is known as the "house of cards."

- The **"slippery slope"** maintains that if one exception is made, any number will follow from it, with dire consequences: *If I let one student bring coffee to class, and another a doughnut, soon they will bring in entire lunches and will be serving four course meals;* or, *If I let Suzie bring her gerbil to school, all the children will be able to bring their pets. Patrick will bring his turtle, Jemima her dog, and soon we will be run over with horses, and possibly elephants.*

- The **"straw man"** involves setting up a false opponent merely to advance your own position, or strengthening your own position by attacking an unrepresentative or weak oppositional argument. Usually, two methods are used to employ this fallacy: first, making an appeal to the general audience and, second, misrepresenting someone's position to set up your own: *Freud showed that his patients in Vienna suppressed their sexual feelings and experiences, and that is exactly why, as I shall show, civilization since him has been in great difficulty.* Freud's theory about suppressed sexuality is the straw man, an excuse for the arguer to advance his own theory about present-day civilization. This argument also shows the *post hoc* fallacy. In another example, the arguer uses a politician's comment as a straw man for an attack on an entire political agenda: *When the mayor cut the milk and lunch subsidy for school children, his comment that they only spend it on candy exposed everything about the city council's agenda.*

Fallacies in Formal Logic

In formal logic, a fallacy is a violation of the rules of a syllogism, namely, that they contain only three terms (for instance, *mortal, human, Socrates* in the example above), that all terms are used in the same sense throughout, and that the middle term must be distributed in at least one premise. *Distributed* means that the information about the middle term must apply to all members of the class. Hence, what is said about humans being mortal is said about all members of that class. Finally, if either term is distributed in the conclusion, then it must be distributed in the premises. We give only a few instances of the most common formal fallacies here, and leave the more complex problems to discussions given in Further Readings and on the *Foundations* Web site.

1. Fallacy of four terms (*quaternio terminorum*):

    > All dogs are mammals.
    >
    > All cats are animals.
    >
    > Therefore, all dogs are animals.

2. Fallacy of the ambiguous middle, or fallacy of equivocation (implies fourth term):

    > Power tends to corrupt.
    >
    > Knowledge is power.
    >
    > Therefore, knowledge tends to corrupt.

    This example equivocates because the middle term, *power,* means different things, "political control over others" in the major premise and "mental ability or authority to control ideas" in the minor premise. If *power* is used in one sense throughout, one premise is false (Copi and Cohen 262).

3. Fallacy of the undistributed middle:

    > All dogs are animals.
    >
    > All cats are animals.
    >
    > Therefore, all cats are dogs.

    The middle term, *animals,* is not distributed; nothing is claimed about the whole class of animals.

    Some other fallacies depend upon some condition, an "if/then" statement, with the "if" part being the antecedent, and the "then" part being the conditional. The valid form of the conditional syllogism (*modus ponens,* way of affirming) is as follows:

    > *If A, then B.*   If it is raining, then the streets are wet.
    >
    > *A.*   It is raining.
    >
    > *Then, B.*   Therefore, the streets are wet.

Some invalid forms of the conditional syllogism:

1. Affirming the consequent:

    > *If A, then B.*   If it is raining, then the streets are wet.
    >
    > *B.*   The streets are wet.
    >
    > *Then, A.*   Therefore, it is raining. (No, the street washer might have gone by.)

2. Denying the antecedent:

    > *If A, then B.*   If a bottle is marked "poison," it will kill me.
    >
    > *Not A.*   This bottle is not marked "poison."
    >
    > *Then, not B.*   Therefore, it will not kill me.

3. The way of denying *(modus tollens)*:

If A, then B.	If it is raining, the streets are wet.
Not B.	The streets are not wet.
Then, not A.	Therefore, it is not raining.

A number of excellent Web sites deal with logic, especially traditional formal logic and fallacies. The Longview Community College site is especially helpful in identifying fallacies, reconstructing arguments to show their parts, and understanding the arguments of complicated discussions (**www.kcmetro.cc.mo.us/longview/CTAC/corenotes.htm**). As well, the introductory logic page from the San José State University Critical Thinking page includes many do-it-yourself exercises for beginners in logic (**www.sjsu.edu/depts/itl/ graphics/main.html**). For other helpful information about logic, see the *Foundations* Web site.

CHAPTER SUMMARY

In Chapter 6, we have shown how arguments work, highlighting logic, induction and deduction, and fallacies. We have also stressed that an awareness of arguments can be used both to criticize arguments by others as well as in formulating your own. You now understand the fundamentals of arguing and assessing a position:

*   You can locate and identify arguments in what you read and hear and in your own work.
*   You have developed some experience and expertise in both inductive and deductive methods and have a sense of when each can best be used to make a case.
*   You have learned how to avoid mistakes in arguments and can identify some of the major fallacies in your own and others' arguments.
*   You have consolidated what was introduced in Chapter 3 and have now moved from developing a critical attitude to being able to implement it.

Now that you have the fundamental building blocks for critical thinking—not just the formulation of logical arguments but also, in the whole of Part II, the development of a critical attitude, sophisticated reading practices, and various means of extending your reading and writing vocabulary—we now move to another set of skills, undertaking research for your assignments on the Web and in the library and learning how to document it.

FURTHER READINGS

Bergmann, Merrie, James Moor, and Jack Nelson. *The Logic Book*. 3rd ed. New York: McGraw-Hill, 1998.

Copi, Irving M., and Keith Burgess Jackson. *Informal Logic*. 3rd ed. Upper Saddle River, NJ: Prentice Hall, 1996.

Copi, Irving M., Keith Burgess Jackson, and Carl Cohen. *Introduction to Logic*. 9th ed. New York: Macmillan, 1994.

Govier, Trudy. *A Practical Study of Argument*. 5th ed. Belmont, CA: Wadsworth, 2001.

Groarke, Leo, Christopher Tindale, and Linda Fisher. *Good Reasoning Matters!* 2nd ed. Toronto: Oxford UP, 1997.

Hansen, Hans V., and Roberts C. Pinto, eds. *Fallacies: Classical and Contemporary Readings*. University Park, PA: Penn State UP, 1995.

Jason, Gary. *Introduction to Logic*. Boston: Jones and Bartlett, 1994.

Johnson, Ralph J. *The Rise of Informal Logic*. Newport, NJ: Vale Press, 1996.

Kelley, David. *The Art of Reasoning*. 2nd ed. New York: W.W. Norton, 1994.

Ruggiero, Vincent Ryan. *Becoming a Critical Thinker*. Rapid City, SD: Houghton Mifflin, 1992.

Thomson, Anne. *Critical Reasoning: A Practical Introduction*. 2nd ed. London: Routledge, 2001.

Toulmin, Stephen. *The Uses of Argument*. Cambridge: Cambridge UP, 1969.

Toulmin, Stephen, Richard Reike, and Allan Janik. *An Introduction to Reasoning*. New York: Macmillan, 1984.

Weston, Anthony. *A Rulebook for Arguments*. 3rd ed. Indianapolis: Hackett, 2000.

part three

Researching on the Net and in the Library

chapter seven

Researching Electronic Sources

The third part of *Foundations* will help you to apply your critical thinking skills to university research. You will learn how to gather essential material for your courses and assignments, how to annotate and digest it, how to keep files about it, and how to document it to prepare for using it in your essays. You will also learn how to avoid charges of plagiarism. Above all, you will become familiar with the written and electronic tools of research.

Chapter 7 begins this exploration by introducing you to the vast new world of electronic information and provides a guide through it to help you get what you want and assess what you find. Libraries use electronic methods for cataloguing, storing, and retrieving information and make huge amounts of material available to students online. We open up this world to you and make it accessible both in the library and from your home computer.

LEARNING OBJECTIVES

This chapter answers questions about how to use the libraries' electronic resources and the unlimited resources of the Internet:

- How do you extend your research capabilities to the new technologies and resources?
- How do you conduct academic research on the Internet?

166

- How do you save and use what you find?
- How do you evaluate what you find?
- How do you access and use the electronic resources of the library effectively?
- How do you apply critical thinking to your research on the Internet?

THE RESEARCH STAGE

In Chapter 3, we discussed the ways to assess the scope and limits of an assignment topic and to position yourself in relation to what the assignment is asking you to do. We discussed an important pre-writing stage, when you consider your audience or reader and determine the purpose and subject of your paper. The next step is to plan your research and writing time and decide how much time you need for revision, final typing, and other preparation of the final form of your essay or other assignment. A schedule that accurately and realistically outlines your time is often a great help.

In reading an assignment critically, you will have become aware of the areas of your topic that need further research. For instance, in one of the assignment examples given in Chapter 3, on Thomas Hardy's despair or optimism, a survey of the critics of Hardy and knowledge of the scope of his writings are fundamental. Your research will involve some library work for this topic and careful note-taking, which entails indicating all direct quotations in quotation marks and noting the sources to avoid later accusations of unscholarly methods. You will also be evaluating the kinds of materials that you locate. The research stage will involve, as well, the careful reading of the relevant novel or poems of Hardy to select those examples from which you will finally develop your position. When you have gathered your notes, you will be able to determine how much more research is necessary. The principles laid out in this and the next chapter stress that the procedures for researching such a paper are applicable to any topic in any discipline because research is systematic, based upon the ways in which information is organized and communicated. This section of *Foundations* will give you the tools for understanding those systems.

NEW RESOURCES AND NEW METHODS

The fundamental problem in researching a topic is finding a match between the specifics of what you are looking for and the general categories by which information is organized on the Web and in your library. Indeed, the idea that knowledge can be classified is itself puzzling to many people, but most students are familiar in some sense with the fact that different sections of the library hold different kinds of books. This awareness is one of the first steps in recognizing how knowledge is classified in the library. Almost all students have searched the Web and have probably used a keyword search engine—again, a first step in recognizing how knowledge or information on the Web is organized—far more inclusively than in libraries, with many other criteria for its various categorizations, including modes of storage and retrieval, popularity, and consumerism, as well as traditional and developing areas of knowledge.

The widespread use of computers has not in itself revolutionized research. But libraries have adopted new electronic technologies with astonishing speed, and now university libraries have their catalogues online for all to use, retaining card catalogues, if at all, only for small special collections. The library's home page also leads you to other resources:

- Access to other libraries in the province or state through the Internet
- Access to huge resources available to you and the general public
- Access to online databases and other e-resources for which your library has protected access, limiting use to registered members of the university
- Access to all of the other libraries throughout the world through the Internet
- Access to thousands of Internet information and research sites for books, collections, and other research materials

This availability on the library's Web page of the Internet and Web resources greatly expands the possibilities for systematic research, but it also complicates that research. University reference librarians have been thoroughly trained in the older book technologies and can greatly assist you in using the reference collections and other materials in your library. Most are also experts in the new computer technologies. These resources have necessarily involved new methods for research, which we address in this chapter.

For other information on Internet library research, Net tools, evaluation, Web browsers, and Netscape, tutorials on search engines, and a glossary of computer jargon, see the following comprehensive site: **www.lib.berkeley.edu/TeachingLib/Guides/Internet/ FindInfo.html**.

RESEARCHING ON THE WEB

A number of strategies are particularly helpful to you when starting research on your essay, both in the pre-writing and the drafting stages. These methods include accessing online research and reference tools, accessing large online collections of standard texts in what is, in effect, a virtual library, and accessing the university library and its online facilities over the Internet—as well as printed sources that we deal with in the next chapter. In what follows here, we first discuss Web browsers, search engines for getting the information from the Web, evaluation procedures, and downloading. Then, we review accessing your university library and some online resources.

You will probably use the Web at an early stage of your research for an essay, first consulting the materials available in your university library and then searching on the Web. You first need to determine exactly which aspects of the topic can be best researched on the Web, which are best looked for in the library in print or electronic sources, and which are best researched in your textbooks and other assigned readings. Whatever method you decide to follow for your research, you will have to spend some time reading what you have found—at least as much time as it took you to find it.

The Internet links two or more networks of computers together to enable them to share information. They all share particular software protocols, known as TCP/IP (transmission control protocol/Internet protocol). Basically, the Internet is the vehicle that transports information (the *net* part) and sends and receives information stored in documents or files from computer to computer (the *inter* part), though they are connected through vast transnational networks of links. Hence, the Internet does not contain information but links you to a computer file somewhere else where the information you want is located.

The World Wide Web (www) is interactive with the Internet, but its revolutionary advance is the use of a programming language called HTML (hypertext markup language). Hypertext is the ability of HTML to enable Web pages to have links or hot addresses (URLs, uniform resource locators), which are activated simply by your clicking on them with a mouse, thereby moving you to the new location within a document or to a new document.

You search the Web using the Internet, but your means of access on your own computer is your Web browser, very likely either Internet Explorer or Netscape. Using them enables you to view Web pages, move between documents using hypertext or hotlinks, view images both still and moving, hear audio, and download anything you want, keeping track of your favourite sites by bookmarking them and using a host of plug-ins to make your browsing more successful. We discuss how to use search engines to canvass the Web below.

The Internet is an excellent resource for all kinds of current information and contemporary topics, such as computers and technology, recent developments in the natural sciences, current news, information from the governments of the world, information about products and business, including the possibility of buying almost anything online, and popular culture (music, films, other kinds of entertainment, travel, hobbies, food, and so on). But even with so-called current information, you will often find that Web sites have not been updated recently (you should examine the date at the end of the page or note the date specified on the Web search engine), and soon, some of your favourite Web sites will have moved or died.

TIPS Researching on the Web

Open your search engine and choose a keyword or phrase to search for.

If searching for one term does not give any useful results quickly, move to another term, or try a different search engine. Be open to a number of different approaches to your topic.

1. Resist the temptation to follow up on every site found, however trivial.

2. Distinguish between researching and surfing. To do research on the Net means to work on some of your academic projects. To surf is to spend time on the Net for entertainment purposes.

3. Keep a sharp eye on your topic, and re-focus your research every few minutes to use your time on the Web to the best advantage.

4. If you find a useful site that you want to explore in greater detail, bookmark it or add it to your favourites in a special folder with your topic as a title, and return to it later when you have accomplished the main purpose of your search. Delete the folder when you are finished with it.

Other fields, including many that are taught at universities, are still developing on the Web. In the humanities and social sciences, many new Web sites are being added daily. Many university courses have Web sites; universities have ample student support pages; writing centres have online tutorials and printouts; and sophisticated search engines review millions of Web pages. However, historical or contextual information about many topics in these fields remains more limited than current information: it is harder to get older information in the Web's rush to remain up to date.

Hence, it is more important than ever that you are aware of the purposes and functions of the various Web search engines. It is also crucial that you continue to focus on your topic and set limits on the amount of time that you spend searching. If nothing shows up within your time limit, you should re-formulate your search or change search engines. You might also try searching at a different time of day if you find that the Web is slow because of heavy traffic during peak hours.

INFORMATION ON THE INTERNET

Web pages on the Internet are indexed, by the title of the page, the address, a keyword, the subject matter of the page, or the entire contents of the page. This information is gathered in different ways by different kinds of search engines and directories, by *spiders* (electronic robots) that continuously scan the Web and sort data electronically and by human researchers who group Web pages into categories. The resulting indexes are the databases which the Web browsers and their search engines have access to. Of course, the Web database and its many parts are never completely indexed. Perhaps only about two billion out of about three billion are indexed at any one time. Thousands of new pages are added every day, just as thousands of other pages disappear through lack of servicing, loss of the Internet provider, inactivity, or cancellation.

WEB BROWSERS

Web browsers are software programs installed on your computer (such as Internet Explorer and Netscape) that let you view hypertext Web pages and undertake Web searches. They have add-on programs that let you set up Web pages and also have facilities for e-mail, conferencing, and many other capabilities. You can customize the way your browser functions for your own needs, including changing its home page (go to your home page of choice, perhaps your university library's home page, and in Explorer select Tools/Internet options, in Netscape select Preferences). The home sites for both Explorer and Netscape have lots of additional information, and their help function gives direct access to the features of each program. Above all, a Web browser enables you to undertake a search for information on the Internet using search engines.

SEARCH ENGINES

Four different means of searching the Web are currently available, and they vary in usefulness and capabilities: a keyword search engine, a metasearch engine, a subject directory, and a specialized database. There are more than 500 of these search engines. Usually, your

TABLE 7.1	Kinds of Search Engines

A. KEYWORD SEARCH ENGINES

- fast and thorough full-text search of selected Web pages
- search by keyword or exact phrase (in quotation marks)
- database compiled by electronic computer robots (spiders)
- size from small to vast, more than two billion pages, and are unevaluated
- examples: Google, Teoma, AltaVista, Northern Lights, AlltheWeb

B. METASEARCH ENGINES

- fast but superficial search, using several keyword search engines at once
- search by keyword
- compile results, often clumping them; limited by characteristics of search engines used
- gather about 10% of results of each search engine they use
- examples: MetaCrawler, Vivisimo, SurfWax, Ixquick, Copernic

C. SUBJECT DIRECTORIES

- requires searcher's choice to navigate sites pre-selected by human searchers
- search by selecting highlighting topic to narrow search by hierarchical categories
- sites are generally well evaluated and usually up to date
- can browse through subject categories and descriptions
- no full-text document searches
- examples: Librarian's Index, Infomine, AcademicInfo

D. SPECIALIZED DATABASES

- sometimes found through a subject directory or hotlink
- are part of *Invisible Web* that cannot be searched by spiders. Require user's input to access them. Use Google to search for your topic and database. E.g. **subsidized housing database**
- use the search box on the home page of the database to search the site
- limited search capabilities, dependent on the size of the site
- can be very useful if on your search topic and totally useless if not
- use the directories of databases like Complete Planet, Direct Search, Internets

Adapted from the Teaching Library Internet Guides from the University of California at Berkeley: www.lib.berkeley.edu/TeachingLib/Guides/Internet/ToolsTables.html

university will have some of these engines already listed as hotlinks on the Internet access or search page (click on the name for access). Otherwise, you enter the URL of a particular search engine (see the addresses below) in your browser's location toolbar and click Enter. If you find the search engine useful, you can bookmark it and save it in a bookmark folder of search engines. Their differences are set out in Table 7.1.

For further information about search engines in general, you can consult the extensive pages on the Internet and Internet searches from the University of California at Berkeley: **www.lib.berkeley.edu/TeachingLib/Guides/Internet**.

The "Searching the Web" link at the Yahoo! site compares the features of many engines and offers further information on conducting an effective search and comparing search engines: **dir.yahoo.com/Computers_and_Internet/Internet/World_Wide_Web/Searching_the_Web/**.

Keyword Search Engines

Keyword search engines are connected to vast Internet databases of millions of references through spiders or robots that circulate throughout the Web and collect information from millions of sites. Normally, these spiders read and index either several hundred words on a Web page or the entire document page (full-text engines), as well as any keywords that the author of the page has built into the page. They then alphabetize the results and add them to a master list, giving greater stress to keywords in headings and to greater frequency of key-words in the body of the text (HotBot, for instance, indexes 110 million Web pages, and Google over two billion). The results that they return give preference to the closeness of the match as well as the site popularity based on the number of hits or visitors. Most have advanced search features that allow you to put limits on the language used, the dates, and other constraints. Some search engines offer a specialized or dedicated toolbar that becomes resident on your Web browser's page for quick access. Search engines allow you to search by keyword, a complete phrase in quotation marks, or a personal name and allow various inclusions (e.g., dates, countries) or exclusions (based on linking your terms with "operators," such as NOT, OR, and so on). AND is the default link between two keywords. Some allow wildcards (*) for words you cannot recall ("*Harry Potter and the Order of the* *")

The information that keyword search engines return can be just the URL or Web address, the heading information, or a short abstract (the most useful). If you already know more or less what you want, such general search engines can be very helpful. On the other hand, if you are not focused, you will waste a great deal of time wading through several hundred irrelevant sites that are evaluated mechanically only according your search criteria. For further information, see **www.searchenginewatch.com/**.

For Web addresses for a number of keyword search engines, see the Weblinks for Chapter 7 on the *Foundations* Web site.

Metasearch Engines

These engines use the term you provide to combine information from a number of other search engines. Because they combine the resources of different engines, they have to suppress the specialized search functions of those engines to achieve a common denominator, thereby bypassing some of the refined capabilities that you might wish to use. Some (such as MetaCrawler) collate the results; others (such as Dogpile) do not. Two of the newer and more sophisticated metasearch engines are Vivísimo, which compiles sites in clusters of like-subjects, and SurfWax. Generally, the metasearch engines are not recommended for a first search since you do not have the ability to control where your search is being undertaken. They all omit searching through Northern Light (an excellent academic search engine), and most do not use Google because it is so large and takes time for the search. Nevertheless, sometimes, they do turn up something that you would otherwise have missed.

For Web addresses for metasearch engines, see the *Foundations* Web page. Further information is provided by each of the Web sites for the browsers themselves. Using each search engine's optional or advanced features will help you to refine your search significantly. For a discussion of the different characteristics of metasearch engines, see **www.lib.berkeley.edu/TeachingLib/Guides/Internet/MetaSearch.html**.

> ## TIPS   Using Search and Metasearch Engines
>
> 1. Use the appropriate search engine.
> 2. Start with a broad category search engine, such as Google, or Vivisimo, especially if you are uncertain about what you might find. If you are looking for information on current entertainment but do not have a category in mind, such an engine works best. Begin with a keyword search engine, then a metasearch engine.
> 3. Use the engine's advanced search options, if available.
> 4. Search by topic, keyword, person, or phrase (use quotation marks around it to get sites with the exact phrase). Search for several words, rather than just one, or use a wildcard (*).
> 5. Be aware of the search conventions. Narrow your search by date, country, or kind of site (for instance, .com for commercial, .edu for educational). Use limiters. All of the keyword search engines accept the limiters for a search used in Boolean logic. That is, the words AND (usually a default), OR, and AND NOT may be used to include or exclude specific items in your search. Limiter words must be typed in capital letters.
> 6. If you are clear about what you want, say, the most recent Steven Spielberg film, enter either his name or the name of the film into a more specific topical index, such as All Movie Guide (**www.allmovie.com**) or CineMedia (**www.cinemedia.org**).
> 7. Read the search engine's help files for useful tips and hints.

Subject Directories

Subject guides categorize Web sites according to content subject area. That is, the directory's staff assigns a site to a specific topic category, based on the Web page's content: computers, education, entertainment (books, movies, music), news, sports, and so on, and then arranges sub-topics within that in what is known as a hierarchy: you start with the broadest and narrow it down. You can narrow your search using the subject guides and options to access advanced features. This search will often lead you to good sources quickly, though there are fewer resources available in the database than in those of general search engines. Subject directories include the following:

- AcademicInfo: **www.academicinfo.com**
- Andersonian Library in Glasgow for academic subjects: **www.bubl.ac.uk/link**
- The Argus Clearinghouse: **www.clearinghouse.net/searching/find.html**
- Galaxy: **www.einet.net**
- Infomine: **www.infomine.com**
- Inter-links: **web.bilkent.edu.tr/nova/start.html**
- Librarians' Index to the Internet: **www.lii.org**
- Yahoo!: **www.yahoo.com**

Specialized Databases

The Web has thousands of databases that are not subject to indexing by spiders because they require a user to enter a special search request to search that database only. Hence these databases are part of what is known as the *invisible Web*. Only rarely are they found in subject directories, but they are sometimes referred to in specialized Web sites directly on your topic, or you might search for them in a keyword search engine (Google, for instance) by adding the word *database* after your keyword. You might then find a library catalogue (all of them are specialized databases that let users search for individual books on their database), or a statistics database. When you activate the search, you generate a page on your browser with information that only you have requested, and it is not retained for anyone else after you leave it.

Guides to databases include the following:

- Complete Planet: **www.completeplanet.com**
- Direct Search: **www.freeprint.com/gary/direct.htm**
- Internets: **www.webpromotion.com/internets/**

For further information, see Robert J. Lackie's invisible Web page at Rider College: **http://library.rider.edu/scholarly/rlackie/Invisible/Inv_Web.html**.

Strategies for an Effective Search on the Internet

What kinds of information are on the Web that might be of use to you in your research, and how might you find it? The secret lies in conducting an effective search. The new generation of keyword search engines has taken over from the metasearch engines and is far more precise. With the speed of modern communication lines, computers can do vast searches in split seconds.

1. Define your search topic. As with traditional methods for research in print texts, you have to focus precisely on your topic for searches in electronic media. You should determine whether it is best to search your library catalogues or other electronic resources before going to the library to consult print copies. If you decide to use an online search of the Internet, you need to consider carefully how your topic can be defined or analyzed to make best use of the various search engines and their features. Make your term sufficiently general and sufficiently focused. Try to use two or three keywords that define your topic closely to limit the search to what is most useful. If you search for "revolution," you will get far too much information. If you narrow your search to "French Revolution," you will be somewhat more successful. If you specify a specific figure, say Marat or Robespierre, you will be far more successful.

2. In the first search, use the search tool with the most information for your topic and the largest search capacity, such as Google or AlltheWeb, each with over two billion pages, or Teoma, which is seeking to challenge them. Use their advanced search capabilities. Bookmark the sites that seem most promising and consult them in detail later. Avoid waste of time, loss of references, and needless returns to Web sites or the library by noting down or printing at least some of the pages you find you will eventually need for your references and bibliography when you use these materials in your essay.

3. In the second search, look for bibliographies or other indexes concerning your topic by consulting the subject directories. Go to Librarians' Index, AcademicInfo, or even to Yahoo! if you are looking for a topic in popular culture. Even in Yahoo!, you can add the term *Web directories* to the search to find collections of information or bibliographies on your topic. Use the available limiters: "topic" + indexes OR Web directories. These limiters will restrict the search to those indexes that list information on your topic. Other places to look include the following:

    • Librarians' Index to the Internet: **www.lii.org**

    • WWW Virtual Library: **http://vlib.org**

    • Purdue University's Internet Gateway: **www.lib.purdue.edu/vlibrary/inet_resources**

4. You can follow up with one of the new compiling metasearch engines such as Vivisimo to check out anything else that you might have missed. Avail yourself of the various options to define the way the metasearch engine will look for your information.

5. Vary your search terms, re-assessing them in the light of your earlier searches. Then, go back over earlier strategies and try other terms or another search engine. Avoid general searches of databases without narrowing your topic.

6. You almost certainly will have found a wealth of information. But if you are stuck or need further help, seek help from the library reference desk or check out the general help at the British Universities' online help: **http://bubl.ac.uk/searches/guides.htm**.

EVALUATING WHAT YOU READ: CRITICAL THINKING AND THE INTERNET

The Web has vast amounts of academic information available on all topics in all disciplines and is now far from being merely an entertainment provider or source for adult sites, by far the most popular and profitable of all categories of Web sites. All universities maintain Web sites, making some course materials available online, along with all kinds of online tutorials and hand-outs connected with student study helps, writing centres, and Internet access. The Web can be a wonderful research tool. However, it must also be said that cranks and crackpots maintain Web sites, along with others that promote racial hatred and religious and other kinds of intolerance, along with thousands of sites that are ill-informed and poorly designed. How do you know the one from the other? The Web can also give you lots of information about popular culture, contemporary events, recent news items, and trivia, as well as access to libraries around the world, some reference books, many journals, and official data from almost every nation. But some of this information is hard to find, though you are becoming an experienced Web researcher and, by now, will be able to locate what you want.

The principles of critical thinking demand two preliminary cautions. First, much of the information that you will find on the Web appears to be anonymous, with no visible author, so the question is—who is the author? And how reliable is that author? Hence, the question of how you evaluate a Web site is crucial to your research. Second, the very anonymity of a Web page and its easy accessibility are great temptations to you. It is so effortless to lift sections of what you find directly into your word processor without acknowledgment, thereby committing plagiarism. But remember that just as you found them fairly easily, so can your instructor. So, a second set of questions arises about academic integrity and the legitimate use of Web resources. We discuss proper documentation of what you find on the Web in Chapter 9, along with the related issues of plagiarism. We consider the issue of the evaluation of what you find on the Web here.

When you search the Web, you should be aware that while many search engines (such as Yahoo! or Excite) monitor and sometimes limit what they carry, the Web itself is open to all who want to set up a page. There is no vetting of it by the Web for factual accuracy, grammatical correctness, freedom from bias or prejudice, currency or anything else, although the makers of the Web page may be careful about these matters. Each site, then, needs to be assessed for its validity, and your guide here should be enquiring skepticism.

Web sites have been classified as having eight purposes: (1) personal sites that give biographical information (often academic, sometimes for vanity purposes), (2) promotional (to sell a product), (3) current (such as newspaper sites), (4) informational (sharing information on millions of topics, hobbies, lifestyles), (5) persuasive (propaganda to convert you to a point of view), (6) instructional (to teach or set out a course of study), (7) registrational (to register for courses, information, or products), and (8) entertainment (**www.iss.stthomas.edu/studyguides/evaluate.htm**). Obviously, several such purposes have potential for your search, but you will need to check each site for its reliability, accuracy, coverage of your topic, and so on. It often helps to bear in mind that there is a user and a Web context for each site. The user context is how a site meets your needs, and here you have to be ruthless, or you will end up surfing for hours. The Web context is where your critical thinking kicks in, helping you determine its validity. Does its content measure up to the elegant design, background, flashing lights, and colourful graphics?

In recent years, universities and other Web users have developed recognized procedures for evaluating Web pages, and such procedures should become a normal part of your research techniques. For instance, Elizabeth E. Kirk of Johns Hopkins University (**www.library.jhu.edu/elp/useit/evaluate/**) lists six categories in evaluating a Web site that we summarize and adapt here:

1. **Authorship.** Who wrote the page? Is the author reliable on the basis of institutional affiliation? Is an affiliation stated, or can you deduce it from the URL? Is there information about an address, e-mail, biographical information, and so on?

2. **Publishing body.** Is the Web page part of an institutional site, such as a university? Does it have some credentials? Can the domain (the part of the URL that gives the Web address's category) be identified? The *domain name* might include a suffix that identifies it as a particular kind of site: .com (commercial site), .edu (educational site), .gov (government site), .net (network site), .org (non-profit organization). A two-letter code often gives the country of origin: .ca (Canada); .au (Australia).

3. **Objectivity, point of view, or bias.** Does the author or corporate Web page have a stake in the topic? Is it engaged in advertising a position or product? Does it have a political, ethical, or philosophical agenda that it is seeking to promote?

4. **Reference to other sources.** Is there a bibliography? Are there additional links, and are they relevant? Check some of the links and see if the site you are considering is cross-linked. Are there acknowledgments of particular schools of thought on your topic? Are other views represented, along with disagreements?

5. **Verifiability.** Can the information and argumentation be tested? Do the cited sources for the documentation back up the position that is argued? Can the methodology be tested in other ways? Is it appropriate, and can it be reproduced?

6. **Currency.** How up to date is the information? Is it dated, or can a date be determined from internal evidence? Is the Web page dated, or is there information about how recently it was updated? You can check how recently it was modified by right clicking with your mouse, and selecting Properties from the drop-down list.

In addition, there are other considerations that you should keep in mind. Is the site that you have found popular or academic? Numerous popular sites have vast amounts of useful information, but you may have to sift through large amounts of trivia on the way. Is the coverage, then, at a level that you can use? What is its focus, and what is its presumed audience? If the site on fairy stories is just to introduce young readers to the genre, it might not

---

TIPS What to Do When You Have Problems

Too few results:

1. When your search turns up few or no locations, first check your spelling.

2. Be less specific in your search terms.

3. Try some variations on the terms you are using.

4. Try another search engine.

Too many results:

1. Use more specific terms to narrow your search.

2. Link the words that narrow the topic even more, using Boolean logic terms (AND, OR, NOT).

Error messages:

1. *Error 404: Page/File not found.* The most common reason for this frequent error is that you have made a spelling mistake or the URL is no longer functional. It may have changed, or the server may no longer carry this site. In any case, check the URL address again, paying particular attention to the upper and lower case characters, to special signs, such as _ or - or ~. Failing all else, move up one level in the address by omitting the last level after the slash (/) and try again.

2. *No answer* or the message that the server is not answering or might be down. Wait a few minutes or perhaps a few hours.

3. *Page has moved.* If you are lucky you may be directed to the new address. If not, try moving higher in the address hierarchy by omitting what follows the last slash. Or try searching for the topic or location again on another search engine.

4. *Permission denied.* Sometimes, sites have restricted access during certain times of the day. Other sites are restricted to a specific membership.

be what you want. Try also to draw a distinction between the design of the site and its content. Many sites have wonderful sonics and graphics, but the content is slim. Look carefully at the home page to determine whether it is accurate. Is the layout clear and accessible? Are there spelling mistakes? Is there a statement of purpose?

It is also wise to consider the accountability of a Web site. Knowledge presented in a scholarly format strives to be accountable by recording its sources, contextualizing its argument in relation to other scholarship, considering opposing views, and using language that is conventional and appropriate for the particular discourse. You can evaluate Web sites according to these criteria and judge the reliability and soundness of the information that a page presents. The key question underlying these criteria is whether or not the site is accountable—that is, whether or not it positions its information appropriately. For instance, there are several sites on the Web dedicated to white supremacy. Racist terms used as descriptives for groups of people clearly mark these sites as biased and as virtually useless as sources of information for any academic topic, except for a study of hate groups themselves.

DOWNLOADING INFORMATION FROM THE INTERNET

Having found information on the Internet that you wish to use in your research, how can you convert it from images and text on your screen to research notes in your assignment file or to essential data in your paper? One of the first steps to preserve research references is to bookmark the page. You can then use other procedures for saving text or graphics to your hard drive or for printing your present document.

Bookmarks

When you find a site that you want to make reference to or that you wish to return to later, you can file it in your own bookmarks or in a course or essay folder for immediate use. In Netscape click on Communicator/Bookmarks/Add; in Explorer click on Favorites, Add to Favorites, OK. The name of the site includes its URL in hypertext, so it is hot to be activated when it is clicked. You can edit your bookmarks by adding or deleting them, adding or moving sites into folders, and so on. Check the help tab in your Web browser.

If you find Internet addresses when using a computer in the computer lab or library, you can either save them to a floppy disk or e-mail them to your address to file them later on your home computer.

Text

Text on the Internet is usually encoded in HTML format (hypertext markup language), which must be converted to be read by your word processor. So, your first choice is to save the file you have found as an HTML file, which you can convert later. To save the file, you click on the File tab in the toolbar of Navigator or Explorer, and choose Save As. You have the choice of designating where you want the file saved and can change the name of the file to fit with your research needs. After you have logged off the Internet, you can recall the file (Navigator or Explorer will run, but not online, to give you access to the file), and then proceed with the next step. You should be aware that Netscape and Explorer will not save graphics in this process automatically, or if they do, the files may be very large.

Perhaps a more useful method is to block the entire document (Edit/Select All) or the part of it you need using your mouse and save it to your word processor. Consult the Help tab in your Web browser for details.

Some texts are encoded in yet another format, PDF (portable document format), which preserves page font and format and can be opened by Adobe Acrobat Reader. This reader can be downloaded free from any number of sites, but especially from the home site (**www.adobe.com/products/acrobat/readstep.html**). This program is often bundled with software that comes with your computer. Once downloaded and installed (by following the advice given at the download site), this reader will be invoked to read Adobe files automatically; they can then be saved in whatever format you wish.

TIPS Using Your Mouse

Even faster than blocking a whole document is the efficient use of your mouse. Clicking on the right button when in an HTML document automatically gives you a variety of choices, including Properties (when the document was created or modified), Copy, Save, or Print. A little experimenting with these procedures will greatly improve your speed, efficiency, and accuracy in downloading research materials.

Graphics

Sometimes, you want to save graphics (illustrations, maps, charts, tables, graphs, headings, or banners) for use in your research or essay. Most Internet graphics are encoded in gif (graphic interchange format) or jpeg (joint picture experts group) format, indicating the kinds of capture and compression used in transferring an image into electronic bytes. To save a graphic image, you should follow these steps:

1. Right click the mouse on the graphic and choose Save As.

2. Save the image to the file that you designate on your hard drive, normally one of your research files for this assignment. Note that it will be saved in the same format that it was in when on the Web page.

3. Your saved image can be imported into a document in your word processor or saved to a file for later use.

4. Various graphics viewing and editing programs have the function of calling up your saved graphic, modifying it, and saving it again in whatever format you wish. It can also be animated, prepared for another Web page with special software like Macromedia products or Flashware. For some graphics viewing and editing programs, see the Weblinks for Chapter 7 on the *Foundations* Web site.

Saving and Printing from the Internet

Sometimes, you may want to save the text or graphics material you have found by printing it (using the Print icon in the browser's toolbar), so you will have a hard copy of the information on the Web page. To incorporate any of this material into your own writing, you will have to either cut and paste it or re-type it.

You may find that modifying your printer's formatting instructions will get you a better output, perhaps by choosing the landscape, rather than the portrait, orientation. You can also use your word processor and printer to print Web pages as a small booklet, or you can use a special utility that prints Web pages and other documents automatically in small booklet format. For instance, the utility "ClickBook" from Blue Squirrel software (**www.bluesquirrel.com/clickbook/**) allows you to print a Web document in a booklet format automatically. It reduces a full Web-sized screen page to half of an 8.5 × 11 inch page (printed in landscape or horizontally) and prints on both sides of the page, formatting them so that they read from front to back when stapled together. It also includes all of the graphics, prints the address of the page and the name of the site, and dates and numbers the pages. The same program can be used in printing from your word processor.

DECODING AND UNSCRAMBLING FILES YOU DOWNLOAD

Before you can use files in your essays, you need to be certain that you have the reference recorded accurately, in case you have to return for further information. If you refer to this document in your paper, you also must note it in your "works cited" list according to the proper form for citing electronic sources. Furthermore, many files that you download include their own HTML or other formatting codes and have to be re-formatted with hard returns, margins, spacing, and so on. Hence it is better to save a file stripped of its formatting codes. You can choose how to save a file (in your Web browser click on File/ Save As and choose the format you wish). If you choose rtf (rich text format), the file is stripped of most of its formatting codes and is easier to edit on your word processor once it is cut and pasted into a document or a new folder. Unless you already have a macro (an encoded command sequence that you initiate through a macro shortcut with only one or two keys) to re-format such files, you will have to re-format the file manually. You should check the manual with your word processor to see whether yours has such a macro. Usually, manual re-formatting involves using the search-and-replace function to convert all single hard returns into spaces (thereby correcting line endings to conform to your line length), five spaces into left tabs, and remaining double spaces into single spaces. Fancier macros will convert double hyphens to the longer en-dashes, triple hyphens into em-dashes, and plain quotation marks into "smart," or typographical, quotation marks (shaped like 6s and 9s).

Your word processor will usually convert files from other word processors automatically, or if you have difficulty, you can save them by accessing your word processor's Save As feature and choosing the Save as ASCII or generic word processor or rtf format. Of course, the formatting codes (italics, underlining, and sometimes paragraph indentations) have to be re-inserted.

INTERNET ACCESS TO LIBRARIES

Your University Library

The libraries of most public and university libraries are now accessible over the Internet. Universities have blocks of terminals in the library, but you can search for materials from home. You can also check whether the book is in the library or on loan, and what other books are available on similar topics, as we explain below. We deal with the Internet and the library and its electronic resources here instead of in the next chapter because that chapter involves print resources. While Internet library catalogues lead you to print sources, they also have large capabilities in e-resources, and some brief discussion of them is appropriate here. For further information on your library's e-resources, see the hand-outs at the reference desk.

To access your university's library, you need an Internet connection with access numbers and codes for the university system, provided as a package of software that makes online connection easy. The advantage of having such an account is that you will then have access to some materials that are reserved for university users, rather than the general public.

To access your university's catalogues, you go to your university's main Web page via Netscape Navigator or Microsoft Explorer, locate the library tab or icon, and you then have a variety of choices, including searching the online catalogue. You can add the library's address to your bookmarks, or make it your home page if you want to have it there each time you are on the Web (Explorer—Tools/Internet Options; Netscape—Edit/Preferences).

Electronic searches of the catalogue enable you to hunt for an author, title, subject, and shelf number. Once you have found a book you are interested in, you can find others on the same topic by clicking on the shelf number or tab, scrolling forward and backward from that number. Or, you can use the subject classification codes or words that are used as descriptors in your book's information pages, listed below the publication data. By clicking your mouse on those hot or hypertext words (usually showing in blue), you can search the catalogue for other books on the same subject.

Catalogue information can be very useful in compiling a working bibliography. You might begin your library research on a topic by gathering one or two pages of bibliographical entries together and then checking the shelves of books in the library. Rather than transcribing all of that information manually, with the potential for errors, you can save it to your word processor where you can compile and edit it later. From the library you can send it to your e-mail address, or print it. You may block and save a single item, items from one screen, or even larger lists. Or you may compile many items to make a single list.

Other Libraries

You might wish to have information about a book that your university library does not own, or you might wish to see whether another university library nearby or a public library has materials you can use. You can access their information by going to your own library and clicking on "Other Libraries" or a similar link on the library's home page. That will give you access to libraries in your area, in the country, and on other continents. One of the largest sources for bibliographical information is the Library of Congress in Washington D.C., which you can access in this way.

Once you have gained access, you can continue your search in the usual way. You can also make a request to borrow those materials from another library (sometimes for a small fee) through the interlibrary loan office of your library. You should allow plenty of time for the materials to arrive before your research is needed. There are many good collections of library links and catalogues on the Web, such as LibCat's guide to Internet library resources (**www.metronet.lib.mn.us/lc/lc1.cfm**) and LibDex's library index (**www.libdex.com**).

Online Indexes, Databases, and Journals

Universities maintain subscriptions to thousands of online databases, e-books, e-journals, and newspapers. For instance, York University's library has over 12 000 e-resources, vast amounts of research information available to users. The many volumes of the *Oxford English Dictionary* are available online. So are the indexes of scholarly work completed in specialized fields over the many years, for instance, those compiled by the American Psychological Association and the Modern Language Association. Similar indexes and databases are available in the sciences, social sciences and humanities, business, education, law, and religion. Some universities also make these resources available to the general public, but most require a user to log in to the library through a university-maintained server or a proxy account (see the library help desk for information) that is accessible only to members of that university community. In this way, the universities can provide the best service to their own members and also maintain the copyright and user restrictions placed on e-resources by the sellers. Any of this material, once accessed, can be saved to your word processor, sent to your e-mail address, or printed.

Similarly, universities have hundreds of journals online, which has become the normal way for them to publish now, rather than in hard copy. Again, access may be restricted to registered university members or through library terminals. It is also worth checking some sites that archive runs of journals, such as the University of California at San Diego Library (**gort.ucsd.edu/ejourn/jdir.html**) and the University of Florida Virtual Library (**www.clas.ufl.edu/users/gthursby/socsci/**).

If you find a journal index that is useful to you, you can make a note of the reference information and look it up in the hard copy in your library. Or you can look further to see whether the article has been stored electronically and you can access it. If so, you can read the article online (although access time through your server might cost you money), download it to read later, or block and copy the text you want to use directly into your word processor. Be careful to clearly mark out what you have copied from the Web, and do not incorporate anything into your submitted work without attribution. You should always keep a careful record of the source. Alternatively, you can print the article or a blocked section of it using the print function on Netscape Navigator or Microsoft Explorer.

Downloading Information in the Library

In the library, you can download information in the same way as at home. You can send materials that you locate on the library catalogue to your e-mail address and print or save to a floppy disk information from the CD-ROMs. The library staff can provide further information.

ONLINE REFERENCE TOOLS AND BOOKS

Dictionaries (English and other languages), style guides, handbooks of quotations, shorter encyclopedias, and so on, are also available online. Some might be available from your university's Web page. You can use, as well, the vast resources provided by Bucknell University at "A Web of Online Dictionaries," which offers over 500 dictionaries in 140 different languages and links to specialized dictionaries in popular and technical fields (**www.facstaff.bucknell.edu/rbeard/diction.html**). Numerous other reference resources are available at **www.yourdictionary.com**. You can search the *Merriam-Webster Dictionary* at **www.m-w.com/home.htm**.

You can also use one of the numerous online reference shelves:

• Columbia University Bartleby Library: **www.bartleby.com/**
• Internet Public Library Reference Center: **www.ipl.org/ref/CenterNG.html**
• Research-It!: **www.itools.com/research-it/research-it.html**
• The Virtual Reference Desk: **www.refdesk.com**

The *Encyclopaedia Britannica* has now set up a free-access Web site (**www.britannica. com**).

Newspapers and other sources of daily information are also widely available, usually by entering the newspaper's name followed by .com. A long international list of newspapers generally available on the Internet is given at *The Reference Desk* (**www.refdesk.com/ paper.html**). Many newspapers have online sites:

• *The Globe and Mail*: **www.theglobeandmail.com**
• *The Toronto Star*: **www.thestar.com**
• *The Times* (London): **www.the-times.co.uk**
• *New York Times*: **www.nytimes.com**
• *Washington Post*: **www.washingtonpost.com**

Information about particular countries can be found on the site maintained by that country:

• Canada: **canada.gc.ca/main_e.html**
• United States of America (US Government's Official Web Portal): **www.firstgov.gov/**
• United Kingdom (Central Office of Information): **www.coi.gov.uk** and the Brit Index: **www.britindex.co.uk**

A wide range of links is collected about many countries at the Web site for Planet Earth (**www.tidusa.com/PEHP2000/Planet_Earth/info.html**). Other specialized information is available also in the *Country Studies,* originally commissioned by the Central Intelligence Agency (CIA) (**lcweb2.loc.gov/frd/cs/cshome.html**). Virtually every country in the world is covered, with information that the CIA thought its agents should know when visiting, dealing with, or writing about such countries. Awareness of the political purposes originally involved in gathering this information should warn users to exercise appropriate judgment and methods of evaluation.

You might want to refer to a standard reference book and can, of course, look for it in the print books in your library. But another possibility is searching for it as an electronic text (called e-texts). There are several repositories of online books on the Web. The University of Michigan has been putting many books online (**www.ipl.org/**). Another collection is Project Gutenberg (**www.promo.net/pg**), named after the founder of the printing press. Many volunteers enter texts by scanning and typing them into electronic format. All of their books are available in ASCII format (that is, with no or very little formatting), to give easy access to all users. Other repositories include Great Books of Western Civilization (Mercer University) (**www.geocities.com/Athens/Atlantis/4360/**) and

Alex: A Catalogue of Electronic Texts on the Internet (**www.lib.ncsu.edu/staff/morgan/alex/alex-index.html**).

If you wish to buy an inexpensive CD-ROM that contains many of these titles, you might try the widely available CD-ROMs produced by Walnut Creek Software or the collection *World Literary Heritage* produced by Softbit, Inc.

One of the advantages of online books is that you can search for information in them. You can download the book, convert and format it for your word processor, and search for the relevant information using your word processor's Find or Search utility. Once you are finished with the book, you can archive it onto a floppy (perhaps using a compression tool, such as WinZip or PKZIP, to make it fit on a floppy) or delete it. For WinZip (shareware), see their Web site at **www.winzip.com/ibrowser.htm**. For PKZIP (shareware), see **www.pkware.com**. Shareware indicates that you pay for the product if you like and use it. Some universities have an onsite licence to distribute these products.

CHAPTER SUMMARY

In this chapter, we have introduced you to research by stressing its systematic nature: to use electronic resources effectively, you must adopt a logical method and must not proceed randomly as if you were surfing. There is no one way or correct logic to discover relevant materials. You need to adopt some basic methods laid out in this chapter, adapting them to your needs. You have already mastered a number of research skills:

- You have learned to use the resources of the Web for your research on essays and assignments.
- You can use a variety of search engines, including their advanced search features.
- You can evaluate what you find for accuracy, currency, and authority.
- You know how to use the e-resources of your university library.
- You can document your sources and save and annotate them in your computer files.

FURTHER READINGS

Blaxter, Loraine, Christina Hughes, and Malcolm Tight. *How to Research*. 2nd ed. Philadelphia: Open UP, 2001.

Burkle-Young, Francis A., and Saundra Rose Maley. *The Research Guide for the Digital Age: A New Handbook to Research and Writing for the Serious Student*. Lanham, MD: UP of America, 1997.

Calishain, Tara. *Official Netscape Guide to Internet Research*. New York: Netscape Press, 1996.

Crump, Eric, and Nick Carbone. *Writing Online: A Student's Guide to the Internet and World Wide Web*. New York: Houghton Mifflin, 1998.

Fielden, Ned L. *Internet Research: Theory and Practice*. Jefferson, NC: McFarland, 2001.

Forrester, William H., and Jane L. Rowlands. *The Online Searcher's Companion*. London: Library Association Publishing, 2000.

Harnack, Andrew, and Eugene Kleppinger. *Online! A Reference Guide to Using Internet Sources*. New York: St. Martin's Press, 1997.

Mann, Thomas. *The Oxford Guide to Library Research*. New York: Oxford UP, 1998. [Includes a wealth of information on Internet searches.]

Pomeroy, Andrew M. *The Research Book: Internet Research: Mastering Research Engines*. Placentia, CA: Creative Continuum, 2002.

Thiroux, Emily. *The Critical Edge: Thinking and Researching in a Virtual Society*. Upper Saddle River, NJ: Prentice-Hall, 1999.

chapter eight

Researching Print Sources

Moving from a high school library to the one in your university can be intimidating. This chapter guides you through its resources, shows you how to find books and articles for your courses and assignments, explains the library's range of printed and electronic reference books, and helps you with basic research methods in many areas.

LEARNING OBJECTIVES

This chapter deals with the following:

- How do you search for the library's materials systematically?
- What are the five basic search methods in the library's online catalogue?
- How do you develop more advanced searches or search for complex materials?
- How do you find relevant articles, reviews, or other materials in the library's print and e-resources?
- What is in the reference section, and how can it be used?

RESEARCH METHODS AND LIBRARY CLASSIFICATION SYSTEMS

Libraries organize knowledge according to institutional norms, which depend on modes of knowledge derived from the enlightenment tradition of the 18th century, as well as from the humanistic views of human nature and social activities that have dominated Western thought since the Renaissance. These traditions tended to stress the works of major writers, thinkers, politicians, and artists which were regarded as classics, and hence these writings came to be regarded as primary texts and the writings about them as secondary texts. This distinction was incorporated into library classification systems, so that in the humanities and social sciences, these works are privileged over secondary works of a critical, historical, and often technical or scientific nature. Much work in contemporary critical theory has challenged the ideological assumptions underlying this distinction. However, you should be aware that the systems of classification do have consistency—for instance, much of the classification system in the humanities is organized around concepts of nation, century, and individual author.

Critical thinking about where this information comes from and how it is organized should alert you to the fact that these systems of knowledge are deeply attached to the value systems and political affiliations of universities, libraries, and the Web. Such systems of organizing knowledge are not divine or written in stone; instead, they are chosen by a library or university for specific reasons of utility and conformity to the systems in other institutions. Awareness of at least some of these implications makes you a more questioning and perceptive user of the library and its facilities. Searching for information about your topic involves you immediately in these value systems and in the way they are put together.

The organization of any information retrieval system, such as the library or the Web, is set out according to topics, which are, in turn, broken down into complex sub-sets. Knowledge of these topics and their sub-sets enables access to the specifics of your topic. The more knowledge you have about how information is organized and classified in the library (and, as you have seen in the previous chapter, on the Web), the better you will be able to conduct a search in order to access this information.

TIPS Using the Library

1. The library offers general tours, instruction, and tutorials, on the online catalogues and workshops on e-resources, as well as many other services.

2. Many of these programs are offered regularly throughout the year. You should certainly take advantage of them early in your university career to get the most out of your research.

3. Your university's library is prepared to welcome you at the beginning of term with all kinds of orientation and instructional programs to acquaint you with its resources.

4. Additional tutorials are available online.

BOOK CLASSIFICATION SYSTEMS

All university and public libraries classify their books according to subject, then break down the subject within each broad general category. Two main systems are used: (1) the Library of Congress (LC) classification system (devised by Charles Cutter and used in the re-organization of the national library of the United States when it moved into its present location in 1897), and (2) the Dewey decimal system (first formulated by Melvil Dewey for the Amherst College Library in 1873 and later refined and expanded for the New York State Library and elsewhere). Most universities and colleges use the Library of Congress system, while most public libraries use the Dewey decimal system. For brief outlines of the Library of Congress and Dewey systems of classification, see the *Foundations* Web site.

At the reference desk in your library, there will be a bound copy of the *Library of Congress Subject Headings (LCSH),* in which each subject is broken down into its components, so that you can search the headings efficiently to find your topic; see also the Library of Congress site (**www.loc.gov/catdir/cpso/lcco/lcco.html**). For a discussion of the LC classification system, with example searches, see **www.lib.duke.edu/libguide/fi_books _sh.htm**. Extensive information about the Dewey decimal system can be found at a useful Web site at Middle Tennessee State University (**www.mtsu.edu/~vvesper/dewey.html**).

YOUR LIBRARY AND ITS GENERAL REFERENCE MATERIALS

All university libraries publish guides and offer tours to introduce students to the libraries' different departments and collections. Most libraries have several departments, such as reference (with librarians on duty to help with finding materials and to consult about library resources), periodicals (where current periodicals, serials, and newspapers are housed), a media library (with sound, film, and video resources), and perhaps specialized libraries, such as a map library, a law or science library, and a rare books library. The reference section also has hand-outs and guides available to make your searches for materials easier, and probably has online tutorials to lead you through the early stages of becoming familiar with the materials and methods for researching.

The general reference area of your library contains a kind of summary of the total library: here are located those books that are deemed essential reference sources in all of the subjects that the library contains. Reference books do not circulate, but are available for all to consult. Many are now online, and more are going online every year. You should take a tour of, or walk through, your library's reference room, browsing to see the materials available. Becoming familiar with the kinds of resources located in your library's reference area is an essential step to becoming a good researcher. To indicate the kinds of books and research tools in the reference section, we give some of the more important categories, with examples.

- *Abstracts* are summaries of larger books or periodicals. Many disciplines summarize the research in their fields in abstracts or digests. For instance, *Historical Abstracts* indexes summaries of articles of almost 2000 journals relating to all areas of the world, except Canada and the United States. For these two countries you have to use *America: History and Life.* Major journals in the humanities and social sciences are covered in both. They are indexed by subject and author.

- *Almanacs* are registers of the days, weeks, and months of the year, with much other information on specific topics.

  The Almanac of Canadian Politics. 2nd ed. Ed. Munroe Eagles. Toronto: Oxford UP, 1995.

- *Atlases* are bound volumes of maps or charts or, sometimes, illustrations of a specific subject, such as an atlas of human physiology.

  The Atlas of African Affairs. 2nd ed. Ed. Ieuan L. Griffiths. New York: Routledge, 1994.

- *Bibliographies* are lists of books about a topic. Many writers and topics have bibliographies compiled about them. General bibliographies are guides to those bibliographies.

  Bibliographic Index. New York: Wilson, 1938 to the present.

  Guide to Reference Books. Ed. Robert Balay. Chicago: American Library Association, 1996.

  Harney, James L. *Literary Research Guide: An Annotated Listing of Reference Sources in English Literary Studies*. 4th ed. New York: Modern Language Association, 2002. A comprehensive guide useful in many fields other than literature.

- *Biographies and biographical indexes* provide information about people living and dead. Such books include the various national biographies and the *International Who's Who* (London: Europa, 1935 to the present), as well as various *Who Was Who* volumes. Many countries also have compiled indexes of their famous people, such as the following:

  Dictionary of American Biography. 11 vols. and supplements. Ed. Allen Johnson, and Dumas Malone. New York: Scribner's, 1973–.

  Dictionary of Canadian Biography. 11 vols. and supplements. Ed. George W. Brown, David M. Hayne, and Francess G. Halpenny. Toronto: U of Toronto P, 1966–.

  Dictionary of National Biography. 22 vols. and supplements. Ed. Leslie Stephen, and Sidney Lee. London: Oxford UP, 1967–68. British biography.

- *Dictionaries* contain information about words, and, sometimes, also subjects, in various languages, arranged alphabetically. Comprehensive reference dictionaries of the English language are listed and discussed in Chapter 5.

  There are many dictionaries of other languages, of course, as well as specialized dictionaries, such as the following:

  A Dictionary of Slang and Unconventional English. Ed. Eric Partridge. London: Routledge and Kegan Paul, 1984.

  Brewer's Dictionary of Phrase and Fable. 15th ed. Ed. Ebenezer Cobham Brewer. New York: HarperCollins, 1995.

  Familiar Quotations. 16th ed. Ed. John Bartlett. Boston: Little, Brown, 1992.

- *Encyclopedias* are large compendia of information about specific topics or national cultures, for example:

  Encyclopedia Americana. 30 vols. New York: Grolier, 1994.

  Encyclopaedia Britannica. Chicago: Encyclopaedia Britannica, 1999–. Also available online (**www.search.eb.com**).

> *The Canadian Encyclopedia*. 4 vols. Toronto: McClelland and Stewart, 1996. CD-ROM edition: *2000 Canadian Encyclopedia World Edition*. Toronto: McClelland and Stewart, 1999. Also available online (**www.thecanadianencyclopedia.com/index.cfm**).

- *Handbooks* provide specialized information or technical instruction. Almost every subject has one or more handbooks or guides, which are invaluable in critical reading for their definitions of terms, statistics and chronologies, and outlines of procedures or methods. Such data can fill in the blanks that inevitably come up in your reading. Some examples are as follows:

  > *Handbook of American Women's History*. Ed. Angela Howard Zophy. New York: Garland, 1990.

  > *A Handbook to Literature*. 9th ed. Ed. William Harmon. Upper Saddle River, NJ: Prentice-Hall, 2003.

  > *Eerdmans' Handbook to the Bible*. Ed. David Alexander, and Pat Alexander. Grand Rapids, MI: Eerdmans, 1983.

- *Indexes* point to where information can be found on a specific topic. For instance, the *Social Science Index (SSI)* indexes materials from some 350 journals related to anthropology, economics, environmental science, geography, law and criminology, public administration, political science, psychology, and sociology. The *Humanities Index* does the same for humanities disciplines.

- *Reviews* are books, collections, or articles that comment on or review other books, films, music, novels, or research. Reviews are useful both for summarizing the content of a text as well as for situating its scholarly, critical, or popular reception. Many indexes to these reviews may be consulted, including the following:

  > *Book Review Digest*. New York: Wilson, 1905 to the present.

  > *Book Review Index*. Detroit: Gale, 1965 to the present.

- *Serials* are regularly published periodicals and scholarly journals that contain research reports or summaries of recent research in a specific field, often in the form of a year-end review. Many thousands are online and accessible for university members. For example, the journal *Victorian Studies* publishes annually a large survey of scholarship in the field.

SEARCHING THE LIBRARY CATALOGUES

Like the strategies for researching on the Web, discussed in the previous chapter, a library search calls for a logical and systematic effort to match what you are looking for with the ways that the information is catalogued. Your first line of approach in researching a topic in the library is to consult the online catalogue. Unlike the system of classification on the Web, which is somewhat arbitrary, inconsistent, and changing, the library catalogues are based on established and stable categories (see Library of Congress on page 188). When entering into the library catalogue, you immediately have a choice of one of five methods.

Author Search

Authors include people, companies, organizations, government agencies, universities, societies, and so on. Type in the author's last name followed by the first name or initials.

If you know only the last name, type it and you can search through all of the authors with that name to find your author, or if you get too many entries, limit your search by using the keyword search (see below). If your book has more than one author, all are listed in the catalogue.

Examples

atwood, margaret
microsoft corporation

If you want books about an author, search by *subject* using the author's name.

Example

hardy, thomas

Title Search

Titles may be of books, journals, films, government documents, music, or computer databases.

Examples

[The] Mayor of Casterbridge
Alice's Adventures in Wonderland
University of Toronto Quarterly
Apocalypse Now

Ignore *a, an,* or *the* in any language if it is the first word of the title. Include *a, an,* or *the* if the word is within the title. For a long title, enter just the first few words. If you have information about an article, search by the title of the journal or other source, not by the title of the article.

Subject Search

The organization of subject headings for a library search depends on the kind of classification system your library uses—Library of Congress or Dewey decimal. The system is important because it determines the specific way that you define your subject. Hence, when you search for a topic, you need to be aware of the kind of logic used in the classification system. If you search for a proper name, such as Margaret Atwood, Melanie Klein, or Pierre Elliott Trudeau, giving the family name first, you should have little trouble and will immediately find a sequence of categories that lists, in order, works by your author, followed by letters, biographies, criticism, and detailed studies according to a wide variety of other sub-fields. Scroll down until you find the category you want, and then search for individual titles that are appropriate.

If necessary, consult the *Library of Congress Subject Headings* index or a librarian for more sophisticated subject searches. Some subject searches may give related terms (with the words *see also*) or refer you to the correct subject term used in the catalogue. If you are having difficulty with a subject search, try using a keyword search.

Keyword Search

Keyword searches look for the word or phrase you type anywhere in a bibliographic record. That is, the words you search must be somewhere in the bibliographic entry, in the author's name, a word in the title, a subject as designated in the *Library of Congress Subject Headings* (specified in the long form of the bibliographic entry), the publisher's name, or the date. If you know one of the words in the title that you are searching for, you can enter that word in the keyword search category, and if that word actually occurs in the title, it will be located. Or you can enter a phrase (such as French Revolution or war movies) or combine two areas of interest, such as an author's name and a subject term. Keyword searches usually display the most recent information first.

When searching by keyword, certain conventions are followed according to a system known as Boolean logic (based on connectives between keywords using words or mathematical symbols):

1. Use ? as a wildcard to search for variations in word endings:
   - politic? [return] finds politics, political, politician, and so on.
   - litera? [return] finds literal, literate, literary, literacy, literature, literatures.

   You can also use $ to indicate a truncated word: govern$ finds governs, governing, governor, government, governmental, and so on. Avoid using ? or $ with very short words, as this will produce long lists of words, most of them irrelevant to your search.

2. Use ? with a number to search for a specific number of additional letters:
   - litera?2 [return] finds literate, literary, literacy, but not literal or literature.

3. Use AND, OR, or NOT to combine keyword search terms:
   - AND finds records with both (or all) of the terms (Shakespeare AND women).
   - OR finds records with either (or any) of the terms (copyright OR photocopying).
   - NOT finds records with the first term but not the second (Santa NOT Claus will find such instances as Santa Barbara, Santa Clara, Santa Scala, and so on).

4. Use adj. to specify that keywords must be next to each other (asian adj. american). An alternative is to put the term in single quotation marks, such as 'gulf war.'

TIPS   Searching the Library Catalogue

1. If you are looking for a title with *good* in it and you search good?, you will get hundreds of entries; you need to be more specific. For instance, if you are looking for the novel *The Good Soldier Schweik* but cannot remember the last name or how it is spelled or the author's name, you can search under keywords for "good adj soldier," which will quickly produce *The Good Soldier Svejk* by Jaroslav Hasek.

2. If you do not know which system of searching your library uses for keywords, you can consult the Help button on the online catalogue, or the reference librarians in the library.

3. If your search results in NO ENTRIES FOUND, you can check for spelling errors, try a keyword search, or make your search more general.

5. Use parentheses to express relationships among keywords:

   • (jazz OR ragtime) AND 'New Orleans' will search for either of the first two terms only in relation to the city of New Orleans.

Some libraries also set up their keyword searches so that you can narrow the field, limiting the items found to those within a range of publication years or to works published in a certain language. Then, the items found can be arranged by date or by year of publication.

Call Number Search

A call number is the shelf mark that indicates a book's location in the library. Searching by call number will lead you to a specific location in the catalogue. You can then look as far as you wish on either side of that call number by keying or scrolling forward or backward to see other books on the same or similar topics.

For instance, if you want to look up Thomas F. Kuhn's *The Structure of Scientific Revolutions* (1962), you will find that it is located in two different places in the Library of Congress catalogue and possibly also in your university library. First, it is catalogued by call number as part of the series in which it was first published:

Q   This letter is the Library of Congress letter designation for Science in general.

121   The number designates the sub-category of general encyclopedias and indexes of science.

I5   The letter *I* designates the first letter of the title of the publication or series in which the volume was published: *International Encyclopedia of Unified Science: Foundations of the Unity of Science*, vol. 2, no. 2.

The book is also listed as a separate publication by Kuhn and is catalogued along with other books in the field of scientific revolutions:

Q   This letter is the LC designation for Science in general.

175   The number designated as the sub-field of scientific revolutions.

K95   Within this sub-field, the books are arranged alphabetically by author. Sometimes, the date is also added.

If your search results in a list, you can obtain more detailed information about your request by clicking on, highlighting, or entering the number of the item for one of the titles, authors, or other search results. Help screens are available at each stage of your search. You may start a new search from any screen. Additional commands appear near the top or bottom of each screen or are available as buttons or as highlighted hypertext links.

TWO SAMPLE CATALOGUE SEARCHES IN HARD-TO-FIND AREAS

In the introduction to this chapter, we discussed the ways that knowledge is organized in libraries, and made general reference to the kinds of intellectual compromises and hidden value systems that characterize those classifications. Here, we set out two methods of searches for information that is hard to get at because the subject classification systems of libraries make access difficult.

Search in a Field that is Quickly Changing Because of Technological Developments

For more difficult topics, such as computers and writing, where would you begin? Since computers and writing is one of the topics of this book, we undertook a search for recent work in the area. The general topic of computers or writing appears to be too large and undefined. So, how can it be narrowed? Furthermore, the area is relatively new, and so the traditional systems of classifying subjects have trouble accommodating it. Here, it is useful to consult the Help buttons on the library catalogue main page or subject page to see how you might search for this topic.

For instance, if you do a subject search for "computers" (without the quotation marks) you will get a large number of entries that will take you a long time to sift through. One of the headings near the top will be "see related headings for Computers" or some such advice to direct you to the cataloguing entries used in arranging this particular online library catalogue. Accessing that entry provides a number of useful lines to pursue. One is "Computer literacy," but that turns out to be related to a user's knowledge of and ability to use computers, not to the connection between computers and English language literacy and writing proficiency. The advice at the end of such a list to search also under headings beginning with the word "computers" eventually might lead you to "Computers and literacy," a far more promising heading, and there you will find a number of titles, most of which likely were written in the last decade, all of them dealing with how literacy can be addressed by computers, but not offering advice on how to improve your writing through the use of computers. If, by any chance, nothing shows up there, you might continue by searching the "related headings for Computers and literacy," which will eventually lead you into a search for the more general heading of "Literacy," and perhaps further off the topic.

Another approach to the subject search after the first failure is to use a different term, say, "writing." If your library uses this classification, you may find the category "Writing computer-assisted instruction" and a reference to the periodical *Computers and Composition,* published since 1983 by Michigan Technological University. If your library subscribes, you can consult this journal for reviews of recent books in this field or other relevant articles. If your university does not subscribe, you can see if it is held by a library near you or is accessible online. Looking at the full bibliographical entry will show you that there is another Library of Congress subject classification specified for the journal, "English Language—composition and exercises—Periodicals," which suggests that "English Language" might be another subject field to search. In that category, another journal turns up, *Kairos: A Journal for Teachers of Writing and Webbed Environment,* which will also provide you with recent reviews and articles.

As you read through the subject classification headings, you will soon be aware that the term *writing* has a number of very different meanings, including writing style and rhetoric (which is the central topic we are looking for), writing in various genres, such as poetry or science fiction, and writing as the physical act of forming meaningful letters on a page or through some other medium (such as penmanship or the study of petroglyphs), along with the history of various kinds of writing or scripts from cuneiform to hieroglyphics. But ultimately, the subject search online will be time consuming and fail to yield many significant materials, except for the periodicals.

A second approach is to use the keyword search. If you enter the phrase "computers AND writing," you will immediately find a number of items, some of which are almost certainly directly related to your topic. Some will relate to using computers to teach writing in the classroom, while others will relate to the actual practice of using the computer to improve your writing. Among these sources, you might find *Writing, Teaching, and Researching History in the Electronic Age: Historians and Computers,* edited by Dennis A. Trinkle (1998). The LC subject headings for this book include "History—computer-assisted instruction," which suggests another place to look in the subject search. You might also find *Transitions: Teaching Writing in Computer-Supported and Traditional Classrooms* by Mike Palmquist et al. (1998), with seven LC subject headings, including "English Language—Rhetoric—Study and teaching—Technological innovations." Further examination of this LC subject heading will lead to many other books on computers and writing style, including handbooks and guides and scholarly discussions of the impact of computers on writing in and for the classroom. Another related subject heading is "English Language—Rhetoric—Study and teaching—Data Processing," which again turns up several useful books: *New Worlds, New Words: Exploring Pathways for Writing about and in Electronic Environments* by John Barber and Dene Grigar (2001); *The Online Writing Classroom*, edited by Susanmarie Harrington, et al. (2000); and *From Disk to Hard Copy: Teaching Writing on Computers* by James Strickland (1997). You will then find that the books are located in the library stacks in a range beginning with the letters PE and then the numbers 1401 through to 1404, and you can search through the shelves for other appropriate books.

This subject heading is not one that might have popped quickly into your head, but the method for searching for it was quite logical and systematic, and it is a method that can be followed for most topics. Here, the keyword search will prove most fruitful and yield a lot of information fairly quickly. You can use this method efficiently if you have learned some of the Boolean shortcuts to make your keyword search more precise. The subject search, however, will be time consuming and will not yield many items quickly. A combination of the two methods, using a keyword search to find relevant books and then searching the bibliographical entry for the appropriate LC subject headings, which you then examine in a subject search, will yield a good number of items. Of course, if you are physically present in the library when you are conducting your online search, you can consult the *LCSH* yourself, or you can ask a reference librarian for suggestions and help.

Search in a Field that Challenges the Assumptions Built into the Classification System

A more difficult kind of search is one in a relatively new field of enquiry that combines older subject headings in innovative ways, or one that relates specific texts to these categories in ways that challenge the assumptions built into the classification system. For instance, Peter Pan from J.M. Barrie's *Peter and Wendy* (1911) is traditionally seen as an eternal boy in a children's text, one who is always at play and who is often associated with the many spin-offs, from stage plays and musicals to Walt Disney's version of 1953. Recent work has begun to question the accepted view of the novel's innocence and has seen the story as reflecting the imperial politics of the late British Empire. In particular, the story has been read as promoting the education of Edwardian children in the "white man's burden" ideology of the empire, which rationalized the right to conquest and colonize by purporting that it was the white man's responsibility. So, while you might legitimately expect to find a lot of material on Peter Pan and children's fiction, how might you begin to look for the more difficult topic that relates it to education and empire building?

One way, of course, would be to look up books under the subject heading of the author of *Peter and Wendy,* J.M. Barrie. There, you will find a list of sub-fields: a number of books will be on Barrie himself, mostly biographies and appreciations, followed by an alphabetized list of headings for adaptations, bibliography, biography, characters, criticism and interpretation, dramatic works, and so on. A check of the entry on "Criticism and Interpretation" will likely produce Bruce K. Hanson's *The Peter Pan Chronicles: The Nearly 100 Year History of the "Boy Who Wouldn't Grow Up"* (1993), an account of the versions, publication history, and reception of the novel and its variants. While this book will contain some material that is appropriate for you, the book by Jacqueline Rose, *The Case of Peter Pan, or, The Impossibility of Children's Fiction* (1984), deals critically with the general acceptance of Peter Pan as a children's classic. It is highly pertinent to your topic:

PR   subject classification letters [here for British Literature]

4074   subject sub-category classification numbers [Victorian and Edwardian number sequence where J.M. Barrie is located]

P32 R6   title and/or author numbers [*P* for Barrie's titles beginning with *P,* as *Peter and Wendy* or *Peter Pan,* with *R* as the author identification letter (Rose)]

1984   date of publication

The rest of the subject search, and even the LC subject headings in the main bibliographical entry for Rose's book, for instance for "Children's stories, English—History and criticism," do not carry you much further.

Since you are not looking for traditionalist interpretations, but, rather, for critical discussions of the British Empire and imperial education in relation to children's fiction, the next route to follow is to search for the keywords for the topic you are going to examine and into which you want to integrate your discussion of *Peter and Wendy.* It will be important for you to have some knowledge of the current discussions about the role of education in training citizens of empire. Here, the first keywords you might try would be "education AND empire," but such a search will turn up a lot of extraneous materials, from the Roman and Byzantine empires through to missionaries and education policy in colonial Canada. One relevant book, however, is John Willinsky's *Learning to Divide the World: Education at Empire's End* (1998). The shelf mark, LC 1090 W53 1998, will lead you to other materials on education in Great Britain and the British colonies in a shelf check. Willinsky's book is a useful find for researching your topic, but the search really does have to be narrowed.

For one thing, you are not really looking so much for the notion of empire, though that word might appear in the titles or subject classifications of works that might be appropriate. Another word you might try is "imperialism," and since you are looking for materials that are also classified as literature, that would be a combination to try. In fact, a search for "imperialism AND literature" turns up a wealth of materials, some of which are not directly related to Peter Pan or Barrie, but that could prove very helpful. For a list of these books, see the *Foundations* Web site.

At least one book, Laura E. Donaldson's *Decolonizing Feminisms: Race, Gender, and Empire Building* (1992), deals with the use of race and gender in defining the role of imperial colonizers, and, in fact, one of her chapters deals explicitly with *Peter and Wendy:* "The Problem of Discourse in a Marxist Never-Never Land: Of 'Piccaninnies' and Peter Pan."

One more route would be to check the subject heading for "Education—Great Britain—Colonies—History," where you will locate several books by J.A. Mangan that deal directly with the topic of imperial education. For the results found, see the *Foundations* Web site.

TIPS Finding More Information on Your Topics

Once you have found at least one book on your topic, preferably published recently, there are various ways of using it to locate other information:

1. Looking at other books that are near it on the shelf might yield other books on the same or similar topics.

2. There are three places in the book to find other information:

    • The first is in the bibliography or the works cited list at the back of the book. Here, you are depending on the reliability of the author and the publisher for the integrity of the scholarly sources.

    • A second place is the preface, where often an author will give a brief summary of the recent scholarship on the topic.

    • Finally, the back of the title page includes details of the book's publication history but also yields various kinds of information, usually about the author (possibly birth and death dates, allowing you to look further into this period of history), and, most importantly, Library of Congress subject headings (enabling you to activate a subject search for other works classified there).

Finally, each of these books can be checked on the shelves for other books you or the cataloguers might have missed in the process, and each of the books you find can spur you on to other subject searches, based on either the bibliographical record in the online catalogue or on the verso of the title page, in the book's publication data in the print copy.

Perhaps a better way is to do a Boolean search that links two words in a string, in the form "empire+education" or "empire AND education" (omitting the quotation marks, of course, in the keyword search).

Another angle would be to look up the most general topics on the British Empire and imperialism, looking, especially, for studies written at about the time of the publication of J.M. Barrie's *Peter and Wendy* (1911). One of the first books to be located would be J.A. Hobson's *Imperialism: A Study* (1902). The catalogue entry gives other information about the Library of Congress subject headings that are used for this book, "Imperialism," "Great Britain—Colonies," and "Imperial Federation," so any of those headings could be searched for other titles.

At this point, you may wish to go to the *MLA Bibliography,* which has a different system of classification—the subject categories are called descriptors. Since it catalogues journal articles as well as books, the *MLA Bibliography* also contains different materials. A search of "peter pan" turns up 50 items, the majority of which are on psychology and gender. A refined search of "peter pan AND imperialism" turns up one item, *Forever England: Reflections on Masculinity and Empire* by Jonathan Rutherford (1997). This book is not classified in the library search under "peter pan" or "literature and imperialism," and so would have been missed had you not gone to the *MLA Bibliography.*

As our two sample searches demonstrate, to be a good researcher takes persistence and flexibility. If you do not find what you are looking for, that does not mean that there is no information available. You probably should adjust the categories you are using to search for that information and make adjustments until you find avenues that lead you where you want to go. Having found book titles and call numbers of books that are in your library, you are well on your way. You can now go to the stacks and follow the call numbers. A shelf search involves looking for books adjacent to those you have already found in your catalogue search related to your topic.

SEARCHING FOR RESEARCH MATERIALS IN NEWSPAPERS, PERIODICALS, AND JOURNALS

To find articles in newspapers, periodicals, and scholarly journals, you can either use print copies of indexes or abstracts (if your library still subscribes), or, the preferred method, go online through your university library's home page to e-resources. Or search the online indexes and abstracts by title. Some of the standard indexes follow:

- *Art Index*
- *Book Review Digest* (especially helpful for popular periodicals)
- *Canadian Periodical Index*
- *General Science Index*
- *Historical Abstracts* (scholarly monographs and journals)
- *Humanities Index* (scholarly monographs and journals)
- *International Political Science Abstracts*
- *MLA* [Modern Language Association]
- *International Bibliography* (scholarly monographs and journals)
- *Newspaper Index* (indexes major articles from the *Chicago Tribune, Los Angeles Times, New Orleans Times-Picayune,* and *Washington Post*)
- *New York Times Index* (indexes all major articles in the NYT from 1913 to the present)
- *Psychological Abstracts* (scholarly works)
- *Reader's Guide to Periodical Literature* (for popular circulation periodicals)
- *Social Sciences Abstracts* (scholarly works)
- *Social Sciences Index* (scholarly works)
- *Sociological Abstracts* (scholarly works)
- *The Times Index* (indexes major articles in *The London Times*)

Your reference librarian can help you find the index most appropriate to your topic. The following steps are usually necessary:

1. Define your topic.

2. Go to your library's e-resources page and select the index or abstracts you wish to search for your topic.

3. Enter the topic into the index's search box. Refine, if necessary.

4. Scroll down to an appropriate title, and either view it or click on it for further details, depending on the kind of index. The journal title and publication data are given in full, and include

   • the author's name,

   • the title of the article, and

   • the title of the journal in which the article appeared, with its volume number, date, and page numbers.

5. If your library has the full-text electronic version of the article, click on the hot button to view it. If you save it, save the publication data also for future documentation.

6. If the library only has a print version, record the call number and search for it in the stacks.

7. Some newspapers are now online, while others are stored on microform.

HINTS AND FURTHER REFINEMENTS

You may want to go into greater detail on a topic than the online catalogue, shelf, book, and periodical searches yielded. Your next move is to consult the resources of other libraries. Many larger university libraries have print copies of one or two catalogues of the world's greatest libraries, perhaps the National Union Catalogue published by the Library of Congress (and covering 2500 major libraries) or the British Library Catalogue (sometimes shelved under its old title, the British Museum Catalogue). The Library of Congress Union Catalogue (**www.loc.gov/z3950/**) and the catalogue of the British Library (**www.bl.uk**) are also available online.

TIPS   Recording Sources

Whatever method you use, record the bibliographical details when you record the quotations or information to avoid having to look for it again later or taking the more risky route of using the material without adequate citation of sources.

These catalogues are author catalogues, except for the titles of periodicals that are included in the general author alphabetical sequence and newspapers (in the British Library catalogue, periodicals and newspapers are listed in a separate set of volumes and are classified according to place of publication). Looking up this catalogue can often give you the first date at which a particular work was published, since both of these national libraries are "copyright" libraries, requiring that everything that is published in the United States or in the United Kingdom be deposited free in the national library. The National Library of Canada is online at **www.nlc-bnc.ca/ehome.htm**. You can also consult the major university library catalogues of the world, such as the Bodleian Library of Oxford (**www.rsl.ox.ac.uk/**), Harvard (**lib.harvard.edu/**), and in Canada, the Robarts Library of the University of Toronto (**www.library.utoronto.ca/index.html**).

The Canadian Library Index (**www.libdex.com/country/Canada.html?/**) provides links to Canadian provinces and through them to university libraries. Here, you might find that a library near you has the book that you want; furthermore, your university's interlibrary loan department can locate and borrow books for you from other libraries throughout North America.

RECORDING YOUR SOURCES

When undertaking library research, it is important always to record the bibliographic data for your sources. Some people use index cards, recording the bibliographic information on one side (call number, author, title of book or article, [journal, issue, date], publisher, place of publication, date, and pages), and on the other side a summary of the article, a description of the book, or a quotation or other piece of information. Others prefer to use single sheets of paper for each source or document. Most researchers now keep such records in computer files. If you are making your notes from the Web, it is easy to record the bibliographic information in the format that you will eventually use in your essay the first time that you access the site. You then can save the record (using the block-and-copy method) and all related records in the same file or folder. For information about how to record your sources, see Chapter 9.

CHAPTER SUMMARY

In Chapter 8, you have become acquainted with the resources of a university library, especially the printed books, journals, and reference materials. You have developed practical skills in looking up pertinent materials for your courses, but have also added more advanced skills in library research:

- You have learned about the library's classification systems and can look up materials systematically.
- You can use five different methods of finding materials: by author, title, subject, keyword, and call number, and you are familiar with the advantages of each method and when it can best be used.
- By following through two samples of advanced searches, you have developed different approaches for undertaking research for essays and other assignments.
- You have learned how to use the indexes to find appropriate journal articles, reviews of scholarly books and media, and newspaper articles.
- You have become familiar with the wide range of resources in the reference section, including the use of specialized abstracts, dictionaries, indexes, encyclopedias, bibliographies, and atlases in many fields.

In the use of all of these resources, it is important to take accurate notes, and to keep a careful record of your sources. How you handle those references in your writing is the subject of our next chapter.

FURTHER READINGS

Ballenger, Bruce P. *The Curious Researcher: A Guide to Writing Research Papers.* Boston: Allyn and Bacon, 1994.

Robertson, Hugh. *The Research Essay: A Guide to Papers, Essays, Projects.* Ottawa: Piperhill Projects, 1998.

References and Documentation: Acknowledging Your Sources

In the previous two chapters, you learned how to undertake systematic research on the Net and in the library. This chapter explains how you refer to that research in your writing. When your teachers read your essays or other assignments, they want to know which sources you used and how you used them. Adding proper references to your paper, or documenting your sources, gives your reader the evidence of your scholarly abilities. Most importantly, proper documentation protects you from charges of plagiarism or other breaches of academic honesty.

LEARNING OBJECTIVES

Chapter 9 will answer the following questions:

- How do you avoid plagiarism?

- How do you refer to your research in the body of your essay?

- Do you only acknowledge specific quotations from your sources? What about more general references?

- What is the book list at the end of an essay called, and what do you include in it?

- How do you document films, Web sites, or library books?

- What are the different ways of referring to your research in different disciplines?

- What do you put in footnotes and bibliographies?

PLAGIARISM

You are probably familiar with debates about pirating movies and music and may also be familiar with controversies around the theft of intellectual property, particularly computer software. These are multi-million dollar issues; in universities, we have similar problems that, of course, do not cost that much money but that are, nevertheless, taken very seriously. Plagiarism is an offence against academic honesty. As in any institution, there is a code of ethics for students, which demands that when using someone else's words or ideas you must acknowledge them.

What Is Plagiarism?

Plagiarism is presenting work as your own that originates from some other source, which you have not acknowledged. Sometimes, students fall into plagiarism through carelessness, by neglecting to make clear, when taking notes from books or articles, where the quoted material ends and where their commentary on that material begins; hence, it is important to make careful notes that distinguish between others' words and your own. Students writing in a second language may have a particular difficulty with charges of plagiarism because in their research, they may copy from a source too exactly, trying to avoid mistakes in grammar, syntax, punctuation, and vocabulary. Sometimes, students are caught in a last minute rush, and the temptation to steal someone else's argument, or even a whole paper, is too great. In this case, the act of plagiarism is deliberate and, if detected, as it often is, can result in dire consequences. Plagiarism is a serious academic offence and may result in a range of penalties, from a warning, to failure in an assignment, failure in a course, being reported to the dean, annotation of transcripts, or even suspension from the university.

Plagiarism can include entire papers, paragraphs, sentences, phrases, ideas, lab results, statistics, and graphics. The sources can include books and articles, encyclopedias, the Internet, or your friend's work. Sometimes, students use ghostwriters, an essay service, paying large amounts for even a short paper; sometimes, they simply lift the essay from a Web site that supplies them for a price. Some believe that if they pay for the essay, they can use it as they please—but this belief is simply wrong. Universities have sophisticated means of detecting and prosecuting such offenders. Police recently investigated the use of essay services by students across Ontario. Ryerson, Toronto, and York Universities, among others, charged their offenders. Many were convicted and sentenced to failures in courses, failures for the year, suspensions, and, in the most serious cases, expulsion from universities in Canada for up to 25 years.

With the intense proliferation of Internet access by students, the evidence indicates that there has been a considerable increase in plagiarism in university courses (see **www.academic integrity.org/cai_research.asp**). The most recent *MLA Handbook* summarizes this problem:

> New technologies have made information easier to locate and obtain, but research projects only begin with identifying and collecting source material. The essential intellectual tasks of a research project have not changed. These tasks call for a student to understand the published facts, ideas, and insights about a subject and to integrate them with the student's own view on the topic. To achieve this goal, student writers must rigorously distinguish between what they borrow and what they create. As information sharing has become easier, so has plagiarism (Gibaldi 69).

Highly sophisticated methods and electronic tools for detecting plagiarism from Internet sources are now available for university instructors, and many universities have made such software generally available to them (**www.turnitin.com**). It may well be that if you set about to plagiarize consciously, you will not be caught, but the evidence also shows that the risks involved in stealing from the Web or using an essay service are extremely high. For a discussion of ethics and academic integrity, see **www.brookes.ac.uk/services/ocsd/4_resource/plagiarism.html**.

Forms of Plagiarism and How to Avoid Them

Often, students are unclear about what constitutes plagiarism. The best advice we can give you is that if you have any doubt, err on the side of caution, and cite your sources. However, you need not indicate a source for such things as familiar sayings, for example, "what every schoolboy knows," and knowledge that, indeed, every schoolchild does know, for example, the fact that the date for Canadian Confederation was 1867. It is best to indicate your sources for such things as up-to-date information on population, gross national product (GNP), export figures, and so on, as well as sources for quotations from a poem, novel, play, or famous political speech, even if that quotation has passed into the language as a saying, such as, Hamlet's "To be or not to be" and Lincoln's first words in the Gettysburg Address, "Fourscore and seven years ago." In these cases, it is enough to identify Hamlet and Lincoln. On the other hand, students may not be familiar with some actions that do constitute plagiarism. For instance, submitting work in one course that you have already submitted and received credit for in another course is a form of plagiarism. Furthermore, if you reproduce too much from a single text, even with attribution, you are breaching a practice called *fair use,* an infringement of the copyright law.

Almost all cases of unintentional plagiarism, however, come down to three central problems. First, in your previous education, you were required to simply copy out information as research, relying upon the source as an authority, and you do not realize that this practice is no longer acceptable. Second, in taking notes during research, you became sloppy and did not indicate quoted material or did not separate your comments from your paraphrase of someone else's ideas. Third (another version of the second), you copied and pasted texts from electronic books or articles on the Web into your own notes and forgot to carefully set someone else's text off from your own. Of course, there are numerous ways that students intentionally and deceitfully try to pass off another's work as their own. But in what follows, we give examples to help those who may be less experienced in avoiding plagiarism.

Suppose you were writing an essay on James Whale's 1931 film adaptation (starring Boris Karloff) of Mary Shelley's novel, *Frankenstein.* In the course of your study, you have read a number of books and articles on the film, including Wheeler Dixon's article "The Films of *Frankenstein*" (1990), in which he talks of the film's complicated history of converting the novel to a different medium and its dramatic box-office and cinematic impact.

The full reference in a works cited or references list, in both the MLA and APA styles, discussed below, is as follows:

MLA STYLE

Dixon, Wheeler Winston. "The Films of Frankenstein." <u>Approaches to Teaching Shelley's</u> <u>Frankenstein</u>. Ed. Stephen C. Behrendt. New York: MLA, 1990. 166–79.

APA STYLE

Dixon, W. W. (1990). The films of *Frankenstein*. In S. C. Behrendt (Ed.), *Approaches to teaching Shelley's* Frankenstein (pp. 166–179). New York: MLA.

Dixon refers to the fact that the power of the film's images stopped other directors from taking a more searching look at Mary Shelley's novel. It would be perfectly acceptable for you to comment in your essay that the film caused a sensation in theatres across North America when it was first shown. Virtually all commentaries discuss this fact, and, indeed, it is almost common knowledge. However, if you say that Whale's film inhibited the development of other films that addressed the novel directly, you must give credit to Dixon's argument in one of the following ways:

> Whale's version of *Frankenstein* was so powerful in its images and impact, however, that it inhibited new examination of Mary Shelley's novel for over twenty-five years (Dixon 169).

or,

> Whale's *Frankenstein,* as Dixon argues, arrested fresh thought about the novel for over twenty-five years (169).

If you acknowledge Dixon like this, you are following good documentation practice; if you do not give credit to Dixon, you are using his ideas and argument as your own and are committing plagiarism.

In fact, this is the passage from Dixon:

> With this 1931 film Whale created a series of iconic conventions that rapidly became clichés in the decade and a half that followed and that, until the advent of the 1957 and 1976 productions, severely limited any serious approach to the novel's actual concerns (169).

If you refer to Dixon in either of the forms above, you are correct. However, if you paraphrase his words too closely, you are in danger of being accused of plagiarism. Here are four examples, which lay out a range of problems and solutions.

EXAMPLE 1

In his 1931 film, Whale created a series of iconic conventions that rapidly became common in the 15 years that followed and that, until the productions of 1957 and 1976, limited any different approaches to Shelley's novel.

This close paraphrase is a clear and unambiguous case of plagiarism, even if you acknowledge the source in general. In fact, whole phrases are lifted from the original, and the sentence structure of the original is copied. Only the opening and closing phrases are changed, along with "cliché" and "decade and a half." These changes indicate a calculated attempt to disguise the direct borrowing from Dixon. To avoid a charge of plagiarism, the passages that are quoted from the original should be in quotation marks, and the source must be acknowledged.

EXAMPLE 2

As Dixon indicates, "Whale created a series of iconic conventions that rapidly became clichés" after 1931 and that, until the advent of the film of 1957, limited serious approaches to the novel (169).

The writer of Example 2 does better than that of Example 1, since at least the source is acknowledged, and the first long phrase is in quotation marks. But the conclusion still borrows language that is often identical to the original, even though words are omitted, and the main idea of the passage is claimed as the author's own or is fudged—at any rate, it is not attributed to Dixon. Example 2, though not as serious, also is a plagiarism and is corrected in the same way as in Example 1.

EXAMPLE 3

From 1931 to 1957, new approaches to Mary Shelley's novel were blocked in large measure because of the force and originality of the screen images that James Whale introduced into *Frankenstein*.

Although Example 3 is a clear paraphrase, changing the order of the ideas and the phrases in the sentence, and does not import any actual phrases from the original, it still constitutes plagiarism, since Dixon's original point (concerning the way that Whale's film blocked re-thinking) is not acknowledged. This example would be acceptable with a general reference (Dixon 169), since it avoids the direct but unacknowledged quotations that are problems in Example 1.

EXAMPLE 4

Few film versions of Mary Shelley's *Frankenstein* have followed the novel closely. Instead, many have remained under the domination of James Whale's version of 1931, as Dixon argues. Indeed, he continues, Whale was so successful in creating "a series of iconic conventions that rapidly became clichés in the decade and a half that followed" that his version "until the advent of the 1957 and 1976 productions, severely limited any serious approach to the novel's actual concerns" (169). We could go even further, claiming that Whale's images continue to dominate not only the film versions of *Frankenstein* but are also clichés in popular culture.

There is no plagiarism in this example. Although there is no specific source for the first sentence, the exact reason for blocking new approaches, which is Dixon's main argument, is fully acknowledged by references to Dixon, quotation marks, and a page reference.

These examples demonstrate different uses of sources and ways of acknowledging them. Different cultures have varying views about the authority of the text and the teacher, and so, opportunities should be available to discuss these concepts and ways to avoid plagiarism as defined at your institution. If you are uncertain about the concept of plagiarism or are worried about a particular instance in a paper you are working on, you should seek advice from your teachers or perhaps the librarians. Another good source for information about plagiarism is the Internet, where a number of sites discuss the problem in detail and give elaborate examples.

The best way to avoid accusations of plagiarism is to use appropriate and accepted scholarly methods of study, research, and the presentation of that research in your submitted work. In particular, you need to document all references to the work of others, not only to avoid charges of plagiarism but also to indicate the scholarly basis of your arguments and to lead others to the resources you have relied on. Beginning students have a problem with understanding that such references are not merely copying others' ideas but, rather, that they are providing a reader with a scholarly map and as well are indicating the work that they have put into their assignment. Furthermore, as Example 4 indicates, you can use these scholarly references to extend your argument. That is, the ideas you are citing are a springboard for you. You partially position yourself by what previous scholars have written and develop your own ideas from theirs.

DOCUMENTATION STYLES: ACKNOWLEDGING YOUR SOURCES

Procedures for documenting your sources vary from subject to subject, and so, we outline here the different formats or styles for acknowledging your sources as used by different academic disciplines. The system for providing that information is called *documentation style.* Your course instructor will tell you which documentation style is preferred for the course, and you should check to see what kinds of variations are acceptable. Once you decide on a particular style, you should use it consistently throughout an essay.

In general, the humanities disciplines (English, history, philosophy, and so on) use the style that has been developed by the Modern Language Association of America (MLA style). It focuses on the author-page system in making references in the text.

In the social sciences (political science, psychology, sociology, and so on) scholars usually use the documentation style developed by the American Psychological Association (APA style), called the author-date system.

For scientific citation (in biology, chemistry, engineering, mathematics, medicine, and physics), the standard is set by the Council of Biology Editors in Scientific Style and Format: *The CBE Manual for Authors, Editors, and Publishers.* CBE style follows a number system. Reference is made in parentheses in the text to a numbered work and the page, and in the works cited, the list is numbered and the works appear in the order of their first citation in the text, not in alphabetical order. We do not discuss the CBE style in detail here, but for further information, see McGraw-Hill's *Mayfield Handbook on Technical Writing* with advice on CBE style (**www.mhhe.com/mayfieldpub/tsw/doc-cbe.htm**) and the sites suggested in further readings. Some teachers (and many university presses) use a more specialized documentation style developed at the University of Chicago, summarized in their published manual, the *Chicago Manual of Style.* But in almost all undergraduate courses in the Humanities and Social Sciences, the preferred method of documentation will be either the MLA or the APA style. In the following sections, we illustrate these two major ways of making your references clear.

TIPS Documenting Your Sources

1. Use MLA style for humanities disciplines, APA style for the social sciences, and CBE style for the sciences.

2. Current practice favours incorporating most references to sources within your essay, adding notes (whether footnotes or endnotes) only for additional information that goes beyond citing a source.

3. Some course instructors still prefer that all citations of sources be included in endnotes or footnotes. Check to determine what is acceptable.

4. Use italics for book and other titles, unless your instructor requires you to follow strictly the underlining method that the MLA style recommends.

HUMANITIES FORMAT: MLA STYLE

In humanities subjects, academic essays generally follow the MLA style (before 1984 MLA style involved footnotes and endnotes with a bibliography for all references). The current method is easy and efficient for both writers and readers. MLA style documents sources in two ways: first, references to sources within the text of the essay are given in short citations (in-text citations), and second, a list of works cited is included at the end of the essay. The in-text reference, then, points clearly to a source in the list of works cited. For a complete account of the MLA style, see their Web site: **www.mla.org**.

In-Text Citations in MLA Style

Within the body of your essay, you include references to each source you are using in parentheses right after your quotation, paraphrase, or summary, usually at the end of a sentence. These in-text citations allow a reader to refer to your works cited list for further information. Usually, an author's last name is used in an in-text citation to identify a source, together with the exact page numbers from which the cited material is taken. The author's name may be mentioned either in your sentence or in parentheses at the end of your sentence (or quotation); the page number is always given in parentheses, not in the text of your sentence.

For the references in the text of your essay, after a quotation or use of an author's ideas, include the author's last name and page number(s) with no comma or page abbreviation, and double hyphen (or en-dash) between multiple consecutive pages (Frye 354) or (Frye 354–56). The final period follows the citation reference. For instance, you might be working on an essay on the social and literary background to dystopias, including Margaret Atwood's dystopian novel *The Handmaid's Tale,* about a patriarchal republic called Gilead, where women are controlled as "breeders." You may quote from the novel by summarizing, commenting in general, or citing the author:

SUMMARY

Confined to her room for the most part, Offred memorizes all of the parts of her new world in the Commander's house, as a prisoner knows the parts of his cell. At the same time, she rejoices in the fact that at least she is alive (Atwood 7–10).

COMMENTARY

While Offred's language is descriptive, it also is evaluative, betraying the fact that she remains rebellious or is tempted to find ways to question the absolute authority that she is placed under. For instance, her own thoughts indicate that she is questioning the motives and words of the others in the household and their submission to authority (Atwood 12–13).

CITATION

Illustrating Offred's need for human contact, Atwood writes: "I would help Rita make the bread, sinking my hands into that soft resistant warmth which is so much like flesh. I hunger to touch something, other than cloth or wood. I hunger to commit the act of touch" (12–13).

CITATION OF A LONGER QUOTATION

Offred links word to word, thing to thing, noting every detail and enumerating them, as each stands metonymically for something else, something more important, in the world she has left behind:

> I take the tokens from Rita's outstretched hand. They have pictures on them, of the things they can be exchanged for: twelve eggs, a piece of cheese, a brown thing that's supposed to be a steak. I place them in the zippered pocket in my sleeve, where I keep my pass (Atwood 13).

In the first two instances, the name of the author is given in parentheses right after the passage you wish to document. Since this is the first reference that you are making to the novel, you need to identify the author. If you were writing only about Atwood and were citing only this text, and it was clear from the context that you were referring to the novel, you would not need to include the author's name. In the third example, the author's name is omitted because it is given in the introductory comment. In the fourth example, the quotation is indented because it is four lines (or more). In every case, there is no punctuation between the author's name and the page references, and the page numbers are given with no abbreviation, such as *p.* or *pp.*

In places where you may use an italic font on the computer (for instance, in book titles), MLA style (*Handbook,* 6th edition, 2003) still recommends that you underline to avoid the misreading of fonts. This outmoded convention is a carryover from the days when author's hand-written manuscripts were read by typesetters or compositors and the practice was to use underlining to indicate italics. But now, writers and students as well as printing houses use computers, so the practice of underlining for italics is rapidly fading out. Students can easily format book titles with italics, but you should check with your instructors about their preferences concerning underlining or italics. Furthermore, there is an additional point of possible confusion, since underlining in texts on the Web and often in printed sources now usually indicates a hypertext URL, an active link to the Internet, rather than italics. For all of these reasons, we have adapted the MLA style here by recommending italic fonts throughout where MLA requires underlining.

While this method of in-text citation for a single author and a single work is easy and efficient, it becomes more complex with other kinds of materials, but in every case, the MLA style specifies how to format your references, and the *MLA Handbook,* the foundation reference on all such matters, includes many more kinds of sources and examples. We give the most common kinds of citations below from texts related to Margaret Atwood and women's writing.

Print Media

In each instance of in-text citation below, we first identify the kind of source you are citing, followed by any pertinent instructions on how to refer to it in the text, and then we give an indented example in a different font.

- **One author.** Follow any of the formats outlined immediately above, with no punctuation between the author's name and page number.

  "I hunger to commit the act of touch" (Atwood 13).

  Atwood writes, Offred hungers to "commit the act of touch" (13).

- ***Two authors.*** Reproduce the order of both authors' last names from the title page with no punctuation.

    "Significantly, the protagonist of Atwood's novel [*Lady Oracle*] ... projects her anxieties of authorship into the fairy-tale metaphor of the red shoes" (Gilbert and Gubar 57).

- ***Three authors.*** Reproduce the order and spelling of the authors' last names from the title page, with commas after the first two.

    Critics [of Margaret Atwood] have addressed such themes as identity, Canadian nationalism, struggle for survival, sexual politics, and shamanism and concentrated on animal, mirror, camera, and other images in Atwood's work (Wilson, Friedman, and Hengen 2).

- ***More than three authors.*** Name all, or use the abbreviation et al. (Latin, *et alii,* and others) after the first name.

    Women's development involves fostering independence of selfhood, the speaking voice, and the questioning and challenging mind (Belenky et al. 24).

- ***More than one source by an author.*** Include the title in a shortened form (one word, if possible).

    Again and again we find [Moodie] gazing at the sublime natural goings-on in the misty distance—sunsets, mountains, spectacular views—only to be brought up short by disagreeable things in her immediate foreground, such as bugs, swamps, tree roots and other immigrants (Atwood *Survival* 51).

- ***Two or more authors with the same last name.*** To avoid confusion, use the first initial and full last name for each author you cite. Usually, the full first name is used in your own sentence.

    Old patriarchal psychologies of women that relate power to masochism have been radically challenged by Jean Baker Miller's claim that power is "the capacity to implement" (121), a claim that is negated in Offred's helplessness, historically established in one of Atwood's source books on puritanism (P. Miller 28–33).

- ***Group or corporate author.*** Use the group name as an author.

    In *Our Bodies, Ourselves* the authors allude to current kinds of oppression that Atwood fictionalizes: "In the broadest sense, violence against women is any violation of a woman's personhood, mental or physical integrity, or freedom of movement through individual acts and societal oppression" (Boston Women's Health Collective 246).

- ***Work cited by title*** (with no primary author). Shorten the title in the parenthetical reference to the first words of the title as it is alphabetized in your list of works cited.

    A brief but dated summary of Atwood's life and works is found in the entry in a standard Canadian reference book (*Oxford Companion* 28).

- ***Multi-volume work.*** Include the relevant volume number in each citation, followed by a colon, space, and page.

    Nineteenth-century opinion held that "a woman's commitment to her own writing would destroy her femininity, threaten her marriage, and disrupt her household, and that literary women were often characterized by strong passions and notorious conduct" (Helsinger, Sheets, and Veeder 3: 6).

- *Translated work.* Refer to the work by the author, unless you are giving particular emphasis to the diction or editorial comment by the translator.

  The particular isolation and foreignness of the handmaids makes them into strangers to their families and to themselves, and parallels them with stranger-figures throughout literary history (Kristeva 10–30).

- *Novel, play, or poem.* Often, it is more useful to give chapter numbers, act/scene/line numbers, or stanza and line numbers; when you use a different text from the assigned one in a course, include chapter numbers after the page citations, separated by a comma.

  The story of Orpheus and Eurydice to which Atwood refers on the last page of the novel is found in Ovid's *Metamorphoses* (10: 1–160) and the "vast darkness" perhaps echoes Horatio's phrase to Hamlet concerning the "dead vast and middle of the night" (1.2.199).

- *Work in an anthology or collection.* Use the author of the work in the in-text citation, and include information about the collection in your list of works cited.

  In "Earth" the speaker is digging in the garden but is aware of the dead below the earth in a way that Serena Joy does not realize (Atwood 160–61).

- *Article in a periodical or newspaper.* Use either the author's name method (above, adding a title if more than one work of an author is cited), the title of the article, or the name of the periodical if one of the other options is not available.

  Margaret Atwood often writes newspaper editorials or commentaries, as in her commentary as a "Sophisticated Traveler" on her experience of the Romans and the Celts in Provence ("Provence" S16).

- *Indirect source.* Use the following format for quoted words in another source.

  Christopher Lehmann-Haupt, an editor with the *New York Times,* says that only in the novel's final pages do we realize "how bleak and even terrifying" that world is (qtd. in Atwood, *Handmaid's Tale* 391).

- *Course kit.* If an article or other reference is used from a course kit, treat it as a work in an anthology or collection (above), using the pagination of the course kit.

  Parody takes different forms in Atwood's poetry and fiction (Godard 75–78).

Audiovisual Media

Audiovisual media include paintings, sculpture, architecture, music, television, radio, video, films, and so on. The MLA style covers the various modes of citing such materials, including references in your writing to them. In general, the artist, composer, writer, or producer/director is named, usually with the title of the work cited. Many other forms of media exist and can be referred to in essays—including performances, personal letters, audio cassettes, and so on. In general, they follow the same pattern as that for print media. If you include illustrations in your essay, label and number them with a caption (Fig. 1. Vincent Van Gogh, *Starry Night,* Museum of Modern Art, New York). If you discuss a book illustration, see below. Further details are given in the standard manuals listed in the further readings at the end of this chapter.

- *Work of art.* Include the artist and list the title in italics.

  ... that landscape of greens and blues with a sky of stars (Van Gogh, *The Starry Night*).

- *Book illustration.* If you discuss or reproduce an illustration, you refer to it by the artist's name.

  The cover illustration to *The Handmaid's Tale* depicts not only the handmaids' costumes, but also their isolation and imprisonment (Marcellino).

- *Musical composition.* List the composer and include the title of the recording in italics or the title of the song in quotation marks.

  Apocalypse Now begins with the music from a famous 1960s rock song (Morrison, "The End").

- *Television broadcast.* List the title of the program in italics, the title of the episode in quotation marks, and the date of the first broadcast.

  One episode of the *X-Files* paid elaborate tribute to Mary Shelley's *Frankenstein* ("The Post-Modern Prometheus" 30 Nov. 1997).

- *Radio broadcast.* List the title of the program in italics, the title of the segment in quotation marks, and the date.

  The National Public Radio portrait of Alice Walker related the title of its program to the literary form of *The Color Purple* ("If God" 3 Mar. 1984).

- *Film.* Include the director and give the title in italics.

  In setting much of his film in and around Boston, the director was true to the locale of Atwood's novel (Schlondorff, *The Handmaid's Tale*).

Electronic Media

Students are increasingly using a large and quickly evolving field of electronic sources that they access through computers and related technologies, including video, CDs, and CD-ROMs, much of them containing audio clips and visual images or graphics. Such electronic media sources from the Web and the Internet include scholarly projects, reference books, databases, e-books (electronic books), articles in periodicals accessible electronically, and professional and personal sites. The current *MLA Handbook* gives ample examples of citing electronic sources and relevant references in works cited lists, but notes also that "electronic media ... so far lack agreed-on means of organizing works. Moreover electronic texts are not as fixed and stable as their print counterparts" (Gibaldi 207). Further, it cautions that its recommendations "on citing electronic works are necessarily not definitive and will doubtless change" (208). In general the MLA style for electronic media follows that for the authors of books, both for in-text citation and for the list of works cited. However, it specifies that Web addresses (URLs) should be placed within angle brackets < >, a typographical device also used in instructing most e-mail programs to send to a specific address, and hence confusing to a reader. Accordingly, we have adapted the MLA style for electronic sources following Janice R. Walker and Todd Taylor in the *Columbia Guide to Online Style* and by James D. Lester in *Citing Cyberspace.*

Electronic media change their references frequently, as new Web sites replace old ones. Many also become inactive. Hence, such references often do not have the durability or reliability of print or hard-copy media. Nevertheless, students must make acceptable references for any citations from such sources. In this evolving field, the following procedures are acceptable for in-text citations. Note that the Web address, or URL, may replace the author, title, and publication data. The date the Internet address was accessed (or the date on the Web page if it exists) is added after the Web address. Since Web pages are only one continuous page, regardless of length, a page reference is unnecessary, either in in-text citations or in lists of works cited.

- *Web sites.* Include the author's name, abbreviation, or alias, if known, or the title or file name, or the Web address, along with the date of access.

  At her Web site Margaret Atwood has made available a great deal of additional information about her novel, including detailed responses to questions. To one question about her heroine, she says: "I wanted an ordinary person, for the simple reason that most people subjected to these conditions are ordinary people" (Atwood, 17 Sept. 1998).

- *E-mail, listservs, and newsgroups.* Include the author's name, or alias, if known, with a short title or file address so that a reader can identify it in the list of works cited.

  "Americacentrism and Eurocentrism mean that Canadian authors have never been chosen for the Nobel Prize in literature. It is disgraceful that Atwood has not been awarded a prize for literature given almost four decades of outstanding poetry and prose. Shame to the Nobel committee" (Charles, "Nobel Prize").

Works Cited List in MLA Style

In the MLA style version of the works cited list, a few conventions function to get all of the information down clearly. To simplify these entries, we have provided the citations for each of the examples of in-text citations given above. The list of works cited follows the body of your essay and the page of endnotes (if any). It begins on a new page with the heading "Works Cited" and is numbered sequentially with the rest of your essay. Like the rest of your essay, it is double-spaced throughout. The works cited list contains all of the materials to which you made reference in the body of your essay. It does not include the materials you consulted but did not use.

Each of the three main elements of the entry is set off by a period: the author's name, the title in italics, and the place, publisher, and date of publication. For publishers' names, you can abbreviate *University Press* to UP or its equivalent: U of Chicago P. Everything else follows from this format.

The works cited list is arranged alphabetically, by authors' last names. If there is no author, you alphabetize by the first main word in the title (omitting *A, An, The*). The author's name is placed at the left margin, and all subsequent lines for the same entry are indented five spaces or one-half inch (on a computer, you can use the hanging indent facility).

In detail, that means that you give the author's name with the last name first (inverted order). If there is more than one author, only the first author's name is inverted, followed by a comma and the rest of the authors. If you cite more than one work by an author, you list each in alphabetical order by title, replacing the author's name with three hyphens and a period before each title after the first. If there is no author for a work, but only a title, you use the title in alphabetizing. All words in the title are capitalized, except prepositions, articles, and conjunctions. The first word in a title is always capitalized. Book titles, film titles, newspapers, and periodicals are all italicized. Articles in periodicals and chapter titles in a book are not italicized but, instead, are enclosed in double quotation marks. The MLA style assumes that you are using a font with straight quotation marks instead of curly or typographical quotation marks ("smart quotes") like these (" "); however, most word processors now print typographical quotation marks automatically. We have assumed that you will use this feature of your word processor's program, and accordingly, we have modified the MLA and APA styles in the examples that follow. Furthermore, as we have noted above, the MLA style recommends using underlining to indicate italics for book titles, but we recommend the italic font on your computer.

Print Media

- **One author.** Use the format outlined above.

    Atwood, Margaret. *The Handmaid's Tale.* Toronto: Seal-McClelland-Bantam, 1998.

- **Two authors.** Order and spell the author's names as on the title page. Use a comma after the first author's inverted name.

    Gilbert, Sandra M., and Susan Gubar. *The Madwoman in the Attic: The Woman Writer and the Nineteenth-Century Literary Imagination.* New Haven: Yale UP, 1979.

- **Three authors.** Order and spell authors' names as on the title page; this applies to joint authorship or joint editorship. Note that the MLA style does not underline titles within titles. Many style books (the *Chicago Manual,* for instance) find this method confusing and put book titles within other titles in quotation marks (Chicago alternative style).

    Wilson, Sharon R., Thomas B. Friedman, and Shannon Hengen, eds. *Approaches to Teaching Atwood's* The Handmaid's Tale *and Other Works.* New York: MLA, 1996.

    Alternative form:

    Wilson, Sharon R., Thomas B. Friedman, and Shannon Hengen, eds. *Approaches to Teaching Atwood's "The Handmaid's Tale" and Other Works.* New York: MLA, 1996.

- **More than three authors.** Name all or use the abbreviation et al. (Latin, *et alii,* and others).

    Belenky, Mary Field, et al. *Women's Ways of Knowing: The Development of Self, Voice, and Mind.* New York: Basic, 1986.

- **More than one source by an author.** Include the full title in the list of works cited. Indicate a second work by the same author by three hyphens (or a long dash) and a period instead of the author's name; arrange titles alphabetically.

    Atwood, Margaret. *Survival: A Thematic Guide to Canadian Literature.* Toronto: Anansi, 1972.

    ———. *Wilderness Tips.* Toronto: McClelland, 1991.

- **Two or more authors with the same last name.** Use the full name for each person, alphabetized according to their given names.

    Miller, Jean Baker. *Toward a New Psychology of Women.* Harmondsworth: Penguin, 1976.

    Miller, Perry. *Errand into the Wilderness.* Cambridge: Belknap-Harvard UP, 1956.

- *Group or corporate author.* Use the group name as an author.

  Boston Women's Health Collective. *Our Bodies, Ourselves*. New York: Simon, 1986.

- *Work cited by title (no author).* Expand the shortened title from the parenthetical reference in the list of works cited.

  Oxford Companion to Canadian Literature. Ed. William Toye. Toronto: Oxford UP, 1983.

- *Multi-volume work.* Include the relevant volume number in Arabic numerals directly after the title.

  Helsinger, Elizabeth K., Robin Lauterbach Sheets, and William Veeder. *The Woman Question: Society and Literature in Britain and America, 1837–1883*. Vol. 3. Chicago: U of Chicago P, 1989.

- *Translated work.* List the book by the author, and give the name of the translator after the title.

  Kristeva, Julia. *Strangers to Ourselves*. Trans. Leon Roudiez. New York: Columbia UP, 1991.

- *Novel, play, or poem.* Note that the first example gives the format for a translated work, and the second, for an edited work.

  Ovid. *Metamorphoses*. Trans. Rolfe Humphries. Bloomington: Indiana UP, 1955.

  Shakespeare, William. *Hamlet*. Ed. Barbara A. Mowat and Paul Werstine. New York: Washington Square-Pocket, 1992.

- *Work in an anthology or collection.* Use the author of the work in the in-text citation, and include information about the collection in your list of works cited, where you also list your author.

  Atwood, Margaret. "Earth." *Poetry by Canadian Women*. Ed. Rosemary Sullivan. Toronto: Oxford UP, 1989. 160–61.

- *Editorial, letter to the editor, or review.* List the author if known, title if given, publication name, omitting *A* or *The* from the title, date, and pages.

  Davidson, Cathy N. "A Feminist *1984*." Rev. of *The Handmaid's Tale* by Margaret Atwood. *Ms*. Feb. 1986: 24–26.

- *Article in a periodical or newspaper.* Use either the author's name method (above), the title of the article, or the name of the periodical if one of the other options is not available.

  Atwood, Margaret. "Provence: Romans vs. Celts." *The New York Times Magazine* 12 September 1993: S16.

- *Signed article from daily newspaper.* Follow the format above, but add the name of the city of publication in brackets after the title, not underlined, if it is not part of the title.

  Wright, Robin, and Josh Meyer. "Righteous 'patriots' testing U.S. authority." *Toronto Star* 25 Apr. 1995: A11.

- *Article in a journal with continuous pagination.* Each issue continues the pagination from the previous issue. Cite the volume number only before the year, using Arabic numerals throughout.

  Godard, Barbara. "Telling it Over Again: Atwood's Art of Parody." *Canadian Poetry* 21 (1987): 1–30.

- *Article in a journal with separate pagination for each issue.* Each issue begins on page 1. Cite the volume number and the issue number, separated by a period.

  > Buss, Helen M. "Maternality and Narrative Strategies in the Novels of Margaret Atwood." *Atlantis* 15.1 (1989): 76–83.

- *Course kit.* If the material cited is from an article, use the article format for its original publication data and indicate its present source: Rpt. in (= reprinted in), followed by the name of the course kit as a book title, followed by the name of the compiler (usually the course director), the location, university, date, and pages. For other material from a course kit, begin with the inverted name of the course director, and treat the volume as an anthology or collection.

  > Godard, Barbara. "Telling it Over Again: Atwood's Art of Parody." *Canadian Poetry* 21 (1987): 1–30. Rpt. in *Canadian Fiction: Course Kit for ENGL 2210*. Ed. Sarah Johns. Toronto: York U, 2004. 60–82.

  > Johns, Sarah, ed. *Canadian Fiction: Course Kit for ENGL 2210*. Toronto: York U, 2004.

Audiovisual Media

- *Work of art.* List the artist, title in italics, museum or collection, and location. You may add the date of the work after the title. Also add the publication data for the source for the illustration.

  > Van Gogh, Vincent. *The Starry Night* (1889). Museum of Modern Art. New York. *Varieties of Visual Experience.* By Edmund Burke Feldman. Englewood Cliffs: Prentice-Hall, 1971. 40.

- *Book illustration.* List the artist, the title of the work (if known) or identify it by description in brackets, and its publication data as in a book.

  > Marcellino, Fred. [Cover illustration]. Atwood, Margaret. *The Handmaid's Tale*. Toronto: Seal-McClelland-Bantam, 1998. Front cover.

- *Musical composition.* Include the composer, song title in quotation marks, album title in italics, medium, producer, and date; or, list the composer and musical form, without italics unless the work is titled.

  > Morrison, Jim. "The End." *The Doors*. LP. Elektra Records. 1967.

  > Beethoven, Ludwig von. Symphony no. 5 in C minor, op. 67. Beethoven, Ludwig von. *Moonlight Sonata.*

- *Television broadcast.* List the title of the program in quotation marks, series in italics, writer and director, if known, and date of broadcast.

  > "The Post-Modern Prometheus." *The X-Files*. Writ. and Dir. Chris Carter. 30 Nov. 1997.

- *Radio broadcast.* Cite the title in quotation marks, series in italics, network, call letters and city of broadcast station, and date.

  > "If God." *Writers Today*. NPR. WGBH, Boston. 3 Mar. 1984.

- *Film.* Include the title in italics, followed by other information, such as director, author of screenplay or actors, production company, date, and any subsequent release, as on videocassette.

  > *The Handmaid's Tale*. Dir. Volker Schlondorff. Screenplay by Harold Pinter. Cinecom, 1989. Released on Videocassette by HBO, 1990.

Electronic Media

The general format for citations from electronic media consists of the following details, with punctuation and capitalization for each item. The lines listed separately here are combined in the citation list:

- Author's (Editor's, Compiler's) Last Name, First Name or Initials. [if known]
- "Title of Document Being Accessed." [title of article, Web page, or posting to a discussion list taken from subject line and put into quotation marks]
  - *Title of Complete Work* (*Project, Database, Personal Web Site*) [if known]
  - Version number or file number [if known]
  - Date of document or of last revision of Web site [if known, but often difficult to find]
  - Name of Institution or Organization Sponsoring the Web Site [if specified]
- Protocol and address [URL]
  - Access path [if specified]
  - Directories [if specified]
- Date of access [in parentheses]

The two essential items are (1) the protocol and address, and (2) the date of access. The protocol identifies the kind of electronic communication (such as CD-ROM, e-mail, ftp, gopher, http, or telnet), and the address is the URL. Some manuals specify that the URL is to be underlined. However, as most of you know, word processors automatically underline and highlight Web sites or addresses as hypertext links that can be accessed on the Internet from within those word processing programs. The underlining (and highlighting in blue on the colour monitor) indicates that the address is "hot" and can be accessed on the Internet directly from the document. In a submitted essay, however, a reader would not have access to enter any site directly. Hence, there is no need to underline the URL as a hot address. The MLA style page on the Internet specifies that the URL should be enclosed in pointed brackets like an e-mail address. The preferred method of citing the URL without underlining or other notation is given here. It is a convention to give the URL all on one line; if it will not fit on one line, it can be broken after a slash in the address. The date of access is the date when you accessed the reference, and it marks a time when the address was active and accessible. Most references also include an author's name and the title of the document or Web page. In other electronic media that do not accept italics, such as e-mail, the convention is to use an underline mark before and after text that would normally be underlined, _like this_.

- *Web site.* Include the author's name, abbreviation, or alias, if known, and the title or file name, as in the in-text citation.

  Atwood, Margaret. **http://www.web.net/owtoad/toc.html** (12 Aug. 2003).

- *E-mail, listservs, and newsgroups.* List the author's name or alias, if known, with a short title or file address so that a reader can identify it on the list of works cited.

  Charles. "The Nobel Prize Internet Archive." **www.almaz.com/nobel/wwwboard/ messages/705.html** Posted by Charles on 07 Jan. 1998 at 14:04:37.

There is a large number of printed and electronic guides available for the MLA style for printed materials. Many of these sources will be available at the reference desk of your library. In addition, most style handbooks have at least a summary chapter on how to make in-text references for the most common materials and how to create a list of works cited. The standard reference manuals, however, give detailed instruction on a wide variety of materials well beyond the possibilities of shorter handbooks. We list a number of these resources in the further readings at the end of this chapter.

TIPS   Remembering the Basic Format for MLA Works Cited List

In a works cited list, use the following order:

Jones, Henry. (author's name, inverted)
The World According to Fido. (title in italics and caps)
Boston: New World, 1997. (publication data)

Everything else is a refinement of this basic format.

SOCIAL SCIENCES FORMAT: APA STYLE

In the social sciences, the method of citation usually follows the standard format set out in the *Publication Manual of the American Psychological Association,* called the APA style (2001, 5th edition). Like the MLA style, the APA style uses in-text citation and a list of works cited (titled "References") at the end of an essay or article. The method of citation and reference, however, is somewhat different from the MLA style. You cite the source in your text using parentheses as in the MLA style, but you include the date of publication as well, in the order of author, date, and a page reference (for example, Jonas, 2001, p. 14), with the abbreviation *p.* and *pp.* This author-date system is linked clearly to the list of books, called *references* at the end of your essay. The list of references contains the author's name, alphabetized, followed by the date of publication, title, publisher, and place of publication. The most current information is available at the APA style Web site (**www.apastyle.org**).

In-Text Citations in APA Style

In the social sciences disciplines, you apply the same general principles about how to acknowledge all sources that you use. While the MLA style uses the author-page format, however, the APA style uses the author-date format. If you refer to a source more than once in a paragraph, the APA style specifies that you refer to the author's name, the date, and the page (each separated by commas) for the first entry only and subsequently list only the name and page for references to the same source. The APA style requires page numbers for all direct citations and also recommends giving page numbers if you paraphrase. To be safe, you should include page references for all derived materials, both those directly cited and ideas that are paraphrased. The abbreviations *p.* (page) and *pp.* (pages) are used for in-text citations. Short quotations of fewer than 40 words are incorporated in your text within quotations marks and a citation reference at the end of the sentence. For quotations of more than 40 words, indent the quotation a half inch from the left margin with no quotation marks. The examples provided here all relate to the question of how possible it is to change the priorities of the social structures of society, a topic that can draw on a wide range of materials in the social sciences.

Print Media

- *One author.* Provide the reference after the quotation, outside the quotation marks and within parentheses: (Author, date, p. 143).

  In assessing the potential for change in social policy affecting the most needy in society, a new look has to be taken at the concept of poverty that was defined at the beginning of the century as inadequate earning of the male members of a family, assuming that "every penny earned by every member of the family went into the family purse, and was judiciously expended upon necessaries" (Rowntree, 1902, p. 111).

- *Two or more authors.* Give both names for two authors, all names for more than two for the first citation. In subsequent citations, give the first author's last name, with et al. Note that *and* is an ampersand (&) inside parentheses, but it is spelled out as *and* in text.

  The study of social change is problematic for sociologists because they rely on social order for their analyses, while change introduces the "unexpected and potentially explosive" (Crysdale & Beattie, 1977, p. 75).

  or,

  Crysdale and Beattie argue ... (1977, p. 75).

- *More than one source by an author.* Distinguish sources by dates; several sources in the same year have letters added to the date: 1990a, 1990b.

  Schudson's recent work on change and integration in national societies (1994) builds on his earlier work on newspapers as instruments of popular culture (1978, 1984).

- *Two or more authors with the same last name.* Use both initials for each author.

  The transformation of intercultural groups depends, among many other factors, on overcoming racial stereotyping, or, rather, replacing racist stereotyping with "positive stereotypes that recognize but respect intergroup differences" (W.G. Stephan & C.W. Stephan, 1996, p. 124).

- *Group or corporate author.* Use the group name as an author.

  A government study determined that by 1980 integration was still severely limited in U.S. schools, since 69% of whites attended schools that were still less than 5 percent African-American (U.S. Commission on Civil Rights, 1987, p. 14).

- *Work cited by title.* Use the first words of the entry, usually the title.

  Shifts in "population, income, and church affiliation" have had little impact on the "cultural aspirations of most people" in Montreal ("Social Change," 1993, p. A4).

Audiovisual Media

In general, the APA style follows the same principles for audiovisual materials as for print resources and requires the same kind of data. Works of art, films, graphics, tables, charts, maps, and so on are cited in similar ways.

- *Musical-video composition.* Include the composer, song title in quotation marks, album title in italics, medium, producer, and date; or list the composer and musical form, without italics unless the work is titled.

  > On its twentieth anniversary, Pink Floyd's *The Wall* continues to chronicle some aspects of urban psychological disorder (Waters 1999).

- *Television broadcast.* Identify the source of the citation by producer and date.

  > Urban issues continue to dominate both the daily news and the news talk shows, as in the treatment of urban failures after September 11, 2000 (Crystal 2000).

- *Film.* Use italics for the film title in a citation, and use the date in a reference.

  > The urban conflict between humans and machinery that both beautifies and demonizes the machine in an urban setting, thereby isolating humans, was captured early in film history by Fritz Lang's *Metropolis* (1927).

Electronic Media

The most recent print edition of the APA *Publication Manual* has completely re-written its treatment of electronic media with lavish information about references, but it also comments that these conventions for citation are undergoing rapid change.

The general procedure follows the conventions of HTML language and the Internet in that pages are not referred to; however, if the site gives an author and/or date, that information is included. The URL is given in the list of references without underlining or any other typographical marking. The APA style recommends that personal communications (such as e-mail) are to be referenced as in-text citations but are not to be listed in the references. However, e-mail and other electronic sources (such as chat lines) are becoming standardized for both in-text citation and notation on the list of references. Indeed, the current editions of print and electronic guides that amplify the APA style do give details on just these matters. For instance, Janice R. Walker and Todd Taylor in the *Columbia Guide to Online Style* give further detailed treatment of electronic sources (see Walker's guide at **longman.awl.com/englishpages/citation_walker.htm**), and James D. Lester's *Citing Cyberspace* (**longman.awl.com/englishpages/cyber.htm**).

- *Web sites.* Use the author's name and date, if known.

  > A new "interdisciplinary theory for cultural change" has recently become available on the Web, and the author hopes that it will begin an online discussion of relevant issues (Fog, 1997).

- *Web-accessible journal.* Numerous journals are available through *WilsonWeb, Ovid,* and many other databases. Cite in your text as in the case of any print publication, and do the same for newspapers.

  > Foster's account shows that in Tennessee social change was impeded by the failure of legislatures and police regulators to stop both the drug trade and drug use (1996).

- *E-mail, listservs, and newsgroups.* Use the author's name and the date of posting.

  The impact of new software in the field of cultural change and the role of Internet search engines in reducing student capacity for sustained concentration have been much discussed on the educational news-groups, as Wertmuller has pointed out in an e-mail (May 14, 1998).

References List in APA Style

The list of books referred to in an essay, article, chapter, or book is entitled *References* in the APA style. The APA *Publication Manual* distinguishes between a reference list that includes the sources for all of the citations in your essay and a *Bibliography* that includes "works for background and for further reading" (215). You will usually use only a list of references. The format generally follows the conventions set up in the in-text citations, based on the author-date method, arranged alphabetically. You add the page of references as the last page of your essay, numbered sequentially. The general format of each entry is the author's or editor's last name, followed by a comma and initials, the year of the publication in parentheses (or "No Date," if unavailable), the title of the source (no quotation marks for an article, but italics for a book or journal title), the publisher, and the pages if it is an article. The APA style requires only the initials of the first and middle names of an author and capitalization of only the first word of a title (along with any proper nouns and the first word after a colon); titles of periodicals are capitalized. The current APA style specifies that titles of works use the italics function on your computer. Current practice, changed from the fourth edition, places the first line of the entry out to the margin, and subsequent lines are indented five spaces (use the hanging indent function on your word processor). The names of university presses are spelled out. Other details are in the APA *Publication Manual.*

Print Media

- *One author.* Follow the format outlined above. Only the first word of a title and the first word after a colon are capitalized.

  Rowntree, B. S. (1902). *Poverty.* London: Macmillan.

  or,

  Crane, D. (Ed.). (1994). *The sociology of culture: Emerging theoretical perspectives.* Oxford: Blackwell.

- *Two or more authors.* Reverse the order of both names, and use an ampersand before the last name.

  Crysdale, S., & Beattie, C. (1977). *Sociology Canada: An introductory text.* Toronto: Butterworth.

- *More than one source by an author.* Repeat the author's name for each publication, and put them in chronological order. For an article or chapter, note that there are no quotation marks around the title. The editor's name is in normal order, followed by Ed. in parentheses and the title. The pages of the article follow with the abbreviation pp. and then the publisher.

  Schudson, M. (1978). *Discovering the news: A social history of American newspapers.* New York: Basic Books.

Schudson, M. (1984). *Advertising, the uneasy persuasion.* New York: Basic Books.

Schudson, M. (1994). Culture and the integration of national societies. In D. Crane (Ed.), *The Sociology of culture: Emerging theoretical perspectives* (pp. 21–43). Oxford: Blackwell.

- **Two or more authors with the same last name.** Use both initials for each author, and treat it as a book by two authors, as above.

  Stephan, W.G., & Stephan, C.W. (1996). *Intergroup relations.* Boulder: Westview Press.

- **Group or corporate author.** Use the group name as an author.

  U.S. Commission on Civil Rights. (1987). *The new evidence on school desegregation.* Washington, D.C.: U.S. Government Printing Office.

- **Work cited by title.** Use the format for a newspaper article entry.

  Social change in urban Quebec. (1993, May 23). *Montreal Gazette,* p. A4.

- **Journal article.** Alphabetize by author. Note that both the title and the volume number are italicized.

  Decker, Jeffrey. L. (1993). The state of rap. *Social Text, 34,* 53–84.

Audiovisual Media

- **Music-Video.** Give the data for the music, video, or combined production, listing artists, composers, or directors first, followed by the italicized title, and the publication or release data.

  Waters, R., Gilmour, D., & Guthrie, J. *Pink Floyd—the wall* [DVD]. New York: Columbia Records, 1999.

- **Television broadcast.** List the name of the major producer, the date, the program, and the source.

  Crystal, L. (Executive Producer). (2000, October 29). *The MacNeil/Lehrer news hour* [Television broadcast]. New York and Washington, D.C.: Public Broadcasting Service.

- **Film.** List the film by director/producer, date, title, and other production data. Use italics for the film title.

  Lang, F. (Director) (1927). *Metropolis* [Motion picture] Germany: UFA Studios. Re-released and digitally restored 2002. New York: Kino International, 2002.

Electronic Media

A reference in the APA style to an item cited from electronic media should include the following (with capitalization and punctuation as shown). However, often, no author name is available. At a minimum, give a title, a date (of original publication in whatever media, or of retrieval), and an address. More complete information would include the following, if available:

Author's last name, Initials. (date of publication or "No Date," if unavailable). Title of document. *Title of complete work.* [if applicable]. Protocol and address [complete URL] (date of access: month, day, year).

You should check with your instructor if you wish to vary from the APA style in formatting references to any kind of electronic media.

- *Web sites.* Use the author's name and date, if known, the title, the date accessed, and the URL with no punctuation at the end of the Web address.

  Fog, A. (1997). *Cultural Selection.* Retrieved on October 10, 1999, from **http://www/datrix. co.za/docs/culture/cult.htm**

- *Web-accessible journal.* These journals are available through *WilsonWeb, Ovid,* and other databases. Cite the author, date, title, and journal as for print; add the database producer, title, URL, and date of access.

  Foster, J. C. (1996). The rocky road to a "drug free Tennessee": A history of the early regulation of cocaine and the opiates, 1897–1913. *Journal of Social History 29,* 547–564. Retrieved July 24, 1997, from H. W. Wilson Humanities Abstracts **http://wilsonweb3. hwwilson.com/cgi-bin/auto_login.cgi**

- *Web-accessible newspaper.* These are available through the newspaper's Web page.

  Slater, E. (1999). Ex-wrestler sworn as governor. *The Record Online.* Retrieved January 5, 1999, from **http://www.bergen.com/news/jesse05199901058.htm**

- *CD-ROM.* Indicate the author, title, medium, such as CD-ROM, and journal, as well as the source from which the information was retrieved.

  Mulvihill, C. K. (1996). AIDS education for college students: Review and proposal for a research-based curriculum. [CD-ROM]. *AIDS Education and Prevention 8,* 11–30. Abstract from: SilverPlatter File: PsychLIT Item: 84-20138.

- *E-mail, listservs, and newsgroups.* Indicate the author, the e-mail or other address, the title of the communication, and, if possible, the source from which it is available and the date of access.

  Wertmuller, C. (cwertm@gosec.columbia.edu). Re: Internet distractions... E-mail to Joe Blum (jblum@hotmail.com) (May 14, 1998).

FOOTNOTES AND ENDNOTES

Footnotes (at the bottom of the page) or endnotes (at the end of the essay, before the list of sources) are now used only for two quite limited purposes, although some faculty still prefer notes to the methods of in-text citation we discussed above (see further comments on this matter below). Both the APA and MLA styles discourage the use of such notes, even for additional information, arguing that if it is relevant, it should be incorporated somehow into the text of your essay. However, sometimes, it may be useful to provide in notes some background materials that would interrupt the main flow of your argument. Usually, this kind of note is either a *content note* (containing biographical or other information that expands the point being made in your essay but that does not belong in the body of your argument) or a *bibliographical note* (that comments on the sources, rather like an annotated bibliography). For a detailed discussion of this use of footnotes, as well as the older use of footnotes and endnotes, see the *Foundations* Web site. For other citation problems in using old bibliographic styles, see early editions of the *MLA Handbook* or the *Publication Manual* of the APA in your library.

AN ANNOTATED BIBLIOGRAPHY

An annotated bibliography is a list of citations of books, articles, and other documents, including electronic sources. Each entry is followed by a brief description and evaluation of the citation. This annotation, or comment, informs a reader of the range and depth of the document referred to, and discusses its sources, validity, quality, and accuracy. The annotation is intended, therefore, to do two primary tasks:

1. To describe the contents of the document, assessing its potential audience, level of difficulty, and range of coverage and perhaps providing a quick overview of its contents

2. To evaluate the relevance of the document and assess its accuracy and quality of argument

To create an annotated bibliography, you will first have chosen (or will have been assigned) a specific topic. Perhaps an annotated bibliography is to be appended to one of your essays. You will have to decide what kind of coverage of the topic you wish to have in your bibliography. Do you want all of the books, articles, or Internet/electronic sources to be on one side of the argument? Do you wish to have a balance of pro and con positions? Should a variety of views on your topic be represented? Do you wish to have a balance between general and detailed treatments, scholarly and popular works? Whatever you decide, you need to gather about twice as many titles as you will finally use, and from those, you make your informed selection.

You will have to examine and quickly review each of the texts to determine which are most appropriate. Then, you can create an entry for each citation, using the appropriate style—MLA, APA, or, if in science, CBE. You then add a short annotation that describes and evaluates the citation. Usually, each annotation is not more than four or five sentences long or about 150 words. If you are preparing the annotated bibliography for an assignment, you should check with your instructor about whether it is acceptable to use fragments or point form in your annotations, rather than complete sentences. If so, you can connect the fragments with semicolons.

You can add items to your annotated bibliography that might be useful to a reader, beyond those that you referred to in your list of works cited. You can also arrange the entries in categories ("Overviews of the Field," "Popular Treatments," and so on).

Your evaluation might consider the credentials of the author (institutional position, position in the field, past writings); the date of the work (republished, original date); the edition (first, revised); the publisher (how well known it is in the field); the reputation of the journal for an article and the range of the other articles in the issue; the audience (popular, educated, scholarly); the coverage in terms of providing new materials, updating old views or data, and dealing with primary materials (raw materials of the research process) or secondary materials (commentary on the primary materials); and how well reviewed the source has been. You might find reviews in the major book review indexes (*Book Review Digest, Book Review Index*).

After creating an annotated bibliography, you are well prepared to move into the writing of an essay. For some essays, an annotated bibliography is a valuable scholarly addition to the paper.

CHAPTER SUMMARY

In Chapter 9, we have discussed the major items providing references for all of the sources you used in your research and that you will be able to incorporate into your essay.

- You are familiar with various ways of making reference to your sources in the body of your essay.
- You can link those references directly to the fully documented source on a list of works cited or a list of references.
- You are familiar with the conventions of the two major styles, for the humanities (MLA) and social sciences (APA).
- You can document different types of material, including print, audiovisual, and electronic resources.
- You can use footnotes or endnotes for additional content or bibliographic material.
- You know how to prepare an annotated bibliography.

Now you are well prepared to gather all of these abilities together in writing your essay, which we cover in the next section.

FURTHER READINGS

Amato, Carol J. *The World's Easiest Guide to Using the APA*. 2nd ed. Westminster, CA: Stargazer, 1999. Extracts available at www.stargazerpub.com/.

American Psychological Association (APA). *Publication Manual of the American Psychological Association*. 5th ed. Washington, D.C.: APA, 2001.

The Chicago Manual of Style. 15th ed. Chicago: U of Chicago P, 2003.

Gibaldi, Joseph, ed. *MLA Handbook for Writers of Research Papers*. 6th ed. New York: MLA, 2003.

———, ed. *MLA Style Manual and Guide to Scholarly Publishing*. 2nd ed. New York: MLA, 1998.

Li, Xia, and Nancy Crane. *Electronic Styles: A Handbook for Citing Electronic Information*. 2nd ed. Medford, NJ: Information Today, 1996. Includes both MLA and APA styles.

Lester, James D. *Citing Cyberspace: A Quick-Reference Guide to Citing Electronic Sources in MLA and APA Styles*. 2nd ed. New York: Longman, 2000.

Scientific Style and Format: The CBE Manual for Authors, Editors and Publishers. 6th ed. Reston, VA: CBE, 1994.

Walker, Janice R., and Todd Taylor. *The Columbia Guide to Online Style*. New York: Columbia UP, 1998.

part four

The Essay from First Draft to Final Copy to Getting It Back

chapter ten

The Planning and Pre-writing Stage

In Part IV of *Foundations,* we narrow our focus to concentrate on planning an essay, writing it, and getting it back. All three parts are essential stages in a critical approach to your courses. This part of the book takes you from your research, perhaps not quite completed yet, through to the submission of it—where many people think the exercise concludes—to the day when it is returned, building on your instructor's comments to improve for the next round.

LEARNING OBJECTIVES

Chapter 10 deals with the interim stage between your research and the writing stage—the crucial pre-writing or planning stage. Here, you learn how to draw your ideas together into an argument, how to work on your introductions and conclusions, and how to plan an outline and formulate a thesis statement:

- What are the basic kinds of essay types?
- How can you summarize your research notes by means of précis or paraphrase, and what is the difference?
- What are the basic ways of organizing a formal essay?
- How do you lay out and follow an outline?
- What is a thesis statement, and how does it lead a reader through your argument?

We all face deadlines and wish that we had all the time in the world to complete our research, preparation, and revision before we hand in that important final copy. You know ahead of time the deadlines for your assignments and can usually make reasonable projections about the demands on your time. Many students face the greatest difficulty just before the writing stage. Panic sets in when they have gathered the appropriate research materials and must formulate them into a coherent argument. The transition from research to entering the first page of an essay on the computer is the subject of this chapter.

DIFFERENT EXPECTATIONS AND DIFFERENT ESSAYS

In Chapter 2, we dealt with different expectations and new environments in universities, but it seems as though for many students the essay, in whatever form, is not a new expectation, but an old fear that takes on living form at least once in every course.

Are There Different Essay Standards?

Many students have difficulty writing essays that satisfy their own intellectual standards and that meet the demands of the instructor. But do different instructors have different standards? To be frank, of course they do: some seem to think that this is the only course that you are taking at university and appear to load on the requirements, including essays that they want to be of a high standard. Others seem casual and laid back, but when it comes to written work, they, too, can be demanding. Some others, again, really do give much less weight to written work and are much less strict in meeting format and content requirements. You have to weigh and judge these expectations and have to recognize that they are different and that you have to meet each of them at least halfway.

Further, students are puzzled by requirements that seem to differ from department to department. And they also find that different instructors put different emphases upon writing in what is often called standard written English. At times, it seems that you receive contradictory instructions for almost everything involved in writing an essay: instructors require different formats for essay presentation; they propose different approaches to the materials to be researched for the essay; and they outline different expectations for analyses of texts or problems in the essay topic.

It is true that expectations of essay styles will vary between a course in introductory economics and one in introductory English. But it is equally true that for either course, an essay that is written in standard English, well researched, cogently argued, and presented in an acceptable format will very likely meet the demands of both student and instructor alike. Nevertheless, a student must be aware of the particular demands of individual instructors and of varying disciplinary norms in the presentation of research. Students also need to recognize that they are engaged in a project to focus their own language, to control and shape it, that they are both the producers and the products of their own language, and that in the classroom many different positions are competing for attention.

Pre-writing

Students often feel victimized by these struggles, especially when, for example, they must hand in by Monday four pages on this novel or that topic in Canadian history. They ask themselves, "What can I possibly say? What can I possibly say that is new? What can I possibly say that hasn't already been said before—and better? What can I say to this teacher that he or she won't laugh or sneer at?" Or the questions might move to a more practical level: "What should I assume about my reader? How do I begin? How will I be evaluated?" We all have been students in just this predicament.

Foundations aims to help you by giving voice to your critical language, weight to your words, and power to your position. The pre-writing or planning stage enables you to assemble your research and focus it on your writing.

The pre-writing stage usually involves six major steps:

1. Gathering and organizing your research data
2. Summarizing it by means of paraphrase and précis
3. Organizing it into a logical order
4. Drafting an outline that can be modified as you work
5. Formulating a tentative, working thesis statement (or hypothesis)
6. Drafting an introduction and conclusion in a little more detail, waiting to finish them in the final stages of writing

By setting out these six steps in order, you avoid pre-writing anxiety and have a clear way of proceeding to the writing of your essay. You should plan on spending a good workday on the planning steps, a day that will make the writing stage go much faster.

Kinds of Essays

There are many different kinds of essays, and their characteristics are usually determined by the criteria for scholarship in particular disciplines. For instance, in anthropology, a study of the social practices of First Nations people in a particular geographical area and at a specific time period, say, just before the arrival of the European colonizers, would rely upon all kinds of archaeological evidence, as well as the oral history of the particular people being examined and the records of the Europeans. Such gathering of data could be assembled for an *exposition* of the problem; it could be used for *comparative* purposes to discuss several First Nations groups (or a then-and-now paper); or it could be used for an *analytical* appraisal that is defending a particular thesis about practices, infant mortality rates, longevity, or whatever.

There are five kinds of critical essays, along with the writing of informal essays.

1. An *expository* essay sets out to explain a body of data or information, a series of events, or a narrative sequence. Its aim is to give information and possibly some interpretation to a reader about a specific body of knowledge. For instance, if you were writing about the rising of the Métis under Louis Riel in what is now Manitoba, you would be setting out your research on the events or an interpretation of those events. Or if you are giving an exposition of a Margaret Atwood novel, you would have to decide what kinds of details your essay would be explaining, and in your outline, your paragraphs should lead the reader through that exposition step by step.

2. A *persuasive* essay (sometimes called an *analytical* essay) presents an argument that attempts to persuade a reader that the position you are defending is valid. It takes the expository essay a stage further and adopts a critical position on the material being examined, as we set out in Chapter 3. Your case will depend upon your evidence and how

you marshal it for your purposes. You might also take into account opposing theoretical positions, being fair to them. Your research will have provided evidence for you, and now your task is to organize it effectively by means of a workable outline and a modifiable thesis statement. For instance, in writing about First Nations people before colonization, you could take a position that they were either better or worse off before European contact. The position would require qualification, consideration of conflicting data, and interpretations of those data, all structured in a logical order supporting your position.

3. A *problem* essay involves taking a particular problem in a course, usually of a narrow focus, and working on it to solve the problem. Sometimes, that problem will be the analysis of a body of data (as in some psychology or sociology courses) or the setting out of the construction of a particular literary work (as in the construction of Margaret Atwood's *Handmaid's Tale,* stressing the elements of structure, theme, setting, and so on), or dealing with the specific economic causes of the Métis uprising (in a history course). You have the task of formulating the problem, considering what its component parts are and how those parts can be put together. Hence this kind of essay builds on the skills of a persuasive essay. In part, the handling of the problem will be your own work, but you may also be relying on the work of others to see how they have dealt with the problem. There might be a body of scholarship that you will have to summarize briefly, but you have to resist the danger of letting their views overwhelm your own treatment of the problem.

4. A *research* essay (sometimes called a *formal* essay) necessarily involves a summary of some of the work of other scholars or writers on your topic and allows you to position your argument in relation to theirs. Hence your research involves becoming familiar with their work and being able to assess it critically. This kind of essay nearly always involves some aspects of the expository essay (you have to set out some information), the persuasive essay (you have to convince your reader that your critical position is valid, and you do so by means of a thesis statement, argument, and supporting evidence), and the problem essay (you have to find some thread to trace through your material to articulate your critical position on it). A research essay involves the synthesis and summary of others' arguments, and hence the principles of précis and paraphrase are vital to you. So also is a strong sense of what is required in accurate quotation and the documentation of your sources. Perhaps the greatest difficulty with a research essay is narrowing the topic sufficiently so that you do not have to read all of the material on the history of the Métis people or of Manitoba or the entire body of critical works on Margaret Atwood, as though either of those were possible. Narrowing the topic, then, is fundamental in formulating the precise focus of your research essay. If narrowing the focus is fundamental, the greatest danger here is plagiarism, relying too closely on other writers without acknowledging them, leading a reader to think that their words or ideas are your own. Hence, what you paraphrase must be done carefully, and how you use the paraphrases in your own argument will determine the strength of your essay.

5. A *review* essay involves taking a particular study or group of studies on a topic and writing a review of them. Usually, a review involves some aspects of the expository essay in that it sets out the argument of the author(s) that you are reviewing, but in addition, it makes a critical evaluation of what is being reviewed. That evaluation can be either an assessment of the strengths and weaknesses of the work under review, or it can place the work in relation to other studies on the same topic or the more general

work in the field. Hence, a review of the most recent biography of Adolf Hitler should make some comment about recent work on Hitler and the Third Reich, perhaps alluding to some recent controversies or to new developments in the use of newly opened archives. The review might also make some brief comparisons with other biographies of Hitler. Reviews can be either formal or informal: formal reviews are like those that appear in scholarly journals that take into account new developments in their fields. Informal reviews are those that appear in the weekend papers and are often motivated by an attempt to sell books, though they can sometimes be more serious while still appealing to a broad and literate audience. In between are the collections of reviews (as in the weekly *New York Review of Books* or the *London Review of Books* or the *Times Literary Supplement*) that are really mini-essays on the topic of the book being reviewed. If you have to undertake a review, a useful shortcut is to go to some of the standard references to reviews of books and read some of the earlier reviews on the book(s) you are examining. Each discipline has ways of accessing these reviews (or you can consult some such resource as the *Book Review Digest,* the *Humanities Index,* or the *Social Science Index*). The library help desk can be of great assistance, and usually, the library provides a hand-out on searching for book reviews.

Finally, an *informal* essay is both too familiar and too much the object of dread. It includes the kinds of informal essays that appear on the op-ed pages and special writer's columns of newspapers, sometimes on off-beat topics, as well as the much feared stand-by of composition classes, "What I did in my summer holidays" (though it might be doubted whether any teacher actually had the nerve to assign such a topic). Very fine writers, often specialists in their fields, have made the informal essay into a *tour de force.* For instance, George Orwell was a master of the form, along with Virginia Woolf and many others. In your own writing, the informal essay is often a part of a creative writing class but may also be a part of a course in a standard Humanities or Social Science discipline. It has a more relaxed structure, does not depend upon argument so much as opinion, and sometimes tries to make its point by means of elegance of style or observation of human foibles.

FROM THE READINGS AND RESEARCH DATA TO THE ORGANIZATION OF THE ESSAY

After you have completed your research, you are ready to begin organizing your materials into the shape of an essay. When you were making your notes, gathering references and quotations and accumulating your research data, you were also making specific connections and links, which you now need to articulate directly. You should consider a number of sub-topics for your paper and begin to group ideas, research materials, and quotations together, noting any gaps or further possibilities for extension. For each of the topics, you might try a topic sentence that summarizes, at least in a temporary way, your position.

Another method involves laying out your materials either physically, by grouping your research notes on a desk or on the floor, or by putting them under headings on your computer. Then, you are faced with the challenge of moving from what you have found to what you will try to prove, from the raw materials to establishing a critical position or an argument. That move does not happen magically, randomly, or automatically. You need to think about how the parts of your materials are related, how they can be linked, what kinds of arguments they can support, what kinds of order they can be put into, and what the most effective presentation might be to meet the goals of your assignment.

Most essay topics demand analysis of events, ideas, data, or texts. Accordingly, mere narration, description, or enumeration of data will be insufficient. If you summarize a writer's ideas or arguments, it is important to do so briefly and clearly. Long summaries, extensive re-telling of narratives, and elaborations of facts do not contribute to analysis. You have to gauge the audience that you are writing for and need to remember that your instructors have also read the books. You are expected to understand the material, to be able to derive the key concepts of the course from your reading and research, and to relate them to the assigned topic. Doing so requires the use of all of your critical skills, of logical argument, analysis, and synthesis, a bringing together of ideas in an integrated way, often with a fresh approach. An outline will greatly help you with your organization, but a lot depends on how you set up your arguments to make your research and thinking work for you in your writing. The aim is to make your arguments communicate and to avoid impeding your ideas.

ORGANIZING YOUR READING NOTES ON YOUR WORD PROCESSOR

You can efficiently gather selected notes from your lecture notes and readings in preparation for writing class exercises, assignments, or research essays. Using a word processor will greatly assist you in making the best use of your time and resources.

Making reading or research notes on the computer is an easy task, especially if you are logical about how you organize your files. You may wish to open up a directory or folder for each course and place within that several sub-folders, perhaps one for the reading notes on your course texts, one for each assignment, and one for your notes on lectures, seminars, and summaries for exams. Entering such research notes into your computer makes assembling them later for your essay much easier, and it also eliminates one more step in which errors in transcribing quotations can creep in. In the assignment folder, several methods are possible for keeping your materials easily accessible.

Organizing Your Research Materials by Source

You may organize your materials according to the books or articles you read in preparation for your assignment. As you read each item, you can mark what you want to note afterwards, or you can make notes as you are reading. Frequently, the latter procedure results in making many more notes than you either need or can use, since you have not yet narrowed your topic to allow you to select strategically for your needs. It is important to read your materials critically and to record the pages where you want to make summaries or enter quotations. In either case, it is crucial to reference your work carefully.

Organizing Research Thematically

If you have already decided on your approach and the general topics under which your paper will be organized, it makes sense to set up your file according to the themes, issues, or problems that you will be discussing. Hence, the materials will already be assembled topically in preparation for your final paper.

Grouping Research Materials

A third method is to complete method one first and then to move through each of the sub-folders noting which material is to be grouped together. Then, you assemble the thematic file. As you can see, this method involves a cumbersome additional step. To make this step easier, some students use a printout of the results of the first method, then annotate it, and use that to select material for the preparation of the first draft, avoiding the thematic file completely. Again, it is important to emphasize that you should note carefully the references to all quoted or paraphrased passages that will be incorporated into your working and final drafts.

METHODS OF ORGANIZING AN ESSAY

There are various ways of setting out and approaching arguments, and we have discussed some of these matters as an aspect of critical thinking in Chapters 3 and 6. Here, we extend that discussion toward organizing your raw material into the form of an essay.

Process or Pre-determined Order

Ordering by process means moving through your material according to an order that is implicit in the material itself. Some topics, such as the description of a historical event, lend themselves to chronological order; some, such as scientific experiments, to cause-and-effect order; and some, such as the description of the action of a play or novel, to the order of events given in the work.

While it is effective and usually necessary to follow a process argument for certain stages of your argument, in isolating ideas for particular emphasis, it is important to avoid being dominated by the supposed "natural order," which might give your work an appearance of merely imitating or describing the concepts and patterns of the work, ideas, or event that you are writing on. For instance, a very common problem in ordering by process is summarizing plot in a literary essay or giving a long chronology of events in a historical essay, as if in either case the reader were unfamiliar with the context.

Parallelism, Comparison, and Contrast

A common problem beginning writers have in using comparison and contrast is discussing each item separately, detailing the particular ideas in each of the works without making meaningful connections. Such essays—in which, for instance, work A is linked to work B with very little comparison or contrast, concluding with a summary paragraph—can have the shape of a string of sausages.

An effective method of lending unity and coherence to a paragraph or a whole paper consists of developing a series of possible topic sentences for each paragraph and a working or tentative thesis statement for the whole essay. The paragraphs can then be set out through parallelism, comparison, or contrast. Such an organization of ideas allows you to explain your idea by revealing similarities and differences in relation to other examples. Furthermore, it demonstrates a broad reading background and shows that you are in control of the material that your course covers. An essay on an aspect of Shakespeare's plays, for instance, could draw parallels to his other works or to related ideas, characters, or events. Similarly, contrasts between these items can highlight your main point. In comparing, contrasting, or drawing parallels between works, events, or ideas, you may use one of several methods for structuring ideas in a paragraph or, indeed, in a whole essay:

1. One method is to discuss work or idea A first, and then work or idea B, with cross-references to A, and then to bring in work C to compare with works A and B. This is a ping-pong method, which is often awkward and confusing to both reader and writer. However, because it moves logically through each of the works, it appeals to an inexperienced writer. You need to be careful when using this method to stress the idea that you are explicating: it is your idea that should control your essay, not the logic of a whole work.

2. It is much better to discuss each of works A, B, and C by themselves briefly and then to focus for most of the essay on the particular grounds or ideas that you are comparing or contrasting. The same principle of organization is applicable to disciplines other than literature; for instance, in the sample question on Canadian history in Chapter 3, you could discuss immigration, urbanization, and industrialization by themselves briefly and then write a series of comparisons and contrasts on their effects in the assigned historical period.

3. The best method is to choose key themes or ideas on which to base your comparison and to set each of them in some context ("Three of the central ideas in Shakespeare's tragedies are the role of nature, the freedom of the protagonist to act, and the theme of order. Each of these...."). Then, you can move to compare each work with respect to these key concepts. This technique gives far greater scope for integration of arguments, emphasis, synthesis, and coherence.

Classification and Analysis

By means of classification you group things according to similarities or differences; analysis takes them apart into their elements and examines their relationships. In almost every essay, some classification will have to be undertaken to identify and set together similar ideas and arguments, to subordinate minor to major arguments, and to examine these classifications in a logical order. According to this method, the subject matter is divided into appropriate categories, both positive and negative.

Major point 1	Minor point A	Evidence pro and con
	Minor point B	Evidence pro and con
	Contrary minor point C	Evidence pro and con
Interim conclusions		
Major point 2	Minor point A	Evidence pro and con, etc.
Synthesis of points 1 and 2		
Analysis		

Consideration is given to which units may be related to larger divisions and which separated into smaller parts. When this method of organization is used, a third stage of argument is usually needed—synthesis—in which the parts, analysis, and classification are brought together into a fresh insight to support your thesis.

Illustration and Example

Almost every essay requires some illustration, example, or citation from a text to support your argument, and so this method is used in each of the models of organization. By using illustrations and examples, you develop the thesis from point to point, at each stage supplying some clarification. The method is useful for dealing with subjects that are made clearer with examples. For instance, when writing about freedom of speech and publication, examples of specific cases of the limitations of censorship would be particularly telling.

Illustrations are most effective when commented upon. You cannot expect that the connection that an example or illustration has with the topic will be absolutely clear; examples need your comment to make their place in your argument clear. Examples that are counter to your position are often particularly illuminating because they give your argument something to push against.

The danger of this method is that it may degenerate into points and examples that are merely strung together. You can maintain your reader's interest by moving from minor to major points in an ascending order. A further danger of this method is that it may give example after example of a point that has already been made conclusively and that needs no further argument. This elaboration of examples will try your reader's patience, as you will appear to be either re-stating the obvious or merely filling space to meet the length requirements of an assignment.

THESIS STATEMENT

Once you have stated the general topic, you need to formulate a thesis about the topic. A *thesis statement* puts your argument in a single, assertive sentence. It formulates the position that your essay will try to prove. A thesis statement is not a hypothesis. A *hypothesis* is a supposition or conjecture, which serves as a starting point for further investigation: it responds to questions that you begin to formulate about the topic and that you will revise during your research and reading for the essay. The hypothesis will change and become more carefully framed, taking into account more aspects of the text or problem being considered. A thesis, on the other hand, is a proposition that is stated and that is to be argued and defended. It is the end product of the creation of various hypotheses and represents the argument that the essay will make. In what follows, we go through the steps from a framing generalization or hypothesis to give direction to your research, to a finished thesis statement that instructs your reader in specific terms what and how you will argue.

But, like your hypothesis, the thesis statement will change throughout the planning and writing of your essay. At the planning stage, it is important to have a working thesis, a tentative statement about what it is that you are going to argue. This thesis statement will give focus to your planning and will help keep the outline and anticipated paragraphs under control. But it will have to be modified as you shape your argument. For instance, a tentative thesis statement on Riel and the Métis might be as follows:

> Riel's rebellion of 1885 was a failure in terms of the Métis participants but a success for the government of Canada and its military power because....

The "because" is left hanging because the reasons have been researched but are not yet clarified. The two-part thesis statement about success and failure is a way of focusing the rest of the content. But as the paper is outlined and the kinds of argument are clarified (and perhaps as the authorities are balanced and adjudicated), this working thesis can be refined:

> While Riel's rebellion of 1885 was a failure in terms of the Métis participants and their supporters (because of the humiliation and execution of the leaders and the scattering of Riel's followers), and while it was a success to the military and its government leaders, the very successes and failures gave it powerful symbolic importance to the Métis (the force of resistance to authority), the settlers (hope of self-control free of national constraints), the military (ability to crush rebellion is tested and proved), the government (national concerns can over-ride local issues).

Now the thesis statement is much more focused into an argument, and the two sides of opposition are being clearly drawn. But it is too diverse and too complicated, even though it is properly leading a reader through its parts. But such an elaborated thesis statement will serve throughout most of the planning and writing stages, until a final formulation is called for, perhaps at the end of the first paragraph of your essay, which will include some discussion of the points raised in this tentative statement. The final thesis statement might be as follows:

> In this essay, I shall argue that Riel's rebellion of 1885 is symbolic of the long-standing and continuing tension in Canadian life because it sets out clearly, and for the first time, the conflicts between native peoples' claims for land and traditional rights and the rights of the colonizers; between the federal authority and the local or provincial issues over freedoms, rights, land, and services; between the social and religious issues of the French and the English, the Catholics and the Protestants; and, finally, between the rival national interests of the Canadians and the Americans.

This more complete thesis statement is a clear proposal that guides a reader through what the essay will argue, stating the conclusion (rebellion is symbolic of tension and conflicts) and the terms (land claims; political authority; social, religious, and national interests) on which it will be argued. The "because" notion that was vague in the hypothesis has now been clarified, and the cause-and-effect relations between the symbolic importance and areas of public life where the symbolism applies are also clarified.

Potential problems with a thesis statement include the following:

- The thesis statement violates any of the six marks stated above: it is too long (more than one sentence), not focused, contains several ideas, is imprecise, unclear, or ambiguous (perhaps using terms in more than one sense). It may not take a stand on the topic or make no claim about the importance of the topic.
- The thesis statement is a truism: *The Riel rebellion is an important event in Canadian history.*
- The thesis statement is too broad: *For many reasons the Riel rebellion is symbolic of Canadian history.* When stated like this, the essay will very probably produce a list of reasons or examples without linking them to the topic.
- The thesis statement is too narrow: *The Riel rebellion ended the aspirations of the Métis in Manitoba.* If your assignment was to deal with the larger issues of the rebellion, this focus on only one aspect is much too limited. If you were free to formulate it on your own, you need to make it broader to give balance and make the implications clear from a number of perspectives.

- The thesis statement does not state your position about a critical argument: *I will show that the Riel rebellion illustrated the negative and positive aspects of the conflict between the Métis and the military.* The introduction with "I will show" suggests that you are going to reveal something new, when, in fact, what the phrase allows you to do is simply to list the evidence instead of arguing how it applies. The terms "negative and positive" are weak and do not indicate that the writer has taken a critical stand on the material, and the notion of "aspects of conflict between" does not indicate a critical position or answer the crucial questions about a thesis statement: What is being argued? How is it being argued?

A final thesis statement develops from a working thesis as the essay is written and is incorporated into the introduction after the essay is largely completed. As a student, you are writing as a professional; modern academic essay practice usually welcomes the first person in a thesis statement and opening declarations: "I shall argue that..., and my analysis will make use of the categories of...." Such formal directness is much preferable to the weakly anonymous and concealed agency of "One sees...," "This essay suggests...," or "We shall examine...." But you should check with your instructor if in doubt about using the first-person pronoun *I*. In phrasing your thesis statement, it is best to avoid weak assertions that begin with "It is evident that...," "It is obvious that...," or "It will be made clear that...." Such phrasing in a thesis statement suggests that your whole argument is unnecessary: if it is already evident, obvious, or clear, why are you arguing it? Such weak claims to self-evident truths are just fillers, and the real point that follows, perhaps still a self-evident truth that should be questioned or qualified, is what needs to be re-examined before you continue.

OUTLINE OR ESSAY PLAN

After you have thought about your topic, completed your research, decided on a method of organizing your essay, and developed a working thesis statement, it is time to draw up an outline of what you propose to cover in your paper. It is often necessary to make outlines in your head, as in writing essay questions on examinations. But in preparing formal essays, a careful and thoughtful writer will usually draw up a formal outline, which is usually not meant to be submitted. The following guidelines will help you in creating an outline:

1. An outline should begin with a statement of the tentative thesis or controlling idea that will be included in the opening paragraph.

2. Each major point is put into a numbered list and should support your thesis. There will likely be three or four of these major divisions.

3. Each major division then should be sub-divided into its parts, which are organized according to some coherent plan, and each may have two or three further sub-sections with a note about supporting arguments, data, or evidence. For a longer essay, even these sub-divisions might be further divided into major and minor arguments or sub-categories. However sub-divided the outline becomes, there should be a category in the outline for each of the paragraphs.

4. One way of checking your organization is to consider possible paragraphs that you will include under each of the main points and sub-sections. For instance, you can summarize each paragraph with a key word or idea.

5. In a more detailed outline, you can write a possible topic sentence for each of the paragraphs. Read over the topic sentences of each of the major divisions of your paper and ensure that they form a comprehensible argument. Often, you will complete this step in the actual writing of the paper, but if an essay proves difficult to organize, it could well form an independent step and would ensure a thoughtful and careful construction.

6. A draft of an introduction and conclusion, each in a tentative form, can be added to the introduction so that you have a further sense of focus and shape to your essay.

With this outline in hand, you are ready to write and edit your first draft and to have it read over by a friend in preparation for the preparation of a more finished draft and the final essay.

SUBMITTING DRAFTS OR OUTLINES FOR COMMENT

Many students ask whether an instructor will read outlines or drafts of essays. Many faculty members will agree to do so, especially for students who have shown that they can profit from in-office advice. Usually, instructors will suggest what forms of draft will be acceptable for reading and will indicate whether they will be marked or commented upon orally. You will, of course, be well aware of the deadlines for the finished assignment and should be prepared to hand in a draft or outline, if it is acceptable, well in advance of the due date. You should check with your instructor about an appropriate timetable. It is likely that you will be doing this work before the materials have been covered in class, so you might want an earlier office meeting to check your interpretation of the materials and topic for the assignment.

You should be prepared to suggest what kinds of drafts would be most helpful, from your viewpoint, to submit. You also need to be clear about whether you should submit these drafts or outlines, marked or not, with your final assignment or whether they are for your own preparation only. If your instructor is willing to read a draft or outline, you should submit it in double-spaced format and include questions about places in the argument where you are uncertain about meaning or interpretation. You also should try to make the outline or draft as clear and complete as possible in order to get the most benefit from your instructor's reading. Finally, you should use the information gained from the marked draft or outline to improve the preparation of the final version of your assignment.

CHAPTER SUMMARY

In the pre-writing stage, you have dealt with matters of structure and organization.

- You have determined the type of essay that you are writing and know how to combine your materials into an effective argument.
- You can summarize and organize your research into notes, useful quotations, and collections of data.
- You are familiar with the basic structures for organizing and outlining an argument.

- You can formulate an appropriate thesis statement from a hypothesis and a working thesis in its final and focused form.

This chapter has led you through the major stages of pre-planning your essay, emphasizing that organizing your data and research is a necessary step before moving to the detailed consideration of writing your argument, to which we now turn.

FURTHER READINGS

Paltridge, Brian. *Genre, Frames, and Writing in Research Settings.* Philadelphia: J. Benjamins, 1997.

Roth, Audrey J. *The Research Paper: Process, Form, and Content.* 8th ed. Belmont, CA: Wadsworth, 1999.

Steven, Laurence, Douglas H. Parker, and Jack Lewis. *From Reading to Writing: A Reader/Rhetoric and Handbook.* Scarborough, ON: Prentice Hall, 1989.

Veit, Richard. *Research: The Student's Guide to Writing Research Papers.* Boston: Allyn and Bacon, 1998.

chapter eleven

The Writing Stage

Chapter 11 sees you through the writing stage by giving detailed advice about the three major steps in preparing your essay: (1) writing the first draft on the computer, (2) building paragraphs into an argument, and (3) revising to make your style persuasive.

LEARNING OBJECTIVES

In this chapter, you will find answers to the following questions:

- How do you overcome writer's block?
- How do you use the computer to write and edit?
- How do you move from the outline you prepared to paragraphs that make an argument?
- How do you use quotations effectively?
- What methods are best for revising to correct faults in style and content?

WRITING THE ESSAY

Having completed your research and after planning your essay well in the pre-writing stage, you are now ready to begin writing and are faced with the blank screen on the computer, with your notes and books beside you. It is time to start.

Of course, you already have started and have completed notes, quotations, the beginnings of paragraphs; you have a clear sense of how it is going to be put together and are already launched into the writing process. Indeed, writing is a process, one which you began when you first started thinking about the topic and that you will continue in writing and revising to the final draft.

Now, when you are getting down to working on the first draft, you probably want to begin with page one, paragraph one, but it is almost certainly best to leave that alone for the moment and start with the first big argument for which you have collected most of your material. You will want to have that section in reasonable shape before you move to your supporting arguments. At each stage, you should check what you write against three things: (1) your preliminary thesis statement, (2) your outline, and (3) the assigned essay topic. As you proceed, add examples from your reading and research, deciding what must be cut to save space and what should be expanded for completeness. When you are fairly content with the shape of your main arguments, you can start to assemble them into a more final form. At this stage, you will work on the paragraphs, plan an introduction and conclusion and perhaps print a rough draft to look over. But once the planning is done, you might already be faced with writer's block.

Overcoming Writer's Block

None of the advice in the world will help if you cannot open that first computer file for your essay and apply fingers to the keyboard. Many writers, from the most experienced to the beginner, suffer from writer's block and find elaborate ways to put off starting to write. All writers agree that writing anything helps remove anxiety. Writing letters, taking notes, jotting something down for a future essay, making a note of an idea on the computer in a miscellaneous file—all of these activities will keep you thinking about writing and, more importantly, keep you practising it. A number of tricks are effective.

Writing against the Clock

Timing yourself is one trick. By this method, you start a timer or have a friend time you for five minutes while you write on your topic—you begin writing when the clock starts and then stop after five minutes. You are to begin on your topic, but if you cannot maintain ideas about it, you must write anything that comes into your head. It might well be that all you write has to be discarded; indeed, it very likely will have to be, but the purpose of the exercise is to begin the process of writing. This strategy can be used at any time to overcome writer's block, and you can write on any topic at all (sometimes called *free-writing*), or even by merely setting out your frustrations in language that only you need read.

Talking Through

To talk through a topic involves another person, preferably one who has some knowledge of your topic. As you talk about the topic, your friend takes notes of what you are saying and perhaps prompts with the occasional question or asks if you have thought of this or that argument. You might discuss the best means of organizing the paper or discuss an outline. Some teachers discourage involving other people in generating ideas or in overcoming writer's block because collaboration might undermine the originality of your ideas. If in doubt, check with your instructor. When you use this method, make sure that what you produce is your own work. An alternative is to record your talk-through on a tape recorder, which will allow you to go back and reconstruct what is useful from the exercise.

Brainstorming

Brainstorming consists of setting out as quickly as possible all of your ideas on a topic, however remote they seem from the topic. During brainstorming, little concern is given to specific order—the point is to get the ideas down. Then, you can organize them into a coherent shape, sequence, order, or outline. Several people can contribute to a brainstorming session, with one or more people recording all of the ideas. Again, you will have to find out whether your instructor recommends using such a process for your assignment.

Consulting with Your Teacher

Discussing your essay with your instructor can help you get started. You might test an idea or approach or get some further information about your topic. Perhaps aspects of it remain unclear to you and you need further explanation. Meeting with your instructor will help you refine your topic and often serves to stimulate writing, especially if you take notes during the meeting.

Using Paraphrases

Taking a passage from your research notes or a library book on your topic, reading it over, closing the text, and writing a paraphrase that sets out the same ideas in your own words, but in order of the writer you consulted, can get you started writing. You can write about someone else's ideas without becoming hung up on your own ideas so much. Further, since the paraphrase is a means of internalizing another person's ideas and argument, you can begin to react against them, expanding them, modifying them, and starting to write on your own.

Writing the First Draft on the Computer

Writing your first draft of an essay on the computer makes sense: it is much easier to organize your materials, move them around, correct and add to text, and form your notes into paragraphs. You can jot down ideas, gather them together, change, re-arrange, or delete them, all while editing what you write.

Preparing and Editing the First Draft

You can easily move words, lines, paragraphs, or large sections of your document with the word processor's "block and move" facility, using either the keyboard or the mouse. With this function, you can incorporate your quotations, examples, illustrations, and data from other files gathered during your research and work on your paragraphs and thesis statement.

You will sometimes find that your corrections are not as useful as the earlier version you had written. Word processors have an Undo function that takes you back step by step through your most recent corrections, sometimes for a number of stages so that you can return to earlier versions.

On the other hand, if you are reasonably content with a longer section of your paper, you can save it (as "draft A" or "argument 1"). A different version can be saved as "draft B." Eventually, you might decide that draft A was much better, so you can return to that version by calling up your saved document, which is a more efficient method for longer passages of writing than using the Undo function. You might wish to combine the two drafts, using draft A as your base argument but incorporating elements from draft B. Alternatively, you might have enough in each draft that you want to compare them, perhaps by printing them out and working through them, marking what you want to move to your final draft from the other. Using a hard copy makes some of this editing easier. Then, you have to move to editing the computer text.

Split Screens

For this stage of editing, word processors offer another useful facility, the split screen that allows two or more files or windows open on your monitor at the same time, say the folders draft A and draft B (see the word processor's Help topics on split screen). Using draft A as your basic document, you can move whatever sections from draft B you want into draft A by blocking and moving, and you can edit them there to make them fit into your argument. It may be necessary to reduce the size of the font to make more of the text fit into the screen, which you can split vertically or horizontally. Most word processing programs let you split the screen either vertically or horizontally, as you choose. You can also monitor or track your editing changes in any document and later can save them all, change them, or reject them (in Word choose Tools/Track Changes; in WordPerfect choose File/Document/Review).

Search or Find and Replace

The computer's Find or Search and Replace function helps you organize your paper in the early writing process and correct it carefully during editing the first and later drafts. These options allow you to move through your document to find the occurrences of a character, word, or phrase to modify them. You can find places in your essay where you have used the similar ideas or phrases that you might wish to link with a comment or move together. Or, if you have discovered a spelling mistake or a usage fault, you can check for similar slips in the rest of your essay. You can replace all occurrences automatically or make a decision about each occurrence separately.

BUILDING PARAGRAPHS AND ARGUMENT

Having made an outline and drafted a working thesis statement in the pre-writing stage and having some sketches of paragraphs in your notes, you can now begin to assemble this material, writing the linking paragraphs, working on the coherence and persuasiveness of your argument, and building the bridges between the phases of your thought and between your paragraphs.

A paragraph denotes a substantial division of thought. The movement from paragraph to paragraph through an essay should indicate the stages in the development of your argument. Paragraphs build your argument in stages: short, choppy paragraphs often indicate fragmentary argument and lack of synthesis, and very long ones often indicate problems in defining the stages of your argument.

The Topic Sentence

Each paragraph should develop one main idea or topic. That topic is usually, though not always, announced in the topic sentence that opens the paragraph. At times, however, it is effective to have a paragraph build to a topic sentence at the end. Each sentence in a paragraph should contribute to the logical development of that topic sentence—adding information or examples, bringing out implications, advancing pro and con arguments, and so on (see Paragraph Development below). If extraneous ideas are introduced that go well beyond the topic sentence, your point, and the reader, will quickly become lost.

The topic sentence unifies the argument of each paragraph. Assembled together, topic sentences should provide an outline of your argument.

The Infant and the Overgrown Paragraph

Many inexperienced writers have difficulty controlling larger passages of prose and fear that the topic sentence in a paragraph will be an inadequate umbrella for all of the following sentences. Out of anxiety, then, they break up their writing into "infant paragraphs" not fully grown, consisting of one or two sentences followed by another short paragraph, and then another. Such paragraphs usually need connecting, and so do the ideas. They need to be linked by interrelated ideas using guide or bridge words that inform the reader about the direction of your thought. On the other hand, fear of formulating a new topic sentence leads some writers to construct long paragraphs covering several topics and pages. To create paragraphs of a reasonable length, you should read over such long paragraphs and break them where a new topic begins.

Bridges or Links between Paragraphs

The reader should be able to follow the writer from paragraph to paragraph, and to accomplish that goal, a reader needs bridges, or links, between paragraphs. Bridges help your reader follow the transitions in your argument. Certain signposts help, such as conjunctions and conjunctive adverbs, which indicate where your thought is turning a corner: *accordingly, after, although, because, before, consequently, conversely, finally, first, for example, furthermore, hence, however, instead, on the other hand, moreover, nevertheless, nonetheless, however, therefore, while.*

Summary phrases also indicate these changes in direction clearly: some gathering phrase can summarize the argument or thought from the previous paragraph, for example, "This devastation from the bubonic plague...." or "Such arguments as these, common in the analysis of popular culture...."

Transition phrases that include short summaries also help, such as "I have already shown that...," or "I have argued that...." Then, the next paragraph might begin "A second consideration is...." However, you should avoid clichés, such as "Firstly, I should like to...," "As mentioned earlier...," or "In conclusion...." Such phrases slow your argument down by unnecessary repetition and irritate your reader by stating the obvious.

Paragraph Unity

Paragraph unity depends on the effectiveness of your analysis and argument, on your grammar and style, and on the connection of ideas to the paragraph's topic sentence. In each paragraph, you should stress main ideas and subordinate minor ones. Each part of a paragraph should relate to its central idea. A reader may stop at any point in a unified paragraph and see how the current sentence bears on the main topic. But the unity depends on more than the relationship of ideas to the main idea of the topic sentence. Unity is sustained through the logical development of ideas, so that a reader can follow what is being said. There are various ways of achieving that unity:

1. Unity of ideas is achieved by making sure that the paragraph is controlled by the topic sentence.

2. A key word is repeated from sentence to sentence, or suitable synonyms are used to keep the idea before the reader's eye: "A major factor in the decline of population was the arrival of the <u>bubonic plague</u> in Western Europe. The coming of the '<u>Black Death</u>' caused massive social dislocation. This <u>natural epidemic</u> was often interpreted in religious terms as a <u>judgment by God</u>. It was also interpreted as <u>the beginning of the end of the world</u>." The underlined phrases are partly synonymous and parallel, and they are summarized in the second-to-last sentence by "this natural epidemic."

3. Unambiguous pronouns refer back to key ideas (in the last example, "it" in the last sentence refers back to "natural epidemic" usefully and reinforces the notion in the reader's mind).

4. Demonstrative pronouns are followed with a "gathering word or phrase that focuses the ideas: for example, *this catastrophe; that disaster; these events; those developments*. Avoid using the unreferential "this" or "that" phrase ("This shows that..." or "This is..."), which has no specific antecedent but usually refers to an idea earlier in the paragraph. The vague "this" phrase leaves a reader to summarize the thought contained in the previous sentences without a useful gathering or summary noun and without any clear certainty about the writer's precise meaning.

5. Conjunctive adverbs are used within a unified paragraph to connect thoughts and draw distinctions: *however, moreover, also, nevertheless, therefore, thus, subsequently, indeed, then, accordingly.* When they begin a sentence, they are followed by a comma.

6. The ideas in a paragraph are arranged in some kind of systematic order, perhaps based on chronology (describing the sequence of events: first came this, then that, then that), on logic (stating major to minor premises or cause and effect), or on space (describing a house or journey, for example, in some order).

Paragraph Development

Paragraphs should move out from the topic sentence by way of illustration, contrast, or data. There are a number of conventional ways of developing a paragraph, many of which will occur to you when you are working through your research materials in the pre-writing stage and when you are preparing your outline.

Using Definition, Explanation, and Illustration

1. Terms may be defined, or a topic may be divided into its parts. However, you should not use general dictionaries to reduce complex terms to simplistic definitions. Too simple definitions do not open up the beginning of your essay. You should define technical terms of a course (such as *hysteria, semiotics, paranoia,* or *repatriation*) through course readings or lectures, specialized subject dictionaries, or the *Oxford English Dictionary.* You should provide a definition only if it is integrated into your argument—in other words, you need not feel obligated to define what is common currency in your course unless you are pushing that definition in ways that you will develop in your argument.

2. An explanation may demonstrate how a phenomenon operates.

3. Examples or illustrations may explicate parts of your argument.

4. Persons, places, things, events, or ideas may be explained or described.

5. An anecdote or quotation may expand or qualify the topic.

Providing Evidence

1. Causes or reasons for discussing the subject may be explored.

2. Evidence or data may be cited to support the argument. Information may be in the form of statistics, facts, details, or precedents.

3. An authority may be quoted or paraphrased in support of the argument, with proper attribution of sources. An authority may also be quoted for purposes of disagreement; however, in the logic of evidence, such a statement must prove the contrary of your argument (pro and con arguments).

4. Something related to the topic may be compared and contrasted, or various degrees, conditions, or stages in the topic may be indicated.

5. Effects or consequences may be pointed out.

6. The relevance of evidence to your argument is demonstrated. No evidence is self-explanatory, transparent, or naturally a part of an argument. If it appears to be self-explanatory, consider carefully whether or not you are stating the obvious.

Providing Analysis

1. Analysis moves from definitions and descriptions to using the evidence to build a case, formulate an argument, assess the importance of the parts of a text or problem, and prepare a critique.

2. To do so, an analysis identifies and explains the relationships among parts of a text or problem, assessing the significance of the parts and their place in the whole. An analysis usually requires an argument about *what* is being said and *how* it is being said—how the argument or narrative in the text is put together, how a problem has been formulated, and how that construction contributes to the meaning of the whole. Sometimes, attention is given to how the reader is involved in creating an interpretation.

3. The analysis prepares for an evaluation, a summation of the strengths and weaknesses of the arguments about the problem or the text, a comment on the validity of those arguments, and a critique of its intellectual position.

These ways of developing a paragraph are derived from the five ancient methods of inventing (or discovering) arguments in Greek and Roman rhetoric:

1. *Definition*: defining by kind, or dividing an idea or thing into its constituent parts
2. *Comparison*: showing similarity, difference, or degree
3. *Relationship* (*causation*): showing cause and effect, antecedence and consequence, or contraries and contradictions
4. *Circumstance*: considering the possible and the impossible, fact and future fact, differences or degree, or difference of size
5. *Testimony* (*evidence*): citing authority, testimonial, statistics, law, maxims, precedents, or examples

These methods can still be applied to any subject. You can also review a list of common topics as headings for suitable arguments and as a stimulus to new ideas.

Major and Minor Ideas

Arguments in paragraphs often move most easily from the general to particular details (the deductive method) or from theory to practice. They may also move from an assertion of a main point to a demonstration or analysis of it and then to an explanation or evidence. Mere assertion does not constitute argument, nor does summary of either your material or someone else's ideas. Inductive reasoning, which moves from particular examples to a general theory, is a more difficult method of arguing.

In any case, you should place main ideas in main or independent clauses and more minor ideas in subordinate clauses. Furthermore, you should place the main ideas in positions of emphasis in the paragraph, such as in the topic sentence: "The central reason for the widespread investment uncertainty is the weakness of the Asian economic markets, but other reasons also have an impact: the weakness of the Canadian dollar, soft domestic consumer demand, and wide-scale unemployment." In the paragraph following this topic sentence, each of the three reasons would be discussed in order.

Thesis Statement

Even if you have not yet drafted your introductory paragraph, you will want to put your working thesis statement into your draft near the beginning. Since we discussed the formulation of a thesis statement in detail in Chapter 10, it is sufficient here to review and summarize what we said there.

A thesis statement shapes your specific topic. To your reader, it serves as a map for your essay: it directs your argument and suggests the focus that you will bring to bear on your topic. It also maps out the direction to your conclusion. If your statement is too general, it needs sharper focus and definition, perhaps by sub-division into relevant parts. The more particular your thesis statement and the more focused your topic, the easier it will be to organize and write your essay. Put another way, the thesis statement answers your research question or formulates the controlling idea of your paper. A strong thesis statement answers the question that a reader might formulate: What is this essay going to argue? How will it argue it (both content and form of the argument)? Why is it important to the writer?

There are six marks of a good thesis statement:

1. It can be stated in one sentence.
2. It is specific, restricted, and focused.
3. It is unified—it has only one main idea.
4. It is precise, unambiguous, and clear.
5. It takes a stand or position.
6. It justifies the fact that what is being discussed is important, not by the use of the word *important* but because it makes clear to a reader that the issue is worth discussion.

Usually, the thesis statement is located in the introductory paragraph of an essay, but not as the first sentence. Since you want the reader to be in tune with your argument as soon as possible, you need to prepare for your thesis statement by building to it. Hence, the thesis statement comes somewhere in the middle of the introductory paragraph or at the end of it.

Introductory and Concluding Paragraphs

The opening and concluding paragraphs state your thesis before and after proof. They shape the whole essay and so require a good deal of work in the planning stages. The actual writing of the introductory paragraph, however, might be the last thing you do in your rough draft.

The first paragraph should catch your reader's attention. There are various methods of doing so, such as opening with a controversial opinion or quotation, a counter-position (which can be argued against), a question (which can be answered), or a summary of your position or the issue in a balanced phrase or sentence. The topic and the thesis should appear prominently. For most papers, an introductory paragraph of five or six sentences is usually adequate, moving from the general toward the more specific statement of the thesis (sometimes in the last sentence) and offering a bridge to the main body of the paper. The funnel method shows how an introduction can be structured (see Figure 11.1).

FIGURE 11.1	The Funnel Method for Introductions

Opening statement(s) or hook to catch the reader's attention.

General statement, idea, concept, or allusion. Avoid sweeping and irrelevant generalizations.

More focused points: perhaps leading to the thesis statement saying what and how you will argue.

Most focused position, perhaps qualifications, leading into the body of the essay.

The funnel method for an introductory paragraph involves moving from the general to the specific, narrowing your focus, just as the sides of the funnel come to a point. To find an opening statement as well as the large general idea, move back from your working thesis statement to ask how it relates to the general field or larger issues. Your topic exists in a wider context, and use that to focus. Then narrow the topic further, to lead into your thesis statement. Follow that up with further questions or qualifications, or link the paragraph back to the opening, or build a link to bridge to the body of your essay.

A note of caution, however, is needed here: beginning writers often misuse the funnel method, moving from a generalization to the thesis statement by beginning their introductory paragraph with sweeping generalizations that are only remotely related to or are banal formulations of their topic ("The Holocaust is an unforgettable event in the history of Europe"). Alternatively, they might begin badly by stating the well-known facts of a historical period ("World War I lasted from 1914 to 1918") or of an author's life or work ("The Canadian author, Margaret Atwood, has won many literary prizes"). An opening generalization should always be governed by the specific focus of your topic.

Many students are tempted to go for some peripheral general context of the topic, rather than for a relevant point. For instance, if your topic were Germany's emergence as a world power from its colonization of Africa in the 1880s and how it contributed to World War I, it would be inappropriate to begin with the general effects of World War I, assertions about how terrible that war was, or how it changed the course of history. Such assertions are incontestable but are irrelevant here. Instead, if you could locate a detail in Germany's colonization of Africa that raised the issue of competition with England and France (two recognized world powers), that detail could serve as a general template for your argument. Alternatively, you could formulate a generalization about Germany's emerging nationalism at the beginning of the 20th century and be well on your way. To test whether your opening statement introduces your focused topic, you can ask how closely it is related to the specifics of your topic. If it is an extension of the topic, it is too remote and needs narrowing or re-thinking.

Two very different corrected introductory paragraphs are set out in Figure 11.2. The first introduction (compiled from two students' essays) is marred by faults in both content and form. It begins with a large and obvious pair of poorly linked generalizations that have nothing to do with the topic of the paper. The rest of the paragraph fails to come to a focus, and shifts from idea to idea with almost no relationships among them. The potential thesis statement ("In *The Color Purple* the master/slave ethic dominates") still remains an assertion of what might be argued, but it does not continue to set out how that will be argued. Finally, the numerous mistakes in grammar, punctuation, spelling and style and wrong words indicate that the student has given little time to prepare the essay, revise it, or proofread it.

The second essay (from one student only) follows a logical order, beginning with a general statement about the two characters on which the essay will focus. The rest of the paragraph narrows that focus from "fabrications of science," to "incomplete fabrications," to a claim about what they lack (their "signifier" or real personal name in each case), to their quest to find their names, and to the special focus of that quest in seeking "knowledge, both of themselves and of their worlds." The paragraph builds to a thesis statement in the last sentence, showing what will be argued, and how it will be argued. The sentences are varied stylistically, and the diction is appropriate (except for the lack of definition of technical terms, which could follow in a second paragraph). The format and lack of mistakes in grammar, punctuation, and spelling make this paragraph a pleasure to read and an effective introduction to the argument that follows.

The concluding paragraph is the summation of your essay, where you state the final position for which your argument and examples are the proof. The conclusions you draw should not exceed the limits of what you have argued or your evidence, but they should state your thesis more fully; in other words, you should not introduce new arguments in your conclusion but should explain what you have done. Avoid simply re-stating your hypothesis in the same words as in your introduction. Above all, resist introducing trivial-

---

| FIGURE 11.2 | **Two Corrected Introductory Paragraphs** |

topic stce: is not what para covers

Within every novel there is a wide range of episodes that take place during the process of reading the novel. Each one of these episodes consists of its own beginning, middle and end, and tells a piece of the story, which can then be put together to create the entire novel.

? generalization wrong–first ½ is a truism, 2nd ½ confuses story & reading it. This what? antec *quite* /ww δ to start ¶ here

ital for book title redund. phrase and del pc

This∧ is <u>quite</u> prevalent within the book, The Color Purple, <u>where the entire novel</u> is written in individual letters, that <u>put together</u>, tell the story of the life of a young black girl. Hence

ww

it is a epistol<u>any</u> discourse. Because it is made up of letters,

sp

sp Her name is Celie

ww pretentious usage: misunderstood technical term

it is called an <u>epistolary or epistemology</u>. In *The Color Purple* the master/slave ethic dominates. As <u>Cecile</u> begins to negotiate her reality and create for herself <u>and</u> alternative world, these values and customs are hightlighted. Mr– loves

this stce could be beginning of thesis statement ww cliché no such word /sp contr

note how para moves from structure to genre to theme and then to characters and re-telling of the narrative. No focus

Shug and he continues <u>serinating</u> her as the <u>cream of the crop</u> wherever she sets foot. But Celie <u>can't</u> write. The words Celie uses explain her meaning fully but <u>grammar wise</u> her speech and writing is incorrect. What she is trying to say is understandable∧however, she could better express herself through the use of grammatical correctness.

false modifier subj-vb agr pc and run on stce

/Mary /Gene add first name when first mentioned

The fictional characters of the "monster" and "Data" in Shelley's *Frankenstein* (1818-31) and Roddenberry's *Star Trek: The Next Generation* (1988) are depicted as fabrications of science, but as incomplete fabrications. They lack complete signs themselves and the ability to use sign systems. Once they discover their "signifier" (the "word image" applied to them—their names) they both go on a quest for

Clear topic stce summarizes para

good use of semiotic theory but terms need defining, perhaps in footnote?

pc at end of parenthesis /,

knowledge that includes, in part, some definition of their "signified" (the "concept" that differentiates them from others). ∧ This quest brings hardship to each of them and

close #

forces them to question both their fabrication and their fabricators. They seek the reasons for their creation. This paper will follow a path similar to the fantasy quest that each of these "life-forms" follows, comparing their process of creation and their quest for knowledge, both of themselves and of their worlds.

Thesis statement at end of para

---

izing, throw-away sentences that leave your reader with the impression that you have run out of gas. As in your opening paragraphs, your conclusion should be free of empty generalizations ("Therefore, Margaret Atwood is a great writer" or, "Hence, World War I was hated by all the nations who fought in it").

| FIGURE 11.3 | The Reverse Funnel Method for Conclusions |

Topic sentence of the conclusion again should catch the reader's attention.

Re-formulation of the thesis statement, not just "What I have demonstrated" but a re-writing of it, without introducing new claims, data, arguments, or evidence.

Some claims about how your analysis related to the general field or larger issues/context of your topic.

A concluding statement, perhaps a quotation, perhaps elaborating your opening.

The reverse funnel method for a conclusion moves from the specific to the general, the reverse of the introductory paragraph. The broadening focus opens the conclusion out for your reader, summarizing and re-stating your thesis, not merely repeating it, pointing out how its implications relate to the general field. You might already have alluded to that earlier in your essay, but here you draw attention to it again, showing how your discussion fits in with the larger context.

The reverse funnel method is a good means for structuring your conclusion (see Figure 11.3). A conclusion should gather your argument into its final focus, moving from the details of the essay to the larger idea of your thesis again. Or it may move from a re-statement of the thesis to a consideration of its implications as brought out in your evidence.

This ending should be emphatic and confident, not apologetic. Avoid the inane phrases "In conclusion …" or "In summary…," which try to hide the lack of appropriate integration. Sometimes, a summary of your argument, if it has been complex, will help the reader recall your main points. Or you may wish to point toward the conclusion that your evidence supports. Even a pithy example that summarizes your thesis would make your conclusion strike home. Another strategy for concluding may be to call attention to the limits of your argument as stated in your thesis—that is, to re-state your thesis to draw attention to the propositions and factors that went into your argument and suggest how changing these facts might lead to different questions, arguments, and even conclusions.

USING QUOTATIONS

Appropriate quotations from documents you worked on in the research stage can illustrate your point briefly and pointedly, lead a reader through your ideas by means of example, and allow easy comparison of texts and ideas. But quotations also have to fit in with your argument to provide appropriate evidence. Quotations can be used to support arguments, serve as a point of disagreement in launching an argument, or provide an illustration. They should not be used to support matters of acknowledged fact nor merely to confirm what you have just paraphrased or summarized. Wherever you are using another writer's direct words, you need to use quotation marks and give the source for your quotation. We raise here a number of considerations regarding the use of quotations when building your paragraphs and arguments.

- **Use quotations to support arguments.** Quotations can give powerful support to your argument. Use a quotation if it makes the point you wish to emphasize in a clear and brief passage. However, nothing is accomplished if the quotation supports your argument through a long, tortuous, and many-faceted passage. If the quotation is not brief and clear, you should summarize it in your own words and give a specific reference for the idea.

- **Use quotations for purposes of disagreement.** You may also use quotations effectively to provide counter-positions, which you can then disagree with or qualify. This use of quotations depends upon considerable knowledge about your topic and is most effective when you have a fresh angle to pursue. An intemperate or unreasoned attack on a critic might seem like adolescent iconoclasm. Beware of the fallacy of the straw man (see Chapter 6) in using this approach.

- **Use quotations for illustration.** Complex arguments, difficult philosophical positions, and abstract reasoning often demand illustration, and sometimes a succinct quotation saves much lengthy and tedious explanation. Illustration, especially in essays on literary topics, is one of the primary ways of bringing in supporting evidence for your position. A quotation can summarize a character's qualities of mind, give a vivid description, and allude to figures of speech or qualities of language.

- **Explain your use of quotations.** Because an appropriate quotation can illustrate an argument well, many students think it can replace argument. Experienced writers use quotations to illustrate their own arguments or to summarize them. You should use quotations to support (or counter) a position that you must argue on your own. Quotations need to be introduced with a phrase or an explanation to show how they relate to your argument as evidence or as proof, and they need to be commented on later to draw out their implications or to make a point. That is, the purpose of a quotation by itself is not self-evident, nor can your reader infer easily how you see it as applying to your argument or conclusion. You need to specify how and why you are using it and what you conclude from it.

In what follows, we set out nine areas concerning quotations that deal with ways of using quotations to build your arguments and methods of integrating them into your prose style.

Quoting Accurately

Direct quotations reproduce the words of another writer or speaker accurately. If you are using someone else's words from any source, you *must* use quotation marks (or single space and indent) and give the source for your information. Failing to do so involves you in serious problems concerning the illegal use of other people's words and can lead to charges of plagiarism. See proper methods for documentation and warnings about plagiarism in Chapter 9.

Avoiding Quotations at the Ends of Paragraphs

It is tempting to end a paragraph with a quotation from some authority on your topic, a quotation that sounds strong and unassailable. However, then you move on to the next paragraph, leaving the authority dangling in mid-air. It is much better to comment on the quotation you have used, showing how it makes your point or provides some useful qualification. You may also wish to note what is not said in the quotation.

Introducing Quotations and Commenting on Them

Quotations are introduced with an identifying phrase to show their function in your argument as illustration or evidence. Their role is not self-evident, so your reader needs to know why and how you are using a quotation. Such introductions usually include the author's name to prepare the reader for your evidence and source:

> *As Freud observed, "Hysteria is a fantasy carried to the level of sickness"* (direct quotation). *"Hysteria," as Freud observed, "is a fantasy carried to the level of sickness"* (direct quotation, source embedded).

Or, you might wish to make the most of your own sentence:

> *Commenting on hysteria, Freud called it a "fantasy" approaching a "sickness"* (direct quotation of two words; the rest is paraphrase).

You might wish to turn the ideas into indirect quotation and some paraphrase:

> *Freud said that hysterical persons were suffering from some fantasy that was so serious that it had become a genuine sickness* (the two words could be in quotation marks, but the direct quotation sense is not so clear, and quotation marks would tend to mean that the words are being used in a special sense).

In each case, it is necessary to give the sources for your quotations. A quotation should almost always be followed by some interpretative comment of your own to explain its significance for your purposes.

Using Short Quotations

There is no absolute rule about what makes a quotation short or long, and different sources specify different numbers of lines. Usually, quotations shorter than four lines should be integrated in your own prose, introduced with a colon or a comma and enclosed in double quotation marks. A critic writes: "In the preface to *Jane Eyre,* Charlotte Brontë says that appearances should not be mistaken for truth" (4). If the lines are poetry, it is customary to set out more than two lines as block quotations. Shorter quotations of poetry indicate line endings by a slash with a space on either side: "In *Hamlet,* Polonius offers his conventional advice to Laertes by first giving his blessing: 'There—my blessing with thee, / And these few precepts in thy memory'" (1.3.57–58).

Inserting Long Quotations

Long quotations of more than four lines of prose are usually separated from your own text, usually introduced by a colon, indented 10 spaces, and typed double-spaced (some instructors want indented quotations single-spaced: check if unsure). Indented longer quotations never have quotation marks, unless the passage quoted begins with quotations marks, in which case they are reproduced exactly as in the original. The quotation ends with the source reference in parentheses.

Inserting Explanations

A word or phrase of explanation added to a quotation should be enclosed in brackets. When you omit material from a quotation, you need to use three spaced dots for the omission (called an *ellipsis*), followed by any necessary terminal punctuation.

Setting Quotations within Quotations

Single quotation marks are used for the internal quotation:

> The actor said, "Hamlet's answer, 'Nothing,' is nonsense."

Periods and commas are usually put within the closing quotation marks; colons and semicolons are put outside them. Other punctuation is placed according to sense.

Summarizing Quotations in Paraphrases

You can use various methods to summarize or otherwise change a writer's comments to adapt them to your style:

1. A *paraphrase* reproduces the content of the original in different words, attempting to clarify meaning and perhaps give some interpretation. Often longer than the original, a paraphrase retains all of the central ideas in the order of the original; however, the ideas and examples are all put into the (usually) simpler language of the writer. One method is to read any page of your source, perhaps the introduction or conclusion, and then to shut the book and write out in a single fairly short paragraph the summary of the major points that are made. Now the book can be opened and checked for accuracy. The same procedure can be applied to your notes on what you have read. If you want to use the detailed notes that summarized the argument of a writer's chapter, you have to summarize them or set out individual parts of the argument in a paraphrase. The proper role of paraphrase lies in moving toward understanding difficult concepts or arguments; danger lies in using paraphrase as a *substitute* in a research essay for your own thought or ideas. If it is used as a substitute and the source of the ideas is not properly acknowledged, the student might be in danger of a violation of academic honesty approaching plagiarism.

2. A *précis,* or a succinct summary, condenses the original while retaining the sense; it may omit substantial illustrations or examples, quotations, or subordinate arguments but will include all of the main arguments.

Both these methods "translate" the ideas of the author into the language of the writer; you should acknowledge the source in a reference.

Including References for Quotations

The APA and MLA styles of documentation include references in the text and make them as clear and short as possible (see Chapter 9). Hence, unambiguous references to a document, poem, play, or novel repeatedly quoted in the course of a paper should be given directly after the quotation. References are made to line numbers in standard editions; to page numbers if a common text is used by the reader and the writer; or to chapter, act, scene, and line (for plays):

> Milton tried to "justify the ways of God to men" (*Paradise Lost* 1.26).

This reference would be used in an essay where Milton is cited only occasionally; if the whole essay were on *Paradise Lost,* the book and line references would be sufficient by themselves.

Hamlet said, "What a piece of work is a man!" (2.2.316).

REVISING: CONTENT AND ARGUMENT

Having worked through your introduction and conclusion and set out your quotations in order in your linked paragraphs, you are ready to take a look at the whole draft. At this stage of your writing, and with the deadline approaching fast, it is tempting only to glance over the argument to see if it makes rough sense. But the difference between a C paper and a high B or A paper often comes in right here. Revise so that your content and argument say exactly what you want them to say, with clarity and coherence. Be aware that the most common problems students have with their essays concern four matters:

1. The thesis statement (none at all, or it is too narrow or too broad)
2. The introductory and concluding paragraphs (too general, one simply repeats the other, no focus)
3. The organization (no direction or structural principles, no clear indication about why this order is used, or no bridges or links between parts of the argument)
4. Sloppy formatting (not double-spaced, typos, misspelled words, wrong instructor, course number)

First, do not revise your draft on the computer. You need to move away from it to gain as much objectivity as you can. Print out the draft and move to a clear part of your desk. Clear space as though you are clearing your mind, since you are moving from being the writer to being the editor. You are shifting your mental processes. The editor's function is to evaluate, make judgments, and read critically. Read through your draft carefully, noting inaccuracies, places lacking continuity, as well as unclear phrasing or other faults or places that need re-working. There is no doubt that some of it will have to be re-written.

Use the Self-Evaluating Your Essay questions at the end of this chapter as a checklist to go over your draft. Pay particular attention to the following points:

- Essay title and its relation to your thesis statement
- Introductory and concluding paragraphs where the reader will get a first impression of the quality of your work
- The first main point in your argument and its relation to your thesis statement
- The bridges between your paragraphs

In the revision of content and argument, you should note how your argument develops from the topic sentences of paragraphs. As you are revising, you can ask yourself questions, such as: "What do I mean here?" "Is this point clear?" "Is this argument supported by pertinent evidence?" "How do I know this fact?" Often, the question "What is my point here?" will clarify your argument.

Now see whether the argument as a whole hangs together by reading *only* the first and last sentences in each paragraph throughout the essay. If there are failures in continuity, mark them in the margins, but continue throughout fairly quickly to get to the end. Go back to the places you marked, and tighten up the links and bridges, reading a few paragraphs before and after to see that the continuity problem is solved. Quickly look over your outline and a few of your final notes to see if anything is left out, and if so, add it now.

The last step in the revision of content and argument is to go back to the computer with your corrected copy and enter the changes. Again, you step back into the writing mode, but this time with the editor's hat still on. If everything is now completed, you are ready for the polishing of your style.

REVISING: STYLE AND PERSUASION

Revision has a variety of purposes: to correct mistakes in spelling, grammar, and punctuation; improve paragraph structure and coherence; and especially refine lapses in argument and examples. A thesaurus will help you think of synonyms; a dictionary or a spell checker on the computer is usually more useful in checking proper spellings at the revision stage, rather than at the writing stage when you want to set out your ideas.

Your argument can be very well organized and your paragraphs carefully laid out, but if your writing contains grammatical or punctuation mistakes, your essay needs to be corrected (see Chapter 12). If it breaks with conventional usage or has faults in idiom or phrasing, your reader will be put off and the strengths of your argument will be obscured.

On the practical level, you still need to be working with a printout. Print the draft again (notice that this draft is at least the second, and perhaps the third). And once more go over it with a pen or pencil as an editor, looking this time for faults in your writing style. Some people find that it is possible to combine revision for argument and for style in one exercise on one draft. But if you are having trouble with the revision stage, we suggest that you try dividing the exercise into two steps. When you are a little more experienced, you might find it more efficient to combine the steps into one.

Once again you can use the Self-Evaluating Your Essay section at the end of this chapter to help with your revision of style. Mark the correction as if you were coming new to this draft as a final essay. If you have developed your rhetorical skills—the stylistic strategies to persuade your reader—your argument will be clear. In this section, we address eight common rhetorical problems.

Avoiding Meaningless Abstractions

It is important to avoid generalizations that are undocumented, unsubstantiated, or irrelevant to your thesis. Abstract concepts are used to provide distance from what is often taken to be a singular and common sense meaning of something. As such, they enable us to examine that phenomenon, whether it is sociological data, a historical problem, or a literary text, in new and different ways that open conventional interpretations to question. Such questioning depends on both the adequacy of the abstract argument and the relevancy of the examples.

When using abstract language, you need to be careful that your concepts are actually communicating ideas and arguments that are relevant to your topic. A tendency in beginning writers is to use abstractions that are empty: "The militaristic hostilities of the United

States instituted a process of tremendous deprivation, disorientation, and dislocation that traumatized the citizens of Iraq." This notion could be better expressed without the meaningless abstractions: "In engaging in carpet bombing, the United States caused tremendous suffering for the common people of Iraq."

Modifiers, whether adjectives or adverbs, should have a purpose in qualifying what they modify. Stringing together empty qualifiers, such as *excellent, meaningful, interesting, beautifully, widely,* and especially *hopefully,* makes your prose and argument vapid. As well, you should avoid circumlocutions (beating around the bush, or refusing to come to the point), unless you wish to achieve a special effect. You should also beware of slang, buzzwords (*interfaces, parameters*), colloquialisms (*I eyeballed him*), and technical jargon, such as the now current computer jargon (*boot up these ideas; get online with that plan*). Such language may be appropriate for particular audiences, but generally, in academic writing, it should be avoided. An essay is often much clearer when it uses concrete language.

Avoiding Unnecessary and Pretentious Words

Cutting out wordiness is an essential to revision. Fillers—words that are unnecessary—should be struck out ruthlessly. They are padding that increases your word count but does nothing for your argument:

> *It is very clear that* **when** *looking at and* **assessing this** *very* **historical development, you cannot** *begin to* **review** *aspects of ethnicity in the light of* **multiculturalism without** taking into careful account **both its liberal and conservative goals** *as their supporters have tended to state them.*

Most of this sentence from a student's essay is padding, marked in italics. By changing the underlined phrase to *considering,* the sentence would read as marked in bold:

> When assessing this historical development, you cannot review multiculturalism without considering both its liberal and conservative goals.

Now, the pruned sentence is far clearer.

Edit your text to get rid of the commonest empty words, some substitutes for a single clear term, and others just unnecessary:

> all during the time that, throughout the time of (for *during*)
>
> as a matter of fact
>
> at the moment
>
> at the present (time, moment, period, on the present occasion—when you mean *now*)
>
> because of (due to) the fact that
>
> by means of, by way of (instead of *by*)
>
> for the purpose of …-ing (replace with *to*)
>
> have a tendency to (replace with *tend*)
>
> in a very real sense, in every sense
>
> in connection with (in reference to) (for *about*)
>
> in the case of, in respect to, in reference to, with regard to (for *concerning)*
>
> in the final analysis

in the event that

in process of

last but not least

of a like mind with, one of a kind with (for *like)*

that point in time, at that day and age, in days gone by (for *then*)

type of

Getting rid of most of these redundancies will involve slight revision.

> As a matter of fact, the history of the Second Iraqi War could only have been written because of the fact that the war correspondents accompanied the troops into battle by means of tanks in which space existed for them to be embedded.

Revise to cut out the wordiness:

> The history of the Second Iraqi War could only have been written because war correspondents accompanied the troops into battle embedded in tanks.

A similar problem involves making your writing sound more impressive by using fancy words. Sometimes, your words are unclear because you use *euphemisms* (words that say indirectly what people avoid saying directly, particularly concerning sex, disease, and death). Euphemisms conceal direct meaning, hiding it behind the language of avoidance.

adult entertainment (pornography)	change of life (menopause)
downsizing (firing)	financial incentives (bribes)
passed away (died)	funeral directors (undertakers)

Other words are pretentious because they try to give a more sophisticated tone to your writing and use longer, or more obscure, words instead of simple and direct words:

ascertain (find out)	commence (begin)
endeavour (try)	exists (lives)
facilitate (help)	institution of higher learning (college, university)
finalize (end)	reside (live)
terminate (end)	utilize (use)

Using Active Verbs in Assertive Sentences

Verbs in the active voice usually convey greater precision and power than those in the passive voice. Assertions are more effective than weak, negative evasions. How feeble it is to say, "The memory of that wedding will not soon be forgotten." How much stronger it is to say, "We shall long cherish the memory of that wedding." To avoid introducing a personal perspective, opinion, or argument, many writers for newspapers, journals, and magazines use passive constructions. (Indeed, journalists and their editors would re-write this sentence to read "Passive constructions are used by many writers.") Sometimes, passive constructions use the past participle ending in *-ed*: "This use of language is required by many teachers and editors" instead of "many teachers and editors require this use of language." Turning passive constructions into active ones almost automatically enlivens your prose and makes it more immediate by focusing attention on the doer of the action, rather than on what is done.

You should also try to avoid the almost omnipresent copula verb. Instead of writing "Another set of circumstances is when the spots on the moon were seen by Galileo as bumps," you should write, "The world-view changed when Galileo looked at the spots on the moon and called them 'bumps.'" You should also avoid like the Black Death tiresome phrases, such as: "it is seen," "there is," "there are," or "an example is when." These unreferenced uses of the copula verb conceal the agent of the action.

Introducing Variety into Your Style

Variety in diction, phrasing, sentence structure, and paragraphs will improve your writing. Some of your ideas and sentences should be balanced; some sentences should be simple, some compound or complex. Sentences should begin and end differently, unless you are seeking a particular effect through repetition.

Using Descriptive Adjectives and Adverbs

Appropriate and precise adjectives and adverbs will qualify your position and enable you to convey far more subtle shifts in meaning. Vague and general descriptors will reduce your argument to meaningless platitudes. You should avoid the intensifier *very,* which rarely communicates the enthusiasm that you might feel, and above all, abominate *very interesting,* a bankrupt description. Modifiers should fall close to the words they modify. Other vague intensifiers include both the adjectival and adverbial forms of *apparent* (*apparently*): *clear, evident, obvious*, and other words that assert that something is self-evident. Such assertions of the self-evident indicate problems in your argument.

Using Precise Connectives

You need to be certain about the precise shades of meanings that you wish to convey by your use of conjunctions and conjunctive adverbs. Consider, for instance, the differences in meaning that can be accomplished by using a variety of them between the two clauses of a sentence such as: "Jane's mother was dying; _____ the doctor saved her."

although	because	before	nevertheless	nonetheless	however
therefore	moreover	indeed	while	though	hence	consequently
accordingly	meanwhile				

Inserting the different conjunctive adverbs in the blank space shifts the meaning of the sentence. Some of the subordinating conjunctions have to be used at the beginning of the first phrase, as in "Although Jane's mother was dying, the doctor saved her."

Expressing Parallel Ideas in Parallel Grammatical Forms

Readers follow your ideas according to the patterns in your thought and your language, and they expect that when you set up a parallel, it will be followed through in the thought and expression: "He likes reading and writing"; not, "He likes reading and to write" (linking two different kinds of verb forms, a participle and an infinitive). Verb forms should be parallel, of the same kind: "She was told to report to the teacher and to take her books with her" (parallel verbals). "Dogs are noted for their friendliness and sometimes for their ferocity" (parallel prepositional phrases). "The Bishop stated that he loved Bach, tolerated modern art, and hated contemporary architecture" (parallel clauses).

Avoiding Inconsistencies in Point of View

You should avoid shifts in point of view from first to third person: "I shall argue that…. One can demonstrate from this text that…." Also, you should ensure that moods or tenses of verbs do not shift. Historical events are usually put in the past tense: "Wellington defeated Napoleon at Waterloo." When writing about literary texts or other documents, it is better to use the present tense: "Hamlet kills Polonius before Ophelia goes mad." "Aristotle discusses tragedy; Frye applies his terms to world literature." Other tenses need to be used logically for events before or after the main action: "Othello finally knows Desdemona has been faithful."

AVOIDING COMMONLY MISUSED WORDS AND PHRASES

To say what you mean, you require an adequate vocabulary. Building your vocabulary means regularly using a good dictionary when reading to discover the meanings of any unfamiliar words. Beyond that, saying what you mean involves having a sense of good usage and of the customary connotation of words (denotation involves the dictionary meaning; connotation involves the customary and contextual resonance of a word). Students often misuse a number of common words and phrases. A list of the most common mistakes is found on the *Foundations* Web site.

USING THE SPELL CHECKER, THESAURUS, AND GRAMMAR CHECKER

When revising, you should use three services on your computer that are crucial to you as a writer. Each is found on the Tools pull-down menu.

The Spell Checker

After completing your first draft, you should run the whole text through the spell checker to highlight misspellings or words not in your word processor's vocabulary (such as proper names). However, you will still have to proofread the final copy (not with a spell checker) to catch any words that are spelled correctly but that are misused or any technical or special words that the spell checker misread.

The Thesaurus

A *thesaurus* is a list of words that serve as alternatives (synonyms or close meanings) and opposites (antonyms) to a selected word. The thesaurus function enables you to vary the words you use in your writing. With the cursor on a word, you can click on Tools and then choose Thesaurus to get a choice of possible replacement words. Any replacement should be checked with the dictionary for proper meaning when used in your sentence and context.

The Grammar Checker

This tool can be turned on as you are writing in order to highlight proposed stylistic improvements, or it can be used on a completed draft. You have the option of modifying or customizing the checking style (for example, standard, formal, or casual style). By responding to the prompts on the screen, you work your way through your document. You will be offered corrections and suggestions. With each proposed change, you need to think carefully about what the grammar checker offers: is it making the right assumptions about your audience and style, as well as your argument and its expression? Is it offering to change what you mean as well as how you are saying it? Do you understand why the changes are being proposed? Are the changes being proposed in any quotations? If so, you will not want to have these changed. Sometimes, the grammar checker finds mistakes where there are no problems, so you have to be alert to the changes that are proposed.

SELF-EVALUATING YOUR ESSAY

To give you an idea of the criteria a grader might use to evaluate your essay, we include here a sample essay evaluation. We recommend that you go through the categories carefully and adopt them for self-evaluation of your work.

Organization and Argument

1. Thesis Statement: Is it on topic, clear, brief? Is the statement of claim made with or without reasons? Is the thesis statement well located?
2. Structure of Argument
   - Introduction: Does it relate to the rest of the essay and really introduce it?
   - Main Points of Argument: Are central positions/issues set out?
   - Subordinate Arguments: Do they support, extend, qualify the main argument?
   - Logic: Is there a logical sequence to the argument based on the sequencing of arguments from major to minor, from claim to evidence, or from topic through a middle argument to a conclusion? Is the argument inductive (drawing conclusions from evidence) or deductive (moving from general principles to particular applications)? Are both sides of the question discussed? Is the argument based on information or assertion?
   - Stages and Functions of the Argument: Are they marked in the text with either formal divisions (e.g., sections, sentences, paragraphs) or by indications in the wording (such as *to illustrate, consequently, in contrast, another example*)? Are these stages identified by their subjects or functions (e.g., definition, exemplification, qualification, restriction, illustration)? Is the overall structure coherent? Are non-functional repetition, redundancy, irrelevancy avoided? Does the conclusion follow from the argument? Look again at the thesis statement. Have its demands been met in the conclusion? Does the conclusion actually complete the argument?

3. Analysis

- Is analysis of key words, terms, evidence, and ideas provided?
- Is contextual analysis used, rather than dictionary definitions? If the dictionary is used, how is its authority incorporated, questioned, or located historically?
- Is the analysis of the primary text/document/monument comprehensive or selective? On what basis? What about secondary text(s), reference books? Do your illustrations and examples elaborate the analysis?
- Are quotations used? Are they provided for evidence or illustration? How are they introduced or discussed?
- Is the analysis at an appropriate level of complexity or level of abstraction? Is it supported with concrete evidence?

4. Factual Accuracy and Plausibility: Are data, statistics, dates, and points of fact accurate? Are points of interpretation plausible? Are sources of ideas, quotations, and illustrations acknowledged?

Sentences, Paragraphs, and Language Strategies

1. Introductory Paragraph: Are opening ideas functional and well presented? Is there a "hook" to catch the reader's attention? Is the thesis stated?

2. Sentences: Is standard English used (e.g., correct subject–verb agreement, pronoun form, use of the apostrophe)? Is syntax correct (meaningful arrangement of words, phrases, sentences)? Is sentence structure varied and appropriate to essay's purposes?

3. Paragraph Unity: Is there a topic sentence? Are paragraphs developed? Are they internally organized? Are bridges and links provided between paragraphs?

4. Diction: Are words carefully chosen for contribution to meaning and argument? Is the level of diction consistent, and does it fit the essay's rhetorical demands and argument and level of formality? Are active verbs and descriptive adjectives used?

5. Conventions of Standard English: Is spelling accurate? Is punctuation useful? Is the format for quotations correct? Are the method of citation and format and content of footnotes or endnotes and bibliography consistent? Is the essay format correct?

CHAPTER SUMMARY

In Chapter 11, you have worked through a series of three systematic steps in writing your essay or other assignment: (1) composing it on the computer, (2) building arguments through the use of paragraphs, and (3) revising it to improve your style and meaning. In particular, you have learned how to move from being stuck at the beginning to finishing and revising its persuasive content.

- You have found the ways that work for you to overcome writer's block.
- You have improved outdated or rusty computer skills and have learned some new techniques to make your writing and editing far more effective.

- You have mastered the steps of converting your outline into paragraphs and your paragraphs into sustained arguments, especially the three most troublesome aspects of an essay—the thesis statement and the opening and concluding paragraphs.
- You have learned how to use quotations to make your arguments more convincing.
- You have realized the importance of revision to improve content and argument as well as the importance of style and persuasion.
- You can test your writing for the eight commonest mistakes in rhetoric and for commonly misused words.
- You can use your computer's spelling and grammar checkers as well as its thesaurus and can check the results of revision against the self-evaluation document.

If you are uncertain about any points of grammar, we review them in the next chapter before turning in Chapter 13 to the important matter of formatting your essay before you hand it in.

FURTHER READINGS

Floyd, Richard. *Success in the Social Sciences*. Toronto: Harcourt Brace, 1995.

Lester, James D. *Writing Research Papers: A Complete Guide*. 9th ed. New York: Longman, 1999.

Reeves, Phoebe. *What's the Big Idea? Writing through Reading and Thinking*. Upper Saddle River, NJ: Prentice-Hall, 1999.

Reinking, James A., Andrew W. Hart, and Robert von der Osten. *Strategies for Successful Writing: A Rhetoric, Research Guide, Reader, and Handbook*. Upper Saddle River, NJ: Prentice-Hall, 1999.

Richardson, Peter. *Style: A Pragmatic Approach*. Boston: Allyn and Bacon, 1998.

Troyka, Lynn Quitman, and Cy Strom. *Quick Access: Simon and Schuster Reference for Writers*. 2nd Canadian ed. Scarborough, ON: Pearson Education Canada, 2004.

Winkler, Anthony C., and Jo Ray McCuen. *Writing the Research Paper: A Handbook*. 6th ed. Austin: Thomson & Heinle, 2003.

chapter twelve

Recognizing How Grammar and Punctuation Work

Chapter 12 deals with grammar and punctuation, a topic that many students dread, since they see it in terms of being marked wrong in matters they place little value on and do not understand. In this chapter, we seek to remedy this problem, not by insisting that you memorize obscure terms and secret codes that are of little use to you outside of this narrow field but by making your writing communicate your ideas with clarity and purpose.

We include many of these terms, and you may learn them if you like, but our real purpose in giving them is to allow you to move, at the end of this chapter, to writing better by recognizing and eliminating from your work common mistakes in grammar and punctuation. In order to use the last two sections of this chapter, on punctuation and common errors, you need to be able to identify such matters as word classes, parts of a sentence, clauses and phrases, and so on. You will thereby be able to understand the conventions, which will, in turn, help you to write better.

LEARNING OBJECTIVES

In this chapter, the following questions about grammar are answered:

- What is standard written English (SWE), and how can you learn to communicate effectively in it?
- How do you identify the major components of a sentence?

- How do you use different types of sentences effectively in your writing?
- How do you use punctuation to make your writing clear?
- How can you ensure that you are not committing the most common errors in grammar, punctuation, and usage?

Some students coming to university may suddenly find that their writing is an inadequate vehicle for their ideas and that it is severely criticized by their professors. These students have little equipment to rely on to correct their writing, and they cannot identify the word classes (or parts of speech) and punctuation problems that are marked as wrong in their writing. They need some help with using the conventions of formal writing, which, once started, will continue to improve. Our view is that some knowledge of grammar and rhetoric is an important part of critical writing and that this knowledge cannot be gained without some application and practice, which we give you in the sections that follow.

GRAMMAR AND STANDARD WRITTEN ENGLISH

Standard written English is a convention or form that is the language of power. In one sense, it is no more correct than forms of slang or idiomatic usage, such as rap or chat-talk. But as its name indicates, it is standard in two senses: (1) as the standard practice of the language among literate speakers and writers, and (2) as the standard or benchmark against which speakers and writers are measured. It is what most students call formal writing, and it is the expected form of English in universities and colleges. It is also required in government, business, law, and the rest of the professions. But many students have had little or no formal training in writing skills (rhetoric), grammar, or punctuation and have rarely had their work corrected in ways that will help them improve. Hence, they are at a tremendous disadvantage when they have to write assignments that meet university expectations. Furthermore, standard written English is the acceptable language for job applications, letters of introduction and reference, and all sorts of other communications. This chapter is directed at just those students, to give them the information about the kinds of terminology, concepts, and practices that will help them improve their writing.

Two important components of standard written English are grammar and rhetoric. In the simplest sense, *grammar* (Greek, *grammatikos,* knowing one's language) is the study of the ways that the vocabulary or words of a sentence can be arranged to give meaning. Grammar involves what it is possible to express in a language. *Rhetoric* (Greek, *rhetorikos,* having the skills of an orator or public speaker) enables you to make choices about putting your words together persuasively. Critical writing involves communicating your reasoned ideas in appropriate grammar and rhetoric. We discuss rhetoric throughout this book, particularly in Chapters 3, 5, 6, and especially 11, but here we focus on grammar, which can be defined in three ways.

First, grammar as a *structure* refers to the system of a language according to its word classes (called *lexis*) and its arrangement of words into phrases, clauses, and sentences (called *syntax*).

Second, grammar is also a *description* of how that structure works according to the conventions and practices people follow when writing or speaking. Descriptive grammars are used by linguists to study changes in usage and shifts in conventions, without saying what is good or bad usage. They are also used to describe the structure of a language, setting out its terms and definitions. Such descriptive grammars are often traditional, and most grammar handbooks, including this one, define and classify terms largely according to the conventions derived from the classical languages of Greek and Latin (which dominated so much earlier education). At the same time, this traditional grammar has been modified by other kinds of grammar, such as the study of large sentence structures that transform the relationships of words to meanings by adding endings or other changes and by generating expectations as a sentence unfolds (as in transformational–generative grammar).

Third, grammar is *prescriptive* in that it often refers to what is deemed to be correct or to the so-called rules of grammar when the customs of acceptable usage become obligatory, pointing to the benefits of clarity in communication. Most students have already assimilated many of these conventions and use them acceptably in their writing. They are able to re-formulate sentences and are at least partly aware of the differences in meaning that are open to them. Such choices are both grammatical (that is, students have to meet the conventions of the language) and rhetorical (students are able to assess the persuasive effect of different choices). At times, however, many students get tangled up in their expression of ideas and cannot understand how to improve their writing or even how to follow an instructor's corrections. This chapter addresses such problems by setting out both a description of the structure of standard English grammar and also a guide to usage for those places in student writing where the structure is weak or falls apart. We do indicate unacceptable usage, but rather than asserting that one usage alone is the correct one, we point out that several choices are possible.

We maintain that some knowledge of grammar and rhetoric improves a good writer and is essential for a weaker writer, at least in understanding the corrections and instructions that are marked on returned essays. For some students, practice in correcting faults in grammar will almost immediately improve their writing and grades. For all students, knowledge of grammar basics will enable them to read and write with greater fluency and precision.

WORDS, PHRASES, CLAUSES, AND SENTENCES

The fundamental unit of the English language is the word, and words are combined into larger structures, called phrases and clauses, which together compose a sentence. Sentences are the instruments of thought, and the ways people use words and sentences dictate the ways in which they think. Sentences, then, contain fully formulated thoughts, and analyzing a sentence requires examining its parts.

Word Classes

The basic building blocks of standard English are words held together in sentences. Even in a nonsense sentence, you know whether it fits a standard English grammatical pattern or not. If I say, "The forbles grobed a dindle," you have no difficulty in recognizing that the pattern is correct, even though the meaning is nonsense. We understand that the words *forbles* and *dindle* are the same types of words and that *grobed* is a different type. To verify our understanding we can substitute real words, "The judges picked a winner." So, in the sentence "My brother plays basketball after school," we sense that *brother, basketball,* and *school* are similar types of words. We also know that *brother* and *plays* are different types of words, and we can say that they belong to different word classes. Categorizing words into their classes enables you to describe their relationships and to understand how they function. Words can have different forms *(brother, brothers),* different positions in a sentence (we can rearrange it as "After school my brother plays basketball"), and different functions in relation to each other (*brother* says who is playing; *basketball* says what is played; and *play* says what my brother does). Word classes (called *parts of speech* in some grammars) provide a system of categorizing words so you can identify their characteristics and fit them together coherently.

The Classification of Words

In English, there are eight word classes:

1. Nouns
2. Pronouns
3. Adjectives
4. Verbs
5. Adverbs
6. Interjections
7. Prepositions
8. Conjunctions

There are various ways of classifying them. One method is to distinguish among meaning words, asserting words, and function words:

MEANING WORDS   (specify objects, persons or things, actions, qualities, ideas, or abstractions):
1. naming words (name things, persons, feelings, ideas, or concepts)
   • nouns
   • noun substitutes: pronouns
2. describing words for nouns and pronouns: adjectives

ASSERTING WORDS:
1. action words
   • verbs
   • the verb *to be,* the copula, or other linking verbs
2. describing or intensifying words for verbs, adjectives, and other adverbs: adverbs
3. intensifying exclamations inserted suddenly into a sentence: interjections

FUNCTION OR LINKING WORDS:
1. linking words for nouns or pronouns in phrases: prepositions
2. linking words for words, phrases, and clauses: conjunctions

Nouns

Nouns (French, *non, nom* < Latin, *nomen,* name) are naming words that specify objects, persons, things, actions, qualities, ideas, or abstractions. Nouns may differ with respect to number (singular and plural), gender (masculine, feminine, and neuter), and case.

Case refers to the relationships between nouns and pronouns and the other parts of the sentence. The *subjective* case refers to nouns or pronouns that are the subjects of a sentence or clause; the *objective* case refers to nouns or pronouns that are the objects of the action of a verb or of a preposition.

The third case for nouns and pronouns in English is the *possessive* case, which is used to indicate possession or ownership. Here, the spelling is changed by the use of the apostrophe and the letter *s: the girl's hat* (one girl); *the students' essays* (several students). The case of each noun is indicated in the following sentence:

Mark	delivered	Lucy's	essay	to her professor.
subjective		*possessive*	*objective*	*objective*

Pronouns

Pronouns substitute for, stand for, or replace a noun (Latin, *pro,* for). The *antecedent* of a pronoun is the noun to which it refers. Like nouns, pronouns are distinguished by number (singular and plural), by gender (as with nouns), and by case. However, the case of pronouns is indicated by differences in spelling or by inflections that indicate the case (*who* is subjective, used as the subject of a verb, and *whom* is objective, used as the object of a verb or preposition) as we explain below. There also is a wide variety of pronouns:

PERSONAL PRONOUNS   refer to the speaker or the person spoken to, or about. The subjective case of the first person pronoun is *I* or *we* and is used as the subject of a sentence: *I am sick; we all ate rotten apples.* When used in the objective case, the personal pronouns are *me* and *us: The dog bit **me**, and forced **us** to flee.* Similarly, the possessive case indicates ownership:

the cat is *mine*	singular
the dog is *ours*	plural

The same procedures apply to second and third person pronouns, including archaic forms (in parentheses) found in the Bible and poetic diction until the end of the 19th century:

Person	Case	Singular	Plural
first	subjective	I	we
	objective	me	us
	possessive	mine	ours
second	subj.	you (thou)	you (ye)
	obj.	you (thee)	you
	poss.	yours (thine)	yours
third	subj.	he, she, it	they
	obj.	him, her, it	them
	poss.	his, hers, its	theirs

IMPERSONAL PRONOUNS   refer to no person or thing in particular but, rather, to a general reference: *One must be careful. It is getting late.* Other impersonal pronouns include *there* (*There is no end to the trouble*), the editorial *we* (*We cannot praise the people enough*), and *they* (*They say it will get colder*). A common mistake is to confuse the possessive pronoun *its* (*The dog wags* its *tail*) with the contraction of the impersonal pronoun (plus the verb *is*) as in *it's,* where the apostrophe indicates the missing letter *i* (*It's a sunny day* = *It is a sunny day*).

RELATIVE PRONOUNS   (*who, which, that*) relate a noun to additional information about it: *The ball that was flying through the air smashed a window. The window which was broken was expensive. All people that on earth do dwell. That* refers to persons or things, and *which* refers to things. Among relative pronouns, only *who* has a full range of case forms:

- *who*   (subjective)   *The client, who was always on time, missed an appointment.*
- *whom*   (objective)   *The client to whom you refer had an appointment with me.*
- *whose*   (possessive)   *The client, whose time was up, left suddenly.*

The difference between the subjective and objective cases for *who/whom* gives students the most problems. *Who* is used as the subject of a verb: *The student who is sick missed the exam. Whom* must be the object of a verb or of a preposition: *The student to whom I gave that grade was very pleased.* Another common mistake is to confuse the possessive relative pronoun (*whose*) with the contraction for *who is* (*who's*): *Whose is that? Who's late for class?* (= *Who is late for class?*).

INTERROGATIVE PRONOUNS   ask a question: *Who? Whom? Whose? Which? What?* and the same words with *-ever* added (*Whoever? Whatever?*): *Who called? You gave it to whom? Whose coat is torn? Which is unclear? What is that?*

DEMONSTRATIVE PRONOUNS   point to the thing referred to. They include *this, that* (singular), *these, those* (plural): *This is acceptable work, but that is not.*

INDEFINITE PRONOUNS   imply but do not have a specific antecedent (or the word that the pronoun stands for): *all, each, either, one, someone, anyone, nobody, everything, nothing,* and so on.

REFLEXIVE AND INTENSIVE PRONOUNS   combine some form of personal pronoun with *-self* or *-selves*. Intensive pronouns are used for emphasis: *He himself came. They themselves found her.* Reflexive pronouns signal that the subject receives the action of the verb: *She is working herself to death.*

Adjectives

Adjectives (Latin, *adjicere* < *ad,* to; *jacere,* to throw, to add to) modify nouns or pronouns by describing or limiting them. Adjectives usually precede or immediately follow the noun they modify (*the* red *house, the day* following). Adjectives that follow linking verbs (*This milk smells* sour) or copula verbs (the verb *to be*: *The bus was* crowded) are called *predicate adjectives. Verbal adjectives* are made from the present and past participles of verbs, such as *following* and *crowded* above. A special group of adjectives are called *articles.* The adjectives *a* and *an* are *indefinite articles;* the adjective *the* is a *definite article.* Adjectives may have comparative degrees to indicate greater intensity (positive, comparative, and superlative degrees: stem, stem + *er,* stem + *est:* e.g., *smooth, smoother, smoothest*). Some adjectives are irregular (*good, better, best; little, less, least; much, more, most*).

When many words discussed in the pronoun section above are used to modify a noun, they function as adjectives. That is, a pronoun is an adjective when it is used with a noun. This category includes *possessive adjectives* (*my, your, thy, her, their,* and so on: *my coffee*); *relative adjectives* (*which* and *whose,* as well as *what* and *whatever: We know which road to take and whose car; we shall take whatever car runs*); *interrogative adjectives* (*what, which, whose: What book is lost?*); *demonstrative adjectives* (*this, that, these, those: These exercises are easy*); and *indefinite adjectives* (*all, each, either,* and so on: *Each question must be answered*).

Verbs

Verbs (French, *verbe,* verb < Latin, *verbum,* a verb, a word) designate an action, condition, process, or state of being. That is, they assert or predicate something.

CONJUGATION   To conjugate a verb, we set out all of the principal parts and the tenses and variants of a verb; a *synopsis* summarizes a conjugation in one person and number only, as in the example of *to take* (see below under Inflection). There are three principal parts to the English verb as shown here with the verbs *to walk* and *to be.*

1. infinitive or base form:	(*to*) *walk*	(*to*) *be*
2. past tense, or imperfect:	(I) *walked*	*was, were*
3. past participle:	(I have) *walked*	*been*

Some grammars add two other verb forms:

4. present tense:	I *walk,* he/she *walks,*	*am, is, are*
5. present participle:	(I am) *walking*	*being*

TYPES OF VERBS   *Regular* (or "weak") *verbs,* the most common category of English verbs, form their principal parts by adding *-ed* to the stem; many verbs have omitted the *-ed* of the past tense and so have all three parts identical (*cut, hit, set, shut*). In a few cases, the past participle is formed by adding *t* (*slept*). Fewer than one hundred *irregular* (or "strong") verbs form their past tense and past participles in irregular ways with a change in spelling (*run, ran, run; do, did, done; eat, ate, eaten; begin, began, begun*).

There are 26 *auxiliary* (or *helping*) *verbs* in English that combine with the root form of the verb (e.g., *can walk*) or a participle (e.g., *were walking, had played*) to convey time and other meanings, such as changing the mode of action or the mood in the main verb:

Auxiliary verbs

have, has, had

do, does, did

be, am, is, are, was, were, being, been

Modal auxiliary verbs

can	could
shall	should
will	would
may	might
must	ought to
used to	had better

INFLECTION   Verbs in English are inflected, or change their forms, according to the usage demanded by voice, mood, tense, number, and person.

Voice can be active or passive. In the *active voice,* the subject is the actor and there is a direct statement of the action of the subject: *I walked the dog. The cat eats its tuna. Mike played the guitar.* In the *passive voice,* the subject is acted on: *The tuna is eaten by the cat. The guitar was played.*

Mood signifies a writer's position concerning the fact or action being expressed. Most grammarians say that there are three moods:

1. The *indicative* mood states a fact or asks a question (some linguists categorize the question as a separate mood, the *interrogative* mood): *Susan studies in the library every day. Did you walk the dog?*

2. The *imperative* mood expresses a command: *Study harder and sleep less.*

3. The *subjunctive* mood indicates a wish, desire, regret, or hope: *If I were to win the lottery, I would buy a new car. I wish I were a better student.*

There are six *tenses* in English. For example, here are the six tenses of the active voice of *to take*:

1. Present (simple, progressive, emphatic): *I take, I am taking, I do take.*

2. Past (imperfect): *I took, I was taking, I did take.*

3. Future: *I shall take, I shall be taking* (no emphatic).

4. Present perfect (uses *have, has* + past participle): *I have taken. I have been taking.*

5. Past perfect (uses *had* + past participle): *I had taken. I had been taking.*

6. Future perfect (uses *shall/will have* + past participle): *I shall have taken. I shall have been taking.*

Verbs also change their form according to whether the subject is singular or plural in number and whether it is first, second, or third person: *I take, you take, he or she takes, we take, you take, they take.*

CLASSIFICATION   Verbs can be classified as transitive, intransitive, copulative, or auxiliary.

- A *transitive* verb needs a direct object to complete the meaning: *I told a story.*

- An *intransitive* verb does not need a direct object to complete the meaning: *Birds fly.*

- A *copulative verb,* also called a *linking verb,* links the subject to its description. Common copulas include *be, become, appear, seem, feel, grow,* and *prove*: *the man appears sick.* The verb *to be* is irregular throughout: *The man was/is/will be sick.* An *auxiliary verb* helps form tenses of other verbs, using the forms *have, be, shall, will, can, may, must, ought, do, should, would* (see directly above, Inflection—tenses).

INFINITIVES   An *infinitive* is a verbal noun, adjective, or adverb: *To lie in court is foolish* (noun). *This question is the exercise to write for next week* (verbal adjective, modifying *exercise*). *Use a computer to check your spelling* (verbal adverb, modifying *use*).

VERBALS   Verbals continue to be a verb, but they are used as another part of speech as well:

- A *participle* is a verbal adjective with *-ing* added to the base form. As a verb, it will have tense and voice; as an adjective, a participle will modify a noun: *the coming decade.*
- A *gerund* is a verbal noun with *-ing* added to the base form. Before a gerund, the possessive case of a noun or pronoun is required: *Her working in San Salvador was dangerous; The journalist's departing from San Salvador was dangerous.*

Adverbs

Adverbs modify verbs, adjectives, and other adverbs and often use the suffix *-ly* (*coldly, happily*). Adverbs say where, how, why, when, to what extent, and under what circumstances something happens. Like adjectives, they may be compared (*fast, faster, fastest*); some are irregular (*little, less, least*).

Conjunctive adverbs connect a complete sentence to a preceding sentence (*especially, hence, however, therefore, nevertheless, then, besides, also, so, further, furthermore, moreover, still, only, consequently, accordingly,* and so on).

Other types of adverbs include adverbs of time (*now, soon, never, yesterday*), of place (*away, here, downstairs, outside*), of manner (*bravely, fondly, sadly, wearily*), and of degree (*very, truly, completely, extremely, rarely*).

Prepositions

Prepositions link a noun or pronoun (called the *object*) to other parts of the sentence (preposition + object = a prepositional phrase). Prepositions give the location or position (hence, pre-position is their name) of the noun or pronoun they are attached to. Many of these usages are *idiomatic* (a conventional phraseology accepted in popular usage, but with a meaning that cannot be determined by its separate words). We use specific prepositions in certain phrases: *accuse a person of a crime; different from* (not *to* or *than*); *in respect of* (not *to*); *inferior to* (not *than*); *superior to* (not *than*); *with a view to* (not *of*), and many more. A long list is given in Eric Partridge's *Usage and Abusage.* Other prepositions include *in, over, from, beside,* and *after.*

Conjunctions

Conjunctions link words, phrases, and clauses and indicate whether the relationship between the parts is equal or unequal.

COORDINATING CONJUNCTIONS   connect words, phrases, or clauses of equal grammatical rank:

- Additive coordinating conjunction: *and*
- Contrasting coordinating conjunction: *but, yet*

- Separative coordinating conjunction: *or, either, neither, nor*
- Final coordinating conjunction: *for, so*

SUBORDINATING CONJUNCTIONS connect subordinate clauses with independent ones (minor to major ones). Some of these conjunctions are *after, although, as, as if, as though, because, before, even if, even though, if, in case, in order that, no matter if, once, provided, since, so that, than, that, though, till, unless, until, when, whenever, whereas, wherever, whether,* and *while.*

CORRELATIVE CONJUNCTIONS are used in pairs to join equivalent parts of a sentence: *either … or, neither … nor, so … as, both … and, whether … or, not … but, not only … but also.*

Interjections

Interjections express sudden and strong emotion and are followed by an exclamation point or a comma. They intensify the emotion of the speaker or the assertion being made. Common interjections include *Golly, Gosh, Wow! Oh, Alas! Help! Hurrah! Ouch!* and *Well!* In analytical writing, interjections should be used sparingly, if at all.

Parts of the Sentence

A sentence has two parts, a subject and a predicate (see Figure 12.1). The *subject* names the person or thing that acts, and the *predicate* consists of the verb and all of the words that are associated with it (such as adverbs). The *direct object* of a sentence is the person, place, or thing that receives the action of a transitive verb. A *complement* completes a verb by adding additional information about a subject or object. A *subject complement* is a noun or adjective that describes the subject of a copula verb: *This essay is* excellent. An *object complement* follows a direct object and completes it, with an implied *to be: The examiners found the answer* acceptable (*acceptable* is an adjective modifying *answer* and functioning as an object complement to the direct object *answer*). The sentence could read: *The examiners found the answer* to be *acceptable.*

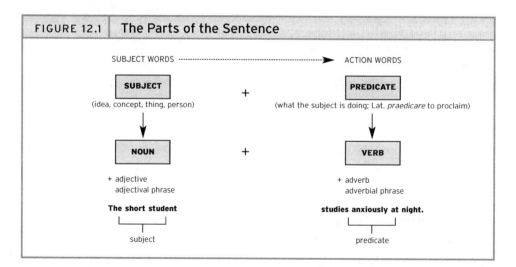

| FIGURE 12.1 | The Parts of the Sentence |

There are five basic sentence patterns in English:

1. Subject + verb: *The cat eats.*
2. Subject + verb + object: *The cat eats its tuna.*
3. Subject + verb + indirect object + direct object: *The student writes her mother letters.*
4. Subject + verb + subject complement: *The student is a visitor.*
5. Subject + verb + direct object + object complement: *Some teachers call articulate students cheaters.*

To add precise details and variety to your writing, you can expand such basic sentence patterns by using modifiers (adjectives and adverbs), by adding phrases or clauses, or by re-arranging the sentence order.

The Phrase

A *phrase* is a group of words that does not contain a subject or a predicate. A phrase is marked by a preposition, an infinitive, or a participle with related words. There are several common kinds of phrase, each of which functions as a single part of speech:

A ***prepositional phrase*** is introduced by a preposition, followed by an object: *in the summer*. Prepositional phrases function as modifiers in either adjectival or adverbial phrases: *The heat* in the summer...; *we came* after the summer.

An ***infinitive phrase*** is introduced by an infinitive: *to try harder.* It may function as a noun, adjective, or adverb: *He hopes* to try harder (noun); *It is time* to try harder (adjective); *He is careful* to try harder (adverb).

A ***participial phrase*** is introduced by a participle: *seeing the end.* It may function as a noun (sometimes called a *gerund phrase*) or as an adjective: *He hated* seeing the end *of a play* (noun—object); seeing the end *of a play was difficult for him* (noun—subject); *the audience,* seeing the end, *understands him* (adjective).

The Clause

A *clause* is a part of a sentence having a subject and a predicate.

Independent (or *main*) *clauses* can stand by themselves as single sentences. An independent clause is not introduced by a subordinate conjunction, but it may be introduced by a coordinating conjunction.

Dependent (or *subordinate*) *clauses* are not complete in themselves and cannot stand as simple sentences. They depend on an independent clause and appear to be part of a sentence. In fact, dependent clauses function as parts of speech—as nouns, adjectives, or adverbs.

Subordinate clauses may also be restrictive or non-restrictive. A *restrictive clause* restricts or limits the meaning to one particular person, place, or thing: *The shirt that you bought yesterday has shrunk.* A *non-restrictive clause* merely adds more information to the idea in the main clause: *Economics, which is a hard subject, is popular among first-year students.* A non-restrictive clause is always separated from the rest of the sentence with commas.

A ***noun clause*** functions as a noun, as the subject of a verb, as the object of a verb, as the object of a preposition, in apposition to a noun, or as a predicate nominative. Most noun clauses begin with *that, what, whatever,* or *whoever*:

That he is right is clear. (subject of verb)

They swore *that he told lies.* (object of verb)

Do you agree with *what she said?* (object of preposition)

The goal *that he accepted* is achieved. (apposition: noun or noun clause in parallel with another noun)

The end is *what I always feared.* (predicate nominative: noun or noun clause in the predicate that renames the subject)

An *adjectival clause* modifies a noun or pronoun. Most adjectival clauses begin with a relative pronoun: *who, whose, whom, which,* or *that.*

The man *who ate the pie* left. (modifies *man*)

The jewellery box, *which I loved,* was stolen. (modifies *box*)

The Dickens character [*that*] *I like best* is Oliver Twist. (modifies *character*)

An *adverbial clause* modifies a verb, an adjective, or an adverb. Adverbial clauses can be recognized easily because they answer the questions When? Where? Why? How much?

He came *when you called.* (modifies verb: when?)

He cried *because you hit him.* (modifies verb: why?)

He is older *than you think he is.* (modifies adjective)

He works faster *than I do.* (modifies adverb)

In addition, there are two special kinds of adverbial clauses. A *conditional clause* describes the condition necessary for the rest of the sentence to be true; it usually begins with *if: If you shout, I'll leave.* The other kind of adverbial clause is a *concessional clause,* which states a concession opposed to the intent of the main clause; it usually begins with *although: Although she is rich, she buys second-hand clothes.*

The Sentence and Sentence Types

The *sentence* is a structural unit of written or spoken composition that contains a subject and a predicate, expressing a complete thought. Every sentence must have a substantive to indicate what the sentence is about (a noun or pronoun, or some other noun equivalent, such as a verbal) and also a verb. *Noun* and *verb* refer to parts of speech; *subject* and *predicate* refer to the functions of those parts in a sentence:

noun	verb
Birds	fly.
subject	*predicate*

The predicate may contain much more than the verb, of course, to complement or complete the meaning of the verb: *Birds fly south in the winter. Fly* and all that follows is a predicate.

In conventional or standard English, ideas are usually put together in sentences that first name a thing or concept and then say what the thing or concept does. There are four kinds of sentences in English (see Box 12.1).

BOX 12.1	The Four Sentence Types

1. **Simple sentence:** one idea or subject + one action
2. **Compound sentence:** two or more simple sentences combined (with a linking word such as *and,* to link equal parts together)
3. **Compound sentence:** one simple sentence + a subordinate clause
4. **Compound-complex sentence:** two simple sentences joined with a linking word + a subordinate clause

---

SIMPLE SENTENCES   contain only one main clause (only one subject and one predicate):

noun	verb
Dogs	howled.
subject	*predicate*

Either the subject or the predicate may be compound:

noun conj. noun	verb
Dogs and cats	howled.
compound subject	*predicate*

noun conj. noun	verb conj. verb
Dogs and cats	howled and fought.
compound subject	*compound predicate*

COMPOUND SENTENCES   combine two or more simple sentences as two parts of one thought, joined by a coordinating conjunction. Each of the former sentences becomes an independent clause. Normally, a comma separates the clauses joined by a coordinating conjunction:

You may not pass. (simple sentence)

You should at least try. (simple sentence)

You may not pass, but you should at least try. (compound sentence)

COMPLEX SENTENCES   have one main clause and one or more subordinate clauses:

If the weather is fine, we shall go on a picnic.

COMPOUND-COMPLEX SENTENCES   have two or more main clauses and one or more subordinate clauses:

If the weather is fine, we shall leave, but they will stay.

PUNCTUATION

Punctuation has a purpose—to mark off the units of thought in your writing so that your reader can understand your meaning fully. In speech, those marks are pauses, intonations, inflections in the voice, and gestures. In writing, these devices are changed into punctuation marks that over time writers and readers have agreed to use in specific ways. That is, punctuation is conventional, and when you break with what a reader expects, such as by putting a comma where a period would be customary, the reader is confused and has to re-read your sentence. Your train of thought is interrupted, and your reader is left unsure of your meaning. Where your punctuation should be helpful, it becomes misleading. Proper punctuation will make your writing clearer and more precise.

Literacy in standard English requires facility in the use of punctuation. An academic essay will not be praised for proper punctuation, but it will be criticized and possibly downgraded if it contains punctuation errors. The discussion of punctuation that follows is intended as an introduction to, rather than as an exhaustive treatment of, the subject. An understanding of the definitions and usage we discuss will enable you to communicate your ideas clearly; you will be able to supply helpful guideposts to lead your reader through your ideas—and through your prose.

Period

A *period* is used at the end of a sentence that is a statement or a command. It indicates a full stop after a completed idea in an indicative or imperative sentence. If a period follows a partial sentence, one lacking a subject or a main verb, the error is a sentence fragment: *The castle, overgrown with moss and cobwebs.* (Incorrect—this fragment needs a main verb.) A run-on sentence omits periods, combining independent clauses, fragments, or complete sentences without the necessary internal or final punctuation:

> ✘ Industrialization began in Canada during the late 19th century it greatly expanded however during World War I helped by European immigration.

> ✔ Industrialization began in Canada during the late 19th century. It greatly expanded, however, during World War I, helped by European immigration.

Comma

A *comma* chiefly connects but also separates the parts of a sentence. It indicates to the reader a pause in the thought, a grouping of words for another thought, and a point of emphasis. It has a wide variety of specific uses, of which we mention the most important. It should not be used haphazardly. When you are writing a first draft or taking notes, you should not get into the habit of adding a comma randomly, just when you stop to think. To guide your reader effectively, you need to use commas deliberately according to the following conventions:

1. Use a comma before coordinating conjunctions (*and, but, yet, or, nor, for,* and *so*) in compound sentences (with two independent clauses, each a complete sentence): *Frankenstein crossed the ice, and the monster moved toward him.*

- Do not use a comma when the compound elements are not independent clauses: *Frankenstein crossed the ice and lost his way* (the *and* introduces a predicate only, not an independent clause with its own subject; hence, no comma is used).

- Do not use a comma to join independent clauses without a coordinating conjunction:

  ✗ The monster leapt toward him, he could not escape. (comma splice)

  ✔ The monster leapt toward him, but he could not escape.

2. Use a comma to separate items (words, phrases, and clauses) in a series of more than two, including before the last item: *The parrot eats carrots, corn, and peas. It fluffs its feathers, clears its throat, and sings "Yankee Doodle."*

3. Use a comma after introductory modifiers (words, phrases, or clauses): *After work, I still had to study.*

4. Use a comma with non-restrictive (non-essential) modifiers, such as dependent clauses, appositives, and participial phrases. Modifiers are non-restrictive when they are not essential to the basic meaning of the sentence, even though they may add important information: *My sister, the smartest of the family, is older than I.* But with a restrictive modifier, no commas are used: *Coppola's film* Apocalypse Now *stars Marlon Brando.* The appositive *Apocalypse Now* restricts or limits the meaning: without it we would not know which of Coppola's films is referred to. Hence, there are no commas. Another way of thinking about restrictive and non-restrictive modifying phrases or clauses is to consider them as essential or non-essential. Commas are used to indicate the fact that this information is not essential. To see whether the information is essential or not, read the sentence without the modifier, and if the meaning is fundamentally unchanged, the modifier is non-essential (or non-restrictive) and should be set off by commas.

5. Use a comma after and around conjunctive adverbs (such as *hence, however, therefore,* and *thus*) and transitional phrases (such as *for example, in addition, it seems to me, on the contrary,* and *that is*): *That is, she died. It is true, however, that Rover has fleas.*

   - Do not use a comma to join a sentence to an independent clause introduced with a conjunctive adverb. You are misusing the conjunctive adverb as a coordinating conjunction and also are committing a comma splice:

     ✗ Our cat never scratches, however it is true that Rover has fleas. (this example also omits the comma after *however*)

     ✔ Our cat never scratches; however, it is true that Rover has fleas. (use a semicolon to separate the independent clauses)

     ✔ Our cat never scratches. However, it is true that Rover has fleas. (separate the independent clauses into separate sentences)

     ✔ Our cat never scratches, but it is true that Rover has fleas. (use a coordinating conjunction with a comma before it)

6. Use a comma between coordinating adjectives (that is, adjectives equal in value that modify the same noun): Death of a Salesman *is a disturbing, absorbing play.* Or, Death of a Salesman *is a disturbing but absorbing play.*

   - Do not use a comma with cumulative adjectives that build meaning from word to word. The order of coordinating adjectives can be interchanged, but that of cumulative adjectives cannot be changed without writing nonsense.

    ✗   The lecturer stressed several, common, grammatical, mistakes. (the three adjectives cannot be interchanged)

    ✔   The lecturer stressed several common grammatical mistakes.

7. Use a comma with quoted words introduced by a verb of saying or an equivalent word: *She said, "It's a cold winter." Or, The poet Blake wrote, "In every cry of every Man ... the mind-forged manacles I hear." Or, "In every cry of every Man," claimed Blake, "the mind-forged manacles I hear."*

    • Do not use a comma when the quoted words are introduced with *that* or *as*. For instance, *Blake referred to the misuse of reason as "mind-forged manacles."* Also, do not use a comma when a quoted phrase is part of your own sentence: *Blake claimed that "mind-forged manacles" were heard in "every cry of every Man."*

8. Use a comma with titles and degrees (*Mary Jones, M.D., gave expert testimony*), addresses (*Regina, Saskatchewan*), dates (*Friday, June 2, 1998*—but omit the second comma when the date is reversed: *Friday, 2 June 1998*), and letter openings and closings (*Dear Cynthia,*).

    • Do not use the comma in numbers to mark off thousands—use a space instead. Four-digit numbers can be grouped together. This usage represents a change resulting from conversion to the metric system in Canada: 333 000 or 4500.

The most frequent comma error is the *comma splice*. This fault joins independent sentences and clauses together with commas (often with no conjunction). It is extremely confusing to a reader: *Johnny flipped the egg over, the lady at the counter watched him.* Comma splices can be corrected by separating the sentences with an end stop punctuation mark, such as a period. Another common comma fault is using it to separate the subject and verb: *The man with the red coat, ran away.* Similarly, a comma is often used mistakenly to separate a verb from the rest of the predicate: *The military defeat of Germany in World War I crippled, the country economically.* Correct these mistakes by omitting the commas.

Semicolon

A *semicolon* is made up of both a period and a comma and has some of the functions of each: it both connects and separates. The semicolon has only two uses. First, it joins two independent and complete statements that form one logical unit. The major use of the semicolon, then, is between main clauses that you want to link together because they are closely related: *It rained incessantly; the camping trip had to be postponed.* Often, the thought in the second main clause contradicts the first. In such a case, the second clause is usually introduced with a conjunctive adverb: *The essay had mistakes in punctuation; nevertheless, it received a good grade for content. It was raining; however, the sun still shone brightly.*

    Second, the semicolon separates items in a series that already has internal commas: *The new student had attended high school in Burnaby, British Columbia; Red Deer, Alberta; and Deep River, Ontario. In his cabinet of 1935, Hitler assumed the role of chancellor; Göring, prime minister; and Goebbels, the minister of propaganda.*

Colon

A *colon* means continue. It is preceded by an independent clause and announces that a continuation of the idea or examples follows in the second part of the sentence. Its most frequent use is to introduce formal lists, illustrations, explanations, and examples. It is often preceded by an expression introducing the list or explanation, such as *the following* or *as follows*. The colon is also used to introduce a direct quotation, to separate the main title from the sub-title in the title of a book (*Essays and Reviews: The 1860 Text and Its Reading*), and to separate the chapters and verses of the books of the Bible (*Genesis* 3:24).

Apostrophe

An *apostrophe* signifies an omitted letter or letters and is used in the following instances:

1. To form possessives: *the boy's cat* (one boy, one cat); *the boys' cat* (several boys, one cat); *the boys' cats* (several boys and cats). The singular possessive is formed by adding *'s*: *John's hat*. English and Canadian usage adds the *'s* even when the proper noun ends in *s*: *Charles's friend*; *Burns's poems*; or *Dickens's novels*. Exceptions to this custom are ancient proper nouns: *Jesus' disciples*; *Xerxes' army*; *Ulysses' wanderings*. American usage drops the second *s* in all possessives: *Charles' friend*.

   Plural possessives ending in *s* add only an apostrophe: *several nations' rights*. Plural and collective nouns ending in a letter other than *s* add an apostrophe and then *s*: *the children's fate*; *the people's choice*. Compound possessives add *'s* after the last subject: *Bill and Jill's home*.

   NOTE: A common and sloppy mistake involves trying to make a plural by adding an apostrophe and *s* to the singular, instead of the simple plural (*link's* instead of *links, essay's* instead of *essays,* and *street's* instead of *streets*).

2. To indicate omitted letters in contractions: *we've = we have; don't = do not*. But in formal essays, such contractions are not used.

   NOTE: The apostrophe in *it's* indicates the omitted letter of *it is*: It's not hard to remember. The personal pronoun in the possessive case (*its*) never uses an apostrophe: *The cat chases its tail*. It is important, then, to distinguish between the possessive (or genitive) case in English and the contraction.

3. To indicate possession by a noun of the action of a gerund (a verbal noun ending in *-ing*): *Alice's falling asleep* or *John's failing his test*.

4. To form plurals of letters, numerals, and symbols by adding *'s*: *Mind your p's and q's! Build it with 2 × 4's. Try not to use &'s; instead, spell out the word*.

Other Punctuation Marks

A **question mark** is used to end a sentence that asks a direct question: *Have you enjoyed that novel?*

- Do not use a question mark for an indirect question. An indirect question is contained in a subordinate clause, often beginning with *if* or *whether,* and the subject and verb are in normal order, unlike in the direct question: *Her friend asked whether she had enjoyed the novel.*

- Do not use a question mark to express sarcasm or irony. Instead, explain your point more fully.

    ✘   The Vietnam War was great (?) for the United States.

    ✔   The Vietnam War was a useful testing ground for American military technology, but for the United States it was a political and military disaster.

An ***exclamation mark*** is used to end a sentence that demands special emphasis or that expresses a strong emotion, such as anger or surprise. It is most often found in dialogue, but it is used rarely in academic prose. *Watch out for that driver! I hate arriving late for class!*

The ***dash*** is inserted automatically by word processors when you activate the automatic replacement function; otherwise, use two consecutive hyphens with no space before or after to indicate a dash. A dash replaces the comma for added emphasis when words are taken out of their normal order. It also should be used sparingly.

Parentheses ( ) are used to interrupt a sentence in order to add information that would otherwise intrude on the flow of thought:

> W.B. Yeats (1865–1939) is probably the most famous Irish poet. The violence in *Alice's Adventures in Wonderland* (unlike that in *The Color Purple*) occurs entirely within a make-believe world.

Brackets [ ] are used to enclose explanatory material within a quotation. They indicate that you have added information to the quotation:

> The Doormouse claimed that "they lived on treacle [molasses]" (*Annotated Alice* 100).

An ***ellipsis*** (three periods) is used to indicate omitted material within quotations. If your omitted material within the quotation includes the end of a sentence, indicate that by using four periods. Current practice discourages ellipses at the beginning and end of quotations to indicate omitted material.

> "So she [Alice] was considering ... whether the pleasure of making a daisy-chain would be worth the trouble of getting up and picking the daisies" (*Annotated Alice* 25).

Italics

The term *italic* derives from 15th-century Italian handwriting, and italic letters are slanted (*like this*), unlike upright roman letters. Italics are used for titles of books, newspapers, magazines, journals, plays, longer poems, TV and radio programs, movies, musical compositions, art objects, and foreign words. Word processors have italic fonts, and you should use them instead of underlining (which formerly, in typed or handwritten essays, indicated italics). Similarly, use your computer's function to indicate **bold face**. Italics and bold face can be used for emphasis, to set off different orders of information, or to help a reader find items in a series, as we have done throughout this book by italicizing key terms before their definitions.

Hyphen

The *hyphen* joins compound words: *a six-year-old*; *twenty-one*; *pre-World-War-One*; *anti-abortion*; *ex-wife*. When a century term is used as a noun it has no hyphen (*the 20th century*); when it is used as an adjective modifying a following noun, it requires a hyphen

(*19th-century literature*). Hyphens also indicate a break in a word at the end of a line. The break comes only after a syllable. A good dictionary will indicate syllabification. Conventionally, each syllable begins with a consonant, double letters are usually split, and prefixes and suffixes (such as *con-, pre-, mis-,* or *-tion, -ing*) are a single syllable.

Quotation Marks

Double quotation marks are used to indicate the following:

- Titles of short works or parts of longer works—short poems, short stories, songs, chapter headings, and magazine and journal articles
- A direct quotation, of either speech or written sources. For long quotations (in verse, three or more lines; in prose, over 10 lines), the convention is to indent the passage and single-space it, omitting the double quotation marks.

Single quotation marks are used to indicate direct speech within the material that you are quoting:

"'Curiouser and curiouser!' cried Alice (she was so much surprised)" (*Annotated Alice* 35).

COMMON ERRORS AND WHAT TO DO ABOUT THEM

Errors in applying the conventions of standard written English get in the way of easy comprehension of your ideas by your readers. As well as minor or mechanical errors in punctuation, they involve problems in grammar, including faults with subjects and verbs (agreements, for instance) or with treating phrases or clauses that lack main verbs as though they were complete sentences. Eight of the most common errors are listed below, along with methods of correcting them. These errors account for most of the basic problems in students' writing. When leaders in education, government, and business complain about students' graduating from high school and university while still functionally illiterate, an important component of their complaint, we believe, is the frequent occurrence of these errors.

An essay that you receive back covered with corrections of your grammar probably consists of the same two or three mistakes repeated: that is, grammar is structural, and if you learn the structure of these eight common errors and how to correct them, then many of your grammar problems will disappear. If you do not learn how to correct them, you will continue to be downgraded by your teachers. Perhaps most importantly, your faults in grammar will not only interfere with how your essay is read in terms of a sympathetic audience, but you will also not be communicating your ideas effectively, and the content of your essay will just not come across.

1. A **comma splice, fault,** or **blunder** is the separating of two independent clauses with a comma:

   ✗ Bush went to Africa, he met many national leaders. (comma splice)

   ✔ Bush went to Africa. He met many national leaders. (The faulty sentence is split into two separate sentences.)

   ✔ Bush went to Africa and met many national leaders. (The two independent clauses are joined with a coordinating conjunction, giving both clauses equal weight.)

✔ Bush went to Africa meeting many national leaders. (The second clause is subordinated with a participle, thereby putting more weight on the first clause.)

✔ When Bush went to Africa, he met many national leaders. (The first clause is subordinated with a subordinating conjunction, thereby giving weight to the second clause.)

2. A **fragment** is a group of words that is punctuated as though it were a sentence but that does not contain a main (or independent) clause: *Such as these fragments. No main verb.* Effective though they may be in creative writing, fragments are hard for a reader to follow in discursive prose. They can be corrected by attaching the fragment properly to a main clause.

✗ Freud who lived in Vienna at the turn of the century. Produced several studies on hysteria.

✔ Freud, who lived in Vienna at the turn of the century, produced several studies on hysteria.

✗ The castle, overgrown with moss and cobwebs. It was transformed from evil to a utopia.

✔ The castle, overgrown with moss and cobwebs, was transformed from evil to a utopia.

Two of the most common forms of the fragment use a *which* clause or a participle instead of a complete verb:

✗ This study of perception involved only adult males. Which is why it was not reliable. The study indicating, of course, the bias against women.

✔ This study of perception involved only adult males, which is why it was not reliable. The study indicated, of course, the bias against women.

✔✔ Because this study of perception involved only adult males, indicating a bias against women, it was not reliable.

3. **Run-on sentences** are a more serious error than either the comma splice or the sentence fragment because they indicate an even more fundamental misunderstanding of what constitutes a sentence. Run-on sentences combine two independent clauses as if they were one without any internal punctuation.

✗ The professor was speaking too quickly the students could not follow him.

✔ The professor was speaking too quickly. The students could not follow him.

✔✔ Because the professor was speaking too quickly, the students could not follow him.

4. **Dangling modifiers** are subordinate phrases that are not clearly related to or dependent on a definite subject.

✗ Going to the store, it was raining. (dangling participle)

✔ Going to the store, I noticed it was raining.

✔ When I went to the store, it was raining.

5. **Incorrectly placed modifiers** are either too far from the words that they modify or divide words that should remain together. Modifiers (such as adjectives or adverbs) should be placed near the words they modify. The parts of an infinitive should not be separated by an adverb: not *to boldly go* but *to go boldly.* The recent editors of the *Oxford English Dictionary,* however, have declared that split infinitives are now acceptable usage.

6. **Agreement problems** usually involve mixing plural and singular subjects and verbs. Verbs agree with the subject in number and person.

   ✗ The national leaders writes e-mails to each other.

   ✔ The national leaders write e-mails to each other.

   The use of a prepositional phrase between the subject and the verb often confuses students:

   ✗ The aim of the leaders' efforts are to gain economic freedom.

   ✔ The aim of the leaders' efforts is to gain economic freedom. (The aim ... is)

   ✗ Chrétien, one of Canada's nationalists, are independent of American control.

   ✔ Chrétien, one of Canada's nationalists, is independent of American control.

   With the conjunctions *or, either ... or,* and *neither ... nor,* the verb agrees with the part of the compound subject next to the verb:

   ✗ During the Second Gulf War, neither Chrétien nor Chirac were under American control.

   ✔ During the Second Gulf War, neither Chrétien nor Chirac was under American control.

   Also, the subjects of sentences beginning *there is [are]* follow the verb: *There is a bird at my window*; *there are many birds at my window.*

   Collective nouns (which refer to a collection of things as one, for example, *nation, army, herd, crowd*) are singular and take a singular verb: *The crowd is unruly.*

7. **Noun–pronoun antecedent problems** usually involve having a plural pronoun refer to a singular noun as its antecedent. A pronoun must agree with its antecedent noun in person, gender, and number.

   ✗ The student must write their essays carefully.

   ✔ The students must write their essays carefully.

   The indefinite pronoun without an antecedent supposes that a reader understands what might be a complicated sequence of ideas, when, in fact, the pronoun glosses over the precise meaning that is intended. The error usually takes the form of beginning a sentence with *this is.* This error is easily corrected by adding a noun that sums up the argument.

   ✗ Nettie, Shug, and Sophia are Celie's role models. Albert is not a role model. This shows the text's feminist strategy.

   ✔ This modelling shows the text's feminist strategy.

8. **Contractions,** such as *I'll, we'll,* and *couldn't,* should not be used in academic essays; they should be reserved for informal use and e-mail. Contractions are often confused with the possessive case of the personal pronoun. Contractions are verb forms that abbreviate (or contract) the verb and connect it to the subject: *it's* (= it is; often confused with *its*); *they're* (= they are, often confused with *their* and *there*); *who's* (= who is, often confused with *whose*). By far the most common of these mistakes concerns *its* and *it's*.

   ✘   This dog walks on it's hind legs when its doing circus tricks.

   ✔   This dog walks on its hind legs when it's doing circus tricks.

There are many resources that you can turn to for help with these and other common problems with grammar and punctuation. Many handbooks for writers have sections on grammar; all discuss style and argument. One of the best is Lynn Quitman Troyka's *Quick Access: A Reference for Writers.* As well, there are many online sites that give help on all aspects of grammar, common mistakes, and usage. The advice in the online manual from the Writing Center at Purdue University is particularly complete and includes many examples of mistakes and corrections as well as other relevant documents. See their site at **http://owl.english.purdue.edu/handouts/index2.html** to access their publications. Another example is the *Grammar Handbook* at the University of Illinois at Urbana-Champagne: **www.english.uiuc.edu/cws/wworkshop/grammar_handbook.htm**.

CHAPTER SUMMARY

This chapter is intended as a guide to proper usage and, unlike most of the other chapters of this book, is not meant to be read through in one sitting. In a sense, it is most useful to you as a reference aid on grammar. You should become familiar with the contents of this chapter so that when questions come up about your writing, you will know how to identify your mistakes and take steps to correct them:

- You are now familiar with standard written English as a convention and as the language of power.
- You have become aware of the different classifications of words, phrases, clauses, and sentences.
- You know the conventions of standard punctuation and know where to look for information when you are uncertain about correct usage.
- You can eliminate the most common errors from your writing.

You can use the grammar checker on your word processor (discussed in Chapter 11), once you have a draft that you want to correct. You should use this chapter to help you understand your instructor's marking of your assignments. Be sure to consult the index on the *Foundations* Web site to find further discussions of particular problems, as well as definitions and discussions of grammatical terminology.

FURTHER READINGS

Handbooks

Buckley, Joanne. *Fit to Print: The Canadian Student's Guide to Essay Writing*. Toronto: Harcourt Brace, 1991.

Connor, William. *Harbrace College Handbook for Canadian Writers*. Toronto: Harcourt Brace, 1994.

Gefvert, Constance. *The Confident Writer*. New York: Norton, 1988.

Messenger, W.E., and Jan de Bruyn. *The Canadian Writer's Handbook*. Scarborough, ON: Prentice Hall, 1995.

Strunk, William, and E.B. White. *The Elements of Style*. 3rd ed. New York: Macmillan, 1979.

Troyka, Lynn. *Quick Access: A Reference for Writers*. 2nd ed. Upper Saddle River, NJ: Prentice-Hall, 1995.

Grammar Reference

Harris, Muriel, and Joan Pilz. *Reference Guide to Grammar and Usage*. Scarborough, ON: Prentice Hall, 1994.

Quirk, Randolph, Sidney Greenbaum, Geoffrey Leech, and Jan Svartik. *A Grammar of Contemporary English*. London: Longman, 1972.

Preparing the Final Copy and Learning from Marked Assignments

Your work on an essay is not complete until you carefully prepare a final copy for submission and later go over your instructor's comments to learn from them when you get it back. Some students move immediately from the first draft to the final draft, revising the first draft on the computer and printing the final copy all in one exercise, most often the night before the essay is due. If you do not treat the final draft as a separate stage of writing and put a proper amount of time into preparing that draft before submitting it, a great deal of hard work that went into the previous stages will be lost by errors in formatting and other sloppy mistakes. In this chapter, we go through a logical order, from revision to proofreading, and then to printing, which establishes a method for preparing your essay before submission. We then go through a process for benefiting from the comments of your professor in marking your assignment, a stage that many students overlook.

LEARNING OBJECTIVES

Chapter 13 deals with the following questions:

- What are the acceptable standards for formatting an essay or assignment? Are there options?
- How do you format title pages, paragraphs, and margins?

- What should you consider in the final steps before you hand your essay in?
- What do a marker's correction symbols mean?
- How do you respond constructively to your instructor's criticisms? What do you do to prepare for an office interview to discuss your paper?

STEPS TO THE SUBMISSION OF THE FINAL COPY

Format of the Final Copy

The final copy should be set out in a format acceptable to your reader. You should print your essay on one side of the sheet only. It should be double spaced, on standard letter-size paper with ample margins: about one and one-half inches on the left and one inch on the other margins, or one inch on all sides, according to the *MLA Handbook* and the APA *Publication Manual.* You should check with your instructor whether the MLA style or the APA style is the preferred model for setting out the format of your essay.

Fonts

The specified length of assignments usually assumes that you are using a 12-point font to print about 300 words to the page. A smaller font will be too difficult to read. Some fonts print smaller than others so that, for instance, Garamond 12 point is about the same size as Times Roman 11 point. You should be aware that your marker probably has a lot of essays to read and, thus, needs a font that is not too small. On the other hand, using a large font with large margins will not hide the fact that your essay is too short. As well, the trick of using a large font and wide margins in order to stretch a short essay to fit the minimum number of pages is immediately recognizable to a reader and creates a very bad impression.

You should choose a legible and conventional font for your assignment and leave the fancy fonts for your birthday cards, or, perhaps, title page (if you have time). Similarly, you should not use an unusual, decorative, or ornamental font throughout your essay to pretty it up; it is hard to read, and so fails to communicate your ideas effectively.

For the body of your essay, you may choose a font from among the following:

- *Roman serif faces* (with feet at the end of strokes), such as Baskerville, Caslon, Garamond, or Times Roman. Courier is a conventional roman serif typewriter-like font that is available on all word processors.
- *Roman sans serif faces* (without feet), such as Arial, Helvetica, or Univers.

Italics (in which the letters slant to the right, based on Italian court or chancery handwriting from the Renaissance) should be reserved for specific purposes, such as book and movie titles. You should not use an italic font throughout your paper or set off quotations in italics (unless they are set in italics in the original). Words to be emphasized can be printed in italics or in bold face. Some writers use bold face for sub-headings in a long paper with sub-divisions, but bold face or sub-headings are usually not needed or useful in a shorter essay.

Paragraph Format

Usually, the first line of a paragraph is indented five spaces or 0.5" tab. In printed books there is no indent, as can be observed readily at the beginning of any chapter. Some writers also leave a larger space between paragraphs to mark them off, which is particularly useful in single-spaced typewritten documents. However, essays for class submission should always be double spaced.

Page Format

Pages are numbered throughout. The title page is unnumbered. The first page is numbered at the bottom. Margins should be one inch on all sides, unless you are instructed otherwise. Use the left-justification option to have your essay printed flush with the left margin. Footnotes are at the bottom of each page; endnotes have a separate page, followed by the Works Cited or References page. Your name should be included on each page in case the pages become separated.

Formatting Details

Your word processor allows you to make systematic changes to a number of variables in preparing your final copy. Often, these variables will already be set up on your computer for your regular work. Many writers prefer to have them in place for the second—writing—stage of assignment preparation. Formatting conventions include *page settings, page numbering* (excluding the title page), *line settings* (use left and right margins set at one inch), *spacing* (double spaced throughout), and justification (justify or align your text flush with the left margin; long quotations and quotations of poetry are indented so that each line of the quotation is also aligned with the indent).

Graphics, Graphs, or Charts

Many other features are available to you on your computer. For instance, you can incorporate appropriate graphics into your writing to make a point, to add a pertinent illustration, or to provide an example. A graphic illustration, however, should contribute to the content and argument of your paper, and it should not be added merely to jazz up the page. It should also be accompanied by an explanation or comment. For instance, if you are writing on the art of the period of the French Revolution and want to discuss David's painting *The Death of Marat,* an illustration of the painting in your paper would be useful. You can do that in one of two ways. The older method is to photocopy an illustration and add the extra page to your printout, referring to it as "Figure 1" (and citing the source in your annotation and list of works cited). The newer method is to scan the image in or download the image.

Other possibilities include using graphics from the Web (such as illustrations from newspapers or magazines, especially for essays on popular culture or related themes), graphs or charts (for instance, showing population or land use, or other data in a schematic way), or summary tables of information. In each case, you will have to explain your illustration or other graphic and integrate it into your argument. Gussying up your paper with happy faces or graphics of Homer Simpson mooning the reader will not predispose that reader to take you seriously.

Title Page and Title

A separate title page is not usually required, but many students use them. If used, it should be prepared last, when you are clear about the precise wording of the title and other details. The title page should contain the essay title (without quotation marks, unless a quotation is included; book titles are set in italics), your name, the instructor's name, the course and section number, and the date. If you give the title on the first page of the essay, the same information should be included. Spelling mistakes on the title page, such as in the instructor's name (which happens more often than you might think), set you off on the wrong foot.

If you do not use a title page, you need to give the title on the first page of the essay. The title should be set two inches from the top of the sheet and should be double spaced if it runs to more than one line. Three spaces separate the title from the first line of text.

Final Steps before Submission

In moving from your working draft to preparing your final copy, you might consider the following steps:

1. When you have completed your working draft, save it both on your hard drive in the assignment file and on a floppy with a short essay title followed by the suffix .dft (draft). The floppy is for this assignment only, to be kept until the end of the year as insurance, showing the stages you reached in preparing your draft. You should also keep your rough notes until you receive your final grade in the course to protect yourself against charges of plagiarism.

2. Print a copy of your working draft.

3. Relax. Then, with a pen or pencil read over your printed copy, as though you were a new reader looking at this piece of work for the first time, seeking to understand the argument and its transitions. This step in the revision process accomplishes two things. First, it makes you into a more objective editor than when you were writing on the computer, since going through your essay in the printed medium will help you look at your writing in a fresh way. Second, it helps you spot errors in punctuation, spelling, grammar, logic, and argument, as these mistakes are easier to see on paper than on the screen. It is particularly important to vet the work that the spell checker has done to ensure that no errors, such as words spelled correctly but misused, have crept in (such as *there* for *their*).

4. After you have gone through your final draft carefully, return to the computer and make the changes you noted.

5. Then, pay attention to the formatting requirements, the references, and all of the finishing details that are necessary. All word processors assist with formatting type size, italics, bold face (which should be used sparingly and in places where you are certain it makes sense), or other variations, and with monitoring indents, tabs, and the like.

6. Read through the essay once more for any mistakes noted in the last minute, and correct them in ink. Many otherwise well-argued papers are marred by slips and mistakes

that are not caught in the final proofreading, an indication of a rushed or careless approach in the last stages of preparation. When done, save your final copy on your hard drive with a backup on a CD or floppy for your records.

Printouts

Any printer attached to your computer, whether ink or colour jet, bubble jet, or laser printer, can do a good job of printing your final copy. You need to be certain that your printer cartridges have enough ink. If you have changed your formatting drastically for your final paper, you should make certain that you have enough time to test your printer before you begin to print your final copy. Some printers do not take kindly to formatting changes; others readily adapt. If your printer has the capability of colour printing, you should use this feature sparingly or for strategic effect. You are not doing a layout for a glossy magazine, where headings should be in a fancy type and rainbow colours. On the other hand, some art reproductions, graphic charts, or tables benefit from appropriate use of colour.

Once the paper is printed, you have two final steps, re-reading it to make any last-minute changes or corrections and fastening it together with a stapler, paper-clip, or transparent binder, following any particular instructions about the preferred or required process in this last step.

Other Formats for Submitting Essays

Of course, with electronic communication the printed essay is not the only possible form of submission. Some courses allow you to submit your assignments electronically on a floppy disk or by e-mail (virtually all journals follow one of these procedures for submission of professors' articles) or through a process of networking and conferencing (in which case you will receive detailed instructions in the course about procedures). Advancing technological developments suggest that the printed essay may, in fact, become obsolete in the not-too-distant future. However, it is still, by far, the preferred method for submitting assignments in university courses.

GETTING THE ESSAY BACK

Many students get papers back and wonder how their instructors want them to improve: how they should develop ideas, correct faults in expression or argument, or push the analysis further. Some instructors mark in great detail, covering each page with corrections. Some markers give attention to one long paragraph, page, or section, marking it in detail. This kind of marking breaks down the whole argument into pieces and critiques the expression, grammar, and analysis. If you receive a paper marked in detail, you are fortunate because the instructor has taken your argument and analysis seriously. In any case, a returned assignment, having been read and evaluated by an expert in the field, is an opportunity to learn. Even if it appears that your grader has been too harsh or has not praised what you consider to be the strengths of your essay, you should take the instructions and markings as an opportunity to rectify and learn from your weaknesses.

Learning from Your Marker's Comments

When many instructors hand back assignments in class, they make detailed comments about how well the class understood and executed the assignment. Those comments can be of the greatest help in the process of re-writing. When papers are given back, you may be too embarrassed to even look at your grade or the annotations on your essay. You should try to get over this block and read the corrections on the paper carefully. Usually, a marker will lay out some of the strengths of your essay, and you should take these remarks not just as praise but as recognition of strengths that you should be able to build on, while putting extra emphasis on those areas of your work that need more attention. It is important that you ask about any corrections that are unclear to you and that you know before you leave the class the instructor's policy about re-writes.

Above all, when the assignment is taken up in class, you should note down on your own paper or in your notebook the instructor's comments on the major faults or problems in understanding or writing the assignment. Often, those comments will be on points that directly concern you and your work, and they will indicate ways in which you might improve, either in a re-write now or in the preparation of a future assignment. With the marker's comments in hand, you should go through *Foundations,* perhaps using the index, to work through the particular problems you find. Remember that the logic of this book is that most problems are structural in that you are often repeating the same mistakes with different contents. If you understand the structures behind your problem, you can address your particular problem in more suitable ways on your own. Teaching yourself in this way is much better than being told by someone else what is wrong.

Recognizing Correction Symbols

It may be difficult for you to recognize what is important in all of the markings on the page. How can you determine what is most significant and to what you should give your attention before the next assignment? What, on the other hand, are the improvements or corrections in expression that might help you to present your case better? You need to be able to distinguish between corrections of major faults or serious flaws in grammar and corrections of more minor kinds. Your instructor can help with this task, but you should be aware of some of the problems yourself.

First, you should correct the serious faults in grammar. These faults include major problems with the comma (the comma splice or the run-on sentence), omitted or partial verbs, writing in clauses instead of complete sentences (the sentence fragment), and faulty agreements between subject and verb (all dealt with in Chapter 12). Faults like these will seriously inhibit a reader's comprehension of your argument, no matter how carefully you have tried to work it out. Second, on the level of argument, you should examine any circumstances the marker has noted where your evidence does not support your case or where there are serious problems in the continuity of your argument. A lack of continuity might involve poor essay organization (missing bridges from paragraph to paragraph or inadequate cause-and-effect sequences), or it might involve an inadequate thesis statement and supporting arguments. In either case, you should examine carefully the way that you have put your essay together.

Other common faults include missing the point of the assignment, failing to pursue the argument in enough detail, failing to support the argument with sufficient evidence, and neglecting to refer to detailed examples. Each of these gaps can be remedied in a re-write, although you should have caught them in the earlier stages of essay preparation and writing. Using an essay-writing checklist, such as the one at the end of Chapter 11, would be helpful.

When you get your paper back, there may be many marks and abbreviations on the page that you do not understand. Some may be quite mystifying. You need to be aware that many markers use the conventions developed by copy editors of manuscripts for publication. Hence, the Greek letter delta (δ) is often used to indicate that a letter, word, or phrase should be deleted. Or the number sign (#) is used to indicate that a space should be inserted where the mark is made, or where the slash-with-a-tail (or the caret, / or ^) is inserted into your text. Table 13.1 lists the various marks that are generally used in the correction of essays, with the abbreviation and a comment on what the mark means. Quickly go through the list, separating the marks indicating mechanical or grammatical problems from those related to conceptual problems in formulating an argument.

If there are other correction marks that you cannot decipher or understand on your marked essay, you should ask your instructor for clarification.

Separating Conceptual and Mechanical Problems

If your instructor has not gone over the conceptual problems in your paper, you should ask for advice about its major conceptual defects and understand them before you get down to details. You need to try to distinguish between the conceptual problems that you have in understanding the topic and the problems you might have in expressing those ideas. You should try to find out what the strong points of your argument are in the estimation of your instructor and also what areas of your paper need improvement. Are there any exercises that he or she could recommend to help you in formulating these concepts better? Did you have problems in understanding the reading for this assignment? If so, you should ask whether you can go over that reading again, now, or look at a short passage with the instructor to see whether you are getting the right points out of what you are reading.

When you are clear about the major conceptual strengths and weaknesses of your paper, you may wish to look again at the mechanical problems in your writing and expression. Again, you should ask your instructor about the major problems in your writing mechanics and style. Are there problems with the organization of your argument, your thesis statement, topic sentences for paragraphs, or grammar and punctuation? Using the index of *Foundations,* locate the solutions to your particular problems. Your instructor might also suggest ways to work on those problems and may suggest exercises, perhaps on the Internet.

Problems in General Comprehension and Analysis of the Topic

You need to look more carefully and systematically at problems in general comprehension of your topic. If you have seriously misunderstood the assignment or the readings involved, you have to get to the bottom of *why* you misunderstood so that you do not make the same mistake again. Had you missed the relevant lectures or seminars in which the work was discussed? Were your notes on these matters unclear or incomplete? If either of these problems

TABLE 13.1	**Correction Marks**

abbrev	abbreviation	**omit—**	omit marked words; do not use parentheses for omissions
act	use active rather than passive voice		
adj	adjective needed or wrong	**p., pp.**	page, pages
adv	adverb required	**par ‖**	parallelism weak
agr	faulty subject-verb agreement	**¶ para**	paragraph problem or start new paragraph
ambig	ambiguous		
amp &	ampersand: write *and* out	**pass**	passive verb construction; use active voice
apost	apostrophe problem		
awk	awkward phrase	**pc**	punctuation problem
bridge	weak link between arguments or paragraphs	**pl**	plural
		poss	possessive problem
case	wrong case of pronoun, often *who* for *whom*	**pron**	pronoun problem or reference
		QED	Latin, *quod erat demonstrandum*: must be demonstrated
cf	Latin, *confer*, compare		
clar	clarify unclear language or argument; needs rewriting	**quest ?**	reader questions validity of marked passage
colloq	colloquial use	**quote(s)**	quotation marks or use needs correction
/, ⋀	comma missing		
comp	comparative form of adj. needed	**red**	redundant/unnecessary
concl	conclusion does not follow	**ref**	reference of pronoun or argument is unclear
conj	wrong conjunction		
contract	contraction (e.g. *they're, I'll*): spell out	**rep**	repetition
		run on	run-on sentence: two sentences joined without punctuation
coord	coordinate stces with coordinating conj. because ideas are related		
		slang	lapse in appropriate language for audience
CS	comma splice		
d or δ	delete	**sp**	spelling mistake
dang part	dangling participle	**splice**	comma splice
det	details needed to support argument	**split infin**	move word that splits infinitive
dic	diction faulty: use dictionary	**stce**	sentence, sentence structure faulty
dict	consult dictionary	**syllab**	syllabification breaks faulty: check dictionary
doc	documentation needed		
e.g.	Latin, *exempli gratia*, for example; distinguish from i.e.	**tense**	verb tenses not in agreement
		thes	thesis statement weak or missing
ellip or...	ellipsis: three spaced periods to indicate omitted material, followed by terminal pc if at end of stce.	**tr ∼**	transpose
		trans	transition faulty; see bridge
		ts	topic sentence absent
frag	sentence fragment	**uc**	upper case, capitals
gr	grammar faulty	**v or vb**	verb problems
½ stce.	half sentence, sentence fragment	**vulg**	vulgarism, inappropriate for formal essay
hy	hyphen		
idiom	idiomatic usage required	**ww**	wrong word
i.e.	Lat. *id est*, that is; see e.g.	**δ**	delete (Greek letter *delta*)
irrel	irrelevant material or argument	**↤ →↦**	move to location indicated
ital	use italic font/underline for italics	**¶**	paragraph
jar	jargon	**‖**	parallelism
lc	lower case needed	**⊙**	period needed
log	logic faulty	**#**	space needed where indicated
mod	modifier misplaced	**∩ ⌣**	reduce space to close up text
nar	narrative being re-told, not analyzed	**/ or ^**	correction location (caret mark)
non seq	Latin, *non sequitur*, it does not follow; a logical fault	**?**	unclear, question the passage
no ¶	no paragraph		
obs	obsolete or obscure		

fits your case, the answer is not hard to find: be certain to attend the classes around the time when assignments are due, and take as complete and careful notes as you can. Often, a lecturer will comment in detail on the requirements for an assignment, give special instruction in a seminar, or answer specific questions that students ask about the assignment.

If the reasons for your misunderstanding really do result from failing to comprehend the course materials, you should use the office time to try to understand them. You should state exactly what it is that you do not understand. Or, if you do not know where to begin (which is often the case for many students), you should say so and ask how you should first move to understand the readings or the topic. Before speaking to your instructor, however, you may want to review the relevant sections in Chapter 3.

The next stage is to consider the defects in your analysis. Often, these defects will result from a failure to ask appropriate and searching questions of your materials in order to answer the problem in the assignment. You might try formulating a different set of questions to see what each set of questions prompts you toward in terms of an analysis. You might bring these questions to the office interview and ask your instructor what set of questions he or she thinks would yield the best results.

You also need to examine the stages in your argument. You should review Chapter 6, which deals with the organization of an argument and see whether you have met those objectives. Your instructor might have marked on your assignment various places where your argument does not measure up, through lack of appropriate evidence, a weak balance of general points and detail, faults in logic, an inability to get beneath the surface of the materials, or an argument based on a too cursory or superficial reading of the materials. For any of these cases, you need to see what kinds of materials would be more appropriate and what kinds of arguments would best present them.

The Office Interview

University instructors hold office hours, and you can take advantage of these special times set aside for consultation. Many students do not realize that office consultation is a regular and expected part of university instruction. You should think about the assignment before you come to the office and re-read your paper and the assignment topic so that you are well prepared. You will want to have some questions in mind (you might want to write some of them down). By referring to them, you are showing to your instructor the seriousness of your intent and indicating that you have given the matter some thought beforehand. You must also bring your marked assignment and any texts that are central to your essay. If your paper was a research paper for which you went to the library or did work on the Internet, you should bring your rough notes and any other materials that were helpful to you in your preparation. Often, a particular problem can be traced to some difficulty in taking notes, evaluating information, or constructing arguments at the planning stage.

When you come to the office appointment, it is a good idea to have some of these materials ready and to have thought about them beforehand. Your aim should be the general improvement of the entire assignment. However, if time is short (either yours or your instructor's), you should try to leave the office with at least one page clear, understanding the revisions that are recommended there, related both to conceptual argument and to mechanical expression in proper grammar and clear punctuation. Having understood at least one page of the corrections and the marking scheme, you can then ask how you can extend the understanding of that page throughout the whole assignment.

You should also have some idea of how long you can spend in the interview. Some instructors are greatly pressed for office time and can afford only five or ten minutes for a first meeting; others are able to give up to half an hour for concentrated work like this. If you need more time, you should ask whether you can book another appointment soon, perhaps outside of regular office hours so that you can spend more time discussing your assignment.

When you are in the office, you need to state your reason for coming and then produce your marked assignment and ask the instructor to go over the first few pages so you will understand the instructor's intention in marking the assignment. Usually, an instructor will want to look over the marked assignment quickly to get a grasp of the mistakes that were pointed out. He or she will then begin the process of re-evaluation and will make comments, ask questions about what you meant here or there, and explain any of the points in the marking scheme that are unclear to you. This office interview is an important part of your learning experience, and most instructors are efficient and helpful in leading you through the process. It is not intended to be a mini-examination or a grilling about what you might have done on your paper. Instead, it is an opportunity for you to understand better what you have written and for the instructor to explain the terms and expectations concerning the assignment and your performance in meeting those expectations. Be sure to take notes during or directly after your appointment.

During the office interview, you might also ask whether it is possible to re-write the assignment. Some instructors allow re-writes, some do not, so it is wise to check about whether it is possible in your course. If you worked hard, or even if you were rushed, you can consolidate your learning and understanding by carefully re-writing the marked assignment having gone over it carefully. Whatever your grade and however you performed, a revision will help you understand and improve your critical thinking and writing skills and your knowledge of the course. Finally, you will be much better prepared for writing your next assignment. If a re-write is allowed, you should be very clear about the terms of the assignment, about what your instructor's markings on your paper mean, and about what your purpose is in revising.

In almost every case, an instructor will want you to re-submit the original marked assignment and any other relevant materials along with your re-written paper in order to assess how well you have profited from the re-thinking stage and to see in detail how you have revised your work. It is important that you submit the final re-write on time (as agreed with your instructor), along with any other materials.

TIPS Re-writing

1. Ask your instructor if re-writing is allowed.

2. Be clear about whether or not the grade can be changed.

3. Find out if there is a possibility of the grade's being lowered if the revision is not sufficiently careful or thorough.

4. Make an appointment with your instructor to go over your paper in detail before you consider a re-write.

5. Re-submit the original marked assignment along with the re-write.

CHAPTER SUMMARY

In this chapter, you have learned how to prepare your assignments and essays in an acceptable format, paying attention to the many details in a step-by-step process that could slip by you in the rush to meet a deadline.

- You have mastered the intricacies of preparing a title page, setting margins, and formatting the body of your essay, as well as the list of books you referred to, secure that you have followed acceptable standards.
- You have learned how to proofread your paper one last time and get it printed.
- You have learned how to interpret your marker's correction symbols and are able to respond constructively to his or her comments.
- You know how to prepare for and benefit from an office interview.

You are now able to use what you have learned about your own work and the course expectations. You can put this knowledge into practice in both future assignments and in tests and examinations, the subject of the last chapter.

FURTHER READINGS

Rosa, Alfred, Paul Escholz, and John Roberts. *The Writer's Brief Handbook*. 2nd ed. Scarborough, ON: Allyn and Bacon, 1999.

Troyka, Lynn Quitman, and Cy Strom. *Simon and Schuster Quick Access: A Reference for Writers*. Toronto: Prentice Hall; Allyn and Bacon Canada, 2000.

Wilson, Wendy. *Print Out: Using the Computer to Write*. Toronto: Harcourt Brace, 1994.

part five

Examinations

chapter fourteen

Preparing for and Writing Tests and Examinations

In this concluding part of *Foundations,* this final chapter draws together the skills you have learned throughout this book, and throughout your course, stressing that a test or an examination should not be considered a negative experience fraught with anxiety but, rather, an opportunity to demonstrate what you have learned.

LEARNING OBJECTIVES

Here, we give practical advice on how to answer the following questions:

- How can you organize your preparation time?
- How can you summarize or map out an entire year's work in a course?
- How do you focus on central ideas or concepts of the course and how can you adapt the examples given in lectures for the purposes of your preparation?
- What do you do about readings and lectures you have missed?
- How do you cram effectively?
- Are there different ways to prepare for a multiple-choice exam, as opposed to an essay exam?
- How do you overcome worries before the exam and anxiety when writing?

RECOGNIZING THE OPPORTUNITY TO PERFORM

Like death and taxes, tests and examinations are inevitable. They come with the territory. All over the world, these spring rituals are played out in different ways. In India, the largest halls are taken over for the dreaded procedures. In Japan, students and parents alike scan the results of examinations to determine who will succeed, who will not. At Oxford, a week of daily examinations in formal dress is the culmination of the B.A. degree, celebrated with friends immediately after the last examination by uncorking champagne bottles in the quadrangle. And in North America, examination time brings the familiar sight of chairs lined up in the gymnasium before desks, where brain and memory are put to the test on the examination paper.

Bound up with tradition, and a characteristic of university teaching from the early Middle Ages, the examination is the culmination of a course, its climax. Mid-term and in-class tests are good preparations for the final examination, but it is the final that carries most weight. Gone, in most instances, are the courses in which the grade depends entirely on this final exercise. Examinations now make up a part of a grade, often about a quarter to a third and so are weighed along with all kinds of other assignments. This re-arrangement, at least in North America, has reduced examination anxiety considerably.

The threat of the examination hangs over a course from the moment the instructor hands out the syllabus and describes the tests and exams in the course. And the threat is the reason behind that banal and all-too-common cry of the anxious student, "Are we expected to know this for the exam?" as though the teacher were simply passing out optional information or as if the course were so full of data that no student could possibly be expected to digest it all for an examination. In fact, most teachers are clear about what will be on examinations, and many go to great lengths to explain the format and kinds of questions beforehand.

It used to be claimed that examinations are an important life experience, forcing you to concentrate in a situation of tension your ability to recall, think through, analyze, and organize a body of material. And it is true that many people will undergo other tests later in life, perhaps not written summaries and analyses of intellectual content in a specific disciplinary field, but possibly tests to show their competence in a job and in a variety of life skills. An examination is an important exercise for you to perform and excel in (it *is* a performance, and as in other art forms, the rules, moves, and procedures can be learned and perfected). Here is an opportunity to pull up a borderline grade and to bring a body of learning into focus.

ORGANIZING YOUR TIME, RESOURCES, AND METHODS

Examination skills depend not necessarily on doing far more work than other students but on taking advantage of all of the learning opportunities that are offered in a course and bringing them into *systematic focus* during the weeks and days before the examination. Many studies have been devoted to knowledge-retention rates. Generally, they demonstrate that without any systematic effort to keep your academic work up-to-date, without weekly and monthly reviews, you will have forgotten more than 80 percent of what you have read and heard in lectures over a four-month period. The effort required to pull that percentage up to an acceptable level in two or three days is enormous. But if you have consolidated your work regularly with reviews, you will have retained about 80 percent by the end of the year and will be in excellent shape to prepare for writing the examination (see Walter Pauk for the grim details about forgetting and retention rates and examination performance in *How to Study in College* 168–69; see Chapter 1).

Bringing your work into focus for the examination requires mobilizing several of your resources. First, you have to be crucially conscious of time. You will be under a lot of pressure to complete courses, assignments, and readings in the final weeks before a test or examination, and other sorts of details in your life will interfere. You need a schedule of your courses, with notes about which courses have term tests (with their dates), which have final examinations, and the weight attached to each exam.

First, when the final weeks before the examinations approach, you are faced with a series of critical judgments:

- Decide which course is in the best shape and which one is in the worst. Arrange your time to devote a proportion to each course. Block off the time in large sections so that you have a morning, an afternoon, or an evening for a specific task that can be completed within that time.
- From your examination schedule calculate how best to divide your study time according to the timetable and your preparedness.

Second, you have to consider your resources:

- Assemble all of your resources for a particular course together. That would include your lecture notes, tutorial notes, essays and rough notes, other assignments, notes for class presentations (your own and others'), the books for your course, reading notes on course textbooks and other books, library research notes, and so on. Generally, some of this material will be in good shape, but some will have gaps. Make certain that you have a complete set of notes, and go over them to make sure they are together and in order.
- Go over your lecture and seminar notes with highlighters. Note in the margins the terms in one colour if you have not already done so. You will have saved a lot of time if you had already prepared your lecture notes week by week in this way. Also, note any concepts that are developed in the lectures, and on separate sheets, begin your summaries—of terms, of concepts, and so on.
- Gather your reading notes together, along with the annotations in the assigned books in your course. You should already have some summaries available. Some will be in the course kits, some will be in your lecture notes, and some you will have made during your reading and studying for that part of the course. If you are missing any of these summaries that are readily available, get them in order now.
- Be realistic in your assessment of what you can do. If you have not read or finished reading some of the books on the course (and who has not been there?), do not try to read them now. Instead, find the summaries to fill in the gaps.

Third, having mapped out your time and assembled your course materials, you are ready to develop a method for moving to the actual preparation for the examination:

- Begin to make your lists of key terms, concepts, arguments, examples, and other details. Put the summaries of course readings together, and start to assess them on the basis of similarities and differences.

- Look closely at the last few lectures on the course for clues about the test or examination. Most instructors give detailed comments about what is expected and what kinds of questions might be on an exam.

- Do not miss the last lecture or class. Most instructors use it for consolidation and student questions, as well as for summary. Many students do miss this review and final instructions for the examination.

- Remember that the last lecture or seminar is often a summary or review of the course, just as the opening lecture or section of the course is often a general introduction. Put these two kinds of materials together for a quick overview. Then, move to your own summaries and charts or study sheets.

MAKING SUMMARIES OF THE COURSE: FROM THE SYLLABUS TO THE TEST OR EXAM

Understanding Course Patterns and Design

In charting out the entire course, your greatest resource is your course syllabus and course kit. These documents set out the goals of the course, usually in a general way, and set out the lectures week by week, providing an overview of the year. Often, the syllabus will contain general materials or weekly assignments that greatly amplify the overall concept and intention of the course, its intellectual goals, and the kinds of skills that you are expected to have mastered.

From this understanding of the course concepts and goals, you can move in your preparation to try to formulate the conceptual framework of the course. What are the first principles of the course? How many are there? Can you state them? Is there one basic concept on which all of the rest of the course depends? Here, you need to be aware of the danger of reducing or oversimplifying a complex subject. You should be able to formulate some of these principles and basic concepts to organize the course.

Now, you can look for the development of ideas. Throughout this book, we have stressed the linking of critical thinking to skills in organizing an argument. As the course comes to a close, you have to draw on those skills to see how the course was developed. You can do so by asking yourself a set of questions: Does this course depend on a series of more or less separate sections with little connection? On the other hand, is the course a progression of ideas, each building on the last? Do the same words recur in the syllabus from week to week as the lectures are outlined? If your instructors wrote outlines on the board for each lecture, was there similarity in the terminology and concepts used there? How are they arranged?

Probably, large sections of the course have sub-headings. The divisions may be chronological: for instance, Canada before colonization; from exploration to colonization; toward Confederation; Confederation: the first years; rail and commerce and the unification of the country; from the turn of the century to World War I; the Great Depression; from World War II to the Cold War; and contemporary issues in federalism. Or, the course may be organized around concepts: for instance, a sociology course stressing the colonial family; the extended family; break-up of First Nations families and cultures under the Native education acts; contemporary stresses on the family; the nuclear family as ideal; and the single-parent family as reality. In a literature course, has the material been covered chronologically or thematically? Have the readings (or novels or plays) been grouped, and if so, how? Why? Whatever the discipline, the important point here is to grasp the organizational principles of the course and to organize your study around them.

When the course was being taught, were you asked to look for connections, to find patterns and design structures? If so, what are they? Were different kinds of information and different modes of analysis used for these different sections? By answering these questions, you are seeking now to "read" the materials on the course inductively to see the patterns and concepts and to derive the organizing principles from the details.

Distinguishing Essentials from Examples

In the section on taking notes in lectures and seminars (see Chapter 1), we discussed the differences between main points in the argument of a lecture and the examples used to illustrate it, and we pointed out that many students get bogged down in the detail of the examples, rather than noting the kind of example or the page reference to be filled in later and concentrating on the main point. In studying for examinations, your purpose is different.

You already have a good outline of the course and have set out the major concepts in a coherent order. Now, you have to fit the details into that same pattern. Your aim is to get one or two examples, perhaps more for important points, which illustrate the concepts you have identified. You might do this by making a chart that lists the concepts on one half of the page, from top to bottom. On the other side you can fill in several columns with appropriate examples, historical events, statistical data, experiments, and so on so that your page, when completed, will include several examples for each of the major concepts of the course. It would be wise to choose examples that fit the concept clearly and to make a note about which particular aspect of the concept the example illustrates. You should note any way in which the example does not fit, either next to each example or in a separate column. You should choose examples from different parts of the course (to exemplify your own coverage of the course materials). You might also pick out similarities from among the examples.

This exercise is important because you must apply critical thinking to the course materials. You have already extracted the main principles, concepts, or terms of the course, and now you have to pull from the full range of the course the illustrations that will make sense of its readings. You are putting the course together for yourself. This synthesis is good for review just before the examination.

Creating Blocks of Material, Details, and Comparisons

Some instructors will spend the last lecture or seminar summarizing the course. They might suggest ways in which you can make your own summaries. Some approaches, of course, work better for one kind of course than for another. In a literature course, for example, one method of preparing your summary is to go through the course from the beginning and note in the left-hand column, week by week, the titles of the readings. In the other columns on the page, you can make your own summaries of the texts in various categories, covering either traditional or non-traditional materials (see Table 14.1).

TABLE 14.1		Summary Outline for a Novel (*Jane Eyre*)					
Author	Title and Date	Major Characters	Minor Characters	Functions	Settings	Summary of Action	Questions or Examples
Charlotte Brontë	*Jane Eyre* (1847)	Jane Eyre	Mrs. Reed	Aunt	Gateshead	[to be filled in as appropriate]	[to be filled in as appropriate]
			John, Eliza Georgiana Reed	Cousins			
			Miss Temple	Teacher	Lowood		
			Helen Burns	Friend			
		Mr. Rochester		Master	Thornfield		
			Adèle Varens	Pupil			
			Blanche Ingram	Rival			
		Bertha Mason Rochester		Mad in attic			
			Grace Poole	Servant			
		St. John Rivers		Teacher	Moor House or Marsh End		
			Diana, Mary Rivers	Cousins			
			Rosamond Oliver	Rival			

The details about the characters, the actions, and the questions and examples will depend on what you have done with the novel in your course. But you might also want to have several kinds of study sheets about such a text, one dealing with the settings in more detail, including specifics about the locations, the kinds of families there, class and economic status, and dominant images and metaphors (such as the chapters at Gateshead, leading to those at the school at Lowood and the contrasting school at Moor House, and the chestnut tree at Thornfield). That is, the summary chart in which you list all of the details of one section after another might draw together the separate charts that you make for each section. If you considered other aspects of the text, you could also include them, such as patterns of sign systems and signification, elements of narratology (plotting, modes of narration, metafiction, and focalizations), historical and political contexts (education in England; colonization, plantation ownership, and interracial marriage in the West Indies; missionary activities, the dominant culture, and racism), or the roles of gender (governesses, inheritance laws, codes of master/servant, and conventions of marriage).

You can make similar charts, though with different headings and categories, for readings in any course. Charts for historical or political readings would list the documents, date them, give something about their historical or social context, and then note the main points, the chief persons or issues that they address, and perhaps their immediate and longer-term impacts.

Assembling the charts is an important stage because you are putting together the large blocks of materials and are setting out the details of the course coherently. But you have not yet moved to making the comparisons. That requires a further step. Once you have your charts together, you need to think more analytically about how the various course materials are linked together, how they can be compared and contrasted. You might find it helpful to jot down possible points of comparison or to draw arrows to make links.

STRATEGIES FOR DEALING WITH PROBLEMS

What You Do Not Understand

The time for dealing with concepts, readings, or lectures that you have not understood is well past once you are preparing for examinations. Most of those difficulties should have been solved much earlier in the year. However, even several days before the examination, it is possible to patch a leaky intellectual boat, to get help about some matters that you do not follow. Your first source of information is your teacher. Some instructors have special office hours for discussing the exam in the final two or three weeks before the examination. Prepare for the office visit in ways similar to our discussion of appointments about returned assignments in the previous chapter. A second source of information is your fellow classmates. Some students study in groups, which often can be helpful in filling in gaps of knowledge, definitions, and so on. A third source is an encyclopedia or other reference books in your subject area. This route, however, is probably useful only in an emergency, since consulting such a book in the library will draw away valuable time from your preparation and might also be a source of distraction. Furthermore, it might not have the kind of focus that was so important in the course that you are gathering together.

What You Do Not Know

There always will be some areas of a course that you know better than others. On the whole, it is wise to try to balance your studying to give attention to all parts of the course, weighted, of course, according to the time your instructors devoted to the various materials. However, there might well be some areas that you know almost nothing about. In the final preparation for an examination, you have to evaluate carefully whether you can safely avoid filling in that gap, whether you can do short-term first aid to patch it up partially or whether you have to sacrifice time from other areas of the course that you know better to devote time to the area that you know nothing about.

If you know nothing about one or two of the course's major concepts—fundamental ideas upon which other ideas are built—it obviously would be wise to recognize that fact and remedy the defect. Otherwise, your lack of a solid foundation will betray you at every stage in your examination answers. It is very difficult to conceal such a gap. On the other hand, if you simply have not covered one of the course topics, perhaps one among many, then your judgment about its importance in the course will be a determining factor.

What You Have Not Read or Researched

Just as there will be some areas in which you lack proficiency, so too will there be some parts of the textbook, other readings on the course, or specific research areas that you have skimmed too superficially or have not read at all and now cannot recall the first thing about. The two or three days before the final examination are not a good time to remedy this defect. You might, in the weeks before, make an office visit to seek help about what to concentrate on, but do not appear to be fishing for exam questions, and try not to win sympathy by complaining or by justifying yourself about the work you did not complete. Either through an office visit or on your own, you need to have some acquaintance with the ideas and topics of the course that you do not know about. You also have to judge the importance of the reading you missed in the overall argument and intellectual framework of the course. Is this reading fundamental? If so, you should find some way to cover it—first by skimming, and then by reading the most important parts more carefully. You might also consider getting an aid to the reading. Some readings have summaries, student cribs, or other reading aids available. Using these tools here is an emergency measure. Study aids (laminated sheets, crib notes, reading guides, and the like) are sometimes recommended by instructors. While some of them are written by leading authorities in the field (some major scholars of John Milton have written crib notes to *Paradise Lost,* and they are used in some courses on Milton to supplement the other readings), some teachers frown on their use, so you should be aware of this potential problem. However, if you decide to simply ignore some of the major readings on the course, you are putting your performance at the examination at risk.

STUDYING ALONE, WITH A FRIEND, OR IN A STUDY GROUP

We have dealt with studying alone and in groups, as well as concentration in Chapter 1 and memory in Chapter 2. These procedures, of course, apply all the more to the crunch time in preparing for tests and exams. With the right people, there are many benefits to preparing for exams in a study group. Having studied a body of material, each of you can explain a concept, a text, or a chapter of the text to the other person, and the other person can then ask questions. You both can then check the materials for errors or deficiencies and assess performance. Then, the roles are reversed for the next body of material.

However, you should set aside enough time to do your individual preparation, too, and you should not plan to study in a group right up to the last minute. A study group made up of people who are willing to work and who can share knowledge with you and use your abilities can give you great support. For your own peace of mind, it is good to find out that others are also worried about this exam, that they share at least some of your difficulties, and that they can help you over hurdles that you thought were impossibly high. At the same time, the approaches that other people use should stimulate you to a better performance level.

CRAMMING TO GOOD EFFECT

Everyone who has studied the technique of cramming, including those researchers who have done it themselves, point out that the short-term acquisition of knowledge is a sure path to quick loss of retention. But for most people it is a sheer necessity. Nevertheless, materials acquired in cramming are not retained. If the course you are taking is a basic course in your discipline, or if it is one that you are expected to use as a foundation to build on later, cramming can get you through the exam, but you will not be able to draw on the course later because much of it will be gone. That said, however, many students have to cram. But there is cramming and cramming. Working hard for the three days before the exam when you have kept your coursework up-to-date is not cramming. It is consolidation. You already have completed what we have discussed above, and you now can take that time to go over your rough notes, draw together your course summaries and charts, and work through the thesis statements, outlines, comparisons, and examples that will set you up for a solid examination. However, seeking to cover coursework in three days that for much of the year you had not consolidated, that you read sketchily in the first place, and that perhaps you only partially understood is cramming. It might bring on a justifiable attack of anxiety. You might be able to impose upon friends, even at this late date, to lend you the notes that they will be needing now or to sit in on a study group, without participating (for who would have you?), to hear what is going on and to get some clues.

You will be tempted to do some of the reading that you had neglected all year. At this stage, some of that reading might still be useful, but it is impossible in a short time to go over all of the material in any detail when you have not looked at it before. So, you need to adopt shortcuts. Read, or at least skim through, the introductions to each of the readings, and fit the introductions into your plan of study, which is now expanding. Add extra pages to it. If you are marshalling this material on the computer, leave spaces where you want to add new information. Do not re-write it, but add. If you are working with pen and paper, use scissors to cut and paste to add new materials from your reading of the introductions. Your aim is to have an overview of the course, not to know it all only superficially. It would be better to have an overview and to have more detailed knowledge about several major parts of the course. In that way, you can write about them with more confidence. Of course, you are taking a chance that those items will be on the examination, so all will depend on choosing the right areas carefully.

Keep a firm eye on the clock, and even though you have had bad study habits in the course throughout the year, redeem yourself now by working solidly and with concentration. Allow yourself short, limited breaks, but then get back to it.

Halfway through your time, turn away from your notes and look at old exams (if they are available) or anticipate the kinds of questions you may be asked. Do an outline for one or two of them, starting with a thesis statement that states what you intend to argue and then presenting three or four major stages to your argument. Quickly flesh out the outline with an example (with similarities and differences) for each of your major stages. Then, leave it and try another. For the third example, choose a question that you cannot answer, and formulate, however shakily, a proposed thesis topic and perhaps some stages, or at least one. Then, go back to your syllabus to locate the place in the course where this material was covered, and consult your notes and try to pull together some of the information that you need. If you draw a blank, look over the books on the course or the textbook to see what should be considered, and by skimming, try to arrive at something. Even if you cannot complete a full outline for this question, get something down so that you are not left with that desperate feeling that your world is slipping away from you.

At the end of the day before the exam, before you go to sleep, plan to know something about several of the major concepts, themes, or divisions of the course. And the next morning, before the exam, go over these major concepts again, and have the examples in mind. After the exam, strengthen your resolve never to let yourself get into this situation again, and write yourself a letter to be opened at the beginning of the next term, as advice from the foolish to the wise.

LEARNING FROM THE MID-TERM TEST

When a mid-term or in-class test is handed back and is taken up in class, you should make notes about the instructor's comments. Often, they will be important clues about what she or he will want you to do on the final examination. Furthermore, these comments provide insight into the marking scheme and into the kinds of errors to avoid. If there are any markings on your paper, you need to make sure that you understand them. Were comments addressed to the way you developed your argument or to your grammar, punctuation, and expression? If so, those points are certainly important in this course, and you will need to improve your exam-writing skills.

Later, you can go over your answers and re-work them to see why your correct or high-scoring answers did well. You should look up your notes from lectures and readings and from your test preparation sheets to see what information you have there about each question. How complete was your response? What were its strengths and weaknesses? If you missed out on a question altogether, you need to determine the reason. Was it because you simply had not covered (and so did not know) that material? Did that omission happen because you misunderstood what was important in the course? Answers to these questions will help you prepare better for the next test or exam in the course.

More generally, you should ask yourself if you were well prepared for this exam and, if not, how your preparations could have worked better for you. Were you prepared for the length and difficulty of the exam? Had you gone over previous exams? Did you complete the exam with time to review your answers? Did you run out of time? If you misjudged the timing or weighting of the questions or did not pace yourself well, how could you correct that for the next test or the final exam?

Above all, you should keep in mind that mid-terms and in-class tests, as well as gauging the work you have done up to that point, are setting out the format, levels of difficulty, and methods used for the final exam, and you should take these tests as a valuable preparation for that section of the course where the grades are heavily weighted. In other words, do not write a test and then simply forget about it, but use it in a critical exercise to improve.

STUDYING FOR DIFFERENT KINDS OF EXAMS

Multiple-Choice and Short-Answer Exams

The so-called objective examinations often test for detail that a student either knows or does not know. Far more demanding are the more sophisticated objective examinations that require distinctions between close alternatives. For instance, the kinds of questions used on the SAT (Scholastic Aptitude Test), LSAT (Law School Admission Test), and GRE (Graduate Record Examination) are very sophisticated methods of evaluation, and analysts of educational trends look over the results of these examinations carefully. Indeed, many universities and private organizations sponsor short courses to train people to perform well in these examinations.

It is crucial that you read the exam instructions carefully. Often, multiple-choice exams are divided into sections, and sometimes different instructions, different numbers of required answers, and different weightings apply to each section. You also need to note whether there is a penalty for guessing. It might still be worth your while to guess if you are fairly certain that you are correct. You should plan your time in relation to the numbers of questions that you have to answer and the weight given to each, then proceed carefully and methodically, pausing from time to time to relax.

Multiple-choice examinations or tests give a variety of alternatives for responding to a particular statement or question. Usually, one alternative will be definitely wrong, but several others will be close to correct. You are looking for the best match between the question and one of the alternatives. You first need to read the opening statement in the question and think about what the answer might be. Then, you can read all of the alternatives before you answer. You should note any qualifying words that determine correct answers. If the root statement is all-inclusive—"All members of category X ..."; or, "Members of category Y always ..."—then the choice you make must fit all of the instances included. On the other hand, if the root statement includes the words *some* or *often*, these relative words allow for a degree of interpretation, and you have to be even more careful.

Yes/no and true/false examinations depend on detailed information that enables you to identify the point being made in the governing statement and judge its truth or falsity. The danger with this kind of examination is lingering or ruminating over a question too long so that eventually your doubts take over and you are unable to decide. If in a true/false examination you are absolutely stumped about which response is correct, you should guess. You have a 50 percent chance of being correct, so you should not leave any question unanswered (unless there is a penalty for wrong answers). Finally, when reading each statement, you should note carefully the presence of any qualifying words (*all, most, some, few,* and so on) and all negative words, especially *not.*

Short-answer exams ask for particular information that you have to supply in a succinct, abbreviated form, often in point form. Such answers require you to know your material well and to be able to summarize it accurately and efficiently.

For each of these kinds of examinations, similar methods of study can be used.

- First, go to the examination record office or to the part of the library or other facility where old examinations are kept. Make photocopies of the most recent examinations, and look closely at the kinds of questions that are asked. Which parts of the course are stressed? Which concepts appear again and again?
- Build your vocabulary in the field of study on which you will be examined. Multiple-choice examinations often hinge on the meaning of a particular crucial word in a statement. If it is close to the materials involved in the question, it might fit the answer; if it is remote from that field, it is likely not the right answer. But your ability to distinguish between possible correct answers and wrong answers will depend, in large measure, on your familiarity with the course concepts and language and on your general vocabulary skills.

Problem-Solving Exams

Problem-solving examinations set out problems and ask you to solve them, using formulas, theories, or mathematics. They are often used in mathematics and computer science examinations, in some areas of sociology and the social sciences, and in economics. More rarely, they are used in humanities courses where the problem might be more closely related to game theory or to the construction of an alternative reading of data based on some stated preconceptions or assumptions. In any case, you are expected to apply the knowledge that you have of techniques, theories, formulas, and practices to new conditions.

If the exam requires you to learn a lot of formulas, you should write them out at the beginning of the examination so that they are clear to you and you can refer to them. Then, you need to read the examination over carefully and select those problems that you think you have the best chance of answering correctly, within the allowances of the exam instructions. When you set to work on a particular question, you should mark or underline the operative words so that you fully understand what is involved in the problem. Then, you can move toward a solution, asking appropriate questions as you proceed: How do I get there? Is this the first step? Are my assumptions correct? Is this formula or principle or theory the right one for the data? You should work in a concentrated and methodical way, solving each step as you come to it. If you get stuck after a reasonable effort, you can move on and come back to it when you have time at the end. You should also try to budget time for a review.

Essay Exams

In preparing for the essay examination, you will have gone over a number of old examinations so that you know the kinds of questions that you will be expected to answer if the exam follows the same format. If you are uncertain about this point, you should ask your instructor. In preparing for the exam, besides all of the preparation we have noted above, you should decide on the major themes, issues, and categories of knowledge covered by the course and make up thesis statements about each. Then, you should list a number of points, at least three or four, in the form of topic sentences for your leading paragraphs. You might create outlines of the kinds of questions that you have been asked on previous examinations and then go over your notes from lectures and readings to see where they could be filled in.

In reading the question, you should re-consider the discussion in Chapter 3 on reading the assignment and be aware that instructors use a variety of different directions. The most common instruction is to "compare and contrast"; you should note that whenever you are asked to compare two or more items, you are expected to give both the similarities *and the differences* and to discuss them. Many students do not consider differences (or contrasts) at all. In such a question, you are forced to make a more complex answer than in a question that simply asks you to provide information. You may have to use specific categories of knowledge in your comparison of two novels, two political parties, or two social phenomena. Or you may have to use certain tools in your analysis, but the essential thing is that you must compare and contrast. It is not sufficient to choose three items, write an introductory paragraph saying that you will compare and contrast the three items in such and such categories, and then write three paragraphs, one about each item individually, without any comparison or contrast, followed by a conclusion. Such an answer fails to achieve its most central goal, that of making a comparison and drawing a contrast. You cannot ask the marker to step in and supply the comparison and contrast for you.

TIPS Writing Essay Exams

1. Write a thesis statement.
2. Do an outline in another examination booklet so that you have it before you as you write.
3. Add key words about details or illustrations to the outline to remind you to include them as you write.
4. Include some details (in parentheses) as you write to show the marker that you know what you are writing about, such as names, dates, historical contexts alluded to briefly, technical terms, and brief quotations of a word or phrase.
5. Give one or two longer examples that you can develop in more detail, and give brief examples to illustrate other points. Again, use parentheses for quick examples to avoid being distracted and writing too much.
6. Make certain at the end that you have not moved too far away from your thesis and also that your main points have covered what was asked for in the question.

Many other words are used in examination questions that require particular tactics for response, as in Box 14.1. For instance, the following questions ask you to do very different things:

1. *Identify* the major results of World Wars I and II as they affected Europe and North America.

2. *Explain* the major results of World Wars I and II as they affected Europe and North America.

3. *Compare* the major results of World Wars I and II as they affected Europe and North America.

4. *Evaluate* the major results of World Wars I and II as they affected Europe and North America.

5. *Justify* the major results of World Wars I and II as they affected Europe and North America.

BOX 14.1 | Common Verbs in Essay Questions

- **Identify:** exemplify, enumerate, list, describe, define, state, summarize
- **Explain:** analyze, discuss, illustrate, interpret, outline, trace
- **Compare:** contrast, distinguish, relate
- **Evaluate:** appraise, criticize, review, weigh
- **Justify:** agree/disagree, debate, defend, prove

Note that each of these verbs has a different connotation. For instance, under *identify,* to *exemplify* means that you have to list specific instances or examples; to *describe* means that you have to specify the characteristics of something; and to *define* means that you have to explain the meanings of a particular term by isolating its qualities. Under *explain,* to *illustrate* means that you have to clarify an issue by means of particular illustrations or examples to illuminate what you are discussing, while to *trace* means you have to set out the development or history of a particular idea or happening. Of course, many of these terms overlap somewhat, but you should be aware of the nuances of the operative terms of each examination question.

In each case, the verb at the beginning of the sentence determines how you should organize your answer. The first question asks for a list of results or effects of the two wars in the form of information. This question demands that you state details, and it is a hard one to fudge. The second asks you to explain or give reasons for the particular results that you already have enumerated: you have to answer the question, Why? The third question asks you to compare two sets of results, and, as always, a comparison asks that you point out both similarities and differences. The fourth question involves evaluation, judging the comparative results of the two World Wars. This question is more difficult than the earlier three because you already will have had to know the information, to make a comparison and then to assess the value or worth of the particular results. Finally, the fifth question asks you to make an argument defending or upholding the results that you have stated.

Here, you have to advance your own view of how those results can be supported (or give the views of others and align yourself with or argue against those views). In this answer, you have to know the materials well enough to position yourself with respect to the details and to defend your position.

It helps to do an outline on the examination itself or on the back of one of the pages (usually in a different book so that you can have the outline before you as you write and can add to it as you are answering the question). You should begin with a thesis statement and re-formulate it if necessary once you have completed the outline. You will recall that a thesis should be a complete statement that summarizes what you intend to argue in the answer. It is not merely a statement of an opinion but, rather, an attempt to state some reasoned position. It should give the main points that you will be developing in your answer. Some students take the terms of the exam question and turn them into a thesis statement, adding their own twist to them and including the three or four points that they will be arguing. However, merely re-stating the terms of the question in the same words does little for you in setting up an argument. You should avoid spending too much time on your outline. Once you have your main points set down, as well as any references to details, illustrations, or examples, you can begin to write. You should copy out the thesis statement and continue from there.

Essay exams have three major dangers: (1) there is the danger that the answer will not address the terms of the question, either by missing some important aspect of the question or by failing to go deeply enough into the material of the course to answer adequately; (2) the answer can be too general, lacking detail, examples, or evidence to back up what you are arguing. This fault is common not only among students who are ill prepared and who do not have the examples in mind at all but also among students who are well prepared but who remain on the level of generalization, never coming to grips with detail; and (3) the detail will take over. This last problem is the rarest, but it happens among students who have done all of the work but who find it difficult to rise above the detail to the terms of an argument. For these students, the outline with a thesis and major points is crucial to keep recalling them to the point that has to be argued. Even if you follow a good outline and have a good balance of general argument and examples, you need to beware of becoming sidetracked by an example that takes over or that draws you into spending too much time. If you find that happening, you should just end it and move on, leaving some space that you can return to during the exam review time to correct with a bridge to the next point.

Take-Home Exams

If you are assigned a take-home examination, you should pay particular attention to the instructions, both in the seminars or lectures before the examination is assigned and in the assignment itself. Are you being asked to use only the course materials, to extend the readings in certain ways, or to research in the library or elsewhere? Answers to these questions will determine, in large measure, how you prepare for and answer the examination. Above all, you will be aware that the kinds of answers you are expected to give are not flip, casual, or superficial. You are being given more time to consult your course materials and are expected to give thoughtful and reflective consideration to the course. You should use the time to prepare your answers carefully, balancing the ideas of the course and illustrating your points with appropriate and detailed examples. You can now afford the time (not available on an essay exam) to write a take-home exam that can be qualified, discriminating, and subtle.

You can get help from the learning skills program at your university or read the information on preparing for tests and exams at various sites on the Internet, such as the York University site (**www.yorku.ca/cdc/lsp/eponline/exam.htm**). The Web site at the University of Victoria also has brief and helpful information on taking multiple-choice, true/false, and essay exams, as well as general tips (**www.coun.uvic.ca/learn/exam.html**). Another site, that of the University of Guelph, has brief tips and advice on exams (**www.learningcommons.uoguelph.ca/ByTopic/Learning/ExamPrep/index.html**).

WRITING TESTS AND EXAMS

Countdown to Zero

On the final day before writing the exam, it is a good idea to go over the syllabus again, to check the study sheets that you prepared, and to look over systematically the thesis statements, the major points you outlined, and the examples you listed. You might add further details. You should also check the readings again to make sure that you have the facts straight and memorize any of the final points that you want to be clear about. During the last day, it is important to eat regular meals and to do some exercise. Finally, the night before the exam, you can get together your equipment (such as books allowed, if it is an open-book exam, pens, pencils, a watch, and any refreshments you need). Above all, remember to take your university photo-ID. Have a good sleep.

Every year students miss the first half-hour or more of an examination because they slept in, missed the bus, or went to the wrong location at the wrong time. Finding out about the time and place of the examination beforehand is your responsibility. Sometimes, the examination halls are in areas of the university that you might be unfamiliar with, so you need to know in advance how to get there. At the exam, listen carefully to any instructions or explanations that the invigilators give at the beginning of the exam. These comments might include explanations of typos on the exam or some other mistake that you should know about.

Special Needs

If you need special consideration for exams because of a physical problem or learning disability, you should make the necessary arrangements well beforehand. Most universities have a special office that deals with students who have such needs. You need to speak to your teacher well before the exam and explain that you are making arrangements to write the exam under the auspices of the student help office (or whatever it is called on your campus). You need to make certain that your instructor knows whether you need extra time or equipment, such as a computer.

Reading the Exam Questions

Even before you read the examination questions, you might want to jot down some of the details of that pesky outline, that trick for remembering those facts in order, or whatever terms you do not want to forget. Then, you can set your mind at rest and get on with reading the exam paper.

We have already stated the basic requirements for any examination in the section above on different kinds of exams. It is important to read the instructions and questions carefully. Then, read them again. Make sure you are clear about the formal requirements (for example, do two of four questions; write on at least three texts, and so on). On any given examination, students lose marks unnecessarily by misreading the instructions and questions. You should note especially any of the words we discussed above (*list, explain, analyze, compare,* and so on). As you go through the exam, you should mark the questions you can certainly answer and those that are possible. Then, you can take at least four or five minutes to read the questions over, circle any words or questions that are confusing, and seek advice from an invigilator if you do not understand either the instructions or the questions. Usually, it is best to begin by answering questions that you are certain of, and a little later, raise your hand and ask the invigilator your questions when he or she approaches your desk.

TIPS   Reading Test and Exam Questions

In reading the exam, note the following:

1. The time allowed for the exam
2. The number of questions required for a complete exam
3. The weightings for each part of the exam and even for each question
4. The key words in each question (underline these key words or use your highlighter to mark them)
5. Any inclusions or exclusions (such as, no material from the fall term may be used on the final exam)

Pacing Yourself

It is crucial that you plan your time and map out your strategy, allowing sufficient time to re-read parts of your exam and to fill in any blanks that you left. You should check again the weighting for each question and plan your answers so that you have enough time for each. Halfway through the exam, you will need to check the time to be sure that you are on track.

You should begin the exam with the questions that you can answer best or with the ones that you want to get out of the way. You do that to build on your successes. But you should not be tempted to overkill on the answers that you are familiar with. It is better to answer what is asked, leave some blank space for later, and go to the next question.

Tactics for Good Answers

Examiners are looking for you to show off what you know, but your knowledge has to be directed to what the question is asking. You should continue to ask yourself at the end of each page whether you are still on topic. You are also being assessed for your knowledge of the course as a whole and its concepts. Are you including the course concepts and the key terms for the course in each of the answers? Are you including concrete examples (dates, authors, events, short quotations, references to documents, and alternative theses)? You should answer short-answer exams by coming to the point quickly. If you are allowed to use point form, using verbs at the beginning of your answers will kick-start your ideas. If you are required to write in paragraphs, you need not waste time by re-phrasing the question, but rather, you should proceed directly to your answer. In essay exams, you can use the thesis-outline method and fill in the references to your examples.

After you have finished, you should still have a small amount of time left for review. That was part of your planning at the beginning of the exam, and now it is vital for you to go over your answers carefully and quickly, adding detail, examples, and comparisons and correcting mistakes as you proceed. Your aim in this review should be to improve your answers, not just to re-read the answers. Finding the energy for this last effort is difficult but important.

Exam Anxiety and What to Do about It

Panic

Everyone feels panic around exam time. Sometimes, it happens before you have started to draw the course together at the beginning of the pre-exam study period and sometimes in the countdown to the exam. Panic and anxiety are counterproductive and form a loop in which they feed upon themselves, inhibiting you from moving forward and getting worse unless you find ways of breaking free of them. Change this unproductive cycle by considering the following:

- You have prepared as well as you could in the time available and given your resources.
- You have a general grasp of the whole course, and you know some of it in detail.
- You might already have a passing grade in the course, perhaps a pretty good grade, and this exam is weighted much less than your other coursework.
- You know enough to get some marks on the exam, and you will pass.
- Even if the exam counts for a lot of marks, you still know enough to pass.
- You have done the best that you could.

Panic during the exam can also be a problem. Now, you have to use your writing and not your studying to get through the anxiety. You should take some deep breaths and focus on some object in the classroom, not the clock. Then, you need to recall that you have done a good deal of work in this course, have attended many lectures, and have read the books, assure yourself that you will do fine, take some more deep breaths, and start writing. It might help to start with an outline or to write out a partial answer in point form—anything to break the circle of panic and anxiety.

Not Knowing the Answer

Many exams, especially essay questions, allow you to choose between alternatives. If the question is compulsory, and you do not immediately see how to answer either of the alternatives, you need to think about it some more. You should choose the most likely alternative and jot down any pertinent ideas you have on the blank page opposite the answer. Then, you can ask yourself questions and write two or three of the questions down: What is this question asking? Then narrow the focus: How might I answer it? What are the possibilities? What would work here? You should not leave the question until you have some ideas written down. Then, you can leave some blank space and move to the next question, reserving time to return to this question later in the exam. Often, ideas will occur to you that you can add to your questions and that you can fill out into an answer before the exam is finished.

IF YOU MISS THE EXAM

If for documented reasons (health, accident, death of a relative, and so on) you missed an examination, you should take the documentation to the course director, who might allow an informal make-up exam. You might have to submit a formal petition (again with all documentation) to allow you deferred standing or to allow you to take a make-up exam. If you miss an examination for undocumented reasons (slept in, mistook the date or time, car did not start, and so on), you can again approach your instructors and hope they are sympathetic. If this procedure fails, you can again submit a formal petition, although your chances for success are more limited.

   If you miss an exam, you should remember that universities have formal petition mechanisms, as well as departmental procedures, which may address your problems. This information is available on the university's Web page under the registrar's office. If you miss an exam for undocumented reasons, you have nothing to lose by seeking permission to take a make-up exam or, if necessary, by trying a formal petition.

CHAPTER SUMMARY

In this chapter, we have examined various resources that you can draw on as you prepare for tests and examinations. You now understand that studying is not merely memorizing facts or remembering isolated bits of data but requires critical thinking. That is, studying for and writing exams is a skill that requires practice and thinking with a purpose. You now can map out a course before you get down to acquiring the details, and you understand that the actual writing of an exam requires planning and organization before you put pen to paper. In preparing for tests and exams, you now are able to address the following areas:

- You have been able to overcome exam anxiety by organizing your time and resources to map out the whole course.
- You have identified the central concepts or problems of the course and have lined up appropriate examples from lectures and course readings, along with particular critical positions that you can adopt.
- You have filled in the gaps in your lecture notes and reading assignments as well as you can.
- You have assembled all of your materials and are ready to review, summarize, and cram, if necessary, to get it all in order.

   In other words, you are now aware that preparing for an exam is not simply a matter of taking your notebook and reading through it from start to finish; and writing an exam is not simply starting at the first question and writing until the time runs out. Neither is a strategic choice.

In many ways, because the procedures outlined in this final chapter apply equally to mid-term tests, this discussion of strategic choices in studying can be applied to your whole year's work. Everything from taking notes in the first lecture to class presentations to the final essay and exam builds cumulatively, but certainly, on the first foundations and comes to its appropriate conclusion with a successful examination. All has depended upon your critical thinking, reading, and writing strategies. In ending with an emphasis on strategy, we have come full circle. You may recall that in Chapter 1, we emphasized becoming an active learner as the key to critical thinking, and we stressed that to do so, you must plan your time and activities with a purpose. In many ways, this entire book has been an elaboration of the parts of strategic thinking introduced in the first two chapters.

FURTHER READINGS

Jalongo, Mary Renck, Meghan Mahoney Tweist, and Gail J. Gerlach. *The College Learner: How to Survive and Thrive in an Academic Environment.* Englewood Cliffs, NJ: Merrill, 1996.

Longman, Debbie Guice, and Rhonda Holt Atkinson. *College Learning and Study Skills*. St. Paul, MN: West Publishing, 1993.

MacFarlane, Polly, and Sandra Hodson. *Studying Effectively and Efficiently: An Integrated System.* Toronto: Guidance Centre, Faculty of Education, U of Toronto, 1983.

Taylor, Catherine, Heather Avery, and B. Lucille Strath. *Making Your Mark: Learning to Do Well on Exams*. Toronto: Harcourt Brace, 1994.

Warren, Russell G. *Carpe Diem: A Student Guide to Active Learning*. Lanham, MD: UP of America, 1996.

Works Cited

BOOKS

Adams, Marilyn. *Beginning to Read: Thinking and Learning about Print.* Washington: Sponsored by the Office of Educational Research and Improvement of the U.S. Department of Education, 1990.

American Philosophical Association. *Critical Thinking: A Statement of Expert Consensus.* Millbrae, CA: California Academic Press, 1990.

Anderson, Richard, Elfreida Hiebert, Judy Scott, and Ian Wilkinson. *Becoming a Nation of Readers.* Washington: Sponsored by the National Academy of Education, National Institute of Education, and Center for the Study of Reading, 1985.

Aristotle. "Posterior Analytics." Trans. G.R.G. Mure. *Introduction to Aristotle.* By Richard McKeon. New York: Modern Library, 1947. 9–109.

Bettelheim, Bruno. *The Uses of Enchantment: The Meaning and Importance of Fairy Tales.* New York: Knopf, 1976.

Board of Education for the City of London. *A Parent's Guide to Whole Language.* London, ON: The Board, 1990.

Breland, Hunter M., Robert J. Jones, and Laura Jenkins. *The College Board Vocabulary Study.* New York: College Entrance Examination Board, 1994.

Brody, Jane E. "Procrastinate No More: You Can Help Yourself." *New York Times* 5 June 1996: C12.

Brownmiller, Susan. *Against Our Will: Men, Women and Rape.* New York: Bantam, 1976.

Card, Claudia. *The Atrocity Paradigm: A Theory of Evil.* New York: Oxford UP, 2002.

Carroll, Lewis. *The Annotated Alice.* Ed. Martin Gardner. London: Penguin, 1970.

Copi, Irving M., and Carl Cohen. *Introduction to Logic.* 9th ed. New York: Macmillan, 1994.

Council of Biology Editors. *Scientific Style and Format: The CBE Manual for Authors, Editors, and Publishers.* 6th ed. New York: Cambridge UP, 1996.

Davidson, Thomas, ed. *Chamber's Twentieth Century Dictionary.* Edinburgh: W & R Chambers, 1901.

Donaldson, Laura E. *Decolonizing Feminisms: Race, Gender, and Empire Building.* Chapel Hill: U of North Carolina P, 1992.

Gardner, Howard. *Frames of Mind: The Theory of Multiple Intelligences.* 10th ed. New York: Basic Books, 1993.

Garner, James Finn. *Politically Correct Bedtime Stories.* New York: Macmillan, 1994.

Gibaldi, Joseph. *MLA Handbook for Writers of Research Papers.* 6th ed. New York: Modern Language Association of America, 2003.

Grimm, Jacob. *Household Stories from the Collection of the Brothers Grimm.* Trans. Lucy Crane. New York: McGraw-Hill, [1882] 1966.

Humm, Maggie. *Dictionary of Feminist Theory.* Columbus: Ohio State UP, 1995.

Joad, C.E.M. *God and Evil.* London: Faber, 1947.

Kolb, D. A., and Roger Fry. "Toward an Applied Theory of Experiential Learning." In *Theories of Group Process.* Ed. C. Cooper. London: John Wiley, 1975.

Lester, James D. *Citing Cyberspace.* New York: Addison Wesley, 1997.

Levy, Harold. "Madame Guilty in Sado-Sex Trial." *Toronto Star* 10 Oct. 1998: A6.

Lieberman, Marcia. "Someday My Prince Will Come." *College English* Dec. 1972: 383–95.

National Council of Teachers of English (NCTE). "Elementary School Practices." *Current Research on Language Learning.* Urbana, IL: NCTE, 1993.

O'Connor, Joseph E., ed. *Image as Artifact: The Historical Analysis of Film and Television.* Washington: American Historical Association, 1990.

Paley, William. *Natural Theology.* London, 1802.

Partridge, Eric. *Concise Usage and Abusage.* New York: Citadel, 1965.

Pauk, Walter. *How to Study in College.* 5th ed. Boston: Houghton Mifflin, 1993.

Pei, Mario. *The Story of Language.* Rev. ed. New York: New American Library, 1966.

Ratnesar, Romesh. "The Homework Ate My Family." *Time* 25 Jan. 1999: 36–45.

Robinson, Francis P. *Effective Study.* 4th ed. New York: Harper & Row, 1970.

Santrock, John, and Stephen Yussen. *Child Development: An Introduction.* Dubuque: Wm C. Brown, 1992.

Sapadin, Linda, and Jack Maguire. *It's About Time.* New York: Viking-Penguin, 1996.

Sexton, Anne. *Transformations.* Boston: Houghton Mifflin, 1971.

Snow, Catherine, Susan Burns, Peg Griffin, et al. *Preventing Reading Difficulties in Young Children.* Washington: Sponsored by the Office of Special Education Programs, the Office of Educational Research, the National Institute on Child Health and Human Development, and the National Research Council of the National Academy of Science, 1998.

Storr, Catherine. *Clever Polly and the Stupid Wolf.* London: Penguin, 1995.

Toulmin, Stephen, Richard Rieke, and Allan Janik. *Introduction to Reasoning.* 2nd ed. New York: Macmillan, 1984.

Traugott, Elizabeth Closs, and Mary Louise Pratt. *Linguistics for Students of Literature.* New York: Harcourt Brace, 1980.

Tuttle, Lisa. *Encyclopedia of Feminism.* Harlow: Longman, 1986.

Walker, Janice R., and Todd Taylor. *Columbia Guide to Online Style.* New York: Columbia UP, 1998.

Williams, Raymond. *Keywords: A Vocabulary of Culture and Society.* London: Fontana, 1981.

Yarington, David. *Surviving in College.* Indianapolis: Bobbs-Merrill, 1977.

Zipes, Jack David, trans. *Beauties, Beasts, and Enchantment: Classic French Fairy Tales.* New York: New American Library, 1989.

———, ed. *The Trials and Tribulations of Little Red Riding Hood.* New York: Routledge, 1993.

WEB SITES

Atwood, Margaret. "Margaret Atwood Speaks to the TCTE May Gathering—May 25/95." *The Margaret Atwood Information Web Site.* 7 Nov. 1997. **www.web.net/owtoad/q.html**

"Coaching Winners." *Critical Thinking Across the Curriculum Project, Longview Community College.* 5 May 1998. **www.kcmetro.cc.mo.us/longview/ctac/winners.htm**

"Concentration and Memory." *Dartmouth College.* 25 Mar. 2002. **www.dartmouth.edu/~acskills/success/study.html**

Dan Kurland's Critical Reading site: **www.critical-reading.com/**

Davis Dyslexia Association Home Page. **www.dyslexia.com/quest.htm**

"Elementary School Practices": *National Council of Teachers of English Positions and Statements.* **www.ncte.org/about/over/positions/level/elem/107653.htm**

"Employability Skills 2000+." The Conference Board of Canada. **www.conferenceboard.ca/education/pdf/emskill.pdf**

Greenberg, Stan. "Politically-Correct Red Riding Hood." **www.otherside.net/redhood.htm**

"Improving the Reading Achievement of America's Children: 10 Research-Based Principles." CIERA (Center for the Improvement of Early Reading Achievement): **www.ciera.org/library/instresrc/principles/index.html** (Nov. 15, 2002).

"NCTE Position Statement on Reading" NCTE (National Council of Teachers of English): **www.ncte.org/about/over/positions/level/gen/107666.htm** (Feb 1999).

Paul, Richard. "Three Definitions of Critical Thinking." *Foundation for Critical Thinking Home Page.* **www.criticalthinking.org**

Special Education Legal Primer. **www.therapistfinder.net/journal/sped/index.html**

Schroeder, Charles C. "New Students—New Learning Styles." *Change in Higher Education* Sept.-Oct. (1993): **www.virtualschool.edu/mon/Academia/KierseyLearningStyles.html**

"Taking Lecture and Class Notes." *Dartmouth College.* 25 Mar. 2002. **www.dartmouth.edu/~acskills/success/notes.html**

Index